AI and ML
for
Coders

*Applying Core ML algorithms, deep learning
models, and MLOps best practices*

Suddhasatwa Bhaumik

bpb

www.bpbonline.com

First Edition 2025

Copyright © BPB Publications, India

ISBN: 978-93-65897-821

To View Complete
BPB Publications Catalogue
Scan the QR Code:

Dedicated to

*To **Atasi** and **Aadriti***
my constant sources of inspiration and joy – this one's for you

About the Author

Suddhasatwa Bhaumik is a seasoned software engineer, passionate about AI/ML. With 18+ years of experience, he has designed data and machine learning systems, led teams, architected solutions, and delivered impactful projects. He has always believed in continuous learning and thoroughly enjoys sharing his limited yet practical knowledge to empower software engineers to embrace the world of data science, machine learning, and AI.

In his current role at Google Cloud India, based out of Pune, he feels extremely proud to be working as a Strategic Cloud Engineer helping customers worldwide in implementing AI and machine learning solutions on Google Cloud.

About the Reviewers

❖ **Sai Chaitanya** is a data scientist with 7 years of experience (8.5 years overall) in building machine learning models and solving real-world problems. He is currently pursuing a master's in data science at Scaler Academy, focusing on **data structures and algorithms** (**DSA**), machine learning, deep learning, and generative AI.

Sai is an aspiring technical author with plans to write a machine learning book that simplifies complex algorithms using a unique visual approach. His aim is to make learning intuitive and long-lasting for readers. This exciting project is set to begin in 2025, reflecting his passion for demystifying data science concepts.

In addition to his professional pursuits, Sai has recently started prioritizing his overall well-being, balancing physical, mental, and spiritual health while expanding his knowledge in personal finance. He is also exploring the stock market and is dedicated to personal growth. Sai envisions a future where his journey inspires others to pursue excellence in the data science field and personal growth.

❖ **Pronnoy Goswami** is a seasoned software engineer and thought leader specializing in distributed systems, cloud infrastructure, and large-scale observability. He has led the architecture and design of next-generation telemetry platforms optimized for high availability, scalability, and operational excellence. With deep expertise in DevOps, AI-driven automation, and performance optimization, Pronnoy builds systems that solve complex problems at scale.

His technical skill set spans Kubernetes, public cloud platforms, ELK, Prometheus, and Terraform, and he is passionate about mentoring, technical writing, and advancing the future of cloud-native technologies. Pronnoy frequently shares insights on cloud computing, infrastructure, and applied AI through articles, tutorials, and expert commentary.

As an active technical reviewer, he contributes to books and publications across top-tier platforms in cloud, AI, and distributed architectures. Pronnoy holds a master's degree in computer engineering from Virginia Tech and spends his free time reading, hiking, and exploring emerging technologies.

Acknowledgement

There are a few people I want to thank for the continued and ongoing support they have given me during the writing of this book. First and foremost, I would like to thank my better half for continuously encouraging me to write the book — I could have never completed this book without her support.

I am grateful to the innumerous amount of courses that I have taken till date from platforms like iNeuron, Udemy and Edureka, my Online Master's programs from Great Learning, and the organisations which gave me support throughout the learning process of Artificial Intelligence and Machine learning, notably my experience at _VOIS and Google Cloud India. I thank all my seniors and colleagues (most of whom are my closest friends!) in supporting me in every possible way to learn and grow throughout my career, especially in the last 12+ years!

My gratitude also goes to the team at BPB Publications for being supportive enough to provide me with enough support and time to finish this book, and in gratefully coordinating in getting the technical reviews and chapter reviews completed on time with the highest levels of dedication and quality.

Preface

This book offers a hands-on, code-centric journey into the world of artificial intelligence and machine learning. Readers will immediately dive into practical coding exercises and real-world examples, mastering fundamental concepts. Starting with machine learning principles, the book progresses through computer vision, teaching image processing techniques like feature detection to enable applications to analyze visual data. It then explores **natural language processing** (**NLP**), equipping software with language understanding and manipulation skills, covering techniques like tokenization and sentence sequencing for applications like chatbots and sentiment analysis. The book also delves into sequence modeling, covering RNNs and LSTMs for handling sequential data.

Building upon these core concepts, readers will learn to develop TensorFlow models and deploy AI solutions across various platforms. The book culminates in strategies for confidently serving models online and in the cloud, ensuring scalable and robust AI applications. By the end of this book, readers will emerge as confident AI developers, ready to contribute valuable expertise to any organization and innovate in the field of AI and ML.

This book is divided into 13 chapters, details of which are listed below.

Chapter 1: Introducing Artificial Intelligence and Machine Learning - In this chapter, we introduce the ever-growing world of AI and ML using practical examples and applications where such systems are in use and where such systems help millions of people worldwide to successfully execute and use products in their day-to-day. This chapter also sets the clear boundaries of what an AI can do as of the current day and what it should be expected to do.

Chapter 2: Machine Learning Fundamentals - Before the readers of the book deep dive into variety of applications of AI and ML, and how to design and develop an entire system covering it, it is essential to know the basics of machine learning, its types, the various algorithms, where they fit into the landscape, and how they are beneficial in solutioning of particular use cases across domains. This chapter provides the landing zone to realize the fundamentals of ML and its use cases. Additionally, it also covers the details around hyperparameter tuning and its importance in production AI/ML systems.

Chapter 3: TensorFlow Essentials - Now that the readers of this book have some idea on what machine learning is and what kind of use cases are catered by their use in the real-world, this chapter sets the stage with the basics of TensorFlow, the most popular and production grade ML engineering library, with Python language as the mode of usage. The readers are assumed to have the very basic hands-on knowledge of the Python programming language to understand all the nuances presented in this chapter.

Chapter 4: Engineering for Machine Learning - It is essential at this stage now for readers of this book to understand and grasp the fundamental ways and tools of programming for machine learning, including how to modularize their software and even design to containerize them later for easy shipments. In this section, we cover the most essential aspects of software engineering required to make the best use of ML driven applications. Additionally, we also introduce the usage and benefits, by some case studies, of RDBMS systems (MySQL and/or Oracle) and EDW (BigQuery, on Google Cloud Platform), for readers to be made aware of how real-world industrial data is stored, managed and processed in both batch and real-time modes.

Chapter 5: Machine Learning Algorithms - Since the basics are now ready with the readers of this book, in this chapter we deep dive into the working of all of the traditional ML algorithms including the most common regression, classification and clustering techniques. Readers are also presented with approaches to use these algorithms given the right use cases, which are suitable for each of these algorithms. We start to implement these algorithms from the next chapter onwards.

Chapter 6: Implementing First ML Models - In this chapter, readers get to learn and focus on the industry recommended and time tested methods of designing and developing all the common ML algorithms using scikit-learn (a starter ML Library, also used in production) and TensorFlow (which is a production grade library for ML). We focus on the nuances of traditional ML algorithms, while the advanced topics like neural networks will be covered starting in the next chapter. From time to time, this chapter refers back to the knowledge gained in Chapters 2,3,4 and 5.

Chapter 7: Computer Vision - We begin this chapter with an introduction on neural networks and the variety of ever increasing use cases where they are finding their place, because of the humongous speed and size at which we (humans) have started to generate and accumulate data. Then, we start to deep dive into one of the most interesting areas in deep learning, a.k.a computer vision, where we understand the basics, the architectures, the use cases, and industries where the methods apply, and the best ways of articulating a successful computer vision project. Readers get to implement the aforementioned computer vision methods using TensorFlow and Keras, another high-level abstraction over TensorFlow library. Readers are also introduced to the challenges in implementing computer vision algorithms in any given project or IT landscape, including relevant portions of data privacy and AI ethics.

Chapter 8: Natural Language Processing - Readers are now introduced to NLP and its nuances in this chapter, which is by far the most common, the most useful, as well as the most challenging category of applications where AI and ML find their use. Readers are introduced to the basics of how to analyze and process text, followed by a variety of methods and algorithms to engineer and recognize patterns from textual data. Finally, readers are introduced to useful case studies covering the most commonly built applications around NLP.

Chapter 9: Sequence Modelling and Transformers - In this chapter, we introduce the importance of sequence models and use cases like forecasting and language translation where there is an increasing use of sequence models. Readers are introduced to forecasting, one of the most common methods used across industries for planning and demand management, followed by modelling language as a sequence of events. We introduce readers to generative adversarial networks which are broadly used in language and image use cases. Finally, readers are introduced to what is today the heart of generative AI systems, a.k.a Transformers, covering what the attention mechanism is. All of these aforementioned topics are implemented hands-on using TensorFlow and Keras for practical realization.

Chapter 10: MLOps and Deployment - In this chapter, we introduce the basic concepts and importance of MLOps in the real-world. MLOps is one of the most important backbone of AI and machine learning applications in Production, which in fact, contributes to more than 90% of the overall components in a system, apart from what the readers have learnt in the earlier chapters, which merely contributes for 5-10% in the overall scheme of things. Once MLOps and its importance are realized, readers are introduced to deployment patterns on-premise and cloud in this chapter, where we use in-house or cloud based IT infrastructure of any given organization to deploy and operate on AI and ML systems. Readers are also briefly introduced to data and model security, along with applicable design guidelines. In this chapter as well, readers are introduced to hands-on MLOps and deployments using **TensorFlow Extended** (**TFX**) and Kubeflow. For cloud implementations and references, readers are introduced to Google Cloud Platform, and the state-of-the-art ML and operations suite of offerings in GCP, a.k.a Vertex AI. We also touch base about model monitoring and CI/CD pipelines for ML models in production.

Chapter 11: Model Serving and Scalability - In this chapter, we introduce the nuances of how to serve models in the real-world, both using in-house IT infrastructure and Google Cloud Platform. This is where readers are also introduced to concepts of model scalability and how to design the right infrastructure for a given application which is powered by AI/

ML. We introduce TensorFlow Serving as one prudent option for effective service of ML models, along with Vertex AI on Google Cloud Platform, and how to design scalable ML infrastructure. Although this chapter is more on system design, readers are also introduced to hands-on practical examples using Python and TensorFlow on aforementioned topics of model serving and scalability.

Chapter 12: Model Deployment for Mobile - In the chapter of this book, we provide the readers with detailed knowledge on how to deploy ML models and make them work on mobile (or related remote) devices. This is a crucial topic to be explored as of date, because of the inescapable rise and role of mobile devices like smartphones, tablets, and smart home devices in our lives! In this chapter, hence, we introduce TensorFlow Lite, which is one of the common methods, along with design and development samples and / or guidelines, to develop and package ML model driven applications for mobile devices. Further, we look at the integration of such applications (driven by machine learning) on Android and iOS platforms. Finally, we conclude the chapter with a couple of interesting case studies on two of the most common current world applications.

Chapter 13: Summary, Future, and Resources - In the last chapter of this book, we provide the readers with a detailed summary of what we have learnt and programmed in this book, touching on the most important design and engineering principles and tools, along with best practices. Readers are introduced to the current state of AI and ML implementations, as a revision/summary, as well as a realization, along with a variety of interesting implications and uses, like generative AI, in the current world. Finally, readers are encouraged with the right amount of additional resources for professional growth in the ever-growing field of AI and ML, including additional focus on AI ethics and data privacy in the age of ChatGPT and similar.

Code Bundle and Coloured Images

Please follow the link to download the
Code Bundle and the *Coloured Images* of the book:

https://rebrand.ly/0184de

The code bundle for the book is also hosted on GitHub at
https://github.com/bpbpublications/AI-and-ML-for-Coders.
In case there's an update to the code, it will be updated on the existing GitHub repository.

We have code bundles from our rich catalogue of books and videos available at
https://github.com/bpbpublications. Check them out!

Errata

We take immense pride in our work at BPB Publications and follow best practices to ensure the accuracy of our content to provide with an indulging reading experience to our subscribers. Our readers are our mirrors, and we use their inputs to reflect and improve upon human errors, if any, that may have occurred during the publishing processes involved. To let us maintain the quality and help us reach out to any readers who might be having difficulties due to any unforeseen errors, please write to us at :

errata@bpbonline.com

Your support, suggestions and feedbacks are highly appreciated by the BPB Publications' Family.

Did you know that BPB offers eBook versions of every book published, with PDF and ePub files available? You can upgrade to the eBook version at www.bpbonline. com and as a print book customer, you are entitled to a discount on the eBook copy. Get in touch with us at :

business@bpbonline.com for more details.

At **www.bpbonline.com**, you can also read a collection of free technical articles, sign up for a range of free newsletters, and receive exclusive discounts and offers on BPB books and eBooks.

Piracy

If you come across any illegal copies of our works in any form on the internet, we would be grateful if you would provide us with the location address or website name. Please contact us at **business@bpbonline.com** with a link to the material.

If you are interested in becoming an author

If there is a topic that you have expertise in, and you are interested in either writing or contributing to a book, please visit **www.bpbonline.com**. We have worked with thousands of developers and tech professionals, just like you, to help them share their insights with the global tech community. You can make a general application, apply for a specific hot topic that we are recruiting an author for, or submit your own idea.

Reviews

Please leave a review. Once you have read and used this book, why not leave a review on the site that you purchased it from? Potential readers can then see and use your unbiased opinion to make purchase decisions. We at BPB can understand what you think about our products, and our authors can see your feedback on their book. Thank you!

For more information about BPB, please visit **www.bpbonline.com**.

Join our book's Discord space

Join the book's Discord Workspace for Latest updates, Offers, Tech happenings around the world, New Release and Sessions with the Authors:

https://discord.bpbonline.com

Table of Contents

CHAPTER 1
Introducing Artificial Intelligence and Machine Learning

Introduction

In a shocking outcome of the infamous Chinese board game *Go*, in early March 2016, the Go champion *Lee Se-dol* and the observers of a historic game were in awe when *Google DeepMind's* AI, AlphaGo, won by 4-1. At least quite a few from the audience had thought that *Mr. Lee's* impressive win in the fourth round of the game not only redefined the final outcome, but also that he was learning how the computer worked and strategized its steps during the game. However, the end result was nothing less than a significant leap forward for **artificial intelligence** (**AI**) systems of the kind being designed by Google DeepMind, in line with many other crucial players around the world. Simultaneously, and in the same game, *Mr. Lee* could be seen to have realized the non-human and eccentric playing style of AlphaGo, hence identifying its weak points and proving that the machine was not infallible.

There are many similar stories, competitions, and applications that we all see around us today, which helps us realize the importance of AI and **machine learning** (**ML**) driven applications and systems, making our lives easy and nothing more. In this chapter, we formally define AI and ML, and look for practical examples all around us. We will finally clear some concepts and boundaries on what an AI or ML system can do as of the current day, along with what it should be expected to do.

Structure

The chapter covers the following topics:

- Introduction to AI/ML
- Applications and use cases
- Responsible AI principles
- Expectations from AI
- Career opportunities

Objectives

By the end of this chapter, you will be able to understand what AI and ML are and how they are used in our day-to-day lives across multiple domains and applications. We will also look at its transformative power (even more with the recent rise in generative AI hype), the career opportunities in this field, and finally, a set of realistic expectations.

Introduction to AI/ML

AI has become an indispensable tool in the professional landscape. From automating repetitive tasks to enabling complex decisions, AI is redefining our working environments in profound ways.

To formally define it:

AI refers to the simulation of human intelligence processes by machines, specifically the ability to acquire, interpret, and apply knowledge and data. It entails developing algorithms and models that can learn and make intelligent decisions without explicit instructions.

As a novice, we can categorize an AI system into one of the following two broad classes:

- **Strong AI (General AI)**: This is where AI has a comparable performance to humans. In simple words, this type of AI can learn, reason, and hence solve problems across different areas of work or domains. General or strong AI remains to be a theoretical concept as of today, and reaching a stage of artificial general intelligence is still a work in progress. Although it sounds intriguing and magnetic, and as we will discuss later in this book, it is imperative to perform our research, development, and applications in line with a solid and broad set of responsible AI principles.

- **Weak AI (Narrow AI)**: This refers to AI systems designed to perform a specific task or set of tasks with high efficiency. Examples include speech recognition, image classification, and game-playing algorithms. These systems form the backbone of many IT systems and would be our primary point of focus during the subsequent chapters of this book. Even if we call this category of systems as weak or narrow

AI, one must realize that the responsible AI principles are equally applicable in these systems, like the former type.

Irrespective of their type, an AI system is designed to process enormous amounts of data to learn and identify patterns, make predictions (and estimations in many cases, as we will learn further in this book) based on the information they have been trained on, and assist humans in unseen cases. This is an important point to note at this early stage of understanding AI, where one must oblige and acknowledge the fact that an AI system is merely an assistant, and in many given contexts and industries, only fits as one or more helpers to achieve a broader goal.

At this stage, it would be logically important to understand the key components of AI so that we can also understand the areas we will be learning in this book, along with hands-on examples. Let us consider the following points:

- **ML**:
  - ML algorithms enable computers to learn from data without being explicitly programmed.
  - They can identify patterns, make predictions and estimations, and improve their performance over time as they are exposed to more data.

- **Deep learning**:
  - Deep learning is a subset of ML that utilizes artificial neural networks, which are loosely inspired by the structure of the human brain.
  - These networks can learn complex relationships within data and make accurate predictions even when presented with incomplete or noisy information.
  - In many practical applications and the onset of exemplary research seen in the last few decades, deep learning and ML have now become interchangeable terms.

- **Natural language processing**:
  - **Natural language processing (NLP)** allows computers to understand and generate human language.
  - NLP algorithms can perform tasks such as sentiment analysis, machine translation, and speech recognition.
  - Both ML and deep learning methods and algorithms are used day in and day out to approach and solve NLP problems. However, since natural language is the most approached method of human communication, it takes a separate stand for itself.

- **Computer vision**:
  - Computer vision algorithms enable computers to interpret and understand visual information.
  - They can identify objects, detect faces, and track movement in images and videos, to quote a few examples in the real-world.
  - Again, similar to NLP, computer vision is a domain by itself, and to approach relevant use cases of computer vision, engineers like us make use of ML and deep learning methods.

- **Robotics**:
  - Robotics combines AI with physical hardware to create autonomous machines that can perform tasks in the real-world.
  - Robots can navigate their environment, interact with objects, and make decisions based on sensor data.
  - One can argue that robotics does not naturally fall in the AI realm by itself, but in our context, these are intelligent machines that are learning to perform human-like tasks using methods like reinforcement learning.

Let us now get over the basics and try to realize the vast number of applications in the real-world that make use of AI and ML.

Applications and use cases

Firstly, let us understand some of the applications of AI and ML from a generalist's perspective. Let us look at a broader set of applications and uses of AI and ML across domains:

- **Healthcare**:
  - **Disease diagnosis**: AI algorithms analyze medical images, such as X-rays, CT scans, and MRIs, to detect diseases like cancer, pneumonia, and bone fractures with high accuracy.
  - **Drug discovery**: ML models help researchers identify potential drug candidates and optimize their properties, accelerating the drug development process.
  - **Personalized medicine**: AI systems analyze individual patient data to tailor treatment plans, predict disease risks, and provide personalized healthcare recommendations.

- **Finance**:
  - **Fraud detection**: AI algorithms analyze transaction patterns to identify suspicious activities and prevent fraudulent transactions in real time.

- o **Credit scoring**: ML models assess an individual's creditworthiness based on various factors, enabling lenders to make informed decisions.

- o **Stock market prediction**: AI systems analyze historical data, market trends, and news sentiments to predict stock price movements and assist investors in making informed decisions.

- **Retail**:

  - o **Product recommendations**: AI algorithms analyze customer behavior, purchase history, and preferences to recommend personalized products and improve the shopping experience.

  - o **Inventory management**: ML models optimize inventory levels by predicting demand, preventing stockouts, and minimizing waste.

  - o **Customer service**: AI-powered chatbots and virtual assistants provide 24/7 customer support, answering queries, resolving issues, and improving customer satisfaction.

- **Transportation**:

  - o **Self-driving cars**: AI algorithms enable autonomous vehicles to navigate roads, detect obstacles, and make real-time decisions, enhancing safety and reducing accidents.

  - o **Traffic management**: ML models analyze traffic patterns and predict congestion, helping authorities optimize traffic flow and reduce travel times.

  - o **Fleet management**: AI systems track vehicle locations, monitor fuel consumption, and schedule maintenance, improving fleet efficiency and reducing costs.

- **Manufacturing**:

  - o **Quality control**: AI algorithms inspect products for defects, ensuring quality and consistency.

  - o **Predictive maintenance**: ML models analyze sensor data to predict equipment failures, enabling proactive maintenance and minimizing downtime.

  - o **Process optimization**: AI systems analyze production data to identify inefficiencies, optimize processes, and increase productivity.

- **Agriculture**:

  - o **Crop yield prediction**: AI algorithms analyze weather data, soil conditions, and historical yields to predict crop yields, helping farmers make informed decisions about planting and harvesting.

- ○ **Pest and disease detection**: ML models analyze images of crops to detect pests and diseases early, enabling farmers to take timely action and minimize crop losses.

- ○ **Precision farming**: AI systems analyze field data to create customized fertilization and irrigation plans, optimizing resource usage and increasing crop yields.

- **Energy**:

  - ○ **Renewable energy forecasting**: AI algorithms predict wind and solar power generation based on weather data, helping grid operators balance supply and demand.

  - ○ **Energy efficiency**: ML models analyze energy consumption patterns to identify inefficiencies and recommend energy-saving measures, reducing energy costs.

  - ○ **Smart grid management**: AI systems optimize the distribution of electricity, reducing transmission losses and improving grid stability.

- **Security**:

  - ○ **Cybersecurity**: AI algorithms analyze network traffic and identify suspicious activities, preventing cyberattacks and protecting sensitive data.

  - ○ **Fraud detection**: ML models analyze transaction patterns to detect fraudulent activities, such as identity theft and credit card fraud.

  - ○ **Risk assessment**: AI systems analyze various factors to assess risks, such as financial risks, operational risks, and compliance risks, helping organizations make informed decisions.

- **Entertainment**:

  - ○ **Personalized recommendations**: AI algorithms analyze user preferences and behavior to recommend personalized movies, music, and other content, improving the user experience.

  - ○ **Content creation**: ML models generate realistic images, videos, and music, enabling artists and content creators to produce engaging and immersive experiences.

  - ○ **Virtual reality and augmented reality**: AI systems enhance **virtual reality (VR)** and **augmented reality (AR)** experiences by creating realistic virtual environments and enabling interactive interactions.

- **Government**:
  - ○ **Public policy analysis**: AI algorithms analyze large datasets to identify trends, patterns, and correlations, helping policymakers make informed decisions.
  - ○ **Fraud detection**: ML models analyze government transactions to detect fraudulent activities, such as benefit fraud and tax fraud.
  - ○ **Emergency response**: AI systems analyze real-time data to predict and respond to emergencies, such as natural disasters and public health crises.

Table 1.1 will help us understand the variety of use cases of AI and ML from a software engineer's or coder's perspective. This gives us a broad perspective on the problem statements these AI systems help to resolve.

Use cases	Applications	Real-world examples
NLP	• Machine translation • Chatbots and virtual assistants • Text summarization • Sentiment analysis • Spam filtering	• Google Translate • Siri, Alexa, and Cortana • Brandwatch Analytics • Gmail's spam filter
Computer vision	• Image recognition • Object detection • Facial recognition • Medical imaging • Self-driving cars	• Google Lens • Facebook's facial recognition software • Zebra Medical Vision's AI-powered medical imaging platform • Tesla's Autopilot system
Speech recognition	• Voice control • Dictation • Customer service • Medical transcription • Language learning	• Apple's Siri • Google Assistant • Amazon Alexa • Nuance Dragon NaturallySpeaking • Duolingo
ML in finance	• Fraud detection • Credit scoring • Portfolio management • Algorithmic trading • Risk assessment	• PayPal's fraud detection system • FICO's credit scoring system • BlackRock's Aladdin investment management platform • Renaissance Technologies' Medallion Fund • J.P. Morgan's AI-powered risk assessment tool

ML in healthcare	• Disease diagnosis • Drug discovery • Personalized medicine • Medical imaging • Clinical decision support	• IBM Watson Health's cancer diagnosis system • Google DeepMind's AlphaFold protein folding algorithm • Insilico Medicine's AI-powered drug discovery platform • Arterys' AI-powered medical imaging platform • Epic's AI-powered clinical decision support system
ML in manufacturing	• Predictive maintenance • Quality control • Supply chain management • Robotics • Automated assembly	• GE's Predix predictive maintenance platform • Amazon's AI-powered quality control system • Alibaba's AI-powered supply chain management system • Fanuc's AI-powered robots • Tesla's AI-powered automated assembly line
ML in retail	• Product recommendations • Personalized marketing • Customer service • Fraud detection • Inventory management	• Amazon's AI-powered product recommendations • Netflix's AI-powered personalized marketing • Sephora's AI-powered customer service chatbot • eBay's AI-powered fraud detection system • Walmart's AI-powered inventory management system

Table 1.1: Use cases of AI and ML

One can now realize the vast places where AI and ML systems are built and made use of. However, before exaggerating ourselves with the magical outcomes of these systems, it is again good to remember that all of these systems and examples are powered by AI and ML and not driven by them in their entirety.

Many of these systems are much more than the ML components learning how to respond to user commands (like Alexa and Google Assistant), which involves software, hardware, and many other facets of engineering. It is rather pragmatic to find holistic solutions to better our lives, where AI and ML would definitely play a major role.

It is important to realize that any given AI and ML model or its implementation only becomes useful when one is able to deploy or install the solution, also known as

productionizing ML in a casual sense. As we go along to learn the various facets of AI and ML, we will cover dedicated chapters in this book to design and develop production-ready ML systems with all other relevant software components.

Responsible AI principles

Before we continue with our exploration of AI and ML, it is highly crucial for us to realize what responsible AI means and the various principles associated with it, as follows:

- **Fairness**: AI systems should be designed to avoid bias and discrimination against individuals or groups based on factors such as race, gender, religion, or disability.

- **Transparency**: AI systems should be transparent and accountable, allowing users to understand how they work and make decisions.

- **Accountability**: Developers and users of AI systems should be held accountable for the consequences of their actions, including any unintended harm caused by the system.

- **Safety and security**: AI systems should be designed to be safe and secure, protecting users from harm and preventing unauthorized access or manipulation.

- **Privacy**: AI systems should respect user privacy and protect sensitive data, ensuring that it is used only for the intended purposes and with appropriate consent.

- **Human values**: AI systems should be designed to align with human values and ethical principles, such as justice, equality, and respect for human dignity.

- **Non-maleficence**: AI systems should be designed to avoid causing harm to individuals or society and to minimize the potential for unintended negative consequences.

- **Responsibility and stewardship**: Developers and users of AI systems have a responsibility to ensure that the systems are used for good and not for malicious purposes.

- **Sustainability**: AI systems should be designed to be sustainable and environmentally friendly, minimizing their carbon footprint and other negative impacts on the environment.

- **Human flourishing**: AI systems should be designed to contribute to human flourishing, empowering individuals and communities to achieve their full potential.

Note: These responsible AI principles are laid out by Google and are available here for reference: https://blog.google/technology/ai/ai-principles/. Accordingly, there are many organizations and governments, for example, which are already in the process of creating a set of similar and better processes and policies for the effective use of AI and ML for society.

Expectations from AI

While we saw a lot of examples of the domains and applications where AI and ML are finding their use, it is imperative that we clear some doubts and common myths to realize what AI is not so that the systems we design and build are realistic and helpful, as follows:

- **AI is not sentient**:
  - AI systems do not have consciousness, emotions, or the ability to experience subjective states.
  - They are not capable of independent thought or action and cannot make decisions based on their values or beliefs.
  - For example, an AI system cannot feel pain or pleasure, and it cannot decide to help or harm a human being.

- **AI is not omnipotent**:
  - AI systems are not all-powerful or all-knowing.
  - They are limited by the data they are trained on, the algorithms they use, and the computational resources they have access to.
  - For example, an AI system cannot solve every problem or answer every question. It can only perform the tasks that it has been specifically trained to do.

- **AI is not infallible**:
  - AI systems are not perfect and can make mistakes.
  - They can be biased, inaccurate, or even malicious.
  - For example, an AI system might misclassify an image, make a false prediction, or generate harmful content.
  - It is important to remember that AI systems are only as good as the data they are trained on, the algorithms they use, and their governance.

- **AI is not autonomous**:
  - AI systems are not independent entities. They are created and controlled by humans, and they are used to serve human purposes.
  - For example, an AI system cannot decide to enable or disable a security system as part of any army installation. It can only do what it is programmed to do.

- **AI is not a threat to humanity**:
  - AI is not inherently dangerous or evil. It is a tool that can be used for good or for bad, depending on how it is used.

- o   For example, AI can be used to develop new medical treatments, solve complex problems, and create new forms of art and entertainment.

- o   However, AI can also be used to spread misinformation and manipulate people.

It is important to remember that AI and ML are a set of powerful tools, and it is up to us to use them responsibly.

Career opportunities

In practice, and looking at the last section where we saw the applications and use cases of AI and ML, there are a plethora of career opportunities, which are approachable in the current day, with the right set of skills and knowledge. By far, the most common job titles include, but are not limited to, ML engineer, NLP engineer, AI research scientist, data scientist, and so on.

All of these opportunities require precise problem-solving skills along with knowledge of the various facets of AI and ML, many of which will be covered in this book. Other than aforementioned, it is important to realize that soft skills are often an overlooked skill for a coder or software engineer who aims to switch careers into AI and ML. Strong software engineering skills, along with knowledge of how to design effective systems, are unavoidable at any level or at any given organization.

Finally, the domains of AI and ML will constantly evolve as we go along. It may well be a fact that by the time a reader of this book finishes reading it, someone at *Microsoft, Google* or *Meta* (for example, which are some of the large players in the big tech arena) have already published another academic paper, with some open-sourced implementation of another novel or better way of performing a certain algorithm or model. Continuous learning and adaptability, hence, are equally essential for an AI or ML Expert so that one can stay up to date with the latest research and industry trends for maintaining expertise. Fortunately, major players always release their research for all on specific websites (like, *arXiv* which is maintained by *Cornell University*, or *Google Research* website, for example!).

Conclusion

In this chapter, we covered the introduction to AI and ML, the variety of use cases, applications, and domains where they find usefulness, and the types or methods of implementing AI and ML for problem-solving. We very briefly realize the importance of responsible AI principles and look into some of the many interesting career opportunities in this realm.

In the next chapter, we are going to learn about the fundamentals of ML.

Join our book's Discord space

Join the book's Discord Workspace for Latest updates, Offers, Tech happenings around the world, New Release and Sessions with the Authors:

https://discord.bpbonline.com

CHAPTER 2
Machine Learning Fundamentals

Introduction

Imagine a typical day in any school. Based on a curriculum and a timetable, the students reach the venue, organize their books and notes, try their level best to study from each class, and are allowed to play as well. Once the kids are back home, they should rest, play, and study or complete their homework with regularity so that a sense of time management and quality is imbided into them from the initial stage of life.

How does one ensure that the core of the subjects which a kid learns in school is with them for a long period, and hence, turn out to be valuable for them in the real-world? The only way to do so is to provide them with high-quality books and teachers, as much as possible, so that students can relate to the concepts with their day-to-day events. Pragmatically, it may not make sense in the long run to remember the postulates of calculus if we do not realize the applications of the rate of change in various activities, we do ourselves, or the various tools we use every day.

Again, one important aspect of any education system is to take evaluations at regular intervals of time to ascertain if the students can recognize and implement the notions of the subjects taught to them. Sometimes the questions are easy, and at times they are deliberately difficult for a beginner to answer. However, overall, the nature of the questions and the expectations from students, unless it starts to impact their health or psychology, helps improve their knowledge.

Although there are very limited institutions which take this leap forward, but ideally, in any given education system, we should also provide every student with a recognized self-evaluation framework, so that once they start living their lives as adults, they can correct their course of action depending on the feedback they receive from the world around them. This is often ignored but is a very important aspect of how good or bad even an educated person responds to a given scenario in life.

Essentially, this is almost the same as what one would need to do to create ML systems. In this context, our students are the computer programs, who would learn how to estimate the future from what they have learnt. They would be taught high-quality information as much as possible, and regularly, one would evaluate to understand how good or bad they are in the real-world. To conclude, we need to provide them with additional assistance to adapt themselves to the changing world around them so that they can improve themselves over time. This is exactly what we will learn in this chapter in depth. We will introduce ML formally, and then discuss in detail every aspect of it, which we need to know to start developing useful software applications for problem statements present all around us.

Structure

The chapter covers the following topics:

- Introduction to machine learning
- Types of machine learning
- Evaluating machine learning models
- Use cases of machine learning
- Common algorithms
- Ways to make ML models better

Objectives

By the end of this chapter, you will be able to understand what is ML, its different types, the use cases which make use of them, how can one evaluate ML models and systems to make them better, the common algorithms which one should be aware of in depth, and finally, how to make any ML model better.

Introduction to machine learning

ML is a subfield of AI that gives computers the ability to learn without being explicitly programmed. ML systems, using researched and time-tested algorithms, can learn sufficiently from data, identify patterns, and make predictions or estimations. It enables such software applications to perform tasks that are tedious or difficult for humans to do manually, although not impossible.

As we briefly looked over in the last chapter, ML is used in a wide variety of domains and applications, including the following:

- **Image recognition**: ML algorithms can be trained to identify objects in images, such as faces, cars, and animals. This is used in applications such as facial recognition, object detection, and medical imaging.

- **NLP**: ML algorithms can be trained to understand and generate human language. This is used in applications such as machine translation, spam filtering, and sentiment analysis.

- **Speech recognition**: ML algorithms can be trained to recognize spoken words. This is used in applications such as voice control, dictation, and customer service.

- **Predictive analytics**: ML algorithms can be trained to predict future events, such as customer churn, fraud, and disease outbreaks. This is used in applications such as risk management, marketing, and healthcare.

- **Recommendation systems**: ML algorithms can be trained to recommend products, movies, and other items to users. This is used in applications such as e-commerce, streaming services, and social media.

ML algorithms work by learning from data. This data can be structured, such as a spreadsheet of customer data, or unstructured, such as a collection of images or text documents. In the industry, most of the time, the data that is required to train and build high-quality ML models reside in a multitude of databases across their respective IT landscape, and hence collating and making the data ready for efficient models to be trained from them requires the organization to invest heavily into data engineering. The algorithm learns by identifying patterns in the data and then using those patterns to make predictions.

Throughout the rest of this text, we would interchangeably use the words system and model to define any given ML model. Interestingly, and without spilling the beans right away, we would realize eventually that a model is a series of numbers, resulting as an output of one or more mathematical equations, which one employs to learn from data so that this learning can be further generalized to similar but unseen instances.

Types of machine learning

Overall, ML can be divided into 3 types, as represented in the following visual:

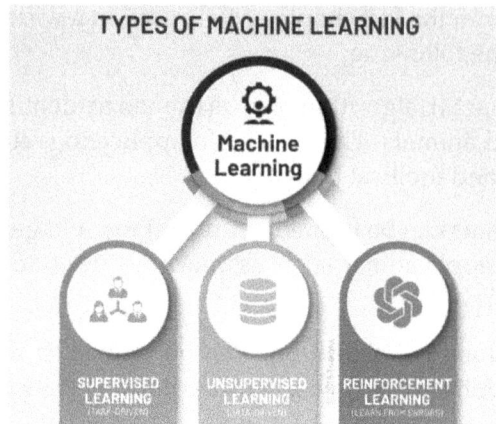

Figure 2.1: *Types of machine learning*

Reference: https://www.linkedin.com/pulse/types-machine-learning-muhammad-imran-arshad-xlswf/

Let us now understand the different types of ML in detail, as follows:

- **Supervised learning**: It is the most common type of ML algorithm. Here, the algorithm is trained on a dataset that has been labeled with the correct answers. For example, an algorithm that is being trained to identify cats and dogs might be given a dataset of images of cats and dogs, each of which has been labeled as either a cat or a dog. The algorithm learns by identifying the features that distinguish cats from dogs, such as the shape of their ears or the texture of their fur. Once the algorithm has been trained, it can be used to make predictions on new data. For example, this system or model, which was trained to identify cats and dogs, could be used to classify a new image as either a cat or a dog.

  - **Classification or regression problems**: Overall, any given supervised learning problem can be further grouped into classification or regression problems.

    - In the case of **classification** problems, like the preceding example, ML is tasked or expected to bifurcate one class from another, or the rest. Examples of this include determining if a customer will default in their loan installments if a bank offers them a loan of a certain amount. Classification tasks like these are also called **binary classification** use cases. There are cases where, given an image or a video, an ML system is expected to determine the animal present in it, which becomes a **multi-class classification** problem.

    - In the case of **regression** use cases, we are trying to estimate the value of a continuous variable. Examples in this category include estimating the salary of an engineer joining an organization given a set of skills and years of experience.

- **Unsupervised learning**: The next common type of ML is unsupervised learning. In this case, we do not have any labels given to the data. Mostly, this happens because of a lack of methods and processes to identify labels in a given dataset. Hence, unfortunately, the model never knows the right answer. A very common use case is that of a retail company that wants to optimize its marketing strategy by identifying distinct groups of customers based on purchasing behavior. The goal is to understand patterns in customer data (e.g., buying frequency, average spend, product preferences) without having predefined labels so they can personalize marketing efforts and improve customer engagement.

- **Reinforcement learning**: Another practical grouping of ML is reinforcement learning. This is quite similar to how a human being may learn from the environment as feedback. Reinforcement learning is like teaching a child to ride a bike. The child (agent) learns in an environment (playground) through rewards (candy) and punishments (falls). The goal is to maximize rewards by learning the best actions. This process is guided by a policy, similar to a parent's instructions.

Further chapters in this book will explore the various applications of these types of ML, the various algorithms used commonly, and how to make them better.

Evaluating machine learning models

Irrespective of the type of ML methods or algorithms which we make use of, to address a particular problem statement, we must understand how good or bad they are when they are created, and then continue repeating this process as long as the underlying data and assumptions change, which for many applications is through their lifetime. Before we explore how to continuously evaluate ML models, let us understand how we can define model evaluation.

As briefly discussed, model evaluation, in simple terms, is analogous to understanding how good or how badly a student has learnt a particular subject by presenting the learner with examinations or quizzes to check the depth of understanding of core concepts, at the least. The questions in these examinations can range from simple to complicated, depending on for what purpose we are preparing the learner or the appropriate way of preparing the learner for unknown scenarios further in their lives. In the same way, in the case of ML models, we make use of metrics to understand how well the model performed learning the data supplied to it, also called the **training data**, and how well it can perform on unseen data, also called the **test** or **validation data**. In different literature, one may often find different names used for the same sets of data, but overall, it is comparable to the textbooks that we use in school or college. For example, to teach a learner, as opposed to the random and out-of-the-book questions that we present to them during their exams, keeping in mind that the subject of both sets of questions should be the same, as of course.

Model evaluation is a critical step in the ML workflow. It allows us to assess the performance of our model and determine its suitability for a given task. By evaluating our model, we can identify its strengths and weaknesses and make informed decisions about how to improve its performance.

There are a variety of different metrics that can be used to evaluate an ML model. The choice of metric depends on the specific task for which the model is being used. For example, if the model is being used for classification, we might use accuracy, precision, recall, or the F1 score as our evaluation metric. If the model is being used for regression, we might use mean squared error, root mean squared error, or mean absolute error as our evaluation metric. It is to be noted that similar evaluation metrics also exist for unsupervised learning problems like clustering, where one may want to use **Within-Cluster Sum of Square** (**WCSS**) errors. For example, to know how good the groups or categories are. At this point, these terminologies may seem alien to many, but as we go along in further chapters in this book and start implementing ML systems of different types and kinds, we will design and develop each of these metrics as they fit into the use case, and see which ones are to be used when.

In addition to choosing an appropriate evaluation metric, it is also important to consider the following factors when evaluating an ML model:

- **Data quality**: The data that is used to evaluate the model should be representative of the data that the model will be used in production. If the test or evaluation data is not representative, the performance of the model may not be accurate, and so our evaluation may be incorrect, too. This is synonymous to asking a student to appear for a linear algebra exam, who has been studying English literature primarily, in some sense.

- **Training and testing sets**: The data should be divided into training and testing sets. The training set is used to train the model, and the testing set is used to evaluate the performance of the model. The testing set must be held out from the training process and should not be used to tune the hyperparameters of the model. Without this being in place, paradoxically means that any student appearing for an exam on history already knows the questions (and sometimes the answers) that are about to come in the exam.

- **Cross-validation**: As we will learn in-depth in further chapters, cross-validation is a technique that can be used to estimate the performance of a model on unseen data. Cross-validation involves training and evaluating the model multiple times on different subsets of the data. The results of the cross-validation can be used to estimate the generalization error of the model, which is the error that the model is expected to make on new data. One must avoid too much generalization of any ML model on one or more facets of the training data to avoid biases in the resulting systems.

Once we have evaluated our model, we can use the results of the evaluation to make informed decisions about how to improve the performance of the model. In the later chapters of this book, we will learn that if any given model is not performing well, as per the chosen metrics, we might try tuning the hyperparameters of the model, collecting more data, or using a different ML algorithm altogether, and so on. At this point, let us keep in mind that the hyperparameters of a model are the nuts and bolts or configurations of any given system. These are similar to the dials we find in our radios, which, with the correct positioning or tuning, help us listen to our favorite shows and speakers.

Use cases of machine learning

Before we investigate the common ways, also referred to as the ML algorithms, which are employed to address specific tasks, it is imperative to understand briefly the types of some common real-world use cases that one can target to address. By the definition of supervised learning, we need labeled data. By label, we refer to what has happened in the past, given a certain property of an observation.

Banks can use customer data and transaction history to detect unusual activity and potentially fraudulent transactions. By analyzing this data, banks can identify suspicious patterns and proactively protect customers from unauthorized access.

Similarly, a particular educational or research institution may want to start labeling each type of flora and fauna they can get a hold of or are researching on, and such data (containing the properties of plants and their labels or names, for example) can be made available publicly for a wider set of audiences. This dataset can further help create ML models, which can make effective use of computer vision and historical datasets with labels to determine the most probable class of a given plant or herb.

Similarly, by the definition of unsupervised learning, one may not always be in a position to easily capture labels in all given cases. For every organization, for example, it may not be possible to collect all the properties of their employees to predict which training plans are best suited for a group of employees or who are more likely to be looking for their next opportunity outside the organization. Finding such invaluable information helps understand the pulse of the organization, as well as helps create or improve processes and frameworks around teams.

One such similar problem statement is when any company wants to rely on customer segmentation to better understand its diverse customer base. Traditionally, this may involve manual analysis of demographics or purchase history, but with clustering, this process becomes more affordable and automated.

Imagine a large online retailer selling diverse products on their website, where one upfront problem is when they have millions of customers with varied preferences and buying habits. It is very difficult upfront to understand how to target marketing campaigns effectively. In such cases, the retailer may want to collect the purchase history of their customers, including items bought or frequency or total spending capacity, etc. After further cleaning and pre-processing the data (which is one very important aspect of data preparation for ML systems), a clustering algorithm is chosen based on the desired segment granularity.

If the system is built effectively, then even the first iteration of the model results in an acceptable grouping of customers, helping the company understand the preferences of each segment or spending behaviour or potential value. Finally, all of these efforts will help perform targeted marketing to each customer segment, resource allocation towards high-value shopping or product segments, and also to identify potential customer churn to enable targeted retention efforts.

These are merely a couple of real-world examples presented for an understanding of the use cases of ML. They expand to any scenario where we have clear patterns in the available data. It is costlier for a human to find these patterns than using an automated approach like ML to help solve them. Some other common day-to-day use cases include applications performing machine transaction, personal assistants and their specific features, deciding how much to charge for your product or service, forecasting customer demand, churn prediction, brand monitoring, and so on.

All of these preceding examples we see indicate some common properties as follows:

- Without quality data and enough history to capture all possible variations, the interpretations of any ML model may not be an acceptable solution.

- None of these examples aim to replace any existing system, but they merely help automate them to some extent.

- A constant feedback system is crucial to not only evaluate how a model is trained or how the data is prepared but also to ensure that when the scenarios of the problem statement evolve, hence changing the patterns and variations in the data, the ML models can adapt to the new changes using model monitoring and retraining.

As we will learn in further chapters in this book, the algorithm of the model itself is a very small part of the ML system in production.

Common algorithms

In this section, we will learn about the most common and traditional ML approaches and algorithms in brief. These are algorithms used in almost all business scenarios across domains wherein ML finds its use. Either these algorithms are used to estimate a continuous value or a categorical one, so in a sense, they help find numeric outcomes or decision outcomes. These are specific examples where we have the history, also known as the labeled data, which is called **supervised learning**, but there are also scenarios where we do not have labeled datasets, which is called **unsupervised learning**. Let us take an overall look into each of the popular ML algorithms in brief, which fall into these categories. In the later chapters of this book, we will discuss in depth the mathematical and design aspects of them when we start to code them. The different types of common algorithms are discussed in the following sections.

Linear regression

Starting with supervised learning, let us see the most common regression method, also known as **linear regression**. This is an algorithm where we try to estimate the value of a continuous value, like a real number. Examples of a typical target variable include salary, age, price demand, and so on. In the case of linear regression, we would want to estimate the value of this target continuous variable based on an assumed linear relationship with the features (which are one or more independent variables).

Let us consider an example of the estimation of the price of a house or the salary of an employee joining a company to understand linear regression better:

- Features or properties like the size of the house, the area where the house is, the number of bedrooms in the house, the number of hospitals in the locality, etc., can be used in a linear regression model to determine the estimated price of the house.

- In this example, since we have more than one feature (or independent variables), hence we will call this a multiple linear regression use case, where if we were simply estimating the salary of a person given the number of years of experience the individual has, then we are talking about simple (or single) linear regression.

- In the real-world, though, we may hardly find a relevant example of simple linear regression, while in most cases, we will have multiple independent features contributing to the estimation of one target continuous variable.

Mathematically, one can think of linear regression as a straight line in two dimensions when we talk about a simple linear regression model, where the Y-axis represents the target (like salary) and the X-axis represents the feature (like years of experience). A quick mathematical representation of a simple linear regression model is as follows:

$$y = mx + b$$

Where:

- **y**: Dependent variable

- **x**: Independent variable

- **m**: Slope of the regression line

- **b**: y-intercept of the regression line

In simple terms, in the case of a simple linear regression, we find the optimal values of m and b (the slope and the y-intercept) so that we can estimate the near to correct values of y given the values of x. Essentially, the y-intercept is the unknown noise from other unconsidered factors that affect the value of y, while the slope (m) is the importance of the input feature or independent variable. As we see in this book later, optimizing values for both of these is a crucial task.

Visually, we can understand the simple linear regression model as follows:

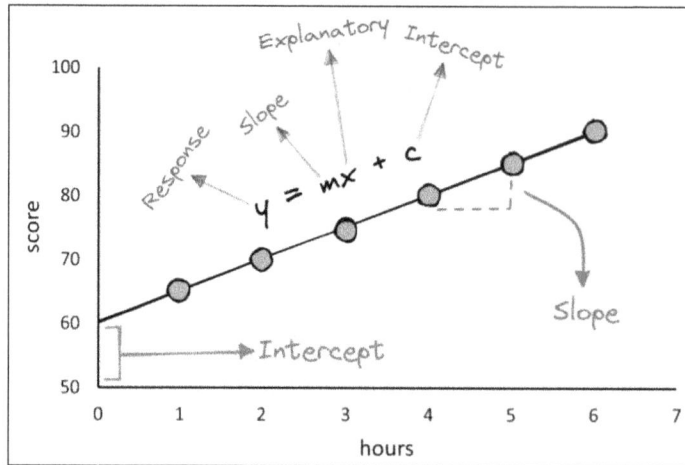

Figure 2.2: *Simple linear regression*

Reference: https://pub.towardsai.net/machine-learning-
the-first-step-is-to-understand-simple-linear-regression-30dde8b4739

We can extend the same concept over to multiple linear regression, where the two-dimensional line above is simply to be replaced to be a hyperplane in n-dimensional space, since in the case of multiple linear regression, we have many features $(x_1, x_2, x_3, ..., x_n)$ and one target (y). To understand this mathematically, let us take an example use case where one would like to estimate the price of a used car. The features (or factors) affecting the price of used cars can range from mileage to model to segment. For the sake of simplicity, if we consider only these three features for our experiment, we can mathematically represent it as:

$$Sale\ price(y) = b + m1(mileage) + m2(model) + m3(segment)$$

Where:

- **y**: Sale price or our target variable
- **b**: y-intercept value
- **m1, m2, m3**: Slopes or weights of each feature

Note that while one explores other literature on the same topic of regression or any other ML models, one may end up seeing different notations representing the same concept or design. For example, at times, the y-intercept value may be represented with notations like w_0 or *c*.

Linear regression is a widely used statistical method because of its simplicity, interpretability, and extrapolation capabilities. However, linear regression expects a linear relationship between the features and the target, so if the relation is non-linear in any given scenario, then linear regression fails to deliver good results. Note that by linear relation, the algorithm assumes that with an increase in the value of a feature variable, the target value increases or decreases, respectively.

It is to be noted that there are cases where any given ML model learns from the training data so well that its performance on the training data is much better as compared to the evaluation or test data. This scenario is called **overfitting**. One can think of it as a student who has potentially mugged up anyone or given a set of books for a particular subject for an exam, but when an unknown or unseen question is given to the student, they do not perform well. Linear regression, unfortunately, is no exception and is seen to be affected by overfitting. In later chapters of this book, we will also define underfitting and see the possible ways to solve this problem.

To sum up, note that every given dataset will contain valid or invalid outliers. These are data points that are quite far away from the rest of the data points in terms of their properties. Imagine an apartment, for example, which was sold historically at a mediocre cost irrespective of being in a posh place. Having this example in the dataset causes substantial problems for linear regression and a substantial number of problems in learning patterns.

Logistic regression

Moving on to classification problems, the most common and very widely used ML algorithm is **logistic regression**. Although the name contains the term regression, logistic regression is used for classification because it models the probability of a binary or multi-class outcome using a logistic function. To clarify, binary classification use cases are where we have two possible outcomes or values of the target variable, for example, whether a transaction done by the customer is fraud or not, or whether it would rain today or not.

Before we investigate the algorithm itself, let us review some basics on odds and probability as follows:

- The theory of chances for success or failure events is often expressed as odds and probabilities.

- In simple words, odds are the ratio of chances in favor by chances against it, and its value lies between 0 to infinity. For example, the odds of getting an ace in a deck of 52 cards are 4/48, where the numerator contains the possible number of aces in a deck of cards, and the denominator contains all other cards.

- Probability is more holistic, where we define it as a ratio of chances in favor of events to the total trials. Hence, in the case of our previous question, the probability of getting an ace in a deck of 52 cards is 4/52 or 7.7%.

It is to be noted that, unlike odds, probability values always range between 0 to 1, where both extremes are near to impossible in the real-world. Simplifying this, we can understand a clean mathematical relation between odds and probability, as follows:

$$oddsratio = \frac{Probability\ (event\ A\ occuring)}{Probability\ (event\ A\ not\ occuring)}$$

Now, we can relate this to probability as follows:

$$oddsratio(A) = \frac{P(A)}{1 - P(A)}$$

Where *P(A)* is the probability of event *A* occurring.

So, we can now deductively say that:

$$P(A) = \frac{oddsratio(A)}{1 + oddsratio(A)}$$

Taking a logarithm of odd ratio gives us the *logit* function, expressed as:

$$\log(oddsratio) = logit(P) = \log\left(\frac{P}{1 - P}\right)$$

The *logit* function is very important in the field of statistics, as it can map the probability values ranging from 0 to 1 to a full range of values in the real-world, from 0 to infinity. The value of the logit function itself varies from negative infinity to positive infinity.

In line with the aforementioned, another important mathematical function, which we will make the most use of in our case, is the sigmoid function, which performs the inverse of the *logit*, i.e., it maps any arbitrary real number into the range of 0 to 1. Here is a quick diagram to understand the function itself:

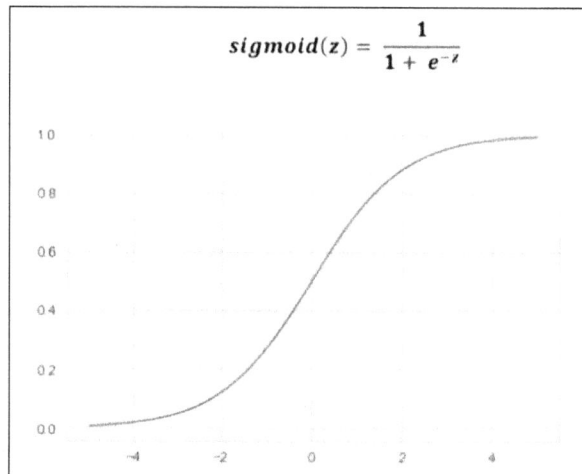

$$sigmoid(z) = \frac{1}{1 + e^{-z}}$$

Figure 2.3: Sigmoid function

It is important to know why we are learning logits and sigmoid in the case of logistic regression. In the case of linear regression, the target is a continuous variable, but in the case of classification problems where the target can have two classes (for example, in the case of binary classification) we cannot use a linear regression model, predicting the exact class for each observation is what the system is meant for, rather than estimating a real number. Also, in the case of logistic regression, since we are fitting a rather straight line or plane, because of the presence of different features, and especially the outliers, the best fit line is often biased and gives inaccurate results.

This is where logistic regression comes in place and uses the concepts of log of odds or logit, and sigmoid function majorly, to realize the scenario. Since in the case of logistic regression, the value we are trying to predict is either 1 or 0 (at least in the case of a binary classification problem), hence it becomes natural to squash the predictions from a model using a sigmoid, since it helps put the outcomes within the range of 0 to 1. Even in the case of multi-class classification problems, we can consider what is often referred to as the **one-vs-rest (OVR)** method, where one class of the target can be signified as 1 and the others being 0.

Imagine the previous diagram as a typical use case where one is trying to predict how likely a student is to pass if they study for 5 hours a day for a given subject. The outcome naturally falls within the range of 0 to 1, and the estimated or predicted outcome can also be very easily represented as a probabilistic value, making it easy to understand and consume. This is the sole reason why many large financial organizations still make use of this classical logistic regression model for a multitude of use cases like credit card or loan lending, transactional fraud detection, and so on. It is to be noted that the ease of understanding the outcome of an ML algorithm is of supreme importance, irrespective of the domain or use case one is trying to solve with it. Overall, logistic regression models the probability of the default class as opposed to the rest of the classes.

Let us also understand the intuition behind the usage of the sigmoid function in the case of logistic regression. Consider the function (as seen in *Figure 2.2*) that looks like a mathematical seesaw. Given a problem statement like which email is spam or not, provided we have the features of the email, like the number of exclamation points, keywords like free money in the email text, sender address, etc., on each side of the seesaw we have the labels, spam or not spam.

The design of the sigmoid function using logistic regression is as follows:

- Using the sigmoid function, logistic regression puts weights on each feature, like pushing down on one side of the seesaw.

- An email can then be classified as spam if the spam side goes down and vice-versa.

- Note that the sigmoid function will return any value between 0 (not spam) to 1 (definitely spam).

- Next, we can multiply each input feature with the weights we learn from the model (using the historically labeled data, remember, supervised learning) and add them up.

- This value acts like a distance from the center of the seesaw. We finally plug this sum into the sigmoid function to get the probability of the email being spam.

- Essentially, during the training phase, we show the model lots of training examples (which are previously labeled data of emails that are spam or not spam), using which the model adjusts the weights to make the seesaw tilt correctly for each email to either side.

With time, the model learns to predict the spam probability for new emails.

Overall, logistic regression is easy to implement and interpret, and fast as well (making it suitable for large datasets as well). However, it is still limited to linear relationships between the features and the target, and, with high dimensional data, it is found to be prone to overfitting. So, when dealing with low-dimensional and linearly separable data, and with interpretability being one major requirement of the ML model in production, logistic regression is a great choice.

Naïve Bayes

Since we started with logistic regression as a classic example of a probabilistic model (which uses the basis of logit and sigmoid function(s)) to determine or predict the output class (given a particular unseen observation), let us look into yet another very commonly used algorithm, called **Naïve Bayes algorithm**, which follows a naturally similar path, but evaluates it from a different perspective. It was the infamous reverend named *Thomas Bayes* who came up with something so elegant that his creation, also called the **Bayes theorem**, drives many uncertainty-driven postulates and experiments in the real-world.

Before jumping into what the Naïve Bayes algorithm is and how it works, one must acknowledge what the Bayes theorem is and its essentials. Imagine that any of us is a detective with a unique superpower; we can potentially update our beliefs based on new evidence. This is the essence of Bayes' theorem, a mathematical formula that helps us recalculate probabilities as we learn more information. Here is shown how it works:

1. **Start with prior beliefs**: We have an initial idea of how likely something is to occur based on our experience or knowledge. This is called the **prior probability**. It is like our starting point before we collect any new evidence.

2. **Gather new evidence**: We encounter new information that could change our beliefs. This is the evidence in Bayes' theorem.

3. **Calculate the likelihood**: How likely is this new evidence, given different scenarios or hypotheses? This is the likelihood, a measure of how well the evidence supports each possibility.

4. **Update beliefs**: Bayes' theorem allows us to combine our prior beliefs with the new evidence to get an updated probability, called the **posterior probability**. This reflects our new understanding of the situation after considering the new information.

The formula (in detective terms):

$$Posterior\ (How\ likely\ is\ the\ culprit, given\ the\ clues)$$
$$= \frac{(Likelyhood\ of\ Clues, given\ the\ culprit) * (prior\ probability\ of\ the\ culprit)}{Overall\ likelihood\ of\ the\ clues}$$

Let one think of Bayes' theorem like this:

- If the evidence strongly supports a certain scenario (high likelihood), our estimation of its probability will increase.

- If the evidence is weak or contradicts our prior beliefs, our estimated probability will decrease.

The question is why we need to know about it, especially before learning the Naïve Bayes algorithm. The following reasons need to be taken into consideration:

- **Makes us better thinkers**: It forces us to consider both our initial assumptions and new information, leading to more informed decisions.

- **Handles uncertainty**: It is a powerful tool for dealing with uncertainty and making the best judgments possible based on limited evidence.

- **Used in many fields**: From spam filters to medical diagnoses, Bayes' theorem is applied in various fields to make predictions and update beliefs based on new data.

Now, let us take a similar example to understand the Naïve Bayes algorithm. Imagine, yet again, that any of us is a detective investigating a crime scene. We have clues like scattered footprints, a broken window, and a mysterious note. To catch the culprit, we need to make predictions based on these clues.

Here are shown the ways to how Naïve Bayes cracks the case:

- **Gather evidence**: Just like a detective, Naïve Bayes begins by collecting clues (features) from your dataset. These might be words in emails, attributes of products, or symptoms of patients.

- **Calculate probabilities**: Naïve Bayes carefully analyzes the clues and calculates probabilities based on past cases and how often each clue appears in different scenarios (our target classes from the training data, for brevity). For example, how often do muddy footprints appear in burglary cases versus friendly visits?

- **Assume independence**: There are ways that make this algorithm Naïve. This happens when Naïve Bayes assumes that each clue is independent of the others, similar to a detective acting as if each piece of evidence is unrelated. This is not always true in real life, but it often works surprisingly well.

- **Combine the evidence**: When faced with a new case, Naïve Bayes multiplies the probabilities of each clue, given different scenarios. This creates a score for each possible outcome.

- **Unmask the culprit**: The scenario with the highest combined probability is most likely to be a culprit. Naïve Bayes points its finger at the most probable class based on the available evidence.

Essentially, one should have received this well by now that the Naïve Bayes algorithm is just like a detective with a knack for pattern recognition, and hence, it comes with the important list of benefits as follows:

- **Simple and efficient**: It is super easy to understand and implement, making it a popular choice for spam filters, text classification, and sentiment analysis.

- **Fast training**: It can learn quickly from even large datasets, making it efficient for real-time applications.

- **Handles diverse data**: It works well with numerical and categorical features, adapting to various types of evidence.

Let us keep in mind that even detectives have their limitations:

- **Naive assumption**: The independence assumption can sometimes lead to errors, especially when features are strongly correlated.

- **Sensitive to irrelevant features**: It can be misled by irrelevant clues, so careful feature selection is crucial.

- **Not ideal for complex relationships**: When features have complex interactions, more sophisticated algorithms might be better suited.

In short, the Naïve Bayes algorithm is like a detective who excels at solving straightforward cases with clear patterns. It is a great tool for quick and efficient predictions, but one should be mindful of its assumptions and limitations when dealing with complex data landscapes.

K-nearest neighbors

What if we could find simple mathematical distances between points and evaluate if they are similar or not? The **k-nearest neighbors** (**KNN**) algorithm tries to do the same by representing the available training data in n-dimensional space. To understand KNN in brief, we will call it a party planner. Let us take the example of organizing a massive party. We have no clue, or it is surely difficult to know exactly who the guests are (other than their names, maybe) and where to seat them so that they are always involved in the proceedings and never feel left off. This can only happen if they are seated with like-minded guests. Think of our guests as data points. Each guest has features, like hobbies, music tastes, and favorite foods. We want to group them with similar guests to ensure a fun-filled bash.

Here are the steps to show how KNN works if we have enough quality data:

1. **Pick a k value**: This is like choosing your squad size, which decides how many neighbors each guest gets.

a. For each new guest, we can calculate the distances between that guest and all the existing guests. Imagine using a ruler or measuring tape based on their features.

b. Next, we find the k number of guests closest to the new guest (the party buddies). Further, we look at the majority group among these k buddies named bookworms, foodies, or dance floor enthusiasts.

c. Finally, we assign the new guest to that group, ensuring they are surrounded by like-minded friends.

Here, we use distance metrics, like Euclidean distance, to measure how far guests are from each other. Think of it as the physical distance between them on the dance floor. Note that Euclidean distance is not the only way to find distances between points. There are other alternative ways, used from time to time in KNN and elsewhere, depending on its suitability as per the data and its properties. Let us look at some of them briefly:

- **Manhattan distance**: Calculates distance as the sum of absolute differences between coordinates, like navigating city blocks.

- **Minkowski distance**: A generalized form that encompasses both Euclidean and Manhattan distances by using a power parameter.

- **Chebyshev distance**: Finds the maximum absolute difference between coordinates in any single dimension.

- **Hamming distance**: Counts the number of differing positions between two strings of equal length.

- **Cosine similarity**: Measures the angle between two vectors, often used for text or document comparison.

- **Jaccard index**: Calculates the ratio of shared elements to the total number of elements in two sets.

Additionally, note that a small k can lead to overfitting (too specific), while a large k might lead to underfitting (too general). This depicts overall how the optimal value of k impacts model performance.

2. **Binary classification of groups**: For binary classification (two groups), we count the majority class among the k neighbors. So, 3 bookworms out of 5 buddies? A new guest joins the book club. We can consider this step as an internal group voting to find the majority and accordingly group the classes.

Note that this does also leave chances for errors, and hence, as we design and develop KNN in further chapters in this book, we will understand the best practices to avoid such scenarios, although the errors in any ML model can never be pushed back to 0.

One should also note, and as we will learn later in this book, that the value of *k* is a hyperparameter (nuts and bolts of ML), which can be tuned to find the best value given a particular data or scenario to get the best possible KNN model.

3. **Multiple classification of groups**: For more complex problems (multiple groups), we might use weighted voting based on distance. Closer buddies have a stronger say in the group assignment.

From this example, one can decipher the quick advantages of using KNN as a classification algorithm for binary and multi-class problems, overall, as follows:

- **Easy**:
    - No complex equations, just distances and majority voting.
    - Perfect for dipping our toes into ML since it is easy to understand and explain, just like the party planner example.

- **Interpretable**:
    - You can see who influenced the grouping of a new data point.
    - It helps us to debug and understand the behavior of the model.

- **Diversified**:
    - There is no need for fancy or complicated engineering.
    - KNN can handle a good amount of data quite well.

However, one should also remember that KNN comes with its own set of unique caveats, some of which are as follows:

- **High-dimensional data**: As the number of features increases, calculating distances becomes computationally expensive.

- **Sensitive**:
    - It includes useless features that can confuse the model.
    - It also leads to inaccurate groupings.

- **Memory**:
    - Storing all the data for comparison can be demanding.
    - This is especially true for large datasets.

Remember, KNN is like a helpful party planner, as per the preceding example, but it also comes with its caveats. It is best for simple problems with clear feature group relationships. Also, one should note that KNN, with some architectural modifications in the way it works, not only helps to solve classification use cases but is also used for regression problems. When used for regression, rather than taking a vote, the algorithm will take an average, for example, of the values part of a particular group where the new observation is found closer.

Decision trees

Decision trees are one of the most common and approachable ML algorithms, which comes as a precious gift from the world of statistics. By its nature or design, it looks almost like a rule book, or a bunch of if-else statements if you like, where a particular set of conditions are validated at each step as the algorithm tries to model the training data in the form of a tree. Note that similar to KNN, the decision trees can also be used for both classification and regression use cases. Let us try to visualize how a typical decision tree looks like using the following representation:

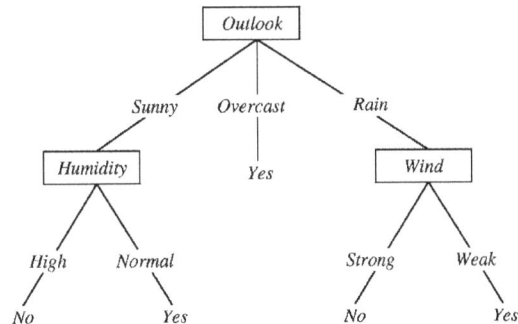

Figure 2.4: *Typical decision trees*

Reference: https://towardsdatascience.com/decision-tree-in-machine-learning-e380942a4c96

Let us try and understand how it works, again using a simple example. Imagine choosing your favorite adventure book where every decision leads you down a different path and shapes your story. Overall, this is how decision trees work, which logically sounds like a bunch of rules or paths or if-else statements. For example, let us think of our data points as adventurers. Each data point has features like age, income, and spending habits. These are the features that one has collected for training and use in the decision tree model. Of course, we want to predict something about them, like whether they will buy a new gadget or not. Other similar examples, the classic decision tree use cases, may include decision-making systems. For instance, whether it would rain or not, or whether a certain team will win a particular match or tournament. However, one important application of decision trees is in the healthcare industry, where, even today, many systems use this algorithm for cancer detection.

Decision trees, in the preceding example, will guide them through a series of choices, like the following:

- **Starting with a root node**: This is the first question, asking if your age is above 30.

- **Branching out based on answers**: Each answer creates a new branch and another question. For instance, do you earn more than $50,000?

- **Keep asking questions**: Each branch gets split further based on answers, forming a tree-like structure.

- **Reaching a leaf node**: These are the endpoints, representing a prediction or category. For example, a leaf might say gadget buyer or gadget ignorer.

Imagine an adventurer starting at the root, answering questions at each node, and following the chosen branches. Their path through the tree determines their final category at the leaf node. Behind the scenes, the mathematics of decision trees is quite intuitive but interesting. Let us try to understand it in brief, as follows:

In the case of decision trees, the algorithm uses information gain to choose the best questions at each node. This measures how well a question separates different data points into distinct groups. Information gain tells us how much a specific feature reduces our surprise about the outcome. The feature that surprises us the least, by neatly dividing the data into predictable groups, is the one with the highest information gain and, therefore, the most valuable for making accurate predictions. Information gain is used in various ML algorithms, particularly decision trees. It helps these algorithms build tree-like structures by choosing the features that best split the data and lead to a more accurate prediction at each level. The algorithm will keep splitting the data until pure leaf nodes are reached or a stopping point, which can be considered as a maximum depth. As a hyperparameter, we can specify which depth we would like to reach in the model with sufficient experiments, as we will find in the later relevant chapters in this book.

Let us look at some important and common advantages of decision trees as follows:

- **Easy**:
  - One can trace the logic behind each prediction by simply following the branches.
  - Later, when we develop decision trees, we will see options to visualize the resulting trees, and clearly, one would be able to identify the rule sets created by the algorithm to model the data.

- **Diversification**: By its design, the decision tree algorithm works sufficiently well with numeric and categorical features, making it versatile for various problems.

- **Effectiveness**: Training and prediction are quick and suitable for real-time applications.

However, some areas of decision trees may also be concerning, depending on the use case we are trying to solve using it, some of which are as follows:

- **Overfitting**: A decision tree model can, more often than not, be inclined to memorize the patterns from the available training data instead of generalizing it to unseen examples in the real-world. This is a very common problem, however, with many ML algorithms, which we would try to learn more about and eradicate to the best possible extent when we learn how to perform hyperparameter tuning.

- **Sensitive**: As seen in many industrial applications, including useless features can create unnecessary branches and reduce accuracy. Hence, it becomes quite important to perform feature selection (i.e., a process to select only the relevant features) and pass them over to the algorithm so that the model is less sensitive in nature.

- **Bias**: If there are obvious biases in the training data, decision trees are unfortunately not able to handle them well, and hence, the resultant model is also equally biased.

It is to be noted that the decision tree algorithm, and hence the resultant model, is similar to branching story paths, which eventually guide data points toward predicted outcomes. They are great for simple problems with clear decision rules but might get tangled with complex data. Let us now see another algorithm where one may want to get over these limitations of decision trees to a good extent. Also, one important point to remember at this stage is that in the future chapters of this book, when we implement decision trees, we will also use methods like pruning to make the trees less susceptible to their fallacies.

Random forests

While understanding decision trees, we realized that often the basis of noise in the data, or outliers, decision trees are prone to some cases of failures. Moreover, it seems as if, going by the example we took of a party planner, there is only one of the multitude of options that we are taking into consideration while placing relevant or like-minded guests alongside each other. What if we could tweak this approach a bit, and rather than taking a single decision tree, we could utilize the power of 100s of them? This is where the random forests algorithm comes into play. Let us try and understand it using an intuitive example.

Imagine we are on a treasure hunt in a dense jungle. Instead of relying on just one treasure map, we have a whole crew of experienced guides, each carrying their map based on different landmarks and pathways. It is tactically what a random forest is. It is a collection of diverse decision trees working together to find the hidden treasure or our desired prediction.

Here is the working of the algorithm with reference to our example:

- **Planting a forest**: Instead of just one tree, we plant many different decision trees, each representing a unique perspective on the jungle. In other words, instead of passing our data to one decision tree, we take a bunch of decision trees and share our data (the one used for training) across them. There are particular ways to do it, which we will learn as we start designing and developing models with this algorithm in the later parts of this book.

- **Random paths**: To avoid everyone following the same path, we give each guide a limited view of the map and instruct them to focus on specific landmarks. This injects diversity into their interpretations of the jungle. In other words, we do not give the entire training dataset to all the decision trees; rather, we take a randomized sample of the training data and pass a particular variety to one particular decision tree and continue the process.

- **Exploring different routes**: Each guide (tree) builds its path through the jungle based on its limited map and the encountered landmarks. They might take different turns, climb different hills, and encounter different clues. In essence, we are letting each decision tree in our current setup learn from the different variations of our data. This brings different perspectives to the table. For example, the lead of a particular team in a software company takes into account the views of all the engineers working in the team for a given problem statement; everyone is allowed to speak and share their different thoughts by looking at different aspects of the problem statement.

- **Sharing findings**: Once everyone reaches the end of their path, they gather and share their insights. Each guide points towards a possible location of the treasure. This method is an inspiration that builds a rather interesting group of ML algorithms, and the approach is called **bagging**. Later, we will learn some of the methods that use another interesting approach called **boosting**.

- **Majority wins**: We do not just trust one guide blindly. Instead, we combine their knowledge by taking the most frequent prediction among all the guides. This collective wisdom leads to a more robust and accurate estimate of where the treasure lies. (Remember our example of the team lead?) In simple words, we take the majority vote from all the decision trees for any particular observation rather than considering the prediction given by one single decision tree.

The result of this exercise is a wiser and more reliable treasure hunt, as follows:

- By combining the insights of diverse and independent decision trees, we reduce the risk of being misled by a single biased or overfitted tree.

- The random element injects diversity and helps the forest navigate complex patterns in the jungle that a tree might miss.

- The majority vote approach minimizes the impact of individual errors and leads to a more reliable prediction of the location of the treasure.

The random forests algorithm is a powerful method for software engineers because it offers the following:

- **Improved accuracy and robustness**:
  - Their ensemble nature surpasses the limitations of individual decision trees.
  - Hence, these models (like bagging and boosting) are also called **ensemble models** in the realm of ML algorithms.

- **Interpretability**: We can still analyze individual trees to understand the logic behind predictions.

- **Versatility**: They handle diverse data types and provide valuable feature importance insights.

However, just like any other jungle expedition, especially the ones where we go with our friends and family for the first time, random forest algorithms have their challenges:

- **Computational cost**: Training many trees can be resource-intensive for large datasets.

- **Black box aspect**: While individual trees are interpretable, the complex interaction within the forest can be less transparent.

- **Overfitting potential**: Not tuning them properly can still lead to overfitting, even with random features.

In essence, one must acknowledge that a random forest algorithm is analogous to a wise council of decision trees, collectively guiding us toward better predictions in complex data domains. It is a powerful methodology, but one must be mindful of their resource requirements and their potential for overfitting. To reduce the overall overfitting potential of random forest models, one may consider one or more of the following approaches:

- **Limit tree depth**: Keep trees shallow by setting a maximum depth to prevent them from learning very specific details.

- **Increase minimum samples per leaf**: Require a minimum number of data points in each leaf node to avoid capturing noise.

- **Control number of trees**: While more trees often improve accuracy, excessively large forests can overfit; find a balance.

- **Adjust number of features**: Limit the number of features considered at each split to reduce complexity and prevent memorization.

Lastly, and just like KNN and decision trees, random forests can also be equally applied for regression and classification use cases alike. The overall method of how a random forest algorithm is applied to a regression use case is similar to how we would have used a single decision tree: find the average or median value within a certain prediction area to find the estimated real number of the target that we would want to estimate. Throughout this book, for all natural reasons, we will always call regression problems estimations since one can never exactly predict the value of a continuous variable, which can take the infinite shape of values.

Other than the handful of most common traditional ML algorithms, which we have briefly learned in this chapter, there are many others in the arena, and the list keeps on growing as ever, with continuous research taking place in AI and ML. One critical point that one must remember is to focus more on the use case, understand more of the data, engineer more of the solution components, and then perform enough experiments to fit and find the right ML model, which completes the picture. Without an approach like this, with relevant modifications as required, the majority of the ML models we come up with may never see the light of day in their lifetime, which is the case for approximately 80% of the ML development today. This is also one of the core reasons why, as part of the curriculum of this book, we would specifically touch base in-depth on ML operations and how to best put ML solutions in production.

For a quick reference, here is a list of some common ML algorithms that one takes into use as per the specific use case in hand:

Name	Type	Description
Linear regression	Regression	Finds a linear relationship between a dependent variable and one or more independent variables.
Logistic regression	Classification	Predicts the probability of an event occurring based on a set of independent variables.
Decision tree	Classification	Creates a tree-like structure to classify data points based on their features.
Random forest	Classification	Creates a forest of decision trees and uses the majority vote to make predictions.
Support vector machine (SVM)	Classification	Finds the optimal boundary between two classes of data points.
KNN	Classification	Classifies data points based on the majority class of their nearest neighbors.
Naïve Bayes	Classification	Uses Bayes' theorem to predict the probability of an event occurring based on a set of independent variables.
Principal component analysis (PCA)	Dimensionality reduction	Reduces the number of features in a dataset while retaining as much information as possible.
Singular Value Decomposition (SVD)	Dimensionality reduction	Similar to PCA but can be used on non-square matrices.
Independent component analysis (ICA)	Dimensionality reduction	Finds a set of independent components that are maximally independent of each other.
Factor analysis	Dimensionality reduction	Finds a set of latent factors that explain the variance in a dataset.
Cluster analysis	Clustering	Groups data points into clusters based on their similarity.
K-means clustering	Clustering	Partitions a dataset into a specified number of clusters.
Hierarchical clustering	Clustering	Creates a hierarchy of clusters based on the similarity of data points.

Name	Type	Description
Density-based spatial clustering of applications with noise (DBSCAN)	Clustering	Finds clusters of data points based on their density.
Ordering Points To Identify the Clustering Structure (OPTICS)	Clustering	Finds clusters of data points based on their reachability distance.
Association rule mining	Association analysis	Finds rules that describe the relationships between items in a dataset.
Apriori algorithm	Association analysis	Finds frequent itemsets in a dataset.
FP-growth algorithm	Association analysis	Finds frequent itemsets in a dataset without generating candidate itemsets.
Eclat algorithm	Association analysis	Finds frequent itemsets in a dataset using a divide-and-conquer approach.

Table 2.1: Common ML algorithms

Ways to make ML models better

Boosting the performance and interpretation of our ML model hinges on understanding its strengths and weaknesses. Remember, building powerful and interpretable models is an iterative process. By taking a data-driven, thoughtful approach, we can unlock the full potential of your ML models and make informed decisions based on their insights.

Here are some key strategies that one should acknowledge day in and day out; we are coming up with new strategies.

Data matters

Without data, there cannot be ML. For appropriate utilization of available data, or to curate it, the following are some of the common strategies:

- **Quality over quantity**: One must focus on clean, accurate, and relevant data and address missing values, outliers, and inconsistencies. Dirty data means dirty predictions. In other words, garbage in equals garbage out. Most of the time, effort, and resources of an AI engineer in the real-world are spent on data engineering while working on the resolution of any given problem statement. This skill is often overlooked, and hence, our readers are strongly recommended to improve their data engineering skills consistently. For example, one should make effective use of handling missing data using data imputation methods (like imputing with mean, median, or mode) or even outlier detection and removal as applicable.

- **Feature engineering**: As part of the AI and ML lifecycle, we should always try to transform and combine features to create more informative ones. Since AI and ML, at their core, are more about experimentation, coupled with solid programming practices, one should always explore different feature sets to see what resonates with our model the best.

- **Balance data**: Real-world data is not only messy but always equally unbalanced. For example, while building a fraud detection system for any financial institution, it is imperative that out of all the available transactions, hardly 1-2% of the examples may contain examples of actual frauds. Hence, we must strive to ensure that our classes are adequately represented, especially in imbalanced datasets. In such cases, and as we would learn specifically in the later relevant chapters in this book, one should make effective use of techniques like oversampling or under-sampling to avoid bias.

Model selection and optimization

Building an ML model is one of the basic steps post we have some quality data available. Here are some guidelines on how one selects and optimizes models for a given use case:

- **Choosing the right algorithm**: Although easier said than done, one must try to align our algorithm with our problem type and data characteristics. It is neither wise nor the best practice to just throw a black box at everything.

- **Hyperparameter tuning**: As briefly stated earlier, one must refine the parameters of our algorithm to find the balance between performance and generalizability. This is one of the reasons why AI engineers make optimal use of validation sets to avoid overfitting as much as possible.

- **Ensembling methods**: In many cases, we combine predictions from multiple models to improve accuracy and robustness. These are cases where we prefer using random forests or other similar algorithms.

Interpretation and debugging

While model building is a crucial part of the process, understanding its intricacies is even more important. Let us look at some guidelines on how to interpret and debug ML models from a technical aspect as follows:

- **Feature importance**: We should understand, in depth, both from a technical as well as a business perspective, which features contribute most to the predictions of the model. Tools like feature importance plots can give us valuable insights.

- **Error analysis**: We should always investigate the errors of our models to identify weaknesses and potential biases. For example, are certain classes or data points consistently misclassified?

- **Visualizations**: We would often use techniques like decision trees or saliency maps to visualize how our model makes predictions. This can help identify biases and complex interactions.

Production readiness

Creating an ML solution is one part of the story, but putting the software in production and being able to constantly update it as the data and requirements change, along with explaining its outcomes to stakeholders, is equally crucial. Here are some ways in which one can achieve this, which will be studied in the later chapters:

- **Regular evaluation**: In production scenarios, we always evaluate the performance of our model over time and retrain it if needed. A well-thought choice of metrics like accuracy, precision, and recall can help track the progress and performance of any given ML system.

- **Explainable AI (XAI) tools**: In any given scenario in production, we should always explore emerging XAI methods to improve interpretability, especially for complex models like deep neural networks. In many cloud platforms, for example, this is a critical aspect of the AI and ML offerings. We will see some specific examples on this topic in this book using the Google Cloud Platform.

- **Domain knowledge**: Often the most ignored aspect, but one must leverage the understanding of the problem domain to interpret the predictions of the model and identify potential issues.

Conclusion

In this chapter, we covered the introduction to ML, the variety of use cases, applications, domains where they find usefulness, and the types or methods of implementing AI and ML for problem-solving.

Here, we briefly realized the importance of ML systems in production and its components, the common ML algorithms that find their places in a variety of relevant applications, and how to make these models better in their lifecycles.

In the next chapter, we are going to learn about two of the most popular and production-grade libraries in Python programming language, scikit-learn and TensorFlow, to further design and develop ML systems.

Exercises

Let us attempt the following questions and tasks to get a better understanding of how ML algorithms work in various situations.

1. From any credible blogs on the Internet (like *Analytics Vidhya, Machine Learning Mastery*, etc.), read about at least 3 other algorithms used in ML and their nuances than the ones mentioned in this chapter.

2. *StatQuest* by *Josh Starmer* is one of such excellent *YouTube* channels that present any given ML model with simple explanations and visuals. Go to his channel and watch at least one video each for all of the ML algorithms that we have discussed in this chapter.

3. Register on the *Kaggle* portal, which is an excellent place to start practicing ML implementations in a variety of different use cases and problem statements. One may want to see the various solutions created by different engineers and data scientists on this platform by looking at their code or notebooks.

4. Read about **machine learning operations (MLOps)** in Google Cloud public documentation. If possible, read the MLOps newsletter from Google, whose PDF is available from a quick internet search. One great resource to start with is this architecture reference: **https://cloud.google.com/architecture/mlops-continuous-delivery-and-automation-pipelines-in-machine-learning**

Join our book's Discord space

Join the book's Discord Workspace for Latest updates, Offers, Tech happenings around the world, New Release and Sessions with the Authors:

https://discord.bpbonline.com

CHAPTER 3

TensorFlow Essentials

Introduction

For coders who would like to learn about AI and ML applications, TensorFlow is a production-ready toolchain. This open-source framework, originally developed at *Google*, empowers one to build ML systems on scale. Although it can be used across a variety of tasks in the ML lifecycle, TensorFlow has a particular focus on the training and inference of a deep neural network, alongside traditional ML algorithms and reinforcement learning. Although we would be using Python in this book while using TensorFlow, however, the library has support for Java, C++, and JavaScript, as well. This flexibility helps to use TensorFlow across industries, even for web and mobile applications where one would like to integrate AI and ML solutions.

In this chapter, we will use both TensorFlow and scikit-learn to build our first set of programs for ML, and then we will learn about another great library, PyTorch, to find where it might fit into our landscape in the future.

Structure

The chapter covers the following topics:

- TensorFlow
- Scikit-learn

- ML models with TensorFlow and scikit-learn
- Merits and demerits of TensorFlow
- TensorFlow vs. scikit-learn vs. PyTorch
- Keras

Objectives

By the end of this chapter, you will be able to understand what TensorFlow is, how it works, what its components are, how to use it effectively for the production scale ML applications, and its comparison with its peers like scikit-learn and PyTorch.

TensorFlow

In simple words, TensorFlow is an AI and ML library in multiple programming languages, like Python. The following are some key points about TensorFlow and its capabilities:

- While the initial reference implementation could run only on a single device, TensorFlow can run on multiple CPUs and GPUs (with optional **Compute Unified Device Architecture (CUDA)** and SYCL extensions support). To understand these terminologies briefly:

   o CUDA enabled TensorFlow to harness the power of NVIDIA GPUs for accelerated computation.

   o SYCL provides a more unified way to write code that can run on both CPUs and GPUs from various vendors.

- TensorFlow is available on all Linux and Windows distributions, along with mobile computing platforms and frameworks like Android and iOS.

- When you write and execute TensorFlow code, computations are represented as stateful dataflow graphs.

- The name TensorFlow itself derives from the operations that such neural networks perform on multidimensional data arrays, which are referred to as tensors.

Building blocks

Let us understand this concept briefly before moving forward, as follows:

- A tensor is a generalization of vectors and matrices to potentially higher dimensions. Internally, TensorFlow represents tensors as n-dimensional arrays of base data types. Remember, when we use TensorFlow, tensors are the main objects passed around and manipulated throughout the program.

- Each of these tensors that we create and maintain helps to represent a partially defined computation step, which will eventually produce a value. This idea is quite similar to the fundamentals of functional programming paradigms as well.

- While we create and ask TensorFlow to use these tensors internally, TensorFlow will acknowledge or understand these objects and their operations in the form of a graph. Since tensors are programmed data objects, each tensor has a data type and size.

For this chapter, we will understand only the basics and delve our hands into some setup and exercises so that we can get a glimpse of how to install and use the library.

Let us briefly discuss the **application programming interfaces** (**APIs**) available in TensorFlow as follows:

- TensorFlow APIs are organized hierarchically with the high-level APIs (also called **Keras**).

- Keras is more object-oriented in its design and has an easier learning curve. TensorFlow also provides reusable libraries and modules for the common ML model components.

- Finally, TensorFlow also provides an extensive control layer to help a coder interact with CPU, GPU, and TPU architectures.

For the current scenario, we would recommend using **Google Colaboratory** to try and learn TensorFlow as follows:

- Google Colab is a free offering from Google to learn, run, and experiment with our ML models, while the data is kept within our realm if we use it in the right way.

- Google Colab is a free online extension of Jupyter Notebooks, which comes preinstalled during on-system installations of data science platforms like Anaconda.

- There are free and paid versions of Google Colab, and we will use the free version throughout this book wherever applicable.

We shall move ahead with the process. Now, go to **https://colab.research.google.com** and log in with your Google ID. The platform works using **single sign-on** (**SSO**). When you are logged in, the first page should look like *Figure 3.1*:

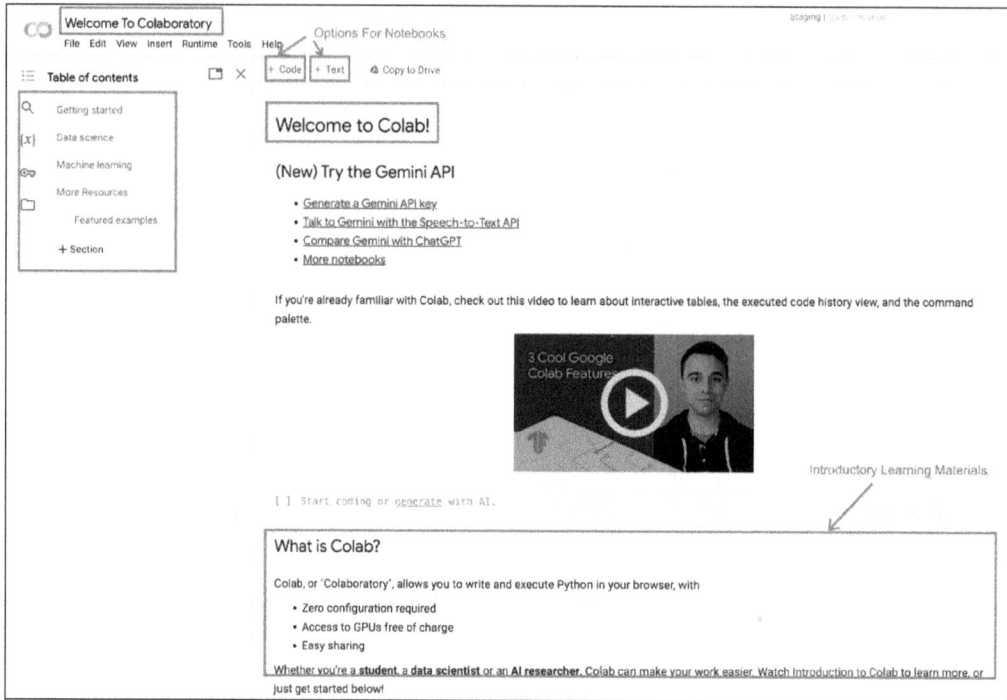

Figure 3.1: *Google Colab introduction*

Getting familiarized with the Google Colab environment is simple, and introductory learning materials are already available in the first notebook, which is shown in the preceding figure. It is to be noted that while working on any project that involves data of any levels of criticality and sensitivity, it is highly recommended that we set up, install, and use local and secured development environments in one's computing devices (desktop, laptop, MacBook, etc.) or Cloud environments like Google Cloud Platform, to ensure minimal chances of data loss or leakage.

Quick hands on

In this section, we will go through the steps of installing TensorFlow as follows:

1. The first step is to click on the **File** option, as shown in *Figure 3.1*, while logged into Google Colab.

2. Open a new notebook and write a code cell using the + **Code** option.

3. Next, even if the Google Colab environment comes with a lot of useful pre-loaded Python packages, one should install TensorFlow using the **pip** utility, which is very useful in the Python package installer and the management system.

4. To do this, in the new cell, we can run the following commands by using *Shift + Enter* or the Run button to run the cell.

See the following example, wherein in a new notebook in Google Colab, we are trying to install the TensorFlow library using the **pip** utility:

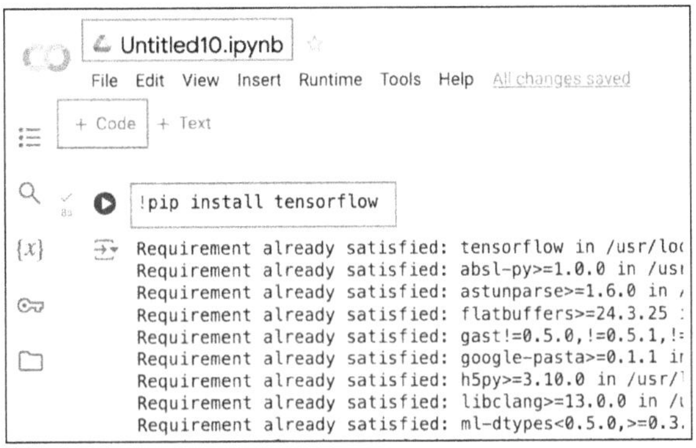

Figure 3.2: Installing TensorFlow

In many cases and as shown in the preceding example, we will find that the Google Colab environment is already preinstalled with the TensorFlow to best available stable version. In the preceding case, for example, the installed version is 2.15. Hence, from the **TensorFlow. org** website, we should be able to find its relevant features and usage documentation with ease.

Note that the TensorFlow website (**https://www.TensorFlow.org/api_docs**) contains excellent documentation on all of its features already, hence, it is helpful to be familiar with TensorFlow official documentation to find quick examples and code.

However, in the case where we were running the installation on a system where we had CUDA-enabled GPU, then we could install the GPU version of the TensorFlow. In Google Colab as well, we can change the runtime of a new or existing notebook to start using some of the available GPU options for free. This is great for trying things and experimenting.

Figure 3.3 shows how we can change the runtime from the **Connect** option on the right corner of our new notebook:

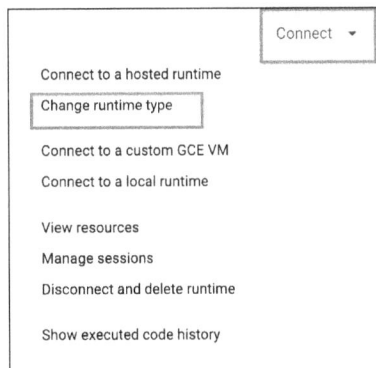

Figure 3.3: Google Colab runtimes

In the preceding example, we observe the following:

- We are keeping the runtime type as the default of Python 3 but changing the hardware accelerator to the T4 GPU, which is generally available for free on Google Colab.

- One must not forget to save the option from this screen, post which the runtime refreshes itself. It is to be noted that any of the previously executed cells are now lost from memory.

- We can imagine this as if the background machine has been restarted; however, the code written until now in the notebook is preserved, and one can restart their coding workflow from where they had left off.

See the following example where we are changing the runtime (using the last set of instructions) in our Notebook in Google Colab from the default value of **CPU** to **T4 GPU**:

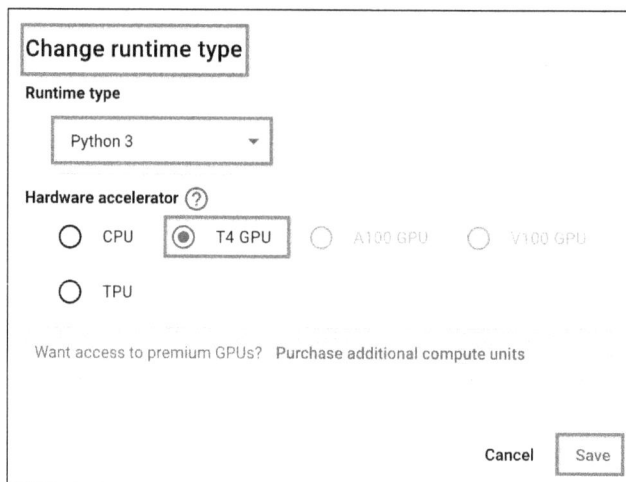

Figure 3.4: *Google Colab runtime changes*

It is the best practice always to comment in each code to the briefest extent possible.

This is to explain why a particular cell contains a particular code or logic, as shown in *Figure 3.5*.

In the following example, we try to install TensorFlow GPU in our Notebook:

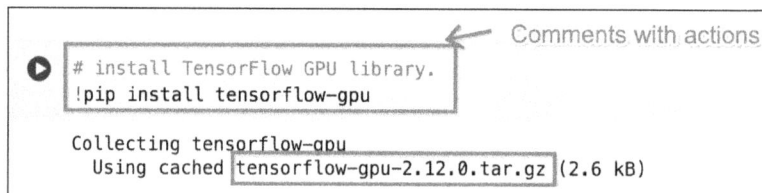

Figure 3.5: *Install TensorFlow GPU*

Creating tensors in Google Colab

The next obvious step is to import the TensorFlow library. This should be quite familiar to any Python developer since, without importing the library, we cannot make use of it.

Once imported, we check the version of the TensorFlow installation before starting to use it. It is shown in *Figure 3.6*:

```
[6]  # importing the tensorflow module
     import tensorflow as tf

[7]  # check the tensorflow version
     print(tf.__version__)

     2.15.0
```

Figure 3.6: *Importing TensorFlow*

Next, let us try to create tensors, which are the building blocks in the TensorFlow world, as follows:

- We can define tensors as a higher-level representation of arrays and matrices where tensors can provide a very easy realization of multidimensional data structures. This is very useful for a multitude of ML systems and data structures.

- Owing to its nature, tensors can be equally useful in representing an array or matrix in 1 or 2 dimensions while even in higher dimensions. Here is an example of how to create a couple of simple tensors, and then we check their rank, which determines their dimensions.

- We can also call **rank** as the degree of a tensor representing the number of dimensions involved in the tensor. It is to be noted that the tensors that we can create can be of rank 0, representing that they are scalar, while higher dimensions represent more real-world datasets.

See this example set of commands in our notebook in Google Colab, where we are trying to make use of basic TensorFlow variables:

```
v  Some Examples Of TensorFlow tensors

[4]  # regular variables.
     text = tf.Variable("Learning TensorFlow", tf.string)
     integer = tf.Variable(100000, tf.int16)
     decimal = tf.Variable(12.345, tf.float64)

[5]  # 1-dimensional tensor
     tensor_1d = tf.Variable([1, 2, 3, 4, 5], tf.int32)

[7]  # 2-dimensional vector
     tensor_2d = tf.Variable([[1, 2, 3], [4, 5, 6]], tf.int32)

[8]  # determine the rank of the 1d and 2d vectors
     # defined in the previous cells.
     print(tf.rank(tensor_1d))
     print(tf.rank(tensor_2d))

     tf.Tensor(1, shape=(), dtype=int32)
     tf.Tensor(2, shape=(), dtype=int32)
```

Figure 3.7: Tensors in TensorFlow

Let us see if we can change the shape of a given tensor or not and also if we can print the shape of a tensor. Note that the shape of a tensor is the number of items that exist in each dimension of that tensor. In some cases (which we will see later in this book), the shape of the tensor may be unknown to TensorFlow.

Here is an example of how to print and change the shape of a tensor:

```
[9]   # print the shape of each tensor
      # which we created in earlier cells
      print(tensor_1d.shape)
      print(tensor_2d.shape)

      (5,)
      (2, 3)

[10]  # example of how to change
      # the shape of a tensor
      tensor_2d = tf.reshape(tensor_2d, [3, 2])
      print(tensor_2d)

      tf.Tensor(
      [[1 2]
       [3 4]
       [5 6]], shape=(3, 2), dtype=int32)
```

Figure 3.8: Tensor operations using TensorFlow

Similar to Python, in the case of TensorFlow, we can observe the following:

- We can perform slicing operations on a tensor so that one can extract specific elements from a given tensor.

- These operations are particularly useful when we slice and dice our datasets to understand elements in the data and help perform deep-dive data analysis and understanding of the data before appropriate ML models are fit on them.

Here is an example of how we are creating a matrix in TensorFlow and checking particular elements:

```
[11] # matrix with 5 rows
     # and 5 columns containing
     # decimal numbers
     matrix_5x5 = tf.Variable(tf.random.uniform([5, 5], 0, 1))
     print(matrix_5x5)

     <tf.Variable 'Variable:0' shape=(5, 5) dtype=float32, numpy=
     array([[0.4790815 , 0.558849  , 0.26568604, 0.8936378 , 0.79865   ],
            [0.68829155, 0.31673968, 0.9043186 , 0.16667676, 0.28446352],
            [0.43490648, 0.6998658 , 0.65408254, 0.42688847, 0.97053814],
            [0.38188362, 0.16170537, 0.4051335 , 0.01381969, 0.86928904],
            [0.08335936, 0.8987994 , 0.644091  , 0.25638652, 0.72783506]],
           dtype=float32)>

[15] # print the 3rd element
     # of 2nd row of the last
     # tensor
     print(matrix_5x5[1, 2])

     tf.Tensor(0.9043186, shape=(), dtype=float32)

[16] # print the 5th element
     # of the 3rd row
     print(matrix_5x5[2, 4])

     tf.Tensor(0.97053814, shape=(), dtype=float32)
```

Figure 3.9: *Tensor operations in TensorFlow*

In the preceding examples, we observe the following:

- We see that we can slice and dice the elements of a tensor in a similar way as any other data structure (like a list) in Python.

- The other point to note is the cell output where we created the 5x5 tensor: we used an in-built function in TensorFlow to randomly generate uniform numbers. Hence, it is called the **tf.random.uniform**, which created the tensor.

- Another important point to be noted behind the scenes is that we could also realize the resultant tensor is powered by NumPy (and hence, deep inside, it is another NumPy array represented as a tensor).

Similar to selecting objects from a tensor, we can also select rows and columns of our need from one, like the example shown in *Figure 3.10*. This is particularly useful when we are trying to understand the features of a handful of observations in a given dataset.

```
[17] # select 1st and 4th row
     # of the last tensor
     print(matrix_5x5[0:2, :])

     tf.Tensor(
     [[0.4790815  0.558849   0.26568604 0.8936378  0.79865   ]
      [0.68829155 0.31673968 0.9043186  0.16667676 0.28446352]], shape=(2, 5), dtype=float32)
```

Figure 3.10: *Tensor slicing*

Quick summary

At this point, one should also note the following:

- TensorFlow offers various types of tensors. These can be categorized as variables, constants, placeholders, sparse tensors, etc. In the preceding examples, we have mostly used variables where the data will or may change as we operate on them. To understand them quickly, here are the most common kinds of tensors:

    - **Variables**: Tensors that can change their values during the computation.

    - **Constants**: Tensors with fixed values that do not change.

    - **Placeholders**: Tensors as placeholders for data that is fed into the model later.

    - **Sparse tensors**: Tensors that are mostly filled with zeros, optimized for efficient storage and computation.

- However, it is good to know about the usefulness of the other types of tensors; the information on them is available from the TensorFlow website. Additionally, note that, currently, we have only covered the bare minimum basics of TensorFlow, which, interestingly, is more than enough of a starting point to analyze the data and build simple and basic ML models.

- It is to be noted that most of the information presented above is taken from the TensorFlow website, and we recommend our readers to perform a quick deep dive on tensors (and try out as many examples as possible) from **https://www. TensorFlow.org/guide/tensor.**

    - On this website, one will find examples of how to run them on Google Colab or options to download the Notebook on local systems for their execution or practice.

    - Experimenting with these examples from official documentation helps us to prepare ourselves with the basics required while building larger and complicated projects.

    - We again strongly encourage all our readers to read the official TensorFlow documentation thoroughly and be familiar with it.

- A very important resource that one must use while learning TensorFlow is the official guide-like Notebooks available as open source on the TensorFlow GitHub repository.

    - One example of the tensor guide in this repository can be found here: **https:// github.com/TensorFlow/docs/blob/master/site/en/guide/tensor.ipynb**.

As we progress with the rest of the chapters and sections in this book, we will make extensive use of TensorFlow in analyzing data and building ML models, along with another starter library in Python, which is not only very easy to digest but is also a good production-ready alternative to TensorFlow, called **scikit-learn**. We will learn about this in the next section.

Scikit-learn

Scikit-learn (sklearn) is one of the greatest starter libraries and provides a simple and efficient set of APIs for predictive data analysis. Being an open source, it is available for anyone to use and has a multitude of reusable components for various parts of the ML lifecycle. Its core strengths lie in its simplicity, efficiency, and wide range of algorithms. Additionally, its emphasis on clear documentation and active community support further enhances its utility and ease of use. Under the hood, it is built with NumPy, SciPy, and Matplotlib, which are the three common data science and ML libraries used by developers across the industry. It is to be noted that sklearn is commercially usable, and currently, there are many varied scales of ML applications that are created using sklearn and that run on production systems. It is essential for us to learn the basics of sklearn so that we can make the best use of it.

Let us start practicing it from a different perspective, which is through analyzing a unique feature where sklearn comes bundled with a lot of starter datasets. This is useful to start exploring the capabilities of sklearn. For this, we start a new notebook in Google Colab and install or import the sklearn library. Usually, the stable version of sklearn is already preinstalled in the available Colab runtimes. Still, it is a good practice to check the installation and the version before we go ahead.

The following is an example of how we can check the installed package and its version:

```
[1] # check if scikit-learn package is installed
    !pip show scikit-learn

    Name: scikit-learn
    Version: 1.2.2
    Summary: A set of python modules for machine learning and data mining
    Home-page: http://scikit-learn.org
    Author:
    Author-email:
    License: new BSD
    Location: /usr/local/lib/python3.10/dist-packages
    Requires: joblib, numpy, scipy, threadpoolctl
    Required-by: bigframes, fastai, imbalanced-learn, librosa, mlxtend, qudida, sklearn-pandas, yellowbrick
```

Figure 3.11: Sklearn on Google Colab

In the preceding example, we can see not only the version of the sklearn library, which is preinstalled in the Colab environment, but also the dependencies. It is clear that many other libraries also use it from time to time. It is built on SciPy and NumPy as the base libraries. This makes the library more of a high-level API abstracted module, wherein one needs to write less code to achieve more.

As seen in the following example figure, let us import one of the datasets from sklearn, which is none other than the infamous IRIS dataset containing a balanced set of examples for the three types of IRIS flowers. This is a useful dataset for starters to practice their ML skills on.

```
[2]  # import IRIS dataset
     from sklearn.datasets import load_iris
     iris = load_iris()

[3]  # print iris data
     iris.data

     array([[5.1, 3.5, 1.4, 0.2],
            [4.9, 3. , 1.4, 0.2],
            [4.7, 3.2, 1.3, 0.2],
            [4.6, 3.1, 1.5, 0.2],
            [5. , 3.6, 1.4, 0.2],
            [5.4, 3.9, 1.7, 0.4],
            [4.6, 3.4, 1.4, 0.3],
            [5. , 3.4, 1.5, 0.2],
            [4.4, 2.9, 1.4, 0.2],
```

Figure 3.12: *Load IRIS dataset*

Overall, it seems like an array if we load the data using its inbuilt .data method or API. There is another method to do this (and, for that matter, all other datasets in the **sklearn. datasets** module), which contains the columns of each of the values.

Here is an example of how to do this:

```
[5]  # print keys in the IRIS dataset
     iris.keys()

     dict_keys(['data', 'target', 'frame', 'target_names', 'DESCR', 'feature_names', 'filename', 'data_module'])
```

Figure 3.13: *IRIS dataset properties*

In the preceding example, we find the columns representing the data, which in this case is the sepal width and length, followed by petal width and length for three classes of the IRIS flowers.

Let us check the classes of IRIS flowers in the example code snippet given in the following *Figure 3.14*:

```
[6]  # check target names
     # in the IRIS dataset
     iris.target_names

     array(['setosa', 'versicolor', 'virginica'], dtype='<U10')

[8]  # print the no. of samples
     # and no. of features in the data
     n_samples, n_features = iris.data.shape
     print((n_samples, n_features))

     (150, 4)
```

Figure 3.14: *IRIS dataset exploration*

In the preceding example, we verify that there are, in total, three classes of IRIS species of flowers contained in this given dataset. We also could find from *Figure 3.14* cell of code that there are 150 rows or observations with these three columns along with an index column (by default for a DataFrame). This is also useful to understand so that later, we can choose the best way of handling data when this ML model is designed to run on production systems. It is to be noted that not all libraries perform similarly in production in terms of performance, and hence, the volume of the data plays a critical role in choosing the right tooling and data design.

At this point in time, we will move on to build some simple ML models with sklearn, along with the TensorFlow library, which we have learnt till the basics now, using the Google Colab.

ML models with TensorFlow and scikit-learn

Let us start with building a quick linear regression model with the sklearn library. Later, we will see more examples of how to better analyze the data before fitting the ML models.

First, we import two important libraries in Python, NumPy and Matplotlib, to generate and visualize some synthetic data, which we would like to use for fitting a regression model.

In the following *Figure 3.15*, we find an example:

```
[9]  # import matplotlib for visuals
     import matplotlib.pyplot as plt

[10] # import numpy for synthetic data generation
     import numpy as np
```

Figure 3.15: *Import NumPy and Matplotlib*

Let us now create the synthetic data, with a sample code as follows:

```
[11] # generate 50 random datapoints
     # with 2 columns, X and Y
     random_number = np.random.RandomState(42)
     x = 10 * random_number.rand(50)
     y = 2 * x - 1 + random_number.randn(50)

[12] # plot the generated data
     plt.scatter(x, y);
```

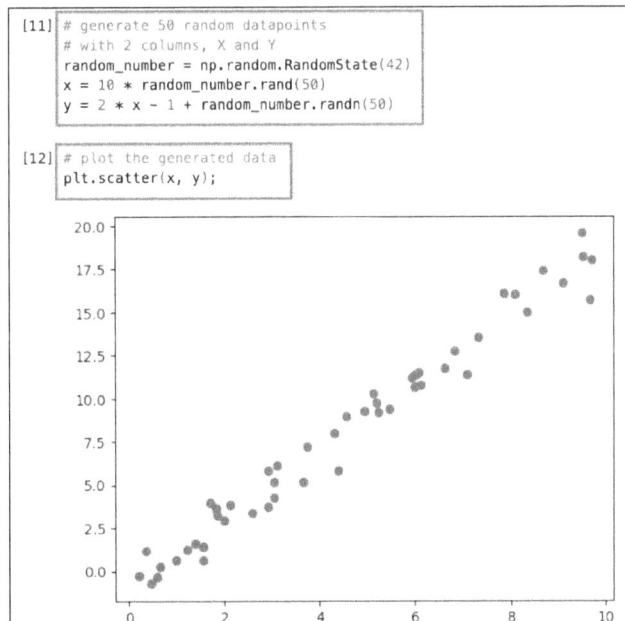

Figure 3.16: *Generate synthetic data*

Some salient points to note on the last code cell are as follows:

- Firstly, we use a predefined equation on the first code cell to generate the data. The x variable we generate can be considered our features (or the properties/ columns of data from which our ML model will learn the patterns). The y variable we generate can be considered our target, which our ML model will be trained to predict or estimate.

- Next, we use the matplotlib library to draw a scatter plot of the data. Note that, in the next chapter, we develop a better understanding of these charts and when to use which one of them.

- Further on, from the plot, the x and y variables look quite well linearly related. This may seldom be the case with real-world datasets. In the real-world, the datasets will be much messier and usually require a separate set of data engineering practices and pipelines to make them usable for ML use cases.

- To conclude, let us import the linear regression module or class from the sklearn library to fit in our first model instantly. See an example below in *Figure 3.17*:

```
[13] # import linear regression
     # module from SKLEARN
     from sklearn.linear_model import LinearRegression


[15] # Fit a linear regression model
     # with x and y variables
     model = LinearRegression()
     model.fit(x[:, np.newaxis], y)

     ▾ LinearRegression
     LinearRegression()
```

Figure 3.17: Linear regression import and object

Let us understand what we did in the preceding example:

- We imported the linear regression class or functionality from **sklearn.linear_ model** module or set of APIs.

- Further, we created an object called **model** of the linear regression class.

Finally, we called the **.fit()** function to pass the x and y variables to create the model.

A very important point to note in the last code snippet is the use of the **np.newaxis** function to broadcast the feature (i.e., the X) variable before calling the **model.fit()** function. By broadcasting, we mean adding a new axis to the specified dimension of the features DataFrame.

This is because sklearn expects a two-dimensional feature data and a one-dimensional target data to create/fit any model. We have randomly generated *x* and *y*, where both *x* and *y* are one-dimensional arrays. Hence, we need to manage the *x* variable (or, in this case, our features) to make it a matrix of size *m*n*, where m is the number of samples in the data and n is the number of features in the data, hypothetically.

Now that our model is fit with a single line of code, let us find the weights of the model. If we recall, when we learned about the linear regression model in *Chapter 2, Machine Learning Fundamentals*, we came across two terms, m and c, which are the slope and intercept, respectively, of the equation of the regression line (remember the regression equation discussed in *Chapter 2*). In the terminologies of the sklearn model, the **coef_** variable (also called the **coefficient**) contains the slope, while the **intercept_** variable contains the intercept value. Here is an example of how to do this in *Figure 3.18*:

```
[16]  # print the coefficient
      # of the model
      model.coef_

      array([1.9776566])


[17]  # print the intercept
      # of the model.
      model.intercept_

      -0.9033107255311146
```

Figure 3.18: Linear regression weights

It is to be noted that the example we took above uses a complete dummy and a synthetic dataset, which has no essence in the real-world since the motivation here was to introduce our readers to the basics of how to use sklearn to fit models. Also, note that at this point, we will not try to find if the linear regression model used in the preceding example is a good one or if there can be a better alternative by choosing the right metric to test it and by tuning the hyperparameters, if all the algorithm or library supports hyperparameter tuning.

Let us see a similar example with TensorFlow. Now, we will make use of yet another simple code to fit a linear regression, using the same synthetic data that we used with sklearn examples. To do so, we will use a neural network modelling style in the TensorFlow, where we fit a sequential model with the dense layer and compile the model with **Stochastic Gradient Descent (SGD)** optimizer looking to improve the mean squared error metric. When completed, we fit the model with our synthetic data for a predefined number of iterations, also called **epochs**. In the later chapters of our book, when we discuss the details of the internal workings of neural networks, we will explain these complex terms in depth and learn how to use them effectively. Here is an example of how to fit the linear regression model using TensorFlow in *Figure 3.19*:

```
[1]   # import tensorflow
      import tensorflow as tf

[18]  # fit linear regression
      # using tensorflow using
      # previous variables
      model = tf.keras.Sequential([
          tf.keras.layers.Dense(units=1, input_shape=[1])
      ])
      model.compile(optimizer='sgd', loss='mean_squared_error')
      model.fit(x, y, epochs=10)

      Epoch 1/10
      2/2 [==============================] - 1s 21ms/step - loss: 4.6028
      Epoch 2/10
      2/2 [==============================] - 0s 10ms/step - loss: 1.1241
      Epoch 3/10
      2/2 [==============================] - 0s 16ms/step - loss: 1.0995
      Epoch 4/10
      2/2 [==============================] - 0s 13ms/step - loss: 1.1046
      Epoch 5/10
      2/2 [==============================] - 0s 7ms/step - loss: 1.0863
      Epoch 6/10
      2/2 [==============================] - 0s 8ms/step - loss: 1.0821
      Epoch 7/10
      2/2 [==============================] - 0s 9ms/step - loss: 1.0791
      Epoch 8/10
      2/2 [==============================] - 0s 7ms/step - loss: 1.0815
      Epoch 9/10
      2/2 [==============================] - 0s 7ms/step - loss: 1.0669
      Epoch 10/10
      2/2 [==============================] - 0s 8ms/step - loss: 1.0498
      <keras.src.callbacks.History at 0x7d62188373a0>
```

Figure 3.19: *Linear regression with TensorFlow*

Note that in this example code, we used a high-level API called Keras to fit the model in TensorFlow with less quantity of code.

By calling another simple API in TensorFlow, we are able to pass a random unseen input to our trained model, and we get back the estimated outcome. Here is an example in *Figure 3.20*:

```
[20]  # estimate for a sample input
      model.predict([10.0])

      1/1 [==============================] - 0s 118ms/step
      array([[18.339676]], dtype=float32)
```

Figure 3.20: *TensorFlow regression model prediction*

Note that, although all the examples may sound like child's play, there is much more to be explored, starting from preparing and analyzing available data, followed by selecting features to train our ML models, followed by evaluation of the model using appropriate metric, and finally by generating an acceptable version of the ML model.

This enables us to plan and design how to put it in production for users and systems to start using this ML model. All of these are essential parts of the ML lifecycle, other than deep-rooted know-how of how the algorithms work.

Merits and demerits of TensorFlow

As a user of TensorFlow, one must be aware of where it works and which are the areas where one may need to be extra careful with regard to its working.

Let us start with the advantages of TensorFlow:

Merits	Explanation
Versatility	Handles diverse tasks like image recognition, NLP, and data cleaning, making it a one-stop shop for various AI/ML needs.
	Can be used to design applications like object detection with models like YOLO or image classification with models like ResNet.
Flexibility	Offers granular control over the model architecture, allowing you to tailor models to specific problems and achieve high accuracy.
Large community and resources	Backed by Google and a vibrant community, it offers extensive tutorials, documentation, and code examples for easier learning and problem-solving.
Scalability	Runs on various platforms, from mobile devices for on-device inference to the powerful servers for large-scale training and deployment.
Keras integration	Provides a high-level, user-friendly API built on top of TensorFlow, simplifying model building and reducing code complexity.
Tensor board visualization tools	Offers visual dashboards to track model training progress, analyze performance metrics, and debug potential issues.
Wide adoption	TensorFlow has become one of the go-to libraries for the ML systems in production, especially for the large-scale systems used in the on-premise installations as well as in the cloud platforms.

Table 3.1: Advantages of TensorFlow

In contrast, now let us also look into some of the observed disadvantages of TensorFlow:

Demerits	Explanation
Steep learning curve	Initial learning can be challenging, especially for beginners in deep learning, due to its technical concepts and syntax.
	The solution is to keep oneself regularly updated with the public documentation and to look at others' work within the team or public forums (like GitHub, Kaggle, etc.).
Performance	While generally fast, it may not be the most efficient choice for specific tasks compared to some specialized libraries or frameworks.
	Leveraging hardware acceleration techniques like using GPUs or TPUs and optimizing model architecture and training hyperparameters can significantly improve TensorFlow's efficiency.
Debugging complexity	Debugging complex computational graphs in TensorFlow models can be tricky, requiring more advanced understanding and troubleshooting skills.
	However, understanding how to trace errors in the computational graph and that tools like TensorBoard and eager execution help mitigate some of these challenges.

Table 3.2: Disadvantages of TensorFlow

It is to be noted that all our ML libraries, like TensorFlow and sklearn, are ever-growing and already have a strong set of long-term contributors. The salient features of both of them are equipped enough for the user to start using them in production systems. In parallel to these, one should be additionally aware of another great library called PyTorch, which also brings similar capabilities for coders, if not less.

TensorFlow vs scikit-learn vs PyTorch

Let us now take a brief look at the salient points to consider when choosing the right ML Library for the given use case. One must note that each of these libraries being compared here is built by different communities for different purposes, and hence, at times, it is quite a daunting task to choose one versus the rest; however, we aim to provide an overall comparison herewith, so that given a particular use case and its approach, one can start with and choose the right toolkit for long term solutions, as follows:

Feature	TensorFlow	scikit-learn	PyTorch
Focus	Deep learning (neural networks)	Traditional ML	Deep learning (dynamic computational graphs)
Ease of use	Steeper learning curve	User-friendly, intuitive API	More Pythonic, easier for prototyping
Model customization	High flexibility	Limited customization within predefined algorithms	High flexibility
Scalability	Excellent, supports distributed training	Limited scalability for large datasets	Good scalability, supports multi-GPU training
Deployment	Supported on various platforms	Primarily for research and prototyping	Primarily for research and prototyping but gaining deployment options
Community and resources	Large and active community, extensive resources	Large community, well-established resources	Growing community, strong support in research
Visualization	Tensor board provides comprehensive visualization	Limited visualization capabilities	Basic visualization tools available
Performance	Faster training time for large neural networks	Comparatively slower for large models in production	Faster training time for large neural networks

Feature	TensorFlow	scikit-learn	PyTorch
Debugging	Challenging as compared to scikit-learn due to static computational graph	Comparatively easy because of its high-level abstraction nature	PyTorch's dynamic graph makes it easier to debug as compared to TensorFlow
Best suited for	Complex deep learning tasks, large-scale projects	Traditional ML tasks, quick prototyping	Research-oriented deep learning, dynamic models, ease of experimentation

Table 3.3: *Comparing TensorFlow, sklearn, PyTorch*

Keras

Keras is a high-level neural networks API, written in Python and capable of running on top of TensorFlow. It was developed with a focus on enabling fast experimentation with deep learning models. Keras is designed to be user-friendly, modular, and extensible. It provides a simple and consistent interface for building and training deep learning models, making it accessible to both beginners and experienced practitioners.

Some of the key features, along with a handful of operational benefits of using Keras, are as follows:

- **User-friendly interface**: Keras features a clean and intuitive API that simplifies the process of building and training deep learning models. It offers a consistent interface across different platforms and backends, making it easy for users to switch between different frameworks or hardware configurations.

- **Rapid prototyping**: Keras is designed to facilitate the rapid prototyping of deep learning models. Its high-level API allows users to quickly build and evaluate different model architectures, hyperparameters, and training strategies. This enables researchers and practitioners to iterate quickly and explore various possibilities before committing to a final model.

- **Modular and extensible**: Keras is highly modular, allowing users to easily combine different layers and components to create complex deep learning models. It also provides extensive support for customization, enabling users to define their layers, loss functions, and metrics. This flexibility makes Keras suitable for a wide range of deep learning applications and research projects.

- **Seamless integration**: Keras can seamlessly run on top of TensorFlow, **Microsoft Cognitive Toolkit (CNTK)**, or Theano, providing users with the freedom to choose the backend that best suits their needs. This interoperability allows users to leverage the strengths of different frameworks and take advantage of the latest advancements in deep learning technology.

- **Extensive community support**: Keras has a large and active community of users and contributors. This community provides extensive documentation, tutorials, and examples, making it easy for beginners to get started with Keras and for experienced practitioners to find solutions to their challenges.

Keras may often come with the following challenges:

- **Limited flexibility**: Keras, while user-friendly, can be less flexible than TensorFlow for complex custom model architectures.

- **Dependency on backend**: Keras relies on a backend engine, like TensorFlow or Theano, which can sometimes lead to compatibility issues or limitations.

- **Slower performance for large-scale models**: For extremely large models and datasets, Keras may not be as efficient as lower-level frameworks like TensorFlow.

Keras is widely used in various domains, including:

- **Computer vision**:

    o Keras is commonly employed for image classification, object detection, and image segmentation tasks. Its user-friendly API and extensive support for pre-trained models make it a popular choice for building computer vision applications.

    o This leads to applications like detecting tumors in X-rays or MRIs, unlocking smartphones with face ID, and identifying pedestrians or traffic signs, or other vehicles in a self-driving car.

- **Natural language processing**:

    o Keras is also widely used in NLP tasks such as text classification, sentiment analysis, and machine translation. Its support for recurrent neural networks and attention mechanisms makes it well-suited for these applications.

    o The most common set of applications that emerge in the real-world from this aspect includes chatbots and virtual assistants, analysis of social media for product/brand marketing, and machine translators like Google Translate.

- **Speech recognition and generation**:

    o Keras is used in speech recognition and generation systems. Its ability to handle sequential data and its support for specialized layers, such as convolutional layers, make it a suitable choice for these tasks.

    o This results in applications like Siri or Alexa, or Google Assistant or transcription services to convert audio recordings to text or even generate audio output from text in case of reading out news articles.

With the aforementioned in mind, let us look at a quick implementation of the linear regression, again using the synthetic data, to understand how easy or difficult it is to use Keras. Here are some steps for our guidance:

1. Firstly, we will import all required libraries, use NumPy to generate dummy data, and reshape the data to make it suitable for Keras. Here is an example in *Figure 3.21*:

```
[1]  # import required libraries.
     import numpy as np
     import tensorflow as tf
     from tensorflow import keras

[2]  # Generate synthetic data
     X = np.linspace(0, 10, 100)
     y = 2 * X + 1 + np.random.normal(0, 0.1, 100)

[3]  # Reshape the data to be suitable for Keras
     X = X.reshape((-1, 1))
     y = y.reshape((-1, 1))
```

Figure 3.21: Import Keras and generate data

2. Further, we create the model object from **keras.Sequential()** class, add one dense layer (about which we will learn more in the deep learning chapter), compile the model by using Adam optimizer to minimize the mean squared error loss, and fit the model with our synthetic data. Here is an example in *Figure 3.22*:

```
[4]  # Create the Keras model
     model = keras.Sequential([
       keras.layers.Dense(1, input_dim=1)
     ])

[5]  # Compile the model
     model.compile(loss='mean_squared_error', optimizer='adam')

[7]  # Fit the model to the data
     model.fit(X, y, epochs=100)

     Epoch 1/100
     4/4 [==============================] - 0s 2ms/step - loss: 359.3369
     Epoch 2/100
     4/4 [==============================] - 0s 2ms/step - loss: 358.2941
     Epoch 3/100
     4/4 [==============================] - 0s 2ms/step - loss: 357.3558
     Epoch 4/100
     4/4 [==============================] - 0s 2ms/step - loss: 356.3596
     Epoch 5/100
     4/4 [==============================] - 0s 2ms/step - loss: 355.3947
     Epoch 6/100
     4/4 [==============================] - 0s 2ms/step - loss: 354.4553
     Epoch 7/100
     4/4 [==============================] - 0s 2ms/step - loss: 353.4731
```

Figure 3.22: Linear regression using Keras

3. In our last step, we try to evaluate the model using the same data that we have available so far. This is not at all a good practice since it is essentially checking our answer sheets in a given exam, even with a reference from a textbook. In reality, and more practical exercises in the later chapters of this book, we will prepare the data and divide it into training, testing, and validation sets to properly evaluate any ML model with data that it has not seen before. For this case, we take the predictions from this model (that we have trained on our synthetic data) and plot the actual versus predicted data. Here is an example code in *Figure 3.23*:

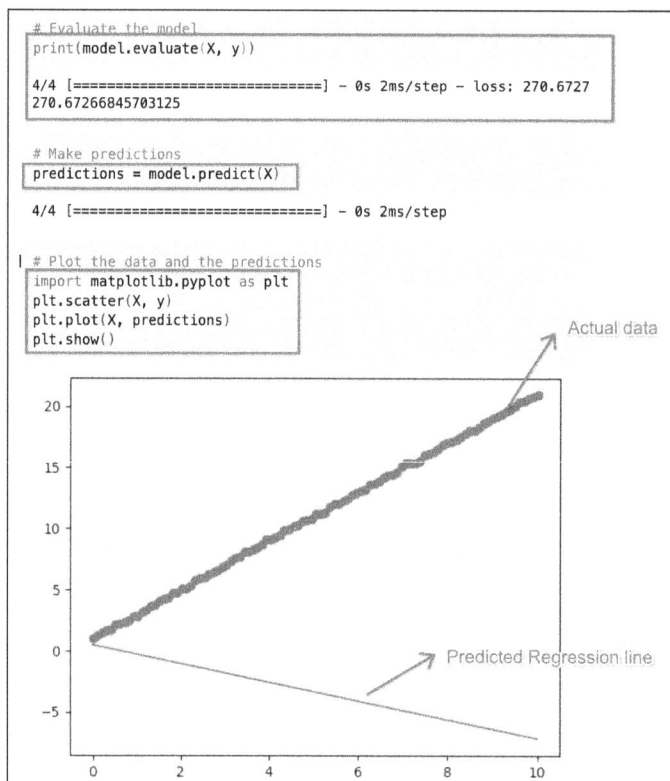

Figure 3.23: Visualizing the regression model

The resultant model is not at all good since the predicted regression line does not represent our synthetic data at all. However, there are time-tested ways to improve its performance, along with better data preparation.

Conclusion

In this chapter, we covered the introduction to TensorFlow and scikit-learn, two of the most common production-grade libraries used for AI and ML applications. We looked into their internals and also compared TensorFlow to scikit-learn and PyTorch to understand which of these frameworks are suitable for what sort of applications or workloads. We saw only a handful of example programs that ran on Google Colab (free) and could realize how data is represented in these libraries and, further, how the data is effectively used for some quick and sample ML implementations.

In the next chapter, we are going to learn about an approximate ideal setup for any software engineer, including the tools we commonly use, how to version our software, and so on. It is done so that we are ready to design and develop effective and production-grade ML applications.

Exercises

Let us make our learning experience interesting by solving (or at least trying to find the right answers to) the following questions. This makes our understanding and exploration stronger.

1. From the TensorFlow website (**TensorFlow.org**), take up at least 3 notebooks, run them on your Google Colab environment, and note down if we get any specific errors while importing and installing the packages.

2. List all the datasets available in the sklearn.datasets module and try to classify them if the problem statement is a regression use case or a classification use case.

3. Similar to our learning and implementing some basic operations on Tensors using TensorFlow, use the official website page of Tensors from the list of PyTorch tutorials (**https://pytorch.org/tutorials/beginner/basics/tensorqs_tutorial.html**) to complete the quick example of tensors in Google Colab notebook.

4. An excellent tutorial on Keras is available on its website (**https://keras.io/getting_started/intro_to_keras_for_engineers/**) to familiarize coders with the Keras framework. Take a copy of the notebook or code and run it on Google Colab.

References

Here are some of the references useful to learn more about the tools explained in this chapter as well as for further reading:

1. TensorFlow official website: **https://www.TensorFlow.org/**

2. PyTorch official website: **https://pytorch.org/**

3. Microsoft Cognitive Toolkit: **https://github.com/microsoft/CNTK**

4. Google Colab: **https://colab.google/**

5. Scikit-learn library (Stable version): **https://scikit-learn.org/stable/**

Join our book's Discord space

Join the book's Discord Workspace for Latest updates, Offers, Tech happenings around the world, New Release and Sessions with the Authors:

https://discord.bpbonline.com

CHAPTER 4
Engineering for Machine Learning

Introduction

Imagine a civil engineer designing or building a multistoried building. Just like good construction depends on strong bricks and a solid foundation, successful ML projects require well-written code and efficient data handling.

One can think of building a complex ML model as constructing a multistoried building. We would not want each floor to be a separate, haphazard structure; instead, we would modularize it and create reusable components that fit together seamlessly. Similarly, well-written ML codes break down complex tasks into smaller, manageable functions, making codes easier to understand, maintain, and share.

At the current state of software engineering, it is essential to be familiar with and make effective use of the concept of containerization, which is like packing our entire building (code, libraries, dependencies) into a neat, portable box. This makes deploying our ML applications to different environments modularized; think of it as building each floor plan as a container and putting the pieces together during the construction phase. This is an example of how many of our modern housing societies are built similarly.

In the real-world, industrial data often resides in large databases or data warehouses. Overall, there are two common types of storage: **relational database management systems (RDBMS)**, like MySQL or Oracle, and **enterprise data warehouses (EDW)**, like BigQuery on Google Cloud Platform. For a production-grade implementation of AI and ML systems, hence, one should have a firm grasp of:

- Fundamental programming concepts in any programming language.
- Software engineering best practices for structuring and modularizing your ML projects.
- The concepts and benefits of containerization.
- How RDBMS and EDW systems are used to manage real-world data for ML tasks.

Structure

This chapter covers the following topics:

- Python for data analysis
- Jupyter Notebooks
- Visual Studio Code
- Version control with Git
- Containers and Docker
- Databases

Objectives

By the end of this chapter, we will be able to understand all the basic engineering tools, frameworks, best practices, basics of containers, and how to effectively make use of databases in AI and ML applications. In this way, we will learn how to efficiently modularize our software, how to package it using containers, how to effectively read/write data to/from enterprise databases, and how to structure a complete ML project.

Python for data analysis

Let us start learning with the most important Python libraries that are used in AI and ML applications. This is a vast topic, however, the motive as of now is to start with the basic and the most important data analysis libraries. We will do this using a sample dataset, then loading and cleaning it, and finally analyzing it.

Before so, let us quickly define the main data libraries, to understand why we are using them so that we can use them effectively:

- **NumPy** is a library for the Python programming language that adds support for large, multi-dimensional arrays and matrices, along with a large collection of high-level mathematical functions to operate on these arrays.

- Similarly, **Pandas** is a software library written for the Python programming language for data manipulation and analysis. It offers data structures and operations for manipulating numerical tables and time series.

- Finally, **Matplotlib** is a Python 2D plotting library that produces publication-quality graphics in a variety of hardcopy formats and interactive environments across platforms. Matplotlib can be used in Python scripts, the Python and IPython shells, the Jupyter Notebook, web application servers, and four graphical user interface toolkits.

For our learning, let us take the Dry Bean dataset from the UCI machine learning repository, which is another great resource to get ahold of free data. This dataset contains images of 13,611 grains of 7 different registered Dry Beans taken with a high-resolution camera. A total of 16 features, 12 dimensions, and 4 shape forms were obtained from the grains. Typically, and as per the UCI repo as well, this dataset is used for multiclass classification use cases of Dry Beans using computer vision and ML techniques.

Let us download and unpack this data:

Figure 4.1: Loading datasets in Google Colab

In the aforementioned code example, we are:

- Importing the NumPy and Pandas library (while we are making use of **pandas** mostly in this example and NumPy will be surely used later).

- Defining the URL of the data using the URLLIB library in Python and sending a request to the link to download the data as a ZIP file.

- Once downloaded, we are finally using the ZIP file library in Python to extract the downloaded file.

- On the left side of our Colab Notebook, we can see the output files.

While analyzing data before preparing and using it for any given ML use case, it is essential to understand each aspect of the data and visualize it as well. We also realize that other than our primary Python libraries, we will end up using as many utilities as essential to load, process, analyze, and prepare the data. This is very important to remember. Additionally, it is also important to note that all these activities must be modularized once they are experimented along with tests to automatically validate their working.

Keeping that in mind, let us now load the data and see the first 10 sample rows:

```
[ ]   # Load the extracted XLSX file
      # using Pandas
      df = pd.read_excel('/content/DryBeanDataset/Dry_Bean_Dataset.xlsx')

 ●    # show first 10 rows
      # of the loaded excel file
      df.head(10)
```

Figure 4.2: Reading data with pandas

The object or data structure we ended up creating while loading the Excel file is otherwise known as a **DataFrame** and is by far one of the most powerful and convenient ways we will be using (most of the time) to load, process, and clean data. Typically, a DataFrame resides in memory and is an exact copy of the data we load into it from the files on disk or elsewhere (even from Cloud storage).

Note: DataFrames are mutable data structures, so one must be careful in choosing the operations on them and test their code systematically to avoid any data quality problems.

We can see the data sample contains a lot of numeric columns (actually, all features are numeric already) and one target column called **Class**. Looks like this data is already prepared to a certain extent since real-world data (for which we will see examples later) will be messier than this.

Further, let us look into the basic statistical properties of the data by describing the dataset as follows:

```
●   # describe the dataset
    df.describe()
```

	Area	Perimeter	MajorAxisLength
count	13611.000000	13611.000000	13611.000000
mean	53048.284549	855.283459	320.141867
std	29324.095717	214.289696	85.694186
min	20420.000000	524.736000	183.601165
25%	36328.000000	703.523500	253.303633
50%	44652.000000	794.941000	296.883367
75%	61332.000000	977.213000	376.495012
max	254616.000000	1985.370000	738.860153

```
[ ]   # describe the data
      # including categorical
      # columns
      df.describe(include='all')
```

	Area	Perimeter	MajorAxisLength
count	13611.000000	13611.000000	13611.000000
unique	NaN	NaN	NaN

Figure 4.3: 5-point statistics

The following are some salient points that we need to pay attention to:

- Notice the difference in calling the function and its parameters to describe either only the numeric columns or to describe all the columns (both numeric and categorical).

- When we look at the numeric columns' description, we get the count, the minimum or maximum values, and the 5-point statistics of the data, namely, the mean, standard deviation, 25%, 50%, and 70%. This is very useful to understand the distribution of the data. Let us take an example of two features:

    o The aspect ratio and compactness features (which are numerical in nature) are two out of many features in this data where one can see that the mean or statistical average of this column is very close to the 50% value, which is the median. This indicates that the data in this column is normally distributed, which is essential for some ML algorithms to perform.

- While we pass **include='all'** inside the **describe()** function, we see the values of the Target column **Class** as well. Seems it has seven unique values (see the 2nd row, which gives the value of the statistical mean; in the case of a categorical field, that is the unique value counts).

- Remember that each of the % values is very important to note in some cases. Let us take an example of one column to describe what these values mean:

    o For the compactness column, for example, 25% of its values are below 0.762, 50% of its values (in this column) are below 0.801, and 75% of its values are below 0.8342. This gives us a good picture of the distribution of the data.

To check the actual unique values of any categorical column, there is another very easy function in Pandas that we can use with the **df** variable, which is our DataFrame, as follows:

```
[13] # check the value counts
     # of values in the Class column
     df['Class'].value_counts()

DERMASON    3546
SIRA        2636
SEKER       2027
HOROZ       1928
CALI        1630
BARBUNYA    1322
BOMBAY       522
Name: Class, dtype: int64
```

Figure 4.4: Value counts

This gives a good but non-visual idea of what this field contains and the common values. Interestingly, if we run the preceding commands in our Colab, we will find that there are no missing values in the DataFrame. This may not usually be the case in a real-world scenario unless we have some great data engineers to thank for their tireless efforts.

Let us check the overall count of missing values in the DataFrame using another approach as follows:

```
[14]  # check info of the dataframe
      df.info()

      <class 'pandas.core.frame.DataFrame'>
      RangeIndex: 13611 entries, 0 to 13610
      Data columns (total 17 columns):
       #   Column          Non-Null Count  Dtype
      ---  ------          --------------  -----
       0   Area            13611 non-null  int64
       1   Perimeter       13611 non-null  float64
       2   MajorAxisLength 13611 non-null  float64
       3   MinorAxisLength 13611 non-null  float64
       4   AspectRation    13611 non-null  float64
       5   Eccentricity    13611 non-null  float64
       6   ConvexArea      13611 non-null  int64
       7   EquivDiameter   13611 non-null  float64
       8   Extent          13611 non-null  float64
       9   Solidity        13611 non-null  float64
       10  roundness       13611 non-null  float64
       11  Compactness     13611 non-null  float64
       12  ShapeFactor1    13611 non-null  float64
       13  ShapeFactor2    13611 non-null  float64
       14  ShapeFactor3    13611 non-null  float64
       15  ShapeFactor4    13611 non-null  float64
       16  Class           13611 non-null  object
      dtypes: float64(14), int64(2), object(1)
      memory usage: 1.8+ MB


[15]  # check null values in each column of the dataframe
      df.isnull().sum()

      Area            0
      Perimeter       0
      MajorAxisLength 0
      MinorAxisLength 0
      AspectRation    0
      Eccentricity    0
      ConvexArea      0
      EquivDiameter   0
      Extent          0
      Solidity        0
      roundness       0
      Compactness     0
      ShapeFactor1    0
      ShapeFactor2    0
      ShapeFactor3    0
      ShapeFactor4    0
      Class           0
      dtype: int64
```

Figure 4.5: Missing values

These are useful statistics to begin with, to know the kind of data cleaning and processing one needs to perform on the available dataset. As we progress further in this chapter, we will see other cases where a data engineer or AI or ML engineer would have to check for data and collect it for training ML models from or using the available databases in the organization. Also, we see (from the output of the **info()** function of the DataFrame) that the data types of each of the columns look correct overall, without any missing values in them, since the total number of rows in the DataFrame matches the non-null values in each of the columns.

In case we had such cases where we see missing values, for example, in a numeric or continuous variable in each or loaded dataset, one can perform a simple activity, like the following, to replace the missing values (in whichsoever applicable rows) with the median value of that column, using a code similar to the following example:

```
# Create a sample dataframe with missing values
df = pd.DataFrame({'Age': [20, 30, np.nan, 40, 50],
                   'Salary': [1000, 2000, np.nan, 3000, 4000]})

# Replace missing values in the 'Age' column with the median age
median_age = df['Age'].median()
df['Age'].fillna(median_age, inplace=True)

# Print the updated dataframe
print(df)
```

Figure 4.6: Missing value treatment with a median

In the preceding example, we end up creating a synthetic dataset and realize it as a Pandas DataFrame, post which we find the median value of the **Age** column and replace the nulls with the median value using the **.fillna()** function.

Note: The use of `inplace=True` replaces the values in the existing DataFrame without copying it. Also, note that this is not always a best practice; one must be careful while replacing values in place.

However, the Notebook, which we have been using all along, provides a reproducible experimentation environment (of sorts), which is great since we can correct the error and rerun the affected cells. Similarly, in case we see similar missing values in a categorical column, one quick way to fill the missing values is to use the mode (or the most frequently occurring value in the entire dataset for this column), like in the example, as follows:

```
[1]  import pandas as pd
     import numpy as np

[2]  # Create a sample dataframe with missing values
     df = pd.DataFrame({'Country': ['US', 'India', np.nan, 'UK', 'Canada'],
                        'City': ['New York', 'Delhi', np.nan, 'London', 'Toronto']})

     # Replace missing values in the 'Country' column with the most frequent country
     most_frequent_country = df['Country'].mode()[0]
     df['Country'].fillna(most_frequent_country, inplace=True)

     # Print the updated dataframe
     print(df)

       Country      City
     0      US  New York
     1   India     Delhi
     2  Canada       NaN
     3      UK    London
     4  Canada   Toronto
```

Figure 4.7: Missing value treatment with mode

Note: Once we learn more about regression and classification algorithms in ML, in further chapters of this book, one may want to fill up missing values in a more intuitive way, by using ML.

For example, we can fit a regression model to estimate the missing values in a continuous variable rather than simply filling it up with the median value. Equally, for filling up missing values in a categorical column, we can fit a classification model (using all other columns as features, for example) rather than using the most common value. This is a statistically better approach since filling up average or common values may render the data or its underlying assumptions incorrect.

Now that we have performed some basic observations on our dataset and have seen at least one good example of how to clean data, let us try to look at the data visually. To do so, we will use the Matplotlib library, along with the Seaborn library, which is built on top of one another, to find patterns in the data.

We start by taking the **Area** and **Perimeter** columns of the DataFrame we loaded and seeing if there is a linear relationship between these variables in the data as follows:

```
# import matplotlib and seaborn library
import matplotlib.pyplot as plt
import seaborn as sns

# plot the scatter plots of Area / Perimeter columns
# in the dataframe to compare them with one another
# using the matplotlib library
plt.scatter(df['Area'], df['Perimeter'])
plt.show()
```

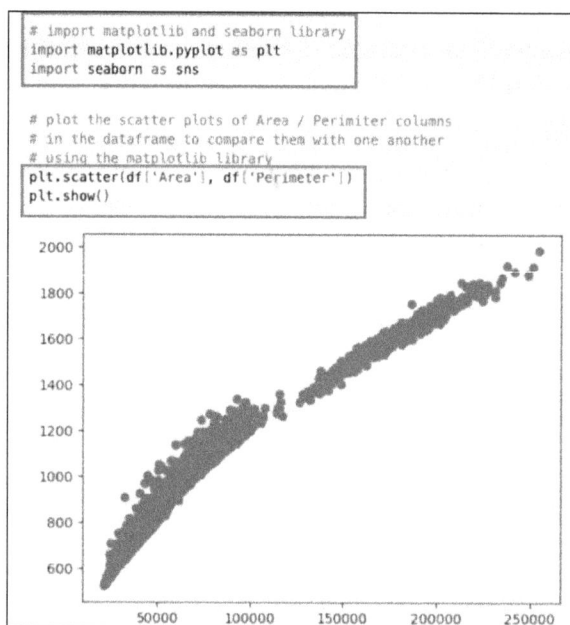

Figure 4.8: Scatter plots

See the use of the **.scatter()** function on the Matplotlib library. This is one of the many built-in functions in this library that can help us pass the data and the specific columns we would like to pass in and find the visuals we are looking for. The output scatter plot, which is the usual go-to way to determine relationships between continuous variables, shows a relation between them; that is, when the **Area** increases (X-axis), the perimeter (Y-axis) increases as well.

Note: In this example, we have not used many features of Matplotlib, like defining the names of the axis and the legends or giving the plot a title, etc., which can be done easily as well, as shown in the following:

```
# generate same scatter plot with title
# axis labels
plt.scatter(df['Area'], df['Perimeter'])
plt.title('Area vs Perimeter')
plt.xlabel('Area')
plt.ylabel('Perimeter')
plt.show();
```

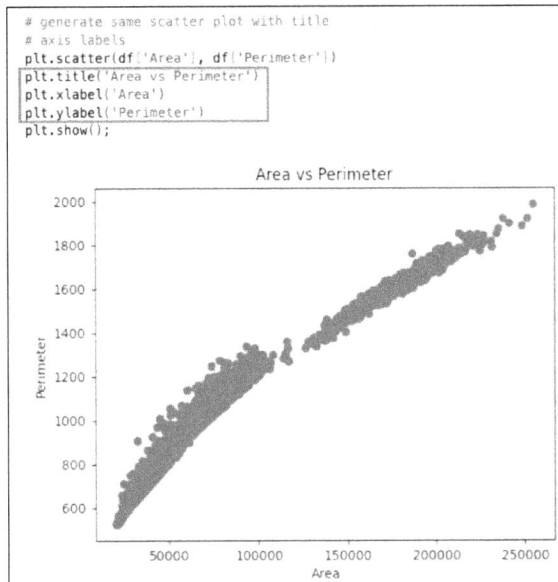

Figure 4.9: Plotting with labels and title

Let us try to perform the same with Seaborn library, and we will find a direct difference between the quality of output we get out of the box. The only line of code we change is to replace the **plt.scatter()** function with the **sns.scatterplot()** function, as shown in the following figure:

```
# create the same scatter plot
# this time using seaborn library
# use title and axis labels
# and show the plot
sns.scatterplot(x='Area', y='Perimeter', data=df)
plt.title('Area vs Perimeter')
plt.xlabel('Area')
plt.ylabel('Perimeter')
plt.show()
```

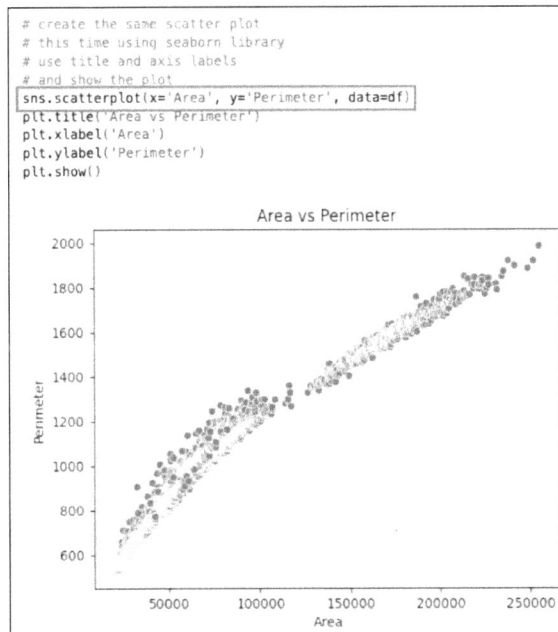

Figure 4.10: Scatterplot in Jupyter Notebooks using Seaborn

As we can see, the out-of-the-box graph from Seaborn is more pleasing to the eye in terms of the use of color, the shape and size of the bubbles as per the density of values, etc. However, if there are, suppose 100 columns in our dataset that are continuous in nature, it would be very cumbersome to check the scatter plots of each combination to find the relations between them. Hence, we need a better and simpler way, which is shown in the following figure, using the **pairplot()** function available in Seaborn.

Note: The following function is good for a dataset with a low or manageable number of columns (like 10 or 15), but the moment it goes out of a certain limit, the output of pair-plotting may not be entirely consumable.

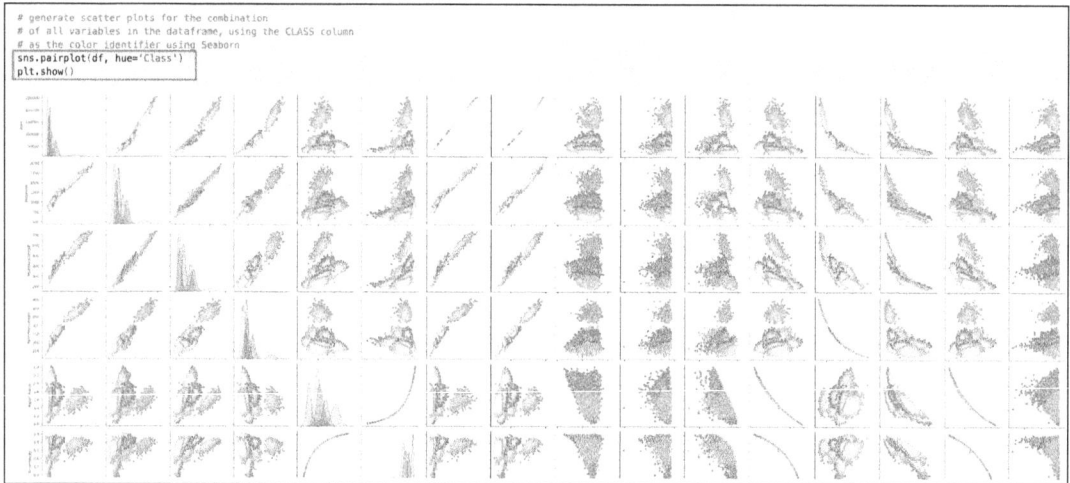

Figure 4.11: Pair plotting

Note: In this output (only a section could be displayed here because of its sheer size), there are legends and axis labels already generated. This is not a bad way to check the relations within columns, but it can become overwhelming (as well as computationally intensive) as the dataset grows.

The most important concept we see in this approach is that, for each of the scatter plots between each combination of the features in the data, we took the **Class** column (which is the target) as the color-coding scheme, giving a very good idea about the features which are excellent determiners of a boundary to segregate one class from the other. For example, look at the fourth or fifth chart in the top row, we can see one class separable from the others. This separation concept is very important, and as we learn more about ML implementations, this one simple concept will be profound in choosing the right algorithm for our data.

Up until now, we have looked into numerical features and not much into categorical features. Now let us experiment to check the relation of a categorical column in our dataset (the **Class** column) with any other numerical column (in this example, the **Perimeter** column) by using a **strip plot**. This type of plotting helps us understand the distribution or footprint of the **Class** column over a range of values of the **Perimeter** column as follows:

```
# draw a stripplot using the Class column
# from the dataframe
sns.stripplot(x='Class', y='Perimeter', data=df)
plt.show()
```

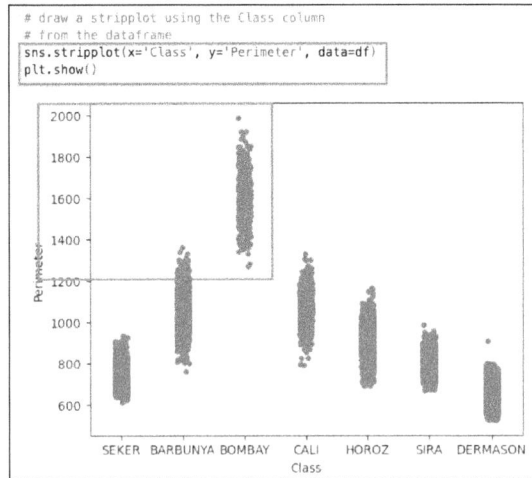

Figure 4.12: Strip plots for categorical features

The reason why we are doing more visual analyses than numeric ones is that such simple plots help us understand the data a lot. For example, it seems that for the BOMBAY type of **Class** column, the range of values of the **Perimeter** attribute or feature falls in a much higher range in our data frame as compared to the other unique categories in the **Class** column. This can indicate that when we create an ML model with this data to predict the value of the **Class** column, the fact that the range of values is quite different for one class can impose some level of bias or dizziness in the model while predicting the values, and maybe, it would be worthwhile to scale the **Perimeter** column. Let us understand how we can scale a particular column and then redraw the same figure:

```
# perform scaling of the Perimeter column
# using Min Max scaler and draw the same stripplot again
# using the scaled column
# and show the plot
from sklearn.preprocessing import MinMaxScaler
scaler = MinMaxScaler()
df['Perimeter'] = scaler.fit_transform(df[['Perimeter']])
sns.stripplot(x='Class', y='Perimeter', data=df)
plt.show()
```

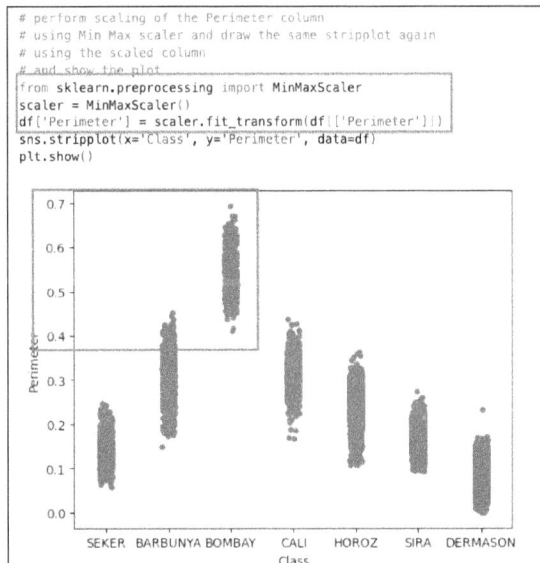

Figure 4.13: Improvements in data scaling

Essentially, what we did over here is, from the scikit-learn library (which we have already discussed):

- We used a **MinMaxScaler** function to put the values in the **Perimeter** column within a range of values.

- Now that we plot the data again using the same **stripplot()** function, the nature or distribution does not change; however, the range of the values over which one class was distributed versus the rest is handled quite well.

- In the case of **MinMaxScaler** in this example, we converted the values of the **Perimeter** column between the range of 0-1, which is the default behavior of the library or function we made use of.

There are other common ways of scaling data as well, like standard scaling, log scaling, decimal scaling, quantile scaling, robust scaling, and so on, which help in the following:

- If or when we scale the data and use it to train a model, the ML algorithm becomes of no use and must deal with the differences in the scales of any feature, and hence, the learning is more effective.

- This is as if in a meeting, every other participant has an equal right to affect the final judgment rather than only the seniors in the room.

- Later, we will also find that scaling also helps prevent overfitting, improves the convergence of the model, and at times makes the predictions from a model more explainable.

Let us step back a little and understand a scenario as follows:

- What if the available data (from our data engineers or collected by an ML engineer from a database, etc.) is not enough to understand or analyze the use case entirely?

- What if we need more data?

One needs to keep in mind that it is a common practice to incorporate additional, and many times external, data along with existing data to make the use case more learnable. For example:

- An ML system trying to recommend the best option to travel from *Mumbai* to *Delhi* may be additionally fed with news information about possible roadblocks or railway installations.

- We can further add data about weather conditions so that the final model can give a more profound reason for deciding on a particular mode of communication rather than others, given the features or the scenario.

Let us take an example of the same (previously created) DataFrame with four rows on **Country** and **City**:

```
# Create a sample dataframe with missing values
df = pd.DataFrame({'Country': ['US', 'India', np.nan, 'UK', 'Canada'],
                   'City': ['New York', 'Delhi', np.nan, 'London', 'Toronto']})

# Replace missing values in the 'Country' column with the most frequent country
most_frequent_country = df['Country'].mode()[0]
df['Country'].fillna(most_frequent_country, inplace=True)

# Print the updated dataframe
print(df)

   Country      City
0       US  New York
1    India     Delhi
2   Canada       NaN
3       UK    London
4   Canada   Toronto
```

Figure 4.14: Missing value treatment with mode

Let us add more valuable data to this frame, like the population of these countries, as seen in the following figure:

```
# download population data
# source: https://raw.githubusercontent.com/datasets/population/main/data/population.csv
# load it as a dataframe
df_population = pd.read_csv('https://raw.githubusercontent.com/datasets/population/main/data/population.csv')

# check top 5 sample rows of
# the population dataframe
df_population.head()
```

	Country Name	Country Code	Year	Value
0	Aruba	ABW	1960	54608
1	Aruba	ABW	1961	55811
2	Aruba	ABW	1962	56682
3	Aruba	ABW	1963	57475
4	Aruba	ABW	1964	58178

Figure 4.15: Read additional data

Note: In pandas, using the `read_csv()` function, we can read a CSV file directly from a public website (or any other HTTP endpoint that has no authentication). Ideally, `read_csv()` is used to read any comma or other delimiter-separated values.

Further, let us perform some basic cleaning of this population data so that we can join it with our earlier data frame, as seen in the following figure:

```
[11] # in the population dataframe, convert the 'Country Name'
     # column to only 'Country'
     df_population.rename(columns={'Country Name': 'Country'}, inplace=True)
     df_population.head()
```

	Country	Country Code	Year	Value	
0	Aruba	ABW	1960	54608	
1	Aruba	ABW	1961	55811	
2	Aruba	ABW	1962	56682	
3	Aruba	ABW	1963	57475	
4	Aruba	ABW	1964	58178	

Next steps: Generate code with `df_population`   ◉ View recommended plots

```
[12] # convert the 'Country' column values
     # in the population dataframe to Camel case
     df_population['Country'] = df_population['Country'].str.title()
     df_population.head()
```

	Country	Country Code	Year	Value	
0	Aruba	ABW	1960	54608	
1	Aruba	ABW	1961	55811	
2	Aruba	ABW	1962	56682	
3	Aruba	ABW	1963	57475	
4	Aruba	ABW	1964	58178	

Figure 4.16: Data cleaning example

Essentially, we are making sure that we have at least one common column in both DataFrames and that the data is camel case (for example, in this case) in the column that we want to use to join the DataFrames. Now, let us try to join the DataFrames as follows:

```
# join our earlier dataframe 'df'
# with the population dataframe 'df_population'
# using inner join in Country column
# and City column
# and save it as 'df'
df = df.merge(df_population, on='Country', how='inner')
df
```

	Country	City	Country Code	Year	Value	
0	India	Delhi	IND	1960	445954579	
1	India	Delhi	IND	1961	456351876	
2	India	Delhi	IND	1962	467024193	
3	India	Delhi	IND	1963	477933619	
4	India	Delhi	IND	1964	489059309	
...	...	...	...	...	...	
181	Canada	Toronto	CAN	2017	36545236	
182	Canada	Toronto	CAN	2018	37065084	
183	Canada	Toronto	CAN	2019	37601230	
184	Canada	Toronto	CAN	2020	38037204	
185	Canada	Toronto	CAN	2021	38246108	

186 rows × 5 columns

Figure 4.17: Merging DataFrames

From this example, we realize that one option is to add external data to an existing Pandas DataFrame by performing an inner join (as used in this case) to match a particular column. Like inner join (where we are keeping only the matching record on one column's value in the final DataFrame), we can also perform outer and full join operations on DataFrames in Pandas, as we could do in SQL. However, in our case, we have 186 rows, one for each **Year** of data that was created as a result of the join.

Let us simplify this only at the **City** and **Country** level, as we see in the following example:

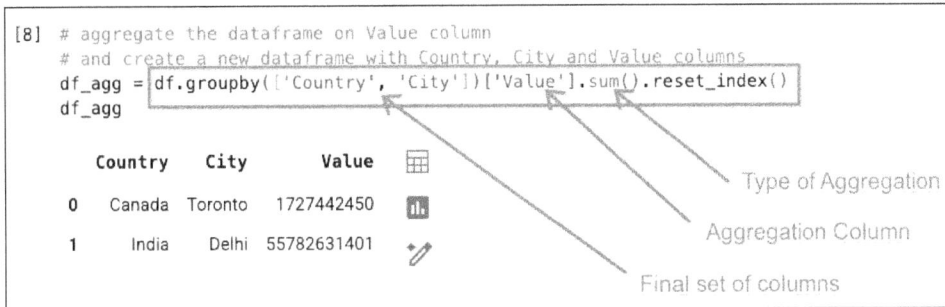

```
[8]  # aggregate the dataframe on Value column
     # and create a new dataframe with Country, City and Value columns
     df_agg = df.groupby(['Country', 'City'])['Value'].sum().reset_index()
     df_agg

        Country    City        Value
     0   Canada   Toronto   1727442450
     1    India     Delhi   55782631401
```

Type of Aggregation

Aggregation Column

Final set of columns

Figure 4.18: Group by in DataFrames

Unfortunately, in this example, it seems the data got lowered a lot in volume, which is not really what we wanted, but it is good to understand this example since that is one common problem of collecting external data that is ungoverned. In this case as well, when we downloaded the data from the GitHub repository (which we will learn later in this chapter), we did not validate its source, how it was generated, if the author was credible, or the methods used to curate and store this data on population, and so on. This signifies that data governance is quite essential, especially while collecting external data.

Now, for a moment, let us get back from our dummy-data-based examples to the previous use case of Dry Beans. As of now, we have only seen a handful of basic properties or relations between the features and the **Class** variable.

Let us now move forward and learn about how to get the **probability distribution functions (PDFs)**. PDFs describe the probability of a random variable taking on a given range of values. When (for example) we plot the PDF of the **Area** column from our DataFrame, using the **Class** column as the hue for clarity, the following is what we see, and gives us some very interesting information not only about the distribution of the data but also about if this feature **Area** can separate one or more particular **Class** from the others, this would signify that when we build an ML model later on this data, the **Area** column will be a very important feature in classifying values in the **Class** column as shown in the following figure:

```
# Probability distribution function
# of the Area column using the Class column
# as the Hue from the dataframe.
plt.figure(figsize=(14,14));
sns.FacetGrid(df, hue='Class') \
    .map(sns.distplot, 'Area') \
    .add_legend();
plt.show();

<Figure size 1400x1400 with 0 Axes>
```

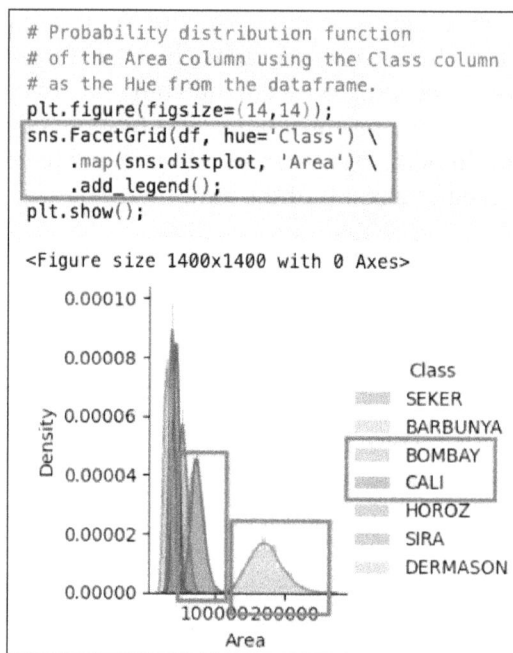

Figure 4.19: *PDF of columns*

From this output, it appears that the **Area** feature will help distinguish between the **BOMBAY** and **CALI** classes of Dry Beans while not so good for the other classes. However, it is not so bad for the other classes as well, especially the **DERMASON** and the **SIRA** ones. This analysis is very important and leads to an area of ML where an ML engineer and a data scientist spend a lot of their time, feature selection, and feature engineering.

As one may have already gathered by now, data analysis (using NumPy, Pandas, Matplotlib, Seaborn, and many other tools and libraries, for example), or also what is commonly termed as exploratory data analysis, is more an art than a science, and hence there are no charted recipes to follow for any given dataset, which work like magic and give insights out of the box. Hence, we can continue learning about the rest of the engineering tools that an ML engineer should be aware of, keeping in mind a couple of points:

In many scenarios, dedicated data analytics software packages like Tableau or Power BI provide easy ways of analyzing and visualizing data.

Note: They come with their own set of engineering guides for installation, management, and cost of operations. At times, one should keep an open frame of mind to learn these peripherals on the job rather than getting overwhelmed.

Other than the libraries that are quickly touch-based in this chapter, there are other interesting toolsets available for a one-time thorough analysis of any given dataset. Some of the important mentions here should be Pandas profiling, SweetViz, and AutoViz, which are the three most interesting libraries we have used over time, which give different perspectives of data exploration, and a combination of the results from all of them can help us understand data to a great extent.

Jupyter Notebooks

As an ML engineer starts to experiment with data to understand it or to try out a specific type of ML pipeline, for example, nothing beats an interactive and free-to-use environment like Jupyter Notebooks.

In a nutshell, this is how one can understand what Jupyter Notebooks are:

- **Interactive data science environment**: Jupyter Notebooks are web-based documents that combine live code (e.g., Python, R, Julia), explanatory text, images, videos, equations, and visualizations. Think of them as a computational scratchpad and storytelling tool all in one.

- **Open-source and versatile**: Jupyter Notebooks are part of the open-source Project Jupyter, used widely in education, research, and industry for prototyping, experimentation, and presenting findings.

Although a Jupyter Notebook seldom provides the ability to run software in a production system (other than some exceptions in cloud platforms like AWS or Google Cloud, where there are services that let us, schedule runs of a notebook or its instance, for example), the Jupyter Notebooks are useful in specific scenarios, a few of which are as follows:

- **Experimentation**: The ability to execute code in small chunks (cells), immediately see results, and easily modify your approach makes exploration and rapid prototyping simple.

- **Documentation**: Text cells let you narrate your analysis, explaining your data, processes, and conclusions.

- **Visualization**: Include plots, charts, and interactive elements to communicate your findings effectively.

- **Collaboration**: Notebooks are portable files (with the `.ipynb` extension of the notebook files), easily shared and worked on by teams.

Note: These are a few of the reasons why platforms like Kaggle, (where one is more interested in the traditional and research approach of AI and ML) provide a Jupyter Notebook interface for AI engineers to try their experiments and move up the leaderboard as their work is liked by others, or when their results are better than others in comparison.

Following is a quick image of how a typical Jupyter Notebook may look in Google Colab, for example. In relevant chapters of this book, we will cover some specific cloud services that an AI engineer uses frequently in their work.

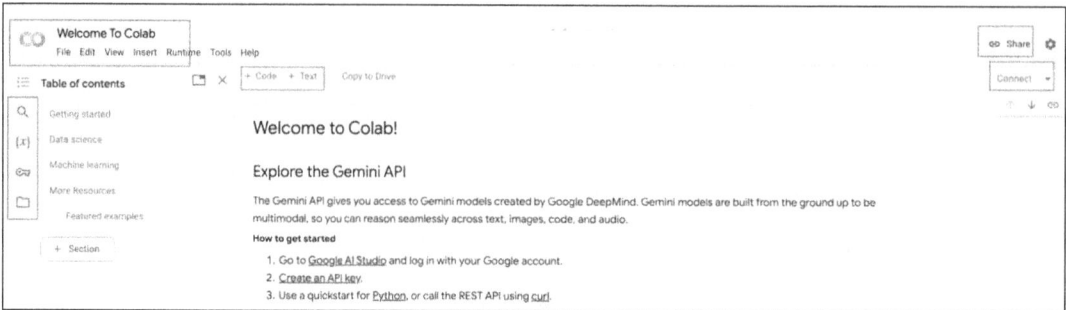

Figure 4.20: *Vertex AI workbench with Jupyter Notebook*

There are multiple ways of installing a Jupyter Notebook environment, other than using a choice of cloud platform, like using the PIP, Python Package Manager, or any predesigned Python distribution like Anaconda, for example. The advantage of the latter is the fact that they usually provide a preconfigured Jupyter Notebook interface, hence reducing the time to set up the work environment for an ML engineer or a data scientist.

Let us dive into its components and see how they fit together.

The launcher of any Jupyter Notebook environment (sometimes called a **JupyterLab**) is the first thing to know about. Typically, in environments like Google Cloud Vertex AI Workbench, this is where one starts to use the features of an experimentation workbench.

So, we can define its properties as follows:

- **Our starting point**: Think of the launcher as your JupyterLab home screen. This is where we will start new projects and access essential tools.

- **Notebook creation**: The primary role of the launcher is to allow us to create different types of notebooks. Each notebook is tailored to a specific programming language (Python, R, Julia, etc.), so we will pick one based on your project's needs.

- **Beyond Notebooks**: While creating notebooks is a significant function, the Launcher also lets us:

  o Create plain text files for notes or simple scripts.

  o Start a terminal session (which gives you a command line interface within our browser).

  o Create folders to organize your project files.

Next up is the File Browser, which gives us the interface to run through the artifacts we use and create during the lifecycle of one or more Notebooks. Our file browser in JupyterLab looks and functions much like a regular file browser on our computer or laptop.

This is the control center for the following:

- **Navigation**: Find, open, and move files within our project's directory structure.

- **Organization**: Create, delete, and rename folders to keep our project structured.

- **Interaction**: Open Notebooks, text files, or other supported file types (images, CSV data, etc.) to use in our current work.

Finally, one has the Notebook Workspace. A notebook workspace is where the magic happens. This is the interactive document where you combine code, explanations, and results. It consists of two primary cell types as follows:

- **Code cells**:

  o **Coding canvas**: This is where we write our programming code (Python, R, etc.).

  o **Execution**: We can use the *Shift+Enter* (or use the Run button) keyboard shortcut to send our code for the computer to process, producing results that appear right beneath the cell.

- **Markdown cells**:

  o **Narrative tool**: One must write text, headings, and lists to explain the code, ideas, and findings.

  o **Formatting**: Markdown uses simple syntax to create headings, bold text, italics, links, images, and even mathematical equations.

Additionally, and interestingly, one should note that beyond just a workspace, Jupyter Notebooks act as:

- **Records**: They preserve a trail of our thought processes, inputs, and outputs, crucial for reproducibility and revisiting our work.

- **Presentations**: Notebooks can be exported into slideshow formats or converted to webpages for sharing results with others.

The one area where all AI and ML engineers should put their equivocal efforts while using Jupyter Notebooks is to put relevant, crisp, and well-organized comments throughout the notebook using markdown cells as well as code cells as applicable. This is to ensure a smooth handover and review of work within and outside the scope of the team where an AI engineer may be working on a particular problem statement. This also makes it easy to later convert the final version of the experiment from a notebook to proper software using an **integrated development environment** (**IDE**), like **Visual Studio** (**VS**) Code, which we will learn now.

Visual Studio Code

Let us start exploring VS Code now as an IDE for creating AI and ML software.

Note: Depending on the tool-set requirements and choices of every organization, the choice of IDE will change; however, most of the IDEs have interchangeable features, and hence, with the knowledge of one of them, it would be relatively easy to learn the others.

Like any other IDEs or editors, VS Code uses a common UI and layout format with an explorer on the left side showing the files and folders we have access to (or the ones we have opened as a workspace) and an editor on the right showing the content of the files we are working with. A typical setup in VS Code looks like the following, as taken from their public documentation:

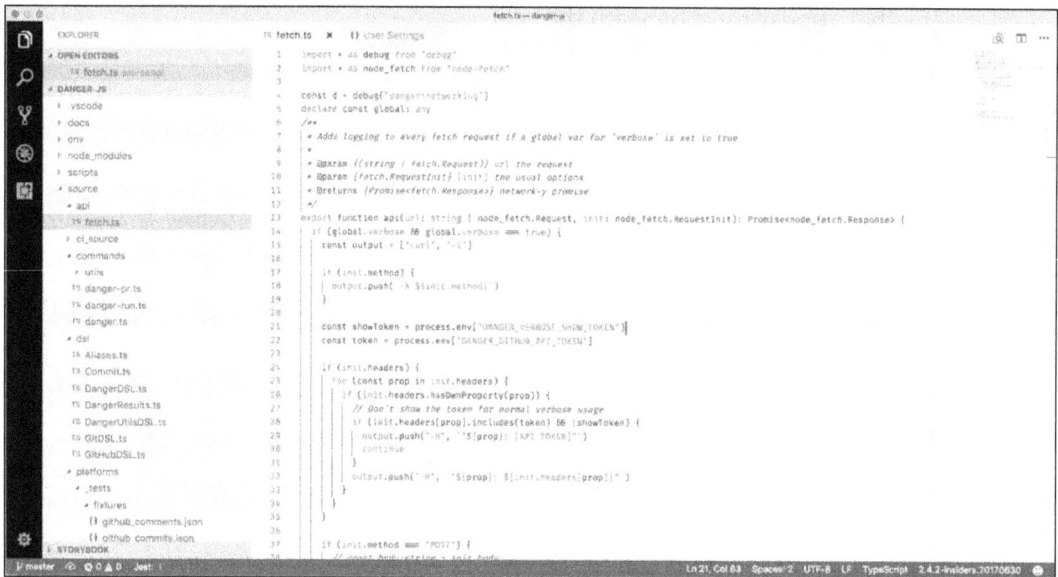

Figure 4.21: Visual Studio overview

One great feature of VS Code is side-by-side editing, where we can work on multiple files at once and even search variables and artifacts through them. This typically helps when we start to modularize our components as part of the AI application we are building, as seen again from the public documentation, as follows:

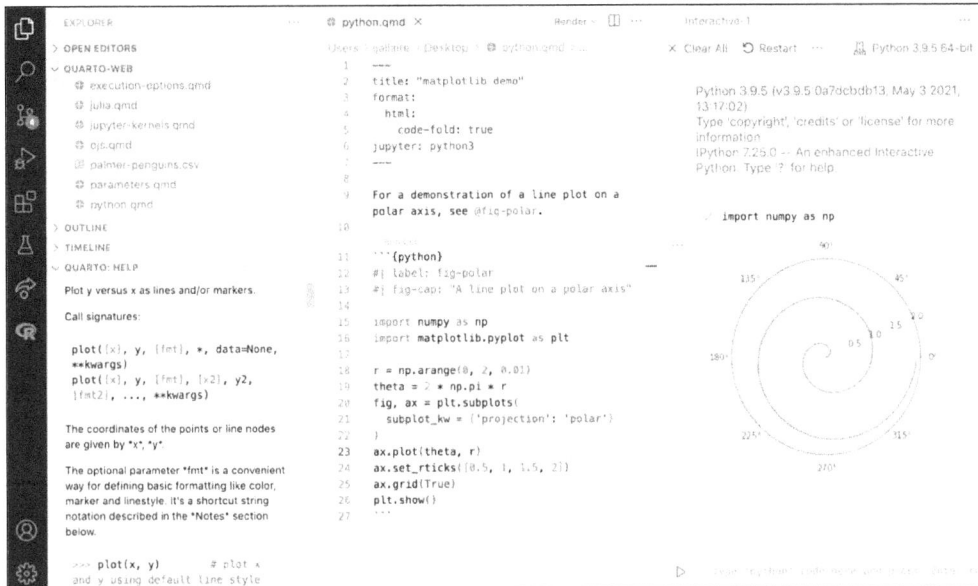

Figure 4.22: Split windows in VS Code

For most of the popular programming languages like Python, VS Code contains utilities or add-ons that help an ML engineer with code completion, style guide checks, linting tests and validations, and so on. These add-ons are called **EXTENSIONS** in VS code, like the example for Python, as follows:

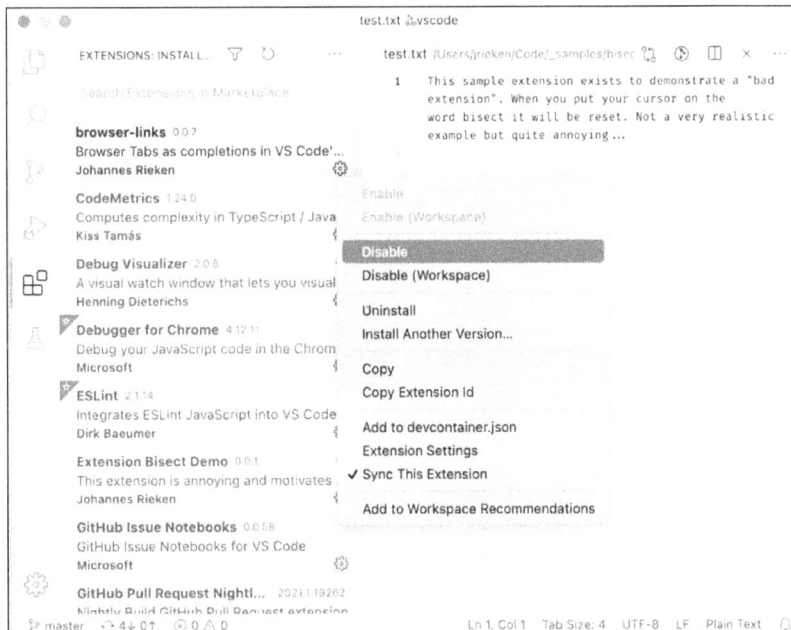

Figure 4.23: Installing extensions in VS Code

Note: VS Code provides the ready interface for AI engineers to get up to speed with their development and testing process and does not impose or carry along any software engineering best practices while writing software, which is a different art that one masters over time and with a consistent amount of practice.

Keeping that in mind, let us go through a quick tutorial to understand how to set up an environment for developing a Python application using VS Code.

Firstly, one can create a separate directory for the utility we would like to develop from scratch (which we will learn about in the later section of this chapter, check existing code). From this directory, we can run VS Code in 2 ways, one with the **code** command in Linux or from the **File** menu option from the VS Code UI, as shown in the following figure:

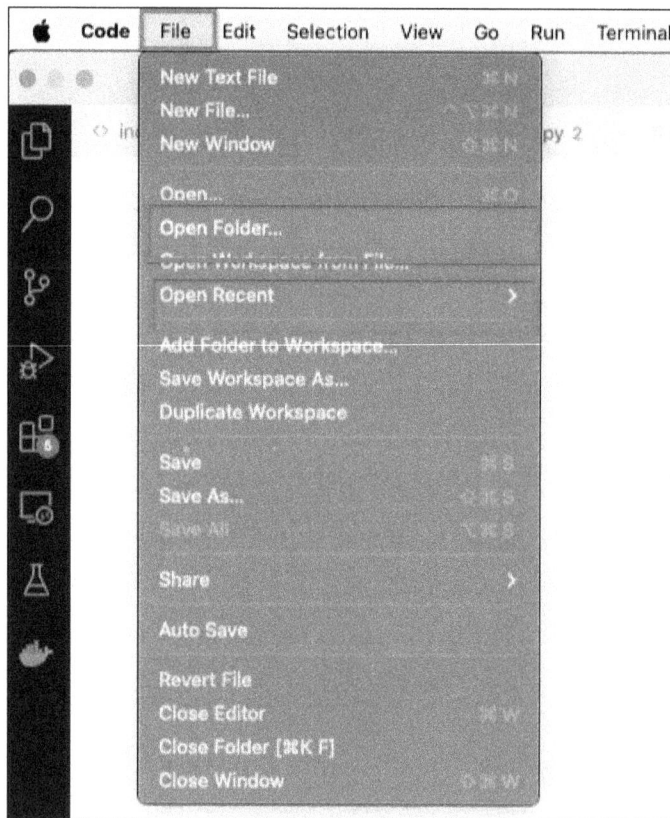

Figure 4.24: Selecting the development folder in VS Code

The best practice herewith, before starting with the development, is to create a virtual environment. This is simply put a separate working directory only for installation of specific libraries and packages in Python, which we would require to install to run our code. We can open the **Command Palette** from the UI (which resides at the bottom left corner of the screen) first, as shown in the following figure:

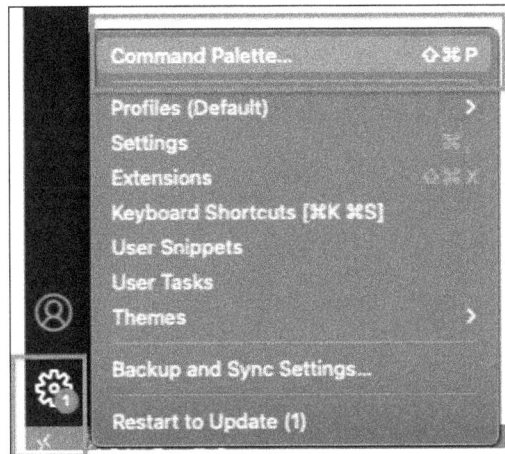

Figure 4.25: Command Palette in VS Code

In the search bar, one can type the **Python: Create Environment** command to search for the appropriate option and select the available commands, as shown in *Figure 4.26*. Usually, **venv** and **conda** are the two most common options presented to the user, both of which are quite similar as a start.

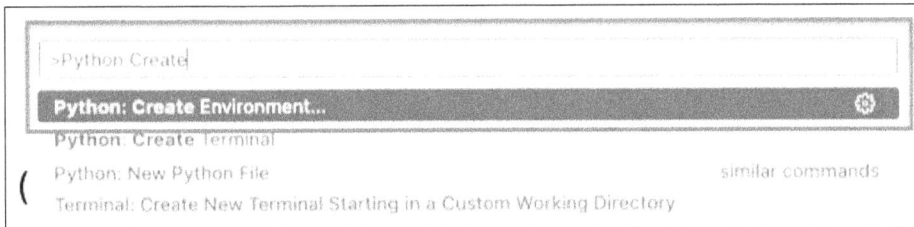

Figure 4.26: Creating Python environments in VS Code

From the preceding option(s), one can further choose to create a Python environment using a virtual environment manager (**.venv**) or conda environment manager (**.conda**). An example of this is as follows:

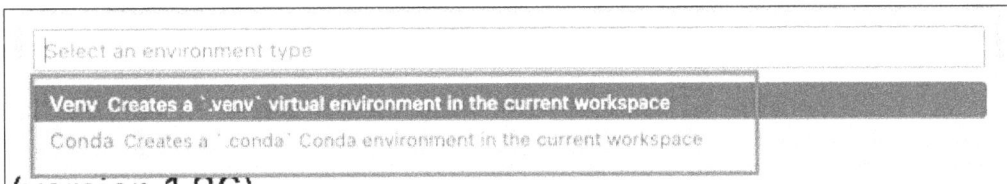

Figure 4.27: Choosing a virtual environment manager in VS Code

From the preceding option(s), one can select any existing Python installation (not recommended for a new project, though) or create a new virtual environment so that there is isolation of packages installed or required for one project as opposed to the other.

The next important thing to do (and this can be automated as well using some existing frameworks or libraries in Python and elsewhere) is to create the skeleton of our project. Typically, an AI engineer would create a folder or work structure like the following; however, some components can change depending on the nature of installation and automation we desire to have in the future:

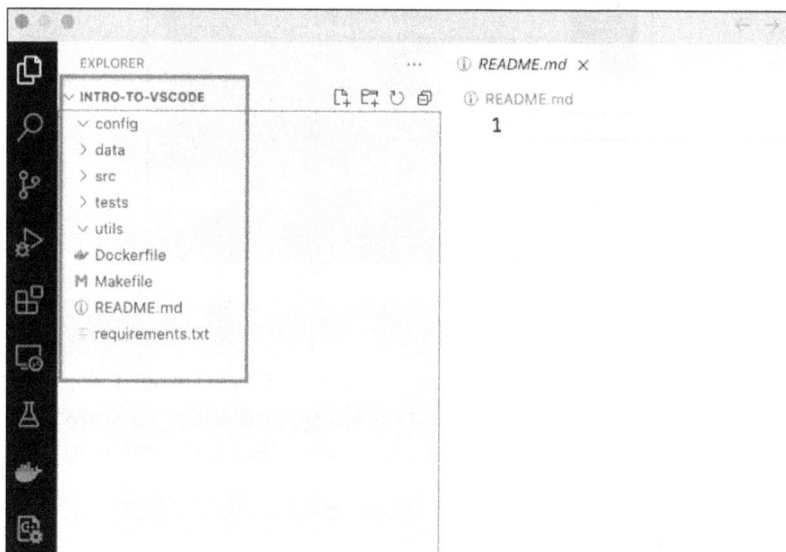

Figure 4.28: Skeleton of a typical ML project

In most cases:

- The **config** folder is expected to have files like **config.py** or **config.ini** from where the default configurations will be read by the application.

- The **src** folder is where the main program will reside.

- The **utils** folder is where we will have utility modules and programs in place to aid our software's working.

- The **data** folder is optional and may contain any test files or temporary datasets we require during the runtime of the application.

- The **tests** folder contains all the unit tests (and other types of tests as well, in the form of Python programs), which will help in running automated tests on the software we write.

- Additional files will include:
  - a **Dockerfile** to create an image (which we will learn about shortly as well),
  - a **README.md** file to (markdown) instructions and information about the software,
  - a **Makefile** to automate the build process of the software,

> o a `requirements.txt` file containing the list of Python libraries and packages we will need to run our software.

By now, one should be set up to create new AI applications using VS Code.

Note: In other IDEs, similar steps are followed with somewhat different user interfaces, and we must know our way around the IDE to make the best use of its features.

Now, let us learn how to version control our code as a first step towards DevOps in ML software.

Version control with Git

Imagine working on a school essay. One may have to save multiple versions as we go along. This gets messy fast, especially if the student must collaborate with others during the writing process. Version control, herewith using Git, is a system that helps solve this matter when we are developing an AI or ML application of any scale. Ultimately, it only helps us create checkpoints or save points of our code throughout the lifecycle of the application, which is usually a very long period. In a nutshell, Git is a powerful, free, and open-source **distributed version control system** (**DVCS**).

Let us clarify some initial concepts first:

- **Repository**: This is our project's home folder, which contains all the files and directories like what we had created in the last section while setting up the VS Code skeleton.

- **Commit**: It is a save point with all changes made at a specific moment. It is like taking a snapshot of our code with a message describing what we have changed, also called the commit message.

- **Branch**: A separate copy of our main code is used to work on new features or fixes without messing up the main working version.

Let us clarify the basic workflow of working with Git, as follows:

- **Make changes**: Edit our code files.

- **Stage changes**: We select which files we want to include in our next *snapshot* (commit).

- **Commit changes**: Create a snapshot (commit) with a clear message describing our changes (e.g., Added image processing feature).

- **Push to remote**: When collaborating, we share our commits with a central repository on a service like GitHub or GitLab.

We can elaborate on these steps with a near-to-real-world AI application like the following:

- Let us suppose we are building a cat image classifier:

○ **Initial commit**: We start with **cat_classifier.py**; this is our first commit, preferably in the **src** folder with optional utilities in the **utils** folder.

○ **New feature branch**: We create a branch called **add_color_filters** to work on a new feature.

○ **Make changes**: We add code, test, and maybe add more files in that branch.

○ **Commits within the branch**: We commit multiple times within our branch (added basic filter, fixed filter bug, etc.).

○ **Merge and push**: When your feature is done, you merge the branch back into your main code and push everything to the central repository.

The advantages that Git brings to the table are as follows:

- **Going back in time**: If something breaks, we can go back to any previous commit to see what went wrong or roll back our code to a working state.

- **Collaboration**: Multiple people can work on the project safely in their branches without stepping on each other's toes.

- **Experimentation**: Branching lets you try out crazy ideas without messing up our main codebase.

Firstly, we need (unless our environment is AWS or GCP) to install Git from the official public website (**https://git-scm.com**). If properly installed as per the instructions on this website, we should be able to run the **git --version** command to see the stable version of Git that was installed in the system.

Note: Installation on Linux and Windows follow different pathways, depending on how these operating system kernels and registries are designed, respectively.

A first-time Git setup is equally important. We need to at least configure the **user.name** and **user.email** configurations (ideally, globally) for the system from where we would use Git to work with our code.

Note: Setting these globally would apply the details for all projects in that system, as shown in Figure 4.29:

```
$ git config --global user.name "John Doe"
$ git config --global user.email johndoe@example.com
```

Figure 4.29: Basic Git configuration

To view the set of all default or newly added configurations, one can use the **git config** command with a **list** option, as shown in *Figure 4.30*. This helps to quickly identify if there are any misconfigured elements in our system and apply it to almost all the repositories that we use in that system at any stage.

Note: By system here, we refer to the desktop, laptop, or even a compute engine VM we use in AWS or GCP.

```
$ git config --list
user.name=John Doe
user.email=johndoe@example.com
color.status=auto
color.branch=auto
color.interactive=auto
color.diff=auto
...
```

Figure 4.30: *List all Git configurations*

Let us say we want to start with initiating a Git repo for the directory we created in the last section (while learning the basics of VS Code). So, we could use the **git init** command to initialize, from where the repo would start reading. This means we are telling Git utility that we would like to start marking our new or existing repository from this folder, as shown in the following figure:

```
for Linux:

$ cd /home/user/my_project

for macOS:

$ cd /Users/user/my_project

for Windows:

$ cd C:/Users/user/my_project

and type:

$ git init
```

Figure 4.31: *Initialize empty repository*

Considering we have the folder now and have initiated a blank Git repo in this folder, we can add further files or modify existing ones that we are working on, add them to the index of files we want Git to know of, and then commit them. When we use these commands (refer to the following example), we are merely pushing some interim changes to what is otherwise called a **local repository** with information about what we have changed:

```
$ git add *.c
$ git add LICENSE
$ git commit -m 'Initial project version'
```

Figure 4.32: *Adding first files in local repo*

Now, this example is where we assumed that we do not already have an existing Git repo. Many times, an AI engineer would end up joining an existing team of developers who are already maintaining their work in any given existing Git repo, usually hosted in an online distributed service or platform, like GitHub, GitLab, Cloud Source Repo in Google Cloud Platform, etc., for example. In this case, the first thing we do is clone the Git repo, as shown in the following figure:

```
$ git clone https://github.com/libgit2/libgit2
```

Figure 4.33: Cloning existing code repository

Note: In this example, we are using an HTTPS-based method to clone a repository.

GitHub or other similar online installations do not allow a developer to enter their username or password combination from the command line to authenticate anymore; instead, it is highly recommended that one uses SSH Authentication keys to clone any existing Git repo. For example, on a Linux system, one can use the **ssh -keygen -t rsa** command to generate the **id_rsa** and **id_rsa.pub** files under the **~/.ssh** directory, post which the contents of the **.pub** file need to be copied over to the GitHub settings page for the user.

Note: This is a one-time setup for any system that an AI engineer or a software developer will use and will be repeated for every new system.

Once configured for one system, unless the OS is wiped clean with a fresh installation, there is no need to generate the SSH keys again. In Windows, one may want to use PowerShell to run similar steps.

At this time, we have a starter Git, either from a local directory from scratch or from an existing remote repository. In our local working directory, either we have a set of already tracked files that Git knows about in terms of their history, or they are untracked since maybe they are not committed or pushed to a remote Git repository yet. As we continue to make changes to our files, Git keeps track of them and marks them either as **untracked** or **modified** from the last commit stage (or as compared to the last snapshot). As we go along, we must stage these changes, commit the files, and carry over this loop as we work on the whole or any part of the project. In a typical lifecycle, the Git SCM public documentation helps us clearly understand the various lifecycle stages of our work with Git, as shown in the following:

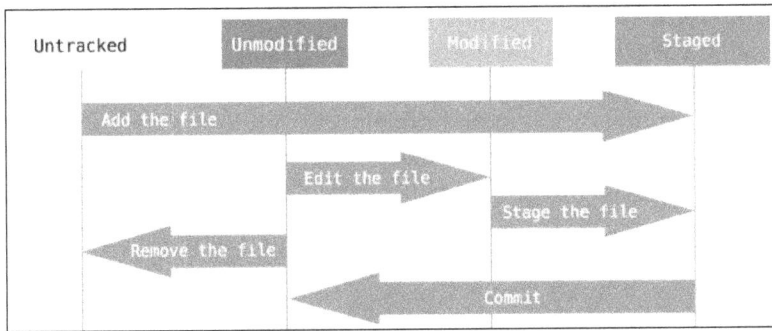

Figure 4.34: Sample Git workflow

At any point in time, a simple **git status** command would let us know which branch we are on, which are the untracked files, etc., along with some easy instructions on what we could do next. Interestingly, we can even ask Git to ignore a certain set of files that we never want to get committed in the repository, using a typical **.gitignore** file in the root directory, from where we started to work on a particular project. A **.gitignore** file can contain full file names of the files to ignore or regular expressions to identify the files to be ignored.

Let us quickly understand what branches are in Git. Think of our main codebase as the trunk of a tree. Git branches are like individual branches stemming from this trunk. Each branch represents a separate line of development within your project.

Here is why this is powerful:

- **Work in isolation**: Create a branch for every new feature, bug fix, or wild experiment. This keeps changes separate until one is sure they work and would not mess with the main stable version of our code.

- **Collaborate smoothly**: Multiple developers can work simultaneously on their branches. Imagine each team member has a mini project within the larger project.

- **Experiment easily**: Branches give us safe sandboxes. Test risky changes, try new approaches, and if they do not work out, discard the branch with no harm done.

Let us say your team is building an Image classifier application, in which case we may see the following set of branches in our Git repo:

- **main**: Production-ready code, what currently lives on the existing running version of the application, if any.

- **feature_engineer**: Separate branch to write the data pipelines for ML training later.

- **training_pipeline**: Separate branch to write the ML training pipelines.

- **hyperparameter_tuning**: Separate branch to write the hyperparameter tuning jobs.

Once a feature on a branch is finished and reviewed, we merge it back into the main branch. This combines all the work from the specific feature branch into our central codebase. This is ideally done when we have all the required components in place: working and tested code, tests (written separately), updated documentation, updated Makefile if applicable, and so on. Once the branch is merged, the specific feature is now available to our code repo and is (or should ideally be) ready to be installed in production.

Some of the key commands that one should keep in mind at this stage are as follows:

- **git branch new_branch_name**: Creates a new branch
- **git checkout branch_name**: Switches to an existing branch
- **git commit -m "Your message"**: Commits changes on your current branch
- **git merge branch_name**: Merges specified branch into your current branch

Let us not forget a couple of very important (industry standard) best practices that one should follow while working with branches in any project, using Git, or for that matter, any other version control system:

- **Short-lived branches**: Branches are meant to be temporary. One should merge them back into the main when the feature or fix is complete.
- **Descriptive names**: One MUST use clear names like fix-search-bug or new-checkout-flow.

We have covered enough to start developing our AI applications (especially as part of a wider team) using Git as the most common version control system.

Now, let us learn how to package the code in the best way using containers.

Containers and Docker

Let us now try to solve a typical problem: The code works on the developer's laptop but does not work in the QA or pre-production environment. This is, or at least was, a typical day in life for many of us as well, until we figured out a better way.

Suppose we have built our initial and working ML model. This is more of a complete software (containing tests, etc.) and works perfectly on our machine, but when a colleague tries to run it, something breaks. Why? There can be many valid reasons behind this scenario, like different software versions, missing libraries, etc.

A **container** packages our code, its dependencies (libraries, specific Python versions), and even the operating system into a self-contained package. Think of it as a little box that has everything our AI application needs to run. The most popular tool for building and running these containers is **Docker**. It is like a reliable shipping company, allowing us to send our software package as a container anywhere (on-premises or cloud infrastructure).

Let us understand why containers and creating images of our work from the development environment for installation in production are useful for AI applications as follows:

- **Reproducibility**: Our ML model will run the same way across different machines, so there should be no more it works on my machine frustrations.

- **Dependency management**: Say our model needs an old version of a library. This could be hard to install everywhere, but our container keeps that old version bundled within, and hence, there should be no conflicts with other projects.

- **Scalability**: Easily deploy our model to multiple servers because the container provides everything the model needs to run anywhere.

- **Cloud portability**: Our container will run with our model smoothly on a local machine or a cloud server on AWS, Azure, or Google Cloud.

In the Docker world, it is good to understand some terminologies first before going in-depth with some practices. The basic definitions we need to know are as follows:

- **Image**: Think of it as the blueprint for our container. Once installed, one can search for Docker images using **docker search <keyword>**. Examples: **docker search python, docker search TensorFlow**.

- **Pull**: To grab a pre-built image, **docker pull python:3.8**

  Note: This command might take a while the first time.

- **Run**: Brings our container to life: **docker run -it python:3.8 bash** (This starts a container using the image we pulled and gives us an interactive shell).

From the Docker official website (**https://www.docker.com/get-started**), one should be able to find instructions on how to download and install the Docker software on their specific workstations depending on the operating system. This would be a good time to perform the installation, as later, we will integrate it with our other systems, like VS Code and others that are used throughout this book.

Quickly, let us create a new directory and create a simple Python script known as **script. py** with a simple command inside it, like the following:

```
print("Welcome to Docker!")
```

Our goal now is to create a quick container that will run this script.

To do so, we create our next file named **Dockerfile** (with no extensions ideally) in the same folder. This file is more of a recipe for what your container will do when used.

Let us write the following in our **Dockerfile** file:

```
# Our base image - we'll use a Python image
FROM python:3.9

# Create a working directory inside the container
WORKDIR /app
```

```
# Copy your Python script into the container
COPY script.py /app

# The command to run when the container starts
CMD ["python", "script.py"]
```

Essentially, our recipe is to create our container **FROM** a base image, create a working directory using the **WORKDIR** command called **app**, then **COPY** our **script.py** program into the working directory, and finally run and command given by the **CMD** when the container starts or is used.

Once the files are saved inside the new directory, one can use the command line utility on their workstation to traverse to this new directory and run the following command, for example, to start creating a new image:

docker build -t my-first-container .

As aforementioned, the **-t** option tags our first image with the given name **my-first-container**, and the **.** sign indicates that the Dockerfile is present in the current path or directory from where the instructions are to be read. Once completed, it will take Docker some time to download the base image and prepare our image on top of it using our recipe. We can then run the image as a container using a simple command as follows. This will run the image we just created in the form of a portable container on our workstation and follow the recipe:

docker run my-first-container

One should see **Welcome to Docker** printed on the terminal. This is also a good test to validate if our installation was done correctly or not. There are many complex things that an AI engineer will perform in their lifetime of software engineering. The steps involved in this particular activity include pushing locally created Docker images to a centralized hub like Docker Hub, Google Container Registry, or Artifact Registry in Google Cloud Platform (for example). Usually, the Dockerfile may well be much more complicated than the one we have built here, and there can be cases when by using services like Google Kubernetes Engine on the Google Cloud Platform, an AI engineer may end up linking and using multiple containers to build complete applications (e.g., a container for our model, a container for our data pipelines, etc.).

We will now continue further and learn more about enterprise databases, which are usually present in organizations of varied scale and domains, from where AI engineers end up pulling data during the lifecycle of the ML application.

Databases

Enterprise databases range from **Online Transaction Processing (OLTP)** to **Online Analytical Processing (OLAP)** to graph, and so on. Let us talk about the role of databases in ML and explore database choices that one might encounter.

Firstly, let us understand databases and their know-how matter for an AI engineer. Then, we will investigate the types of databases in use as well. The most important reasons why an AI application makes use of a particular type of database are as follows:

- **Storing training data**: ML models learn from data. Datasets can be gigantic, so databases provide an organized, efficient way to store and retrieve training data.

- **Data preparation**: Databases make it possible to run, pre-process, and clean tasks on our raw data to prepare it for ML algorithms.

- **Serving model predictions**: Once our model is trained, one may want to store its predictions in a database for applications, user queries, or analytics. This is a good idea to cache the results of an ML model to review later during investigations of production issues.

- **Experiment tracking**: With different experiments and parameters, a database can log metadata about each model one has trained, keeping our research organized.

Let us look into the categories of databases in use and of choice. Broadly, we find two main categories relevant to machine learning as follows:

- **Relational databases (SQL):**

   o **Structure**: Data is organized into tables with clearly defined relationships. Examples: Oracle, PostgreSQL, MySQL, SQLite.

   o **Common for ML**: Often used to store structured data features, experiment results, or well-defined input data to an ML model.

   o **SQL knowledge**: SQL language proficiency is essential to perform data manipulation.

- **NoSQL databases:**

   o **Flexibility**: Comes in various flavors (document, key-value, graph, etc.), each designed for specific kinds of data and scaling needs. Examples: MongoDB, Cassandra, Redis.

   o **When they shine**: Handling massive volumes of data, rapid read/writes, or data without rigid structures (e.g., raw logs, social media data).

While choosing a database type for ML applications, one should consider the following important factors:

- **Data format**:

   o If the data is structured or tabular, one can go for SQL options.

   o If the data is semi-structured, nested, or rapidly changing, then NoSQL might be a better fit.

- **Scale**:

  - For a small experiment, SQLite could be sufficient. If the data is massive, consider distributed NoSQL solutions like Cassandra.

- **Performance**:

  - Our choice will be informed depending on whether we need to read, write data during training or serve low-latency predictions.

- **Complexity**: Some NoSQL options offer great flexibility but can introduce added complexity to manage.

Some very popular choices of databases while working on AI applications are as follows:

- **MySQL, PostgreSQL**: Mature, open-source SQL database. Robust features and is great for structured data. It may also offer specialized data types (like spatial data) used in ML.

- **MongoDB**: Document-oriented NoSQL database, a good fit for JSON-like data (often seen in web apps or semi-structured datasets).

- **Redis**: An in-memory key-value data store great for caching, feature stores, or real-time analytics. This makes it fantastic for low latency serving of predictions.

- **Cloud Databases**: Most cloud providers (AWS, Google Cloud, Azure) offer managed versions of both SQL and NoSQL databases, simplifying setup and scaling.

Note: This is not to be considered a comprehensive list, as the choice of the database will be influenced not only by what the ML application deserves but also by other confounding factors like the Tooling preferences of a certain organization.

Let us take a quick example of storing features for a recommendation system:

- **Relational (PostgreSQL)**: Tables for users, items, and ratings with clear relationships.

- **NoSQL (MongoDB)**: User profiles are stored as flexible documents, potentially making user interaction updates dynamic.

The best database for our ML project depends on our specific data, project goals, and scalability needs. Often, one would find that even multiple databases are used in a single ML system.

Conclusion

In this chapter, we covered how to effectively perform data analysis for AI and ML applications, followed by how to use an IDE like VS Code and how to use version control using Git, basics of how to create containers using Docker, and finally how to effectively use RDBMS and EDW in an existing IT infrastructure.

In the next chapter, we are going to learn about classical ML algorithms in depth and implement them in varied scenarios. We will learn how these ML models are created for a variety of use cases across organizations.

Exercises

Let us try and solve the following questions to understand the concepts in depth. A good AI/ML engineer should study the solutions of different ML use cases shared by other engineers without violating the copyright of assets and code. Feel free to utilize popular websites like *Stack Overflow* and *Kaggle*.

- Download and install the Anaconda distribution on your workstation. Once the installation is complete, start a Jupyter Notebook from the command line. Create and run the first notebook to practice all the codes from *Chapter 3, TensorFlow Essentials,* and *Chapter 4, Engineering for Machine Learning.*

- Load the Iris dataset from Kaggle or sklearn datasets. Perform basic levels of data exploration in a Jupyter Notebook, either using Google Colab or a local Anaconda distribution installation. Note in detail the findings on each feature and target variable as inline markdown cells.

- In the section on VS code, we provided an example skeleton of ML projects or a Python project. Create that skeleton on your workstation and check examples on GitHub on how other projects have made use of configuration file(s), Makefile, Dockerfile, and `main.py` program.

- Take any one ML project notebook from Kaggle on any random problem statement. Download the data and the notebook on your workstation. Open the notebook using Jupyter and study or run each code cell. Add a markdown cell under or above each code cell and write down your findings and questions.

- Create your GitHub account (if not already in place), set up SSH keys from your workstation, add them to your Settings page in GitHub, and create your first repository from the command line. Push a sample Python application, even if it is as simple as a calculator app, with only addition and subtraction, using Makefile and test scripts in Python. To do this, create a feature branch rather than checking out the main branch and pushing code into it.

- Install Docker on your workstation and try the first hello-world container from the Docker examples. Next, perform a Docker search to find images containing installations of Jupyter Notebook. Install any one such image from the Docker Hub with the highest number of stars. Check if you can run the container locally and access the Jupyter Notebook URL.

Note: Some of these exercises may seem difficult at first, but one should get an idea of how to strategize their approach when starting to work on a project or task that they have not done before. This helps get out of the comfort zone and understand what areas of improvement one should be working on.

Join our book's Discord space

Join the book's Discord Workspace for Latest updates, Offers, Tech happenings around the world, New Release and Sessions with the Authors:

https://discord.bpbonline.com

CHAPTER 5

Machine Learning Algorithms

Introduction

This chapter will provide an extensive understanding of ML, introducing key algorithms used to unlock hidden patterns in data. We will further discuss techniques like regression, classification, and clustering use cases.

One need not memorize any complicated terms. We will break down each algorithm, explaining its strengths and when to use it. We will discuss linear regression for understanding data trends, advanced regression techniques like Lasso and Ridge tackle complex data with their unique strengths, followed by intuitive techniques with algorithms like logistic regression and KNN, make smart decisions based on similar data points, and then, powerful methods like gradient boosting and **Extreme Gradient Boosting (XGBoost)** to unlock hidden patterns even complex models might miss. We will also explore traditional clustering algorithms like k-means and DBSCAN to find patterns in unlabeled data.

Additionally, neural networks are fascinating but intricate; get a brief introduction here. However, remember that this chapter provides the knowledge foundation with sample code, which by no means is production. We will make them better by the next chapter while we lay the foundations here.

Structure

This chapter covers the following topics:

- Regression models
- Classification models
- Clustering models
- Neural networks

Objectives

By the end of this chapter, you will be able to understand all the important traditional machine learning algorithms in-depth and understand which one fits into the right ecosystem of solutions for a given use case. In turn, we will learn which ML algorithms are to be used in which use cases, their strengths and weaknesses, and how these algorithms operate under the hood (in simple words, with examples).

Regression models

In this section, let us try and understand the different **regression algorithms** to learn about how they work and where they are used.

Linear regression

Let us quickly understand the basics before we discuss the main concepts.

A linear regression helps to estimate a numeric value while it fits a line in 2D, a plane in 3D, or a hyperplane in n-dimensions. If one wants to estimate the height of a person, having given features like weight, gender, ethnicity, hair color, etc., one may choose a regression model since we are estimating a continuous value. When it comes to linear regression, it assumes that most points lie on a linear surface, and hence, the model tries to generate an equation that best fits the data points. Here is a quick visual of how a typical linear regression model (the blue line) will look like, as one tries to estimate the sale of a given product, having given the ads shown on *TV*, when the actual observations are given by the red points, as shown in the following figure:

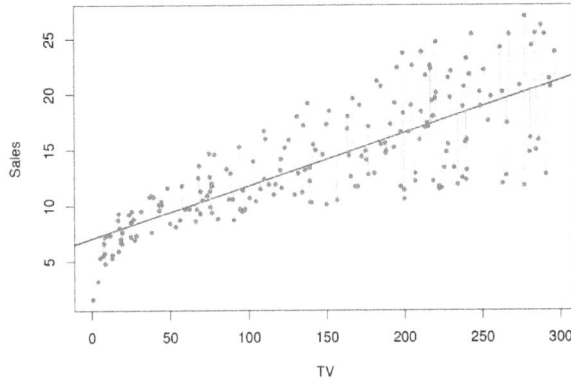

Figure 5.1: *How a regression model looks like*

We can mathematically put the best-fit line as follows:

$$y_i = w_1 * x_1 + w_2 * x_2 + w_0$$

Looking at the preceding line, one thing is clear: many red points are either very close or overlap on the blue line itself. These are cases where the value on the line, at any given value of TV, gives the value of sales that is very close to the actual value. In other words, the actual is almost the same as the estimated value of sales. However, there are even cases where the actuals are very far away from the estimates. Hence, we realize that just like a student making some mistakes in each exam, even our regression line can and will make mistakes. The objective, hence, in the case of creating a linear regression model, is to reduce this error as much as possible. In mathematical terms, we call this the **residual sum of squares** (**RSS**) error, and it is represented by the mathematical formulation as follows:

$$\text{RSS}(\beta_0, \beta_1) = \sum_{i=1}^{n} \left(y_i - \hat{y}_i(\beta_0, \beta_1) \right)^2 = \sum_{i=1}^{n} (y_i - \beta_0 - \beta_1 x_i)^2$$

To put it into simpler terms, what we are trying to achieve here is as follows:

- To minimize the squared error difference between the estimated and the actual values summed over all observations.

- We perform a square of the values so that they become impervious to their scale.

- The RSS equation given here is also called the **cost function**, which we try to minimize over some smart ways or experiments.

- To minimize the cost function, we need the optimal values of the coefficients (the intercept and the slope).

If we find the most optimal regression line or best possible regression model, then the error or output of the cost function will be *0*; that is, there is no difference in values between the actual and the estimate.

Performance metrics, as we understand them now, play a vital role to quantify and validate the performance of an ML model like a regression model. The most common metrics one uses to evaluate a regression model are the R-squared (for simple linear regression models) and adjusted R-square (for multiple linear regression models). Both these metrics typically denote the power to explain the ability of selected features (or independent variables) to the variation or changes in the target (or the dependent variable). Typically, this metric is represented as:

$$R^2 = 1 - \frac{RSS}{TSS} = 1 - \frac{\Sigma_i(y_i - \hat{y}_i)^2}{\Sigma_i(y_i - \bar{y})^2}$$

The numerator term provides the average of squares of residuals (which is the squared differences between the predicted values and the average of the target variable for all N number of observations), while the denominator shows the variation in the response values (which is the difference in the actual vs. the average values). A smaller value of R-square, hence, denotes a poor model. In this equation, RSS is the residual sum of squares, while TSS is the total sum of squared errors.

Note: R-squared is also known as the coefficient of determination as per canonical statistics.

In contrast, the adjusted R-square is represented as follows:

$$\text{Adjusted } R^2 = 1 - \frac{(1 - R^2)(N - 1)}{N - p - 1}$$

Here, N is the total number of observations (or the number of rows in the data), and p is the number of features (or the independent variables). The main reason why one needs an adjusted R-square is because of a slight problem with the R-squared metric; it increases with an increase in the number of features of the model, irrespective of whether these features significantly contribute to the estimation of the target or not. Hence, adjusted R-squared makes use of an additional layer of check so that its value is only affected by the useful features being added to the model. This is also the reason why the value of the latter is always smaller (or equal at times) to the former.

Other than the aforementioned, there are two more common metrics used in regression models, namely the **mean absolute error (MAE)** and the **root mean squared error (RMSE)**. The MAE is the average of the difference between the actual and the predicted values of the actual and predicted values of the target, as follows:

$$\text{MAE} = \frac{1}{n}\sum_{i=1}^{n}|y_i - \hat{y}_i|$$

On the other hand, RMSE merely adds the squared terms to it, making it slightly more robust in cases where features can naturally have outliers in their values, and it is represented as follows:

$$\text{RMSE} = \sqrt{\frac{1}{n}\sum_{i=1}^{n}(y_i - \hat{y}_i)^2}$$

Now, let us continue our discussion on how to find the optimal values of the coefficients so that the error in the model is as low as possible, making the model more accurate to reality. The most common brute-force method to find the optimal values of the coefficients is to try out all possible values and fit a regression model for each of these sets of values. Finally, one can choose the best line out of all the lines, where the cost function returns the minimum value, that is, the error in the model's estimation is the lowest. This method is called **gradient descent**. Imagine plotting all values of errors for different values of coefficients. The resulting visual is represented as follows, where the lowest point (also called global minima) is what we desire:

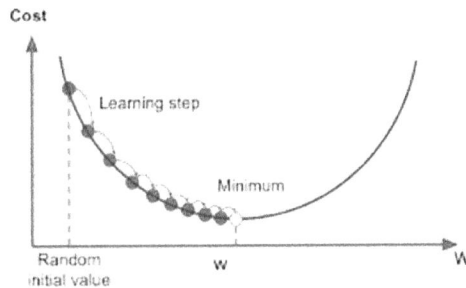

Figure 5.2: *Gradient descent in action*

Mathematically, we do the following:

- We pick a random value of the coefficients and calculate the cost function by fitting the regression line.

- Once we get the error value from the cost function, we change the values of the coefficients by taking their gradients (remember, differential calculus from school).

- The steps of change are usually very small so that one can determine if we are going in the right direction of reducing the error rather than increasing it. Let us keep a note of some of the salient points in a nutshell:

  o The learning steps of change are usually denoted by a factor called **the learning rate**, which is a hyperparameter as well.

  o We can understand the learning rate as the rate at which we make very small changes toward reaching the optimum values of the coefficients or weights of a regression model.

  o The choice of a learning rate is very important; a higher value will lead to oscillations as the gradient descent tries to reach the global minima, while a lower value will simply incur elevated time to reach the minima.

- After a lot of trials, one should reach a state where, after oscillating between higher values of errors, we come to a place where, even with the change in the values of the coefficients, the error does not change much, and we assume that this is our final stage of optimal values.

There are multiple ways of performing gradient descent using dedicated optimizers, which we will discuss further when we start exploring neural networks.

Getting back to our primary objective of cost function, our focus is to make the coefficients as close as possible to the actual values. To do so, we often make use of regularizations, like L1 or L2 regularization. This is because, in every real-world data, despite how well we have collected and maintained our datasets, we still get biases, mostly because of confounding variables that we can never account for. For example, the prices of houses in a particular area, city, or country may be impacted by other conflicts going on at the same time in some other parts of the world. Since these are hard to account for, typically, a regularization unit helps to trim down the values of the weights even more. Think of it as a tug of war between two parts of the optimization algorithm (like gradient descent) where, on one hand, we are updating the values of the weights while, on the other hand, we are keeping the change to their values within check.

The regularization methods help prevent overfitting the training data when the model starts to memorize every pattern, even if they are outliers. Let us discuss these regularization methods in detail, as follows:

- **L1 regularization**: Also known as Lasso regression, it shrinks the absolute values of the model's coefficients. By doing so, it encourages sparsity by selecting only the most important features. For the features where the importance is less (or even lesser), the weights on those features tend to be close to zero. Due to this, the final model is more interpretable now since it has fewer features than originally considered in the training data. So, L1 regularization is used typically when we have too many features and/or we are not sure which ones are important in estimating the target variable's value.

- **L2 regularization**: As opposed to L1 regularization (also called Ridge regression), an L2 regularization method shrinks the squared values of the coefficients towards zero. This makes the model stronger in handling noise in the data and helps to avoid issues with multicollinearity (we will define this term ahead in this section), which is a big issue in any given ML model, especially in regression models. Hence, one chooses to use L2 regularization when one wants to control the overall model complexity and prevent overfitting without any focus on feature selection.

We were introduced to the term, multicollinearity. It is a scenario in which the independent features in the data are not independent of each other, invalidating the basic assumption of linear regression itself. To cater to this scenario, there are multiple methods used to detect and remove features from the dataset that are intercorrelated. One of the common methods is correlation analysis, which gives us a valuation of how closely one value affects any positive or negative change in another value.

Before we move on, let us look at some interesting features of linear regression and understand why it is one of the most loved algorithms:

- Since the equation of the model can be explained very easily, the interpretation of model results is quite natural and easy to convey.

- Since the calculations in the model involve fitting linear lines or planes, it is computationally inexpensive.

- However, since it expects data to be linear and features to be independent, in many complex real-world cases, linear regression may not find its place in cases where we have multicollinearity and non-linear relations; the linear regression may fail to deliver an optimal solution.

Let us now discuss some interesting algorithms to perform regression other than linear regression analysis.

Support vector regression

One surprisingly powerful method is support vector regression, wherein we use the fundamentals of **support vector machines** (or **SVMs**, which we will discuss in the next section of this chapter when we discuss classification algorithms), where the motive is to find a hyperplane in n-dimensions with the maximum margin between the data points and the margin boundaries. This margin represents the model's predictions.

Before understanding it in depth, let us discuss a few definitions to understand the mathematics behind it, as follows:

- **Hyperplane**: Consider this as a line in two dimensions or a plane in higher dimensions that separates data points based on their target values. This is a very useful way to distinguish between observations when they are already labeled. The same method can also be used to estimate a continuous value.

- **Support vectors**: These are quite simply the data points or observations that are closest to the Hyperplane, which help to determine the margin. Consider this as an imaginary area around the hyperplane, which helps to understand the vicinity of the hyperplane.

- **Kernel trick**: This is a mathematical trick or method that helps the support vector regressor handle non-linear data by transforming it into a higher dimensional space where a linear hyperplane can then separate the data. The multiple forms of kernels, like radial basis functions and polynomial kernels, will be discussed in the next section when we use them effectively to solve classification problems. However, it has its use in regression problems as well, which we will see further.

- **Epsilon**: The distance on each side of the hyperplane to the margin around the hyperplane.

The following diagram can help us understand the meaning of some of the aforementioned definitions; the rest will be clear once we discuss the workings of this algorithm:

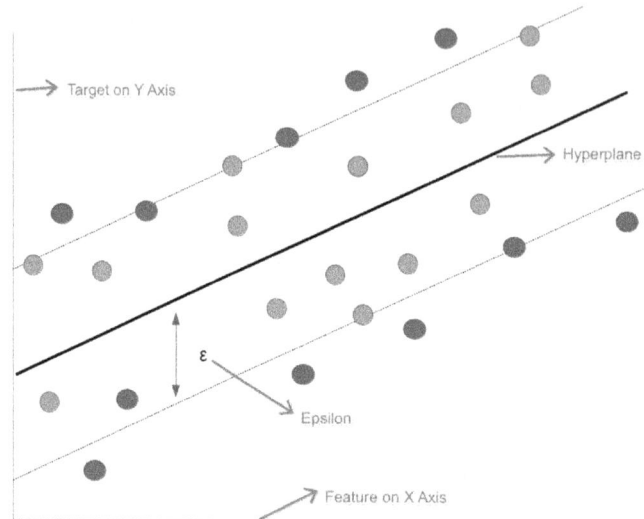

Figure 5.3: Support vectors and hyperplane

Let us now try to understand, in simpler terms, how an algorithm that is predominantly used for classification is used for regression problems. Consider an imaginary dataset with the size and cost of the apartment. Our goal is to estimate the price, given the size. This example makes it easier to understand how the algorithm works. Considering the following data:

- Support vector regressor will first create the regression line, just like it would create the hyperplane while classifying points of two classes.

- Since we have the hyperplane, we would also have the imaginary margin as defined by the **epsilon (eps)** value.

- Our goal now (or mathematically, the constraint of the model put by the algorithm) is to ensure that the absolute difference between the actual and the estimated values of the target variable is less than the value of eps on each side of the hyperplane. In simple terms:

    o   The differences between the original and estimated target values should fall within the margin of the hyperplane.

    o   The additional item added while calculating the constraint is the Eta value, which is the distance of each outlier from the margin around the hyperplane.

    o   The ideology here is to determine not only the fit line but also the optimal value of eps so that all points are near the hyperplane, which models the data points.

- For the points that are still outside the eps or margin range, the algorithm calculates Eta, which is the distance from the hyperplane to these outliers. Our (mathematical) cost function, hence, tries to minimize the hinge loss, which is the sum of squared distances of all such outliers for a factor of C, which is a hyperparameter to the model. Let us look at the most important hyperparameters:

  o The main hyperparameter, in case of regression use cases to consider and tune, is the eps value, since Eta is out of our control unless we can either ignore the outliers from the model (which will be a logically incorrect decision in many cases), or we can treat the outliers to the best possible extent.

    Note: With lesser values of eps, we want fewer errors on the training data, and this will result in overfitting and the model eventually tending towards memorizing the patterns in the data on which it is trained.

  o Again, if the value of eps is too high, it signifies that we can allow errors in the model, resulting in underfitting.

  o We will learn more about the other hyperparameters of SVMs (like the C value) in depth in the next section of this chapter when we learn about their classification capabilities.

- Lastly, it is up to the ML engineer to perform the required amount of hyperparameter tuning to ensure that we have minimal hinge loss so that the resulting best-fit line represents the nature of the data more accurately, as follows:

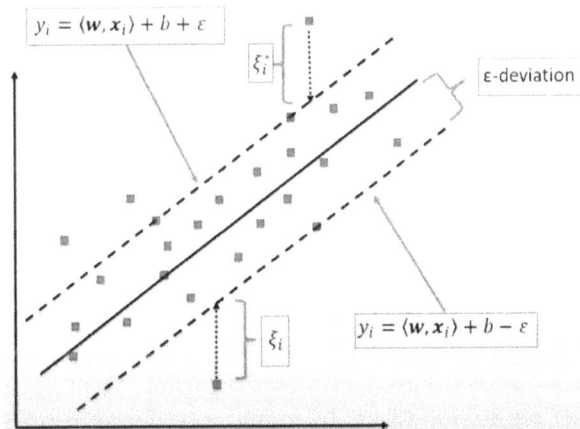

Figure 5.4: Mathematical representation of SVMs

The method we discussed is acceptable in the case of linear data, wherein we are fitting linear hyperplanes, deciding the margin, and so on. In the case of a non-linear hyperplane (where the data itself is non-linear), we need to use the appropriate kernel function, which is another model hyperparameter, to find the best-fit non-linear plane to capture the nature or patterns in the data.

Now, let us look at some salient properties of the random forest regressor while in action:

- The kernel function is a great tool (we will discuss it in detail, in the next section of this chapter) to discover hidden features from the data by combining two or more existing features, and hence, this algorithm out of the box provides feature engineering capabilities, provided one has chosen the right kernel for the right use case.

- In **Support Vector Regression (SVR),** we can choose the nature of the surface (linear or non-linear) depending on the nature of the data. This provides a great amount of flexibility, which was primarily lacking in the case of linear regression. Note that we can still perform polynomial regression, for example, when working with non-linear data, as a parallel option to SVR.

- Since kernel functions are used in the case of non-linear hyperplanes, and they are quite complicated mathematically, SVRs are not as easy to explain as linear regression models in the real-world while modeling complex scenarios.

- It is good news that SVRs are not so impacted by the outliers since we have a cost function to minimize their effect on the model, and also, we mostly care about the support vectors (the points closer to the hyperplane and within the margin). However, in the case of non-linear scenarios, the choice of a kernel may result in unwanted overfitting in search of perfection during the training of the models.

- Large dimensions are not a concern for SVRs in the real-world.

In short, SVRs (and later, we will see this for SVMs as well) with the right kernels and models will perform well. However, note that SVR models can be difficult to interpret or understand, especially when using non-linear kernels.

Random forest regression

Now, let us understand how a random forest algorithm can also be used for regression use cases. We will start by quickly revising what bagging (or bootstrap aggregation) is and how it is used in this context.

Note that we will discuss decision trees later in this chapter for more clarity, but as of now, let us be aware that decision trees are yet another versatile machine learning algorithm that segments data into subsets based on decision rules, creating a tree-like model for classification as well as regression tasks. In regression, decision trees predict continuous numerical values by partitioning the data and fitting simple models to each region.

Given a regression use case with D observations, the algorithm picks K samples of size m each, where K is a subset of the total number of observations in the training data, and m is a subset of features or columns available in the training data. Each of these samples is used to train and model a decision tree separately. We can call all these samples bootstrap samples or row sampling. The process that the algorithm uses to randomly select some features for each base learner is also known as **feature bagging** or **column sampling**.

Once the models are trained, we combine them into a larger model by taking a vote on each observation for each predicted class. Here are a few things to consider:

- For example, if we fit 10 decision tree models, and eight of them predict that for row number 24 in the dataset, the class predicted is *1* or true, then the final prediction for this observation r24 is *1* or *true*.

- The aforementioned example was in the case of a classification use case. In the case of a regression use case, rather than taking a majority vote, the algorithm computes a mean or median value of the estimated value from all the decision tree models.

- Interestingly, under the hood, each of the decision trees also creates the decision boundaries and calculates the mean or median to provide the estimations of the target variable.

- This process of combining the prediction power of all models into one is the aggregation process.

While estimating the values on an unseen observation, using the patterns discussed by our model from the training data, the final model passes the features of the observations randomly (bagging process) to all underlying decision trees, and each decision tree calculates the output for this unseen observation.

The mean or median of all these outputs is then computed (aggregation process) and is assigned an output or estimated target value, as follows:

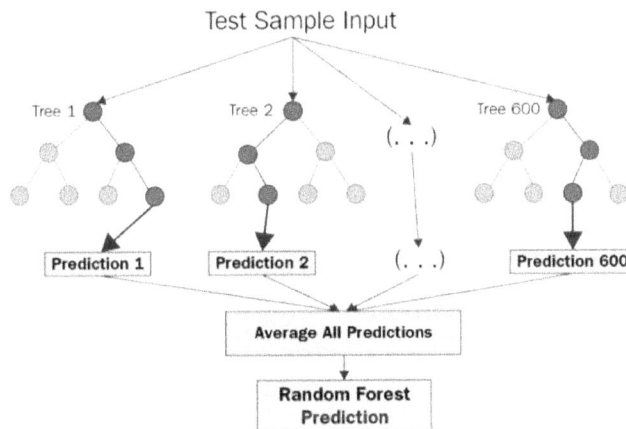

Figure 5.5: How random forest works under the hood

Before we progress to the next section, let us discuss the following points about the random forest regression algorithm:

- If there are any changes in the training data over a period, then as samples are randomly selected, the change in the samples will be less, thereby leading to a very small change in the model(s) trained by these bootstraps, and hence, the aggregation stage is not affected by and large.

- Since the base learners are decision trees in this case, which (as understood in *Chapter 2*) are a set of if-else type systems, hence, random forests are also relatively easy to explain and not at all complicated like support vector regressors. The only challenge at times is to pick the underlying decision trees in case we choose to fit 100 trees in parallel, where one can only choose to visualize a handful of trees to know how they found the patterns in the data.

- Since we are passing bootstrapped samples of rows and columns to each of the base learners (decision trees), the computation of random forests is quite elegant.

Note: In this approach, and even in the case of a random forest classification, which we will learn about later, the base learners (the decision tree models) are trained in parallel rather than running them in sequence.

We will now investigate another interesting algorithm to perform regression, where a typical student learns from their previous mistakes and improves over time.

Gradient boosting regression

Now that we have understood the concept of bagging, let us briefly understand what boosting is.

Imagine preparing for a competitive examination for which one has joined a coaching institute. The way the teachers conduct the flow of operations is such that, every single week there is an exam, let us say on Monday, and then for the following four days, the learners concentrate only on the areas where they did not do well. The cycle repeats every week with an exam on the first day, and the feedback of the exam results is used to learn better throughout the rest of the week. This is exactly how boosting works:

- The base learners are weak, like decision trees with shallow depth (which we will understand in-depth in the next section, along with the bias and variance concepts). Since the trees are shallow, they would not be able to capture enough patterns from the data, and hence, the training error will be high.

- Once the first model is built, we calculate the error we got for each observation by simply finding the difference between the estimated value and the actual value.

- For the next model, the training data is updated with existing observations and the errors from the previous model (that is, the observations of the previous model where we got errors). To emphasize the error made in the last model, the algorithm adds a weight component to the calculation. This is a hyperparameter for this algorithm.

- For the next model, we follow the same recursion: take the previous model(s), add weights to them, and add the errors from the previous model with another weight term. At each stage, like this, we get an additive weighted model.

- We continue the iterations if N models are trained, by the end of which the residual error should be much less since we are retraining every new version of the model (of the base learner, in this case, a decision tree) with the errors from the last step.

What we find is, unlike bagging, where the decision trees were trained in parallel, in the case of boosting the base, learners are trained in sequence, as we see in *Figure 5.6*. However, overall, the algorithm tries to estimate the target variable in the first model, and each subsequent model tries to fix the errors by combining the previous models.

Note: Boosting methods can easily overfit, and hence, we apply tricks like high bias base learners or regularization by shrinkage.

We will learn about them as we progress in developing the models. As a start, let us look at a quick visual of how a typical boosting model operates:

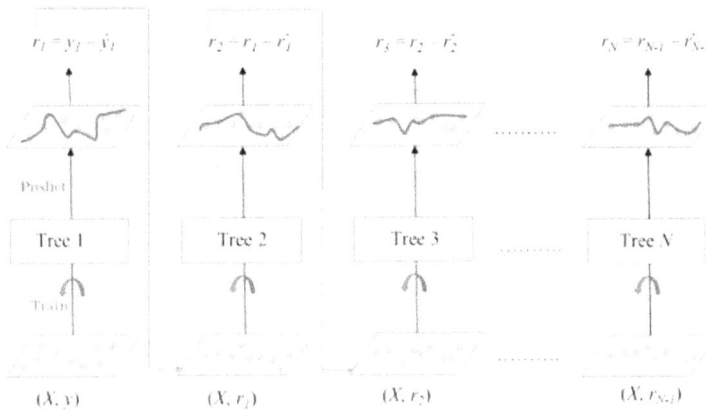

Figure 5.6: Typical boosting algorithm flow

Taking this concept, the gradient boosting regression algorithm uses any mathematically differentiable log function and any base model (like a decision tree) and reduces the errors over each iteration. The overall working of a gradient-boosting regression algorithm remains the same as we discussed earlier. Since we are performing regression, the decision trees, or for that matter any other base learners used in this case that can perform regression, like SVRs, use mean or median to find the estimated value of the target variable, just like in the case of the random forest regressor.

Note: The algorithms that perform regression are merely a handful.

Regression analysis is a separate field of study by itself, inspired by traditional statistical methods and research, followed by improvements until research to date on neural networks. For those interested in learning in-depth, it is recommended to pick up relevant literature specifically focused on regression analysis for in-depth mathematical intuitions.

With this background, we will now discuss classification algorithms, which help in predicting the target classes to which a given observation belongs. In the next chapter, we will take up specific use cases to implement all these models.

Classification models

To classify whether a customer will take up a new offer from a bank, or whether a particular team has higher chances of winning a particular game or not, our scientists and researchers have been discovering new algorithms and improving upon the existing ones every day, and we use them. To quickly revise:

- Classification use cases are those where we want to predict the specific class or type to which a given observation falls. Unlike regression, we are now predicting (rather than estimating) the target class.

- These are use cases with two types (yes or no, pass or fail, win or lose, etc.), which are called **binary classification** problems, while there are use cases with about 40 classes (for example, object detection in images) called **multiclass classification**.

Note: There are a variety of ways to measure how good our predictions are (as compared to the actual observations).

For the sake of simplicity and so that we can focus more on how the algorithms work behind the scenes, we will explore the so-called model evaluation metrics from the next chapter when we start to implement these algorithms using code.

K-nearest neighbors classifier

Let us take an example of a simple binary classification problem, of whether it would rain or not, given we have factors (or features, or independent variables) like temperature and humidity. One easy way to model this scenario is to first plot all the data for our understanding by color-coding each data point as per the class variable. As shown in the following figure, the data points were generated randomly:

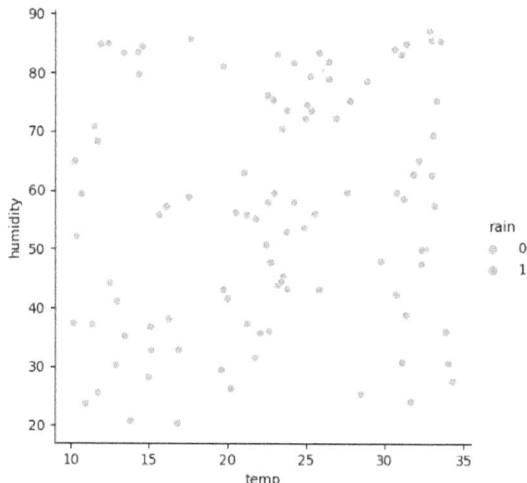

Figure 5.7: Sample classification model output

With this example in mind, let us understand how a KNN classifier works to classify any given unknown point.

For any unknown point, the algorithm can essentially identify its location on the spread of existing data points. Consider this step as adding another random point anywhere in the given dataset or the aforementioned figure. Let us see what we can do with this information:

- For a given input value of *K*, which is a hyperparameter to this algorithm, the algorithm now calculates the distance of all K nearest/closest data points from the new or unknown data point.

- Imaging one is the 5th person sitting at a table in a conference (where any participant could sit anywhere and participate), and the algorithm is trying to find how similar or dissimilar this new person is as compared to the other four people who were already on this table.

- One easy way of calculating the distance in this case is to use the Euclidean distance metric.

  Note: In this step, the algorithm is not calculating the distance from this new point to the other K existing data points, instead, the distance is calculated from this new point to every other data point (that is, all existing observations in the training data).

- For all the K closest neighbors, the algorithm checks the label of these existing data points. Remember that since this is a classification use case falling under the realm of supervised learning. Hence, like in regression, we already have assumed to have labeled data for the history. This is equally clear in our first visual, where we know the target for each observation (hence, they are color-coded).

- Finally, the algorithm takes a majority vote. If most of the nearest K data points from the new or unknown point are near observations of label 1 (that is, it will rain), then for the new data point as well, the algorithm predicts that it will rain.

- The algorithm does not necessarily return a probabilistic value of the chances of it raining or the amount of rainfall, which is expected, since that is not the objective of this use case.

Finally, following is how the resulting model may look like in a given example use case:

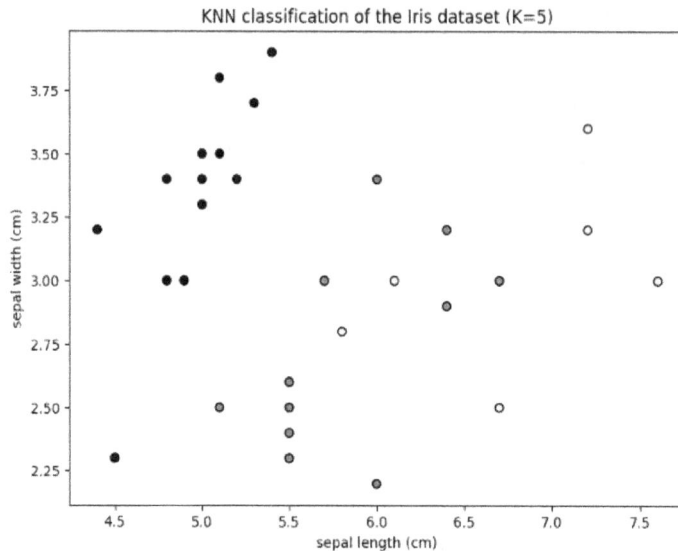

Figure 5.8: Sample KNN classifier output

In short, the class for any unlabeled new data point is decided by calculating the distances from this unknown point to its K nearest data points, followed by taking the majority vote from the labels of the K nearest data points. Now, let us understand what happens in some extreme scenarios, as follows:

- If the data is very randomly spread, then finding the right class for a given unknown or new data point is very tricky for this algorithm and often fails to deliver the right results.

- If the new data point itself is sort of an outlier and falls quite far from all other data points in terms of distance, then again, the algorithm's outcome can be wrong.

Both of these cases are just two of the primary scenarios where we have seen the KNN classifier not working so well; otherwise, for use cases where we have separated data points, KNN does an excellent job.

Note: In the preceding description, we mentioned the Euclidean distance as one way to calculate the distance from the new point to any other point.

Depending on the use case, one may choose to use other distance metrics as well, like Manhattan distance, Minkowski distance, or Hamming distance. This depends on the distribution of the data points or observations, given a particular use case.

Note: Another interesting way of calculating the distance is the Cosine distance or Cosine similarity metric, which also works great given particular types of use case(s).

Let us understand these distance metrics in brief so that one can choose the right metric given the use case at hand:

- **Euclidean distance**: This is where we are simply finding the straight-line distance between two points. When features generally have similar scales, we can use Euclidean distance to measure distance in low to moderate-dimensional spaces. In some literature, this is also known as the L2 distance metric.

- **Manhattan distance**: It is also called L1 distance metric; this calculates distance along a grid-like path (just like traversing from one place to the other in a cityscape). This metric is useful when we are dealing with high-dimensional data and where individual dimensions are not equally important.

- **Minkowski distance**: This metric generalizes both the Euclidean and Manhattan distance based on a parameter. Choosing the parameter as 1 gives Manhattan distance, while choosing the value as 2 gives Euclidean distance.

- **Hamming distance**: This metric is specifically for measuring differences (or the count of the number of mismatches) between each element of two vectors. This is quite useful when performing use cases like sentiment analysis or when one is trying to compare a set of words with another.

- **Cosine similarity and distance**: The Cosine similarity metric helps to measure the angle between two vectors, focusing on their orientation rather than magnitude. To get the Cosine distance, we can simply subtract the Cosine similarity from 1. This metric is useful when the direction or relative similarity matters more than the absolute magnitude of the vectors. For this reason, this metric is used quite frequently for comparing word embeddings or document similarity (more of which will be discussed when we explore natural language processing).

Now, let us revise some of the other common classification algorithms in a bit of depth than what we have seen briefly in *Chapter 2*.

Naïve Bayes

By the design of a Naïve Bayes classifier, this algorithm tries to find the given, unseen data point or observation, the probability that it belongs to one class or the other. Hence, the algorithm's primary task is to calculate the probabilities of each class and determine which one is the maximum. Under the hood, Naïve Bayes uses the Bayes theorem to predict the likelihood of an event based on a set of observed features. The only reason this algorithm is naïve is that it assumes that features are independent of each other or have conditional independence of the features.

Let us understand the algorithm using another Naïve use case to analyze whether it will rain tomorrow, as follows:

- Let us say that we collected at least some past days' data containing the outlook of the day (sunny, overcast, or rainy), the humidity in the air (high, normal), and the wind speed (strong, weak). This is the training data that is fed into the algorithm.

- Next, the algorithm calculates the prior probabilities, which are the overall chances of rain based on our past observations and the overall chance of no rain.

- Next, for each possible condition, the algorithm generates the probabilities. For example, the probability of a sunny outlook on days when it rained, the probability of high humidity on days when it did not rain, and so on.

- When a new observation or a test data point is fed into the algorithm, it calculates the evidence based on the previous calculations. For example, let us say that the new data point has today's forecast of sunny, high humidity, and weak wind. Keeping this in mind, the algorithm calculates the following:

P(Rain | Sunny, High humidity, Weak wind) = (P(Sunny | Rain) * P(High humidity | Rain) * P(Weak wind | Rain) * P(Rain)) / P(Evidence)

P(No Rain | Sunny, High humidity, Weak wind) = (P(Sunny | No Rain) * P(High humidity | No Rain) * P(Weak wind | No Rain) * P(No Rain)) / P(Evidence)

Here, *P(Evidence)* is a normalization factor to ensure probabilities add up to 1, which we can often ignore for simple comparison.

- Finally, the algorithm will compare the results from this last or previous step of calculations. Whosoever probability is higher is our prediction (rain or no rain).

Let us discuss the following features of Naïve Bayes so that one can make informed decisions on when to use it and when not:

- Naïve Bayes performs well, provided the features are independent of each other. Even if the features are slightly correlated, the algorithm does a great job. In some technical literature, we may also find some research and data-driven confirmation about this property of Naïve Bayes, which is probably why it is one of the most common algorithms used in text-related ML use cases.

- For high-dimensional data as well, like text classification use cases, Naïve Bayes performs great and helps to serve as a good benchmark for use cases like spam detection or sentiment analysis, etc.

- Out of the box, Naïve Bayes works great for categorical features; for real value features in the data, we can either encode them to categorical values if applicable or we can make use of Gaussian Naïve Bayes.

- Since it depends entirely on probabilistic values, Naïve Bayes is easily interpretable, and hence, the importance of features (which we will touch on in almost every upcoming chapter from now on) can be easily calculated. This makes this algorithm suitable for problems where interpretability is a very crucial factor, like healthcare-related ML use cases.

- Since the calculations in the algorithm use basic math, the time and space complexity of the Naïve Bayes algorithm is very low compared to the K nearest neighbor algorithm, which makes it suitable for low latency solutions.

- One of the cons, however, of Naïve Bayes is that at times it can easily be overfit on the training data. This is why any Python library, for example, that has a Naïve Bayes implementation may choose to provide an **out-of-the-box** (**OOTB**) Laplace smoothing technique to keep this property under control, with alpha as the new hyperparameter.

Decision trees

Decision trees are like if-else conditional statements in a typical software application. Given the training dataset, this algorithm finds the patterns in terms of decision boundaries under the hood so that it can primarily categorize each of the observations to one of the classes; when their features are given, by finding the patterns in the data recognizable in the form of conditional statements. Let us take an example to understand this in-depth and discuss some key concepts and terminologies.

Imagine we are working for an online retailer specializing in tech gadgets. From our available historical experience (in the form of transactional records in our database), we know that we have collected the age group of our past customers, along with their income levels, followed by how tech-savvy they are, and finally, if they have bought more tech gadgets in the past from our website, as opposed to accessories. Let us look at the design flow:

1. Consider using this history, with whether the customers purchased a past gadget or not, as the training data for our decision tree algorithm.

2. While building the tree, the following are the components that the algorithm ends up creating:

   a. If the algorithm finds that age is the best feature to initially split the data, then this column becomes the root node of our tree.

   b. This decision is made by calculating impurity in the data using metrics like entropy or Gini index, which helps to identify columns or features in them, which creates a clean demarcation of classes as opposed to the others.

3. Next comes deciding the branches based on the next most important feature by calculating the impurity. For example, the first branch can be on a feature, like tech savviness, to recommend high-end noise-canceling headphones to expert audiophiles or otherwise basic starter models to beginners. For customers with no history of purchases, the browsing history feature can become the more prominent feature to create the next set of branches.

4. This process is repeated until the resulting leaf nodes of the tree consist of almost all similar customers together. These nodes are where the actual or final decision lies, which the model is now going to use as a learning to classify unknown or unseen data.

5. During the entire process, the choice of metric to calculate impurity is a hyperparameter. Similarly, the depth of the tree (how long the branching process will continue to give the final leaf nodes) is also a hyperparameter, the choice of which gives a shallow or deep decision tree.

6. Now, for any given unseen observation, the model can be used to utilize this series of if-else style branching strategies to put the record into the final leaf node so that we get the final prediction.

Now, with this basic idea, let us perform each aspect of the algorithm.

First, let us look into the impurity metric, especially entropy. Concerning information theory, entropy helps to find the information gain (in other words, the purity of any feature column) in identifying a clear pattern in the data. Mathematically, it is represented as follows:

$$H(Y) = -\sum_{i=1}^{k} P(y_i) \times \log_b\big(P(y_i)\big)$$

In this equation, Y is the random variable that can take up k values, and the entropy of Y is represented by $H(Y)$. The base of the logarithm is usually equal to 2 or the Euler number (=2.718). $P(y)$ represents the probability of the event for any random value of Y.

Hence, this formulation is used by a decision tree algorithm to calculate the impurity (or the information gained from a given column or feature) for each column, provided we choose entropy as the metric to determine the impurity (since it is a hyperparameter to the algorithm), as follows:

- The value of entropy is maximum, mathematically, when the dataset is equally distributed for a given feature. For example, if the age group column in our fictitious example of an online retailer equally divides customers into the respective sets of classes of the target variable, then its entropy is equal to 1, rendering it to be the most impure column.

- In case we select another column like the tech savviness and find that this feature or column renders one class to take preference over all others, then the entropy for this particular feature is equal to 0 since it is the purest, and it is the best in classifying patterns in the data for all new observations.

- So, entropy remains within the range of 0 to 1, with 1 being the most impure and 0 being the purest. This way, our decision tree algorithm selects one column after the other to create the tree, with the purest column (the column or feature that helps to determine a clear demarcation of the data) as the root node, followed by other features in decreasing order of purity.

In this case, the concept of information gain is made use of, where breaking from the root to the branches and finally to the leaf nodes is determined by calculating the entropy of the parent node and then subtracting the weighted average of the entropy of the child nodes.

This calculation defines the information gain. The objective of the decision tree algorithm is to maximize the information gain at every stage, hence creating the best possible tree-like representation of patterns from the data, as follows:

$$IG(Y, var) = H_D(Y) - \sum_{i=1}^{k} \frac{|D_i|}{|D|} \cdot H_{D_i}(Y)$$

In the preceding mathematical equation, Y is the target variable, D is the dataset that the algorithm is fed with for training, and k is the subsets the data can be broken into using some feature in the data var.

Similarly, another impurity metric is known as the **Gini Impurity,** which is like entropy at first glance but comes with certain salient advantages. Mathematically, we can represent the Gini Impurity measure as follows:

$$I_G(Y) = 1 - \sum_{i=1}^{k} \left(P(Y_i)\right)^2$$

If we draw all possible values of entropy and Gini Impurity on a plot, we will find that while entropy had a range of 0 to 1, Gini Impurity falls within the range of 0 to 0.5, which indicates that Gini Impurity is a somewhat scaled-down version of entropy. However, entropy contains a computationally expensive logarithm term, as compared to Gini Impurity, where we perform simple arithmetic. This may be the reason why many production-grade libraries in Python, like scikit-learn, provide Gini Impurity as the default value of information gain metric while one implements decision trees. The following figure shows an example of decision tree splits:

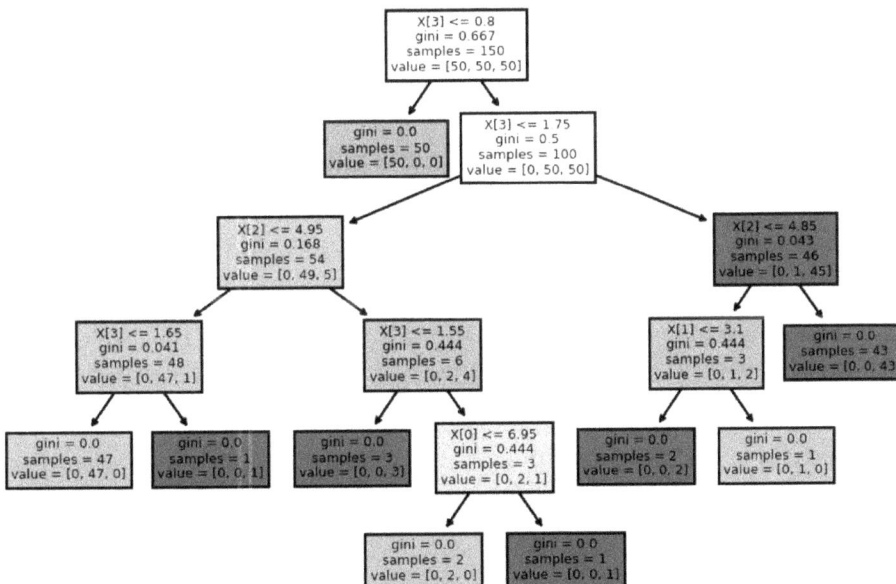

Figure 5.9: Example of decision tree splits

Combining it all, the decision tree algorithm will calculate the information gained from each column on the entire dataset to choose the root node. In this case, the root node is essentially that one feature column which was the maximum information gain. The algorithm further continues to repeat this exercise, potentially reusing features at different levels of the tree, to create branches in the tree, until the required depth of the tree is reached (which is a hyperparameter) or if a pure leaf node is achieved, where the node of the tree contains only one type or class of observations. However, excessively deep trees can lead to overfitting, where the model becomes too complex and performs poorly on new, unseen data. To mitigate this, techniques like pruning can be employed to simplify the tree and improve its generalization performance.

Note: Depth is an essential hyperparameter since with trees with very high depth, the leaf nodes will ultimately result in a smaller number of observations from the training data, representing overfitting on the training data, while having a smaller depth of the tree may never result into pure leaf nodes in the tree, resulting into underfitting.

Hence, in the later chapters, we will aim to find the best value of depth and all other hyperparameters, using techniques like cross-validation as part of hyperparameter tuning.

Before we move on, let us discuss some salient points about decision trees, which will help an ML engineer choose this algorithm in the right use case:

- Given the simple nature or design of the algorithm, it creates a series of conditional statements like apparatus to find patterns in the data, hence, the outcome of any decision tree model is very easy to interpret. This is a very important point to consider where, more than the performance of the model, its interpretability is of primary importance.

- At each stage, the algorithm calculates information gain to create the next branch, and hence, one can perform a good selection of features once the first tree is built and visualized.

  Note: In the next chapters, we will discuss the existing libraries in Python.

- As discussed, decision trees can solve both regression and classification use cases without much change in the approach to its core algorithm or calculations. This makes it suitable out of the box for both types of supervised learning problems.

- Since there are many critical calculations in the algorithm that are dependent on the number of features or columns, the space and time complexity of the algorithm is adversely affected if we have a dataset with many features.

- Similarly, if an ML engineer does not perform in-depth hyperparameter tuning to optimize the model, then decision trees become very prone to overfitting or underfitting at times, depending on the default values chosen to build the model.

- Lastly, in some cases, literature observes poor performance from a decision tree model if there is noise in the data; hence, to get the best value, the key is to get the preprocessing data in the right way.

Let us move on and see our first bagging algorithm, which makes extensive use of decision trees under the hood.

Random forest algorithm

In many cases, rather than using a single model to provide the estimations or predictions, some algorithms make use of multiple, similar, or dissimilar algorithms in parallel to create the necessary outcome, thereby elevating the performance gains that one may have achieved from using only one model. This is how ensemble models work in machine learning. Primarily, there are four ways in which any ensemble is designed from its core: bagging, boosting, stacking, and cascading. The main ideology of an ensemble is that the more different the underlying models are, the better we can combine them.

In this section of the chapter, we will focus more on bagging, which is a quick short form of bootstrap aggregation. In these architectures, the available dataset for training is divided into multiple random bootstrap samples, with combinations and permutations of rows and columns. Each of these subsets of data is then used to train a different model (usually of the same type or algorithm). Once trained, the results of all these models are combined into a larger model. The first part, where we break the data randomly, is called **bootstrapping**, while the latter part, where we combine their power, is called **aggregation**. One typical and very high-performing bagging algorithm, which uses the capabilities of decision trees, is mostly the random forest algorithm. We defined its nature briefly in *Chapter 2*. Let us now understand it using yet another example of predicting customer churn, which is by far one of the most important use cases across industries in general, as follows:

- Let us consider that in the training data, we have collected features like subscription length in months, usage frequency, customer support interactions (in terms of the number of tickets raised to date), payment plan selected, and so on.

- As the first step, the random forest algorithm will take repeated samples from the available data with varied combinations of rows and columns. We call these **bootstrap samples**. Here is a graphical example to better understand how bootstrapping works:

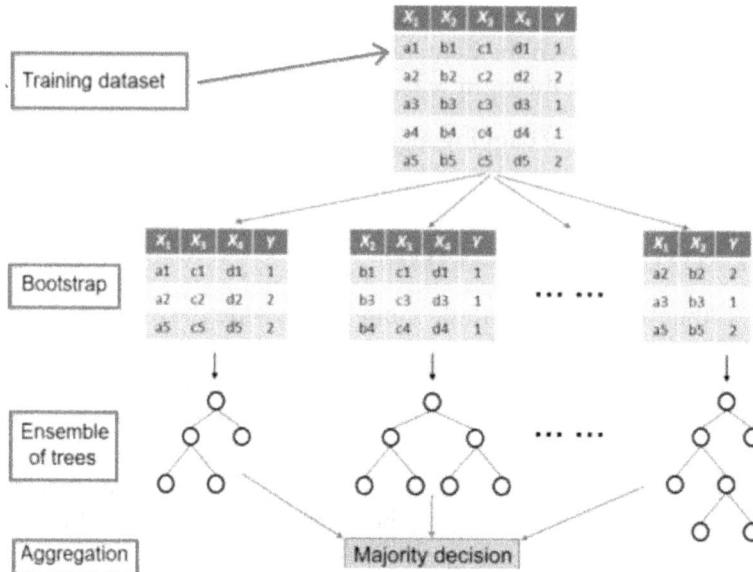

Figure 5.10: Example of decision tree splits

- The algorithm provides us with hyperparameters to decide how this split will take place so that we can choose a random percentage of rows and columns in each split of the data.

- For each sample, a different decision tree is built, and the patterns are understood in the same way in which a decision tree classifier works.

  Note: All of these decision trees can work in parallel since they have their copy of the training data. The number of decision trees to be trained in parallel is a hyperparameter for the random forest algorithm.

- Next, for a given new observation (data of a different customer, for example where we want to find if the customer will churn or not), the data is fed into each decision tree in the forest, and with the patterns already gathered by each of the trees, (each tree predicts the outcome).

- Finally, the random forest algorithm takes a majority vote from all underlying decision trees and outputs the prediction. For example, if in a random forest, we have 100 decision trees, and 73 of the underlying trees predict a churn for a customer, then the final decision or prediction from the random forest model is that this particular customer has a very high chance of churn.

Here is a quick view of how a random forest classifier will look like, similar to random forest regressors, using decision trees as the backbone:

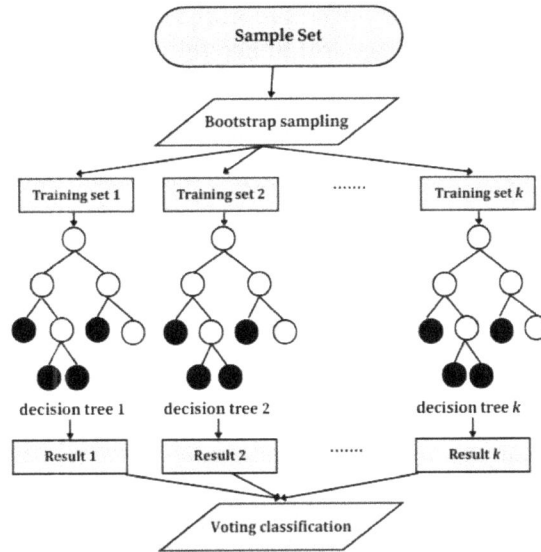

Figure 5.11: Example random forest classification models

The underlying mathematics (including calculation of information gain, metrics of impurity like entropy or Gini index, etc.) are all the same as a decision tree.

The following are some of the many useful points to consider for an AI engineer who is considering using a random forest algorithm for a given use case:

- Out of the box, the performance of a random forest algorithm is comparatively better in many cases and instances than a standalone decision tree-based model due to the ensemble approach.

- Since we are using multiple base learners (decision trees), and that too in parallel, this algorithm is robust for overfitting issues.

- Since the base learners are decision trees that cannot handle high dimensionality in the data (that is, a large number of features), random forests will also suffer from the same scenario.

- Since the number of trees can be chosen to be a very high number, the computation cost (that is, the time and space complexity) of the random forest algorithm is comparatively higher than a standalone decision tree. This also impacts the interpretability of the model since, in case we were using a single decision tree, we could have it visualized, but understanding 100 different trees to explain the model is difficult.

- Finally, depending on the number of trees chosen as base learners, it can become computationally expensive at times to perform hyperparameter tuning on a random forest model.

At times, the random forest algorithm helps in feature selection.

Note: In a decision tree the most important feature is the one with the highest purity (in terms of the Impurity metric chosen and hence the information gain), in the case of a random forest model the most important feature is the basis of the overall reduction of impurity at various levels of each of the base learners.

For example, if a feature is important in many of the base learners, then it is important in the holistic view, too. Let us explore our next algorithm, which makes use of another ensemble design.

XGBoost

While in the case of bagging, we saw a parallel approach of training base learners, in the case of boosting, the overall idea is to reduce the errors and losses from the final model iteratively as the base learners are trained. As seen in *Chapter 2* briefly, boosting is where, in each iteration, we incorporate the errors from the last step with some weight alongside the available training data so that in each iteration, we can reduce the amount of loss and progress further. The overview of the XGBoost is as follows:

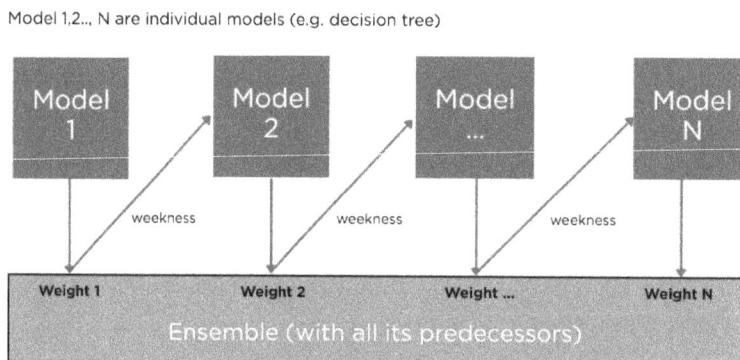

Figure 5.12: *Overview of XGBoost*

Let us take an example of a spam detection use case to understand how boosting (and, in essence, how the XGBoost algorithm) works in detail, as follows:

- Considering our spam identification use case, let us assume that in our training data, we have features like the Sender Address (IP address and Email ID), the subject line of the email, the body content of the email, the time when the email was received, and so on.

- The algorithm starts with an initial model (weak learner) *f0* that predicts the probability of an email being spam *P(spam | x)* where *x* is the set of available features (which we assume to have cleaned and processed). Often, a simple decision tree is used.

- In this step, the algorithm ascertains the observations for whom the predictions do not match the actual class labels.

- For each further iterations *m*:

    o The algorithm calculates pseudo-residuals wherein it computes the difference between the original target class and the predicted probability from the previous model.

    o The algorithm trains a new learner *f1* based on the data points and their corresponding pseudo-residuals. This ensures the new model focuses on the data points the previous model struggled with.

    o The algorithm then updates the ensemble model by combining the predictions of all models using a weighted sum of earlier iterations' prediction and current, using a wright value, also called the learning rate:

        ▪ α_m is the learning rate, a hyperparameter that controls the impact of each new weak learner on the overall prediction.

        ▪ Smaller α_m leads to small weight updates, reducing the risk of overfitting.

    o This series of iterations continues (if we have instructed it to run, the value of which is a hyperparameter to boosting algorithms) while the errors continue to reduce per iteration.

XGBoost builds upon this core boosting framework with several enhancements:

- **Gradient boosting**: Instead of using pseudo-residuals, XGBoost utilizes gradients, which provide the direction of the largest improvement for the ensemble loss function. This often leads to faster convergence towards the final ensemble containing as less errors as possible.

- **Regularization**: XGBoost implements techniques like *L1* and *L2* regularization to penalize model complexity and prevent overfitting.

- **Efficient tree learning**: XGBoost employs algorithms like depth-wise splitting and feature importance scoring to build trees efficiently and focus on the most informative features.

The resultant model at any stage after *K* iterations can be represented as:

$$F_K(x) = \sum_{i=0}^{K} \alpha_i h_i(x)$$

The error or residual at the end of each stage *K* can be given as:

$$error_i = y_i - F_K(x)$$

The salient feature to note here is that the Bagging algorithms like random forests could not minimize all forms of losses since they only focus on minimizing the entropy loss, whereas in boosting algorithms like XGBoost, one can choose to minimize any loss since we are using pseudo residuals and gradients.

Before we move ahead, it is important to know some salient features of the XGBoost algorithm, or boosting algorithms in ML in general:

- By combining multiple weak learners, boosting can achieve state-of-the-art performance in various classification tasks.

- For the very same reasons, boosting algorithms like XGBoost can mathematically capture intricate relationships within data that single models might miss.

- However, XGBoost comes with an elevated potential of overfitting since it requires careful selection of hyperparameters like learning rate and regularization strength to avoid overfitting the training data.

- At times, and depending on the volume of the data, training multiple models iteratively, as opposed to being trained in parallel like bagging, can be computationally expensive compared to single models.

- Finally, understanding and explaining the combined logic of numerous models becomes more challenging.

Now, let us further explore unsupervised learning and discuss the most commonly used clustering algorithms.

Clustering models

Clustering algorithms come under the section of unsupervised learning, wherein because of various valid reasons, one may not have the availability of labeled data, or the given use case labeled data does not have to be addressed at all.

In simple terms, clustering is where one performs the task of grouping a set of objects in such a way that the objects in the same group are more like each other than those in other groups. Each of the resulting groups is called a **cluster**. The observations or data points in one cluster are very close to the other. We emphasize the concept of closeness here, as we discuss further, this concept will play a pivotal role in creating good clusters from our datasets. For now, let us understand that if a group of observations lies in the same cluster, then we call them **intra-cluster** observations, and if a group of observations is spread across different clusters, we call them **inter-cluster** observations.

Overall, the two main methods of clustering (or algorithms) that we will explore in this section are K-means clustering and DBSCAN.

K-means clustering

One of the simplest algorithms for grouping observations into clusters is the K-means clustering algorithm. The value of K refers to the number of clusters we form out of finding patterns in the available dataset. Let us understand how the algorithm works using a classic example of customer segmentation:

- Let us assume we have data for our customers visiting our website, and we want to identify distinct customer groups to tailor marketing strategies and product offerings.

- Now, before the algorithm starts to do its job, we must feed it with the value of K, which is also a hyperparameter to the algorithm. If we give, for example, the value of K as 3, then the algorithm will try and cluster all data points into three separate groups or clusters.

- To create the clusters:

  o With the given value of K, the algorithm creates K number of random points on the space of all observations, and from these random K points, the distance to all other observations is calculated using the coordinates of each observation and the coordinates of the randomly chosen points. These random points are called **centroids**. Usually, a Euclidean distance is chosen.

  o Assign each of the observations to the closest centroid (based on the distance calculation done in the last step).

  o Next, by calculating the mean of coordinates of all data points assigned to a particular cluster, the algorithm recomputes the coordinates of the centroid themselves.

  o This iterative process continues until the centroids stop moving substantially or when a maximum number of iterations is reached, as shown in *Figure 5.13*:

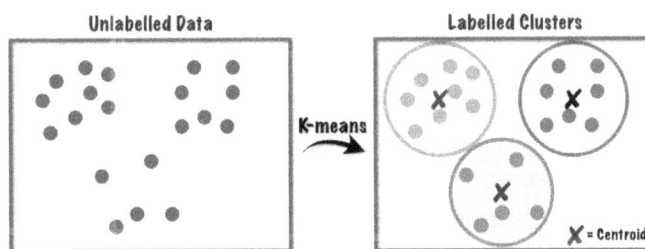

Figure 5.13: Example representation of K-means clustering

While calculating the distance, if the Euclidean distance metric is used, then each observation's coordinates are compared to that of the centroid's using:

$$distance\,(p, q) = \sqrt{\sum_{i=1}^{n} (x_i - y_i)^2}$$

When the data points are assigned to a cluster then the objective of the algorithm is to minimize the distance of the centroid to the data points, as much as possible. That is the overall strategy used in this approach to reduce the errors to the minimum!

One of the key considerations of K-means clustering is to choose an appropriate value of K and use effective randomization methods while selecting the initial random locations of the cluster centroids. There are methods like the elbow method to find the optimal value of K, but more often in reality, there are practicalities and business considerations that dictate the value of K as well.

Let us discuss what the elbow method is and how it is used to calculate a probable optimum value of K:

- One can run or model the data using the K-means algorithm multiple times, increasing K from 1 (all points in one cluster) to a higher value, for example, 10 or more.

- For each K, one can then calculate the **Within-Cluster Sum of Squares (WCSS)**, which measures the total squared distance of all points within their assigned cluster (K) to the cluster's centroid (μ). Lower WCSS indicates tighter clusters.

- Further, we can now plot the WCSS values we have already calculated for each K on the y-axis and the corresponding K values on the x-axis.

- Finally, we would look for an elbow shape in the plot. As K increases, WCSS typically keeps decreasing (tighter clusters). However, at some point, the decrease in WCSS becomes less significant. This elbow is a potential indicator of the optimal K.

Mathematically, WCSS is represented as:

$$\text{WCSS} = \sum_{P_i \text{ in Cluster 1}} \text{distance}(P_i, C_1)^2 + \sum_{P_i \text{ in Cluster 2}} \text{distance}(P_i, C_2)^2$$
$$+ \sum_{P_i \text{ in Cluster 3}} \text{distance}(P_i, C_3)^2$$

While the elbow method is primarily a visual analysis, there is an underlying intuition:

- Initially, increasing K leads to significant reductions in WCSS as data points are grouped into more specific clusters.

- After a certain point, adding more clusters yields diminishing returns on WCSS reduction. This suggests you might be overfitting the data by creating too many granular clusters.

The K value corresponding to the elbow (the point where the decrease in WCSS starts to slow down) is considered a reasonable choice for the number of clusters. Imagine that our plot shows a significant decrease in WCSS up to $K=3$, followed by a more gradual decrease for $K=4$ and onwards. This suggests that $K=3$ might be a good choice for the number of user segments in our customer segmentation use case.

However, one must be aware of the following limitations of the elbow method:

- Identifying the elbow can be subjective and depends on the scale of the plot.
- The method might not always yield a clear elbow, especially for complex datasets.

Other mathematical alternatives to the elbow method are as follows:

- **Silhouette analysis**: Another method that measures the cohesion within a cluster and separation between clusters.
- **Gap statistic**: A statistical method that compares the WCSS of our data to the WCSS of randomly shuffled data.

By combining the elbow method with other techniques and domain knowledge, we can make an informed decision about the optimal number of clusters for your K-means analysis. Considering the example of our customer segmentation use case, if the elbow method suggests a value of $K=6$ being a good choice, one needs to consider if our business can afford to create and follow through with six different marketing plans, one for each of our customer segments.

Let us look at some salient features of K-means clustering, which should help one to choose this algorithm for a given clustering use case:

- The best feature of the K-means algorithm is that it is easy to understand and implement.
- The algorithm does scale well to large datasets with proper optimizations. However, out of the box, it may not be a good solution for high-dimensional data, especially one with many observations.
- The biggest drawback of the K-means algorithm is that it struggles with non-spherical or complex cluster shapes. When the data is separable, K-means works great out of the box.
- Since K-means works well with data containing some inherent cohesiveness, the algorithm is often sensitive to the presence of outliers in the data.
- Lastly, and as we discussed WCSS, the K-means algorithm requires domain knowledge or techniques like the Elbow method to determine the ideal number of clusters.

Now, let us look into the DBSCAN algorithm and how it is employed in clustering use cases.

DBSCAN

In real-world scenarios, especially the ones that are complex and conjugative, there is a need for a clustering algorithm a tad more sophisticated than what K-means can achieve, despite its simplicity. DBSCAN is a clustering algorithm that groups data points based on density and connectivity. Unlike K-means, which requires predefining the number of clusters (K), DBSCAN can automatically identify clusters of arbitrary shapes and handle outliers effectively. Let us understand the intuition behind the DBSCAN algorithm, as follows:

- A data point is considered a core point if it has a **minimum number of points (MinPts)** within a specified radius (eps). These points form the core of a cluster.

- A data point is directly reachable from a core point if it is within the eps radius.

- Clusters are formed by connecting core points that are directly reachable from each other and all points directly reachable from them.

- Points that do not belong to any cluster are labeled as noise.

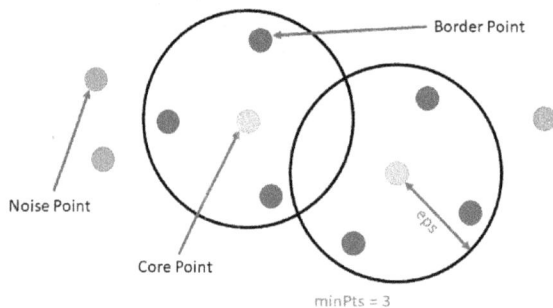

Figure 5.14: Typical DBSCAN clustering model outcome

The most important parameters involving the DBSCAN algorithm (which are briefly mentioned above as well) are as follows, both of which are essentially hyperparameters:

- **Eps**: Maximum radius to consider points as neighbors.

- **MinPts**: The minimum number of neighbors at a point needs to be considered a core point.

In essence, this is how the DBSCAN algorithm works on a given set of training data:

- Identify points with at least MinPts neighbors within eps distance.

- For a point p:

    o A point q is directly reachable from p if the distance between them ($d(p, q)$) is less than or equal to eps, and p is a core point.

- For cluster formation, keeping the aforementioned in mind, the following process is followed:

    o Start with a core point p.

    o Find all points directly reachable from p (including core points).

- o Add these reachable points to the cluster.

- o Repeat for all reachable points within the cluster, recursively adding their reachable points until no new points are added (expanding the cluster).

- Lastly, the data points not classified as core points or reachable from any core point are labeled as noise (potential outliers).

In the next chapter, we will code all these algorithms using TensorFlow and scikit-learn libraries in Python, and we will learn more about hyperparameter tuning, which will help us find the most optimal values of MinPts and eps. However, the following are some considerations while choosing their values as well, which results in a good DBSCAN model:

- **Dimensionality**: Generally, MinPts should be greater than or equal to the data dimensionality (for example, *MinPts >= 2* for 2D data).

- **Density variations**: We should consider the spread of our data points. If the density is relatively uniform, smaller eps might work. For highly uneven density, a larger eps might be needed to capture clusters across sparse regions.

- **Outliers**: If you expect a significant number of outliers, consider a slightly higher MinPts value to avoid mistakenly including them in clusters.

- **Cluster granularity**: A larger MinPts value might lead to fewer but more robust clusters, while a smaller MinPts might yield more fine-grained clusters (potentially capturing smaller, denser regions).

While we perform hyperparameter tuning for DBSCAN, we can use the same elbow plot or Silhouette analysis to find the best values of these hyperparameters for creating the best possible model with the available data. Before closing off with DBSCAN and clustering in this section, let us look into some salient features for one to be able to choose them given the right use case:

- Out of the box, the DBSCAN algorithm can help find clusters of arbitrary shapes without specifying K or the number of clusters we want from the data. With hyperparameter tuning, its performance is seen to improve quite well with complicated datasets.

- In practice, it is observed that the DBSCAN algorithm effectively identifies and isolates outliers as noise.

- The performance of the DBSCAN algorithm depends heavily on choosing the right eps and MinPts values. Hence, hyperparameter tuning is of prime importance.

- The results of the DBSCAN algorithm can vary depending on the chosen distance metric (for example, Euclidean vs. Manhattan distance).

- At times, it is observed that the DBSCAN algorithm can be computationally expensive for large datasets.

Let us now discuss artificial neural networks, the building blocks of very powerful machine learning (also known as deep learning algorithms) architectures.

Neural networks

Artificial neural networks are machine learning models, loosely inspired by the structure of the biological brain. These concepts (borrowed and improved upon from various other scientific fields of study and research) help create the literature and software frameworks, making use of neural networks, which are consistently becoming state-of-the-art solutions and algorithms, irrespective of the use case that an AI engineer is trying to address.

In the following figure, one can see the representation of an actual neuron from our brain as a reference to the artificial neuron, which we designed to emulate a learning paradigm like how our brain works:

Note: We are far from achieving great results as compared to what our imagination and brainpower can do. But as of now, we have reached quite a good stage.

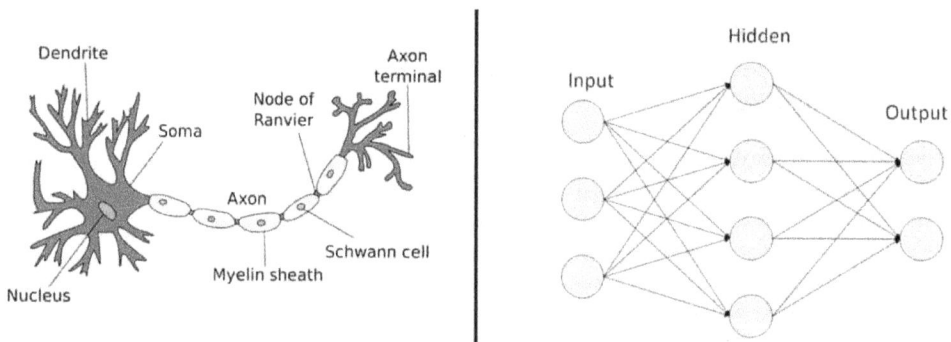

Figure 5.15: Basic structure of an artificial neuron

Here is a simplified breakdown of the components of an artificial neural network:

- **Neurons (nodes)**: These are the basic building blocks that help process information. A neuron takes multiple inputs, performs a weighted sum, and often applies a non-linear function (activation function) to the result. This allows for the capture of complex relationships.

- **Layers**: Neurons are organized into layers. The input layer receives the raw data features (for example, image pixel values or numerical features representing customer behavior). Hidden layers stay between input and output, where complex calculations occur to gradually transform and extract patterns from the data. The output layer, finally, produces the final prediction (for example, the probability of an image containing a cat or the estimated price of a house).

- **Connections**: Outputs from neurons in one layer form the inputs to neurons in the next layer. Each connection has a weight, signifying the influence of the signal.

Under the hood, neural networks use the baseline research of *Geoffrey Hinton* and others to make learning more effective via these layers in a network. This method is generally known as **backpropagation**. Let us understand the components that are involved in it, in a rather simplistic manner, as follows:

- **Forward pass**: Data flows through the network, generating a prediction.

- **Error calculation**: The difference between the actual and predicted values is determined by using a loss function.

- **Backpropagation**: This error is propagated backward through the network. The gradients are calculated to find which weights contribute most to the error.

- **Weight updates**: Weights are adjusted slightly in the direction that reduces the error (often using gradient descent).

- **Repeat**: This iterative process continues for many training examples, refining the network's weights.

Note: A common term frequently used across literature and software implementations is deep learning, which refers to neural networks with multiple hidden layers, enabling them to learn hierarchical representations of data. In this book, we may refer to artificial neural networks and deep learning interchangeably at times.

We will discuss and implement neural networks in the further chapters. Now let us look at the following features, which will help us choose them over others:

- Neural networks can help capture intricate non-linear patterns in data that traditional models might miss.

- Neural networks can perform a sort of automatic feature engineering and hence can learn relevant features directly from raw data, often reducing the need for extensive manual feature engineering.

- However, depending on the chosen architecture variation of a neural network, they can become computationally expensive at times. Training large neural networks can be resource-intensive, depending on their design.

- Lastly, understanding the internal decision-making logic can be challenging, though this is an active area of research.

Conclusion

In this chapter, we covered some of the critical ML algorithms used in AI, ML engineering, and data science practices. We came to know about the internal workings of each of the commonly used ML algorithms, along with the pros and cons of each of the models so that we could choose the right algorithm for the right task to some extent.

In the next chapter, we are going to implement all these algorithms from scratch in a peculiar way that is used by many data scientists and ML engineers in the real-world.

Exercises

Let us now try the following exercises to revise the concepts and explore the possibilities of applications of these ML algorithms:

1. Search for one or more Kaggle notebooks for each of the regression algorithms that we discussed in this chapter and run the notebook with data on Kaggle itself (by creating a free account) or on our local Anaconda (or any other popular ML) distribution. Even if you do not understand how the code is working, the idea is to only have a working setup in place, locally, in Kaggle, or Google Colab.

2. Search for similar examples in Kaggle for classification algorithms that we discussed in this chapter and follow the same exercise.

3. Search for similar examples in Kaggle for clustering algorithms that we discussed in this chapter and follow the same exercise.

4. Glance through credible sources on the Internet like KDnuggets, ML mastery, or Analytics Vidhya, and go through the basic concepts of how an artificial neural network is built and try to write your understanding of why it does not require specific feature engineering before modeling the data.

Join our book's Discord space

Join the book's Discord Workspace for Latest updates, Offers, Tech happenings around the world, New Release and Sessions with the Authors:

https://discord.bpbonline.com

## CHAPTER 6

Implementing First ML Models

Introduction

This chapter will help us in the implementation of our first models, given a handful of variety use cases, with all available datasets (representing real-world scenarios), using software engineering best practices.

The flow of operation during this chapter will be simple: we start with a particular use case by downloading an available dataset. Then, we practice how to perform in-depth exploratory data analysis with the available data. Furthermore, we learn how to fit basic models, followed by the evaluation of the first models. Additionally, we learn hyperparameter tuning using techniques like cross-validation and find the best possible values of hyperparameters before we export the model for usage.

Structure

This chapter covers the following topics:

- Estimating social media interactions
- Prediction of heart disease type
- Clustering water treatment plants

Objectives

By the end of this chapter, you will be able to understand all the lifecycle components of a typical ML project and how to structure our code into an IDE (we will be using Visual Studio Code), covering the exploration and preparation of datasets for ML. Moreover, we will build our models, evaluate them, and make them better by hyperparameter tuning. To learn these aspects of ML, we will use one example each of regression, classification, and clustering.

Estimating social media interactions

For our first use case, we will use the data of *Facebook* performance metrics of a renowned cosmetics brand's Facebook page, which is available for analysis from the *University of California Irwin (UCI) ML Repo*, here:

https://archive.ics.uci.edu/dataset/368/facebook+metrics.

The problem statement is to estimate the possible total number of interactions on a particular page in Facebook (or similar social media installation) for a given brand (in this case, a cosmetics brand) whenever a particular type of media is uploaded or shared amongst customers of this brand. This is a particularly interesting regression use case to understand how much of our products are liked on social media as one of the prominent marketing channels today, followed by the possible upsell and increase of revenue for our products from an online or offline store.

Note: The data is related to posts published during the year of 2014 on the Facebook page of a renowned cosmetics brand.

This dataset contains 500 of the 790 rows and part of the features analyzed by *Moro et al.* (2016), while the remaining were omitted due to confidentiality issues.

The first thing we do (as always) is to create the scaffolding of our project, sort of a skeleton, in our IDE. In this case, we can structure our work in a folder opened through VS Code as follows:

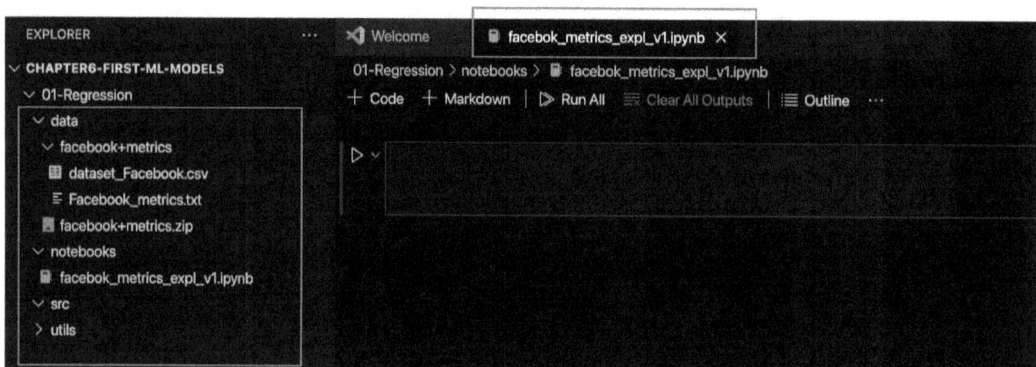

Figure 6.1: Scaffolding example

The separate directories that we have put in place are as follows:

- **data**: To save the data files that we will use for this ML experiment and later to create a software out of it.

- **src**: Where the source code or the main Python files will be saved.

- **utils**: Where the utility functions will reside, like data pre-processing and feature engineering.

- **notebooks**: Where the experimentation notebooks will be kept.

There will be some other files coming in picture shortly, like the **requirements.txt** containing the Python libraries we require, the Dockerfile which we will finally use to create an image of our ML application, and optionally a Build or Makefile which we will use to automate the local runs, tests and deployments. Additionally, as we create software out of our first ML experimentation, we will add a **tests** directory with all the unit test scripts written in Python.

We will begin our machine learning experiments in a Jupyter Notebook. Before we start coding, let us create a **requirements.txt** file to list all the necessary Python libraries. Then, we will use this file to set up a Python virtual environment using **venv**. A **venv** is a tool for creating isolated Python environments, allowing you to manage project dependencies and avoid conflicts between different projects by keeping their libraries separate. This will help us keep our project organized and make it easier to reuse later.

The following figure shows how it would look if we open a new **TERMINAL** and check the installation of all libraries:

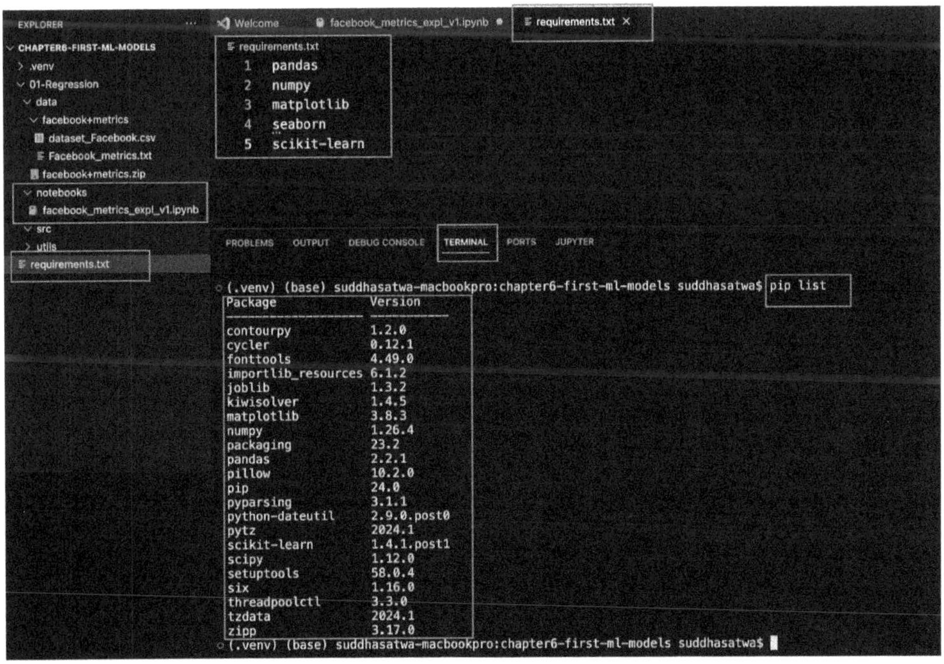

Figure 6.2: requirements.txt for libraries installation

Now, let us head over to the notebook, where we can perform the initial set of structuring. Firstly, it is good to divide the notebook into sections with a common structure, such as data loading, data analysis, feature engineering, initial modelling, model improvements, and (finally) model export.

Before we move forward, it is essential to note again that Python is a great choice for ML solutions because of its vast library support, but there are other programming languages too, which one may make use of in parallel. These languages (like C++ or Java) are where most of the software may have already been developed in one's organization.

Nevertheless, it is a good practice to divide our Python notebook into sections. Here, the first section we can create is to load the required libraries (all at one place, which gets appended as we code) and then load the initially available dataset for analysis and cleaning as follows:

```python
# import all libraries
import pandas as pd
import numpy as np
import matplotlib.pyplot as plt
import seaborn as sns
from sklearn.model_selection import train_test_split
from sklearn.preprocessing import normalize
from sklearn.linear_model import LinearRegression
from sklearn.metrics import mean_absolute_error, root_mean_squared_error, r2_score

# load available dataset
df_all_data = pd.read_csv('../data/facebook+metrics/dataset_Facebook.csv', delimiter=';')
df_all_data.sample(5)
```

Once the data is loaded, in the aforementioned code, we check the sample of the data, using the `.sample()` function on any **pandas** DataFrame, and see what the data looks like. However, this does not tell us about the statistical properties of the data, we would find them as we go. This book assumes that our readers have adequate basic knowledge of the Python programming language. Even so, it is recommended that one constantly upskill themselves in using Python programming language.

Next, we can check the dataframe information using the `.info()` function to check and later correct them and also to see whether the columns available in the dataset are given the right data types or not. This is very important for the analysis and cleaning of data, which otherwise will increase the amount of time we spend on data cleaning unnecessarily. Many times, one will find some or more columns being wrongly interpreted, especially when the data is loaded as a Pandas DataFrame from a database, as we will find in the later sections and chapters.

```
# check basic properties of the data
df_all_data.info()
```

From the given dataset, we should get a result similar to the following:

```
# check basic properties of the data
df_all_data.info()
✓ 0.0s

<class 'pandas.core.frame.DataFrame'>
RangeIndex: 500 entries, 0 to 499
Data columns (total 19 columns):
 #   Column                                                          Non-Null Count  Dtype
---  ------                                                          --------------  -----
 0   Page total likes                                                500 non-null    int64
 1   Type                                                            500 non-null    object
 2   Category                                                        500 non-null    int64
 3   Post Month                                                      500 non-null    int64
 4   Post Weekday                                                    500 non-null    int64
 5   Post Hour                                                       500 non-null    int64
 6   Paid                                                            499 non-null    float64
 7   Lifetime Post Total Reach                                       500 non-null    int64
 8   Lifetime Post Total Impressions                                 500 non-null    int64
 9   Lifetime Engaged Users                                          500 non-null    int64
 10  Lifetime Post Consumers                                         500 non-null    int64
 11  Lifetime Post Consumptions                                      500 non-null    int64
 12  Lifetime Post Impressions by people who have liked your Page    500 non-null    int64
 13  Lifetime Post reach by people who like your Page                500 non-null    int64
 14  Lifetime People who have liked your Page and engaged with your post 500 non-null int64
 15  comment                                                         500 non-null    int64
 16  like                                                            499 non-null    float64
 17  share                                                           496 non-null    float64
 18  Total Interactions                                              500 non-null    int64
dtypes: float64(3), int64(15), object(1)
memory usage: 74.3+ KB
```

Figure 6.3: Dataframe information

Real-world data is usually very messy. However, this does not seem to be the case with our dataset here, which is an indicator of data engineering practices being in place. However, we do see columns with missing values (check the non-null count values for each column in the last command output), which need to be identified and treated accordingly. We treat or correct these values during the data preparation stages since missing values will not add any value (or can even result in operational errors) during the modelling process. Additionally, we see that column names have white spaces and contain long names too at times. It is recommended to put all of these cleaner scripts into **.py** files or at least in the form of reusable Python functions so that we can quickly convert our experiment into software at a later stage. This is a good time to clean it, using a quick utility as follows:

```
# get a list of all columns
# and change their names to
# suitable format

# existing columns
all_columns = df_all_data.columns
```

```
# new col. names
new_col_names = []

# make changes
for each_col in all_columns:

    # remove the word 'Lifetime Post'
    each_col = each_col.replace('Lifetime Post','')

    # remove the word 'Lifetime Post'
    each_col = each_col.replace('Lifetime','')

    # Impressions by people who have liked your Page --> impressions
    each_col = each_col.replace('Impressions by people who have liked your
Page','impressions')

    # reach by people who like your Page --> reach
    each_col = each_col.replace('reach by people who like your
Page','reach')

    # People who have liked your Page and engaged with your post -->
people_engaged
    each_col = each_col.replace('People who have liked your Page and
engaged with your post','people_engaged')

    # remove whitespaces
    each_col = each_col.replace(' ','')

    # convert in lower case
    each_col = each_col.lower()

    # append in final list
    new_col_names.append(each_col)

# print new list
print(new_col_names)
```

In the preceding code example, we merely converted the column names. The new column names should be put back into the DataFrame. One way to do so is as follows:

```
# creating new dataframe with revised set of columns.
df_all_data_revised = df_all_data.set_axis(new_col_names, axis=1)
df_all_data_revised.head()

# checking information of new dataframe
df_all_data_revised.info()
```

If we look at the output of the **.info()** function, which gave the count or volume of missing values in the DataFrame, it seems that for our scenario here, we have much less missing values to be considered a risk, and hence the rows or observations with missing values can be dropped safely. This is usually a technique we employ when less than 1-3% of the data contains missing values, although this number is not an industry standard. In other examples (which we will work on in this book), depending on the % of missing values, we may replace them with the median (in case the column contains numerical values) or mode (in case the column contains categorical values).

Here is an example of how we drop NULL values from the dataset:

```
# remove nulls from the new dataframe
df_all_data_revised.dropna(inplace=True)

# Checking dataframe information.
df_all_data_revised.info()
```

Now that the basic levels of cleaning are completed, we can move to our next section for data analysis, where the first thing we usually perform is a quick five-point statistical summary to find any anomalies in the data, like the presence of outliers or skewness, etc. In our case, there are distribution issues, as shown in the following code cell's output:

```
# checking basic statistics of the data.
df_all_data_revised.describe()
```

Before we check and correct these properties in the data, let us look at another interesting exercise often performed in case of regression analysis, which is to find the correlation of features to the target. To do so, we calculate the Pearson's correlation coefficient and plot the correlation values as a heatmap. Note that the Pearson correlation coefficient measures the linear relationship between two variables, ranging from -1 (perfect negative correlation) to 1 (perfect positive correlation), with 0 indicating no correlation. In this visualization, the higher the value of correlation, the lighter the color. The following is an example of a correlation heatmap on our dataset:

```
# visualizing correlation of all columns.
df_all_data_correlation = df_all_data_revised.drop('type', axis=1,
inplace=False)
plt.Figure(figsize=(18,14))
sns.heatmap(df_all_data_correlation.corr())
plt.show();
```

Let us look at how the output of a correlation map will look when the aforementioned code snippet is run in a Jupyter Notebook or even as a Python script:

```
# visualizing correlation of all columns.
df_all_data_correlation = df_all_data_revised.drop('type', axis=1, inplace=False)
plt.Figure(figsize=(18,14))
sns.heatmap(df_all_data_correlation.corr())
plt.show();
```

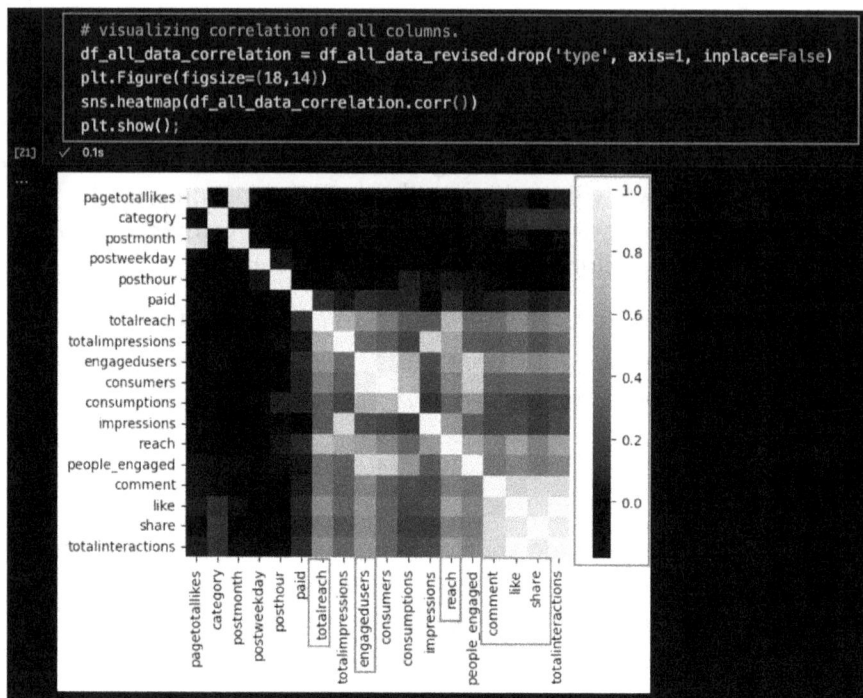

Figure 6.4: Heatmap for correlations

Here, we see that with **totalinteractions** being our target column, the most correlated features are **comment, like,** and **share** (which makes practical sense). Additionally, **totalreach**, **engagedusers,** and **reach** features are also quite well correlated with the target column. This quick visual analysis helps us perform feature selection while modeling and helps us in choosing the right model. From the available dataset and its analysis, we can use a common industry practice in case of regression analysis, i.e., to fit not one but two models in total, one of which will contain all the available features alongside the target column, while the other will contain only the most correlated features and the target column.

From the information of the dataset (output of the **.info()** function), we saw that the majority of the columns in the data are numeric. In place of this, we can perform a quick univariate analysis of each column, which can be achieved with a quick code cell as follows:

```
# perform univariate analysis of each column
# by identifying its type.
for each_col in df_all_data_revised.columns:
    if df_all_data_revised.dtypes[each_col] == 'O':
        plt.Figure(figsize=(8,4))
        sns.histplot(df_all_data_revised[each_col])
        plt.show();
```

```
else:
    plt.Figure(figsize=(8,4))
    sns.displot(df_all_data_revised[each_col])
    plt.show();
```

The `.dtypes()` function call tells us if a particular column is read as numeric or not. This is a naïve approach to finding categorical and numerical columns. In case the data was not read properly (because of encoding issues, etc.) by Pandas, there may be columns (for example) that contain numeric data but are represented as strings. For our case, as of this dataset, this approach is recommended to use better or different approaches to correct data types, one of which we will use shortly. Meanwhile, in the univariate analysis, we find that almost all columns are right-skewed (see the following example of one column) and require processing to bring them in a range:

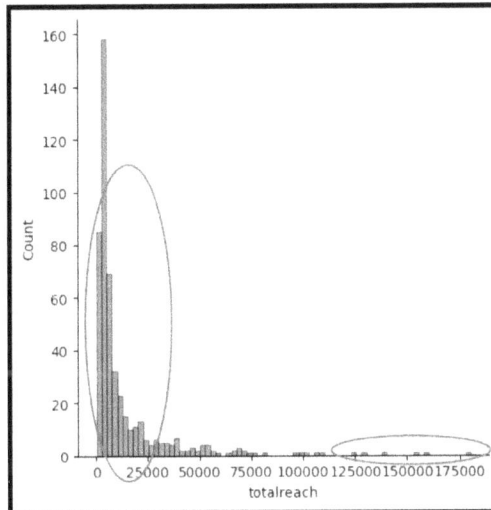

Figure 6.5: Data distribution from univariate analysis

There are some more observations from the analysis when one runs the code given in the accompanied Jupyter Notebook. For example, the type of content on the Facebook page is more videos than any other media, most of the posts are during the month of December as compared to others, the posts are made at 4 am or 12 pm time-slots, and that most of the posts we have are free rather than paid. These are critical pieces of information to keep in mind in case we see unwanted bias in the model during its evaluation (or later, when we productionize it).

Now, we move to the feature engineering section. Here, before we normalize the available data, one should break the data into training and testing and then perform normalization of the data. This is done to avoid overfitting through data leakage scenarios. Let us understand it briefly, as follows:

- **Overfitting**: This is by far the most common reason for an ML model's unreliability, wherein because of wrong practices applied or no penalization being applied to the model, it memorizes the patterns from the training data. This can also happen if the data is artificially created when patterns are hard-coded during the data generation process.

- **Data leakage**: In case we are (by mistake) using some part of the training data for testing our model, we can see data leakage issues, wherein the data ends up having common trends. This is like evaluating a student's exam on questions similar to what they have studied. This can also happen when or if we process the data before breaking it into training and testing sets. If we, for example, normalize the data before splitting it, then eventually, the training and testing data will have similar statistical properties, leading to a very good model during training, but in the real-world, it will fail to understand the patterns.

- **Multicollinearity**: Specifically impacting linear regression or any other similar models where the algorithm demands feature independence, the problem of multicollinearity occurs when one or more features are already highly correlated to the other.

- **Target variable range**: In some rare cases, the range of values in the target variable is in very close proximity, and then the adjusted R-squared values can get inflated as the algorithm is able to model the data very easily. We learned about the R-squared metric in *Chapter 5*.

Now, let us understand the concept of normalization to bring the numerical columns to a range. The one we are going to use is from the **sklearn** library, which uses the L2 normalization method. In simple words, each value in consideration is scaled in a way that the sum of squares of the values in each row equals 1. There are other methods of normalization as well. However, L2 is commonly used to improve ML model performance across a variety of use cases (like ours or computer vision use cases).

Note: Normalization does not change the inherent nature of the distribution but only helps rescale the data. While we perform normalization of any column, its scale will be quite controlled, while its inherent nature of distribution (left skewed, right skewed, or normal) still remains.

Keeping this in mind, here is how we can progress with feature engineering. To create the training and testing splits, in this particular use case, we will use 75% of the data for training and 25% of the data for testing, as follows:

There is no industry standard for these numbers, but these values are a good start. At times, even an 80-20 split is a good starting point.

```
# make a copy of the dataframe
# before performing any feature engineering
df_feature_engg = df_all_data_revised.copy()
```

```
# create features and target sets
all_features = df_feature_engg.drop("totalinteractions", axis=1)
target_variable = df_feature_engg["totalinteractions"]
print("Shape of Features' data: {}".format(all_features.shape))
print("Shape of Target data: {}".format(target_variable.shape))

# let's now divide the data into training and test splits
x_train, x_test, y_train, y_test = train_test_split(all_features, target_
variable, test_size=0.25)
print(x_train.shape)
print(x_test.shape)
print(y_train.shape)
print(y_test.shape)
```

Let us normalize the features available in our **x_train** and **x_test** variables, as we have now broken the data and use that further for modeling purposes. To do so, we can identify the categorical and numerical columns first and then normalize the numerical ones as follows:

```
# create dataframe only with numeric columns
# first identify numeric and string columns
str_cols = []
num_cols = []
for each_col in x_train.columns:
    try:
        _ = df_feature_engg[each_col] / 2
        num_cols.append(each_col)
    except Exception as e:
        str_cols.append(each_col)

# now create dataframe only with numeric cols
df_num_cols = x_train[num_cols]

# normalize all columns in the data
df_num_norm = pd.DataFrame(normalize(df_num_cols), columns=df_num_cols.
columns)
df_num_norm.head()
```

Now that we have processed the numerical columns, there is a type column as well, which contains categorical values. One way to convert such columns into numbers is to encode them. Usually, there are two simple ways of encoding data: one where we give each category a value (called **label encoding**), or one where we create a new column for each category with a value of 1 or 0 depending on its presence in a particular row (called one hot encoding). In this case, we can perform one hot encoding, for example, to see how the model performs. For cases where we already have lots of features, one hot encoding may result in many more additional columns, which can make the model training slower; in that case, we can use label encoding.

Note: For each such operation, we are using a separate dataframe to perform the changes, which we will join back once all the processing steps are completed. At times, resetting the index of a dataframe is necessary to ensure that we have the right set of rows and columns.

Here is an example to perform one hot encoding using the **pandas** library:

```
# perform one hot encoding of the string cols.
df_str_cols = x_train[str_cols]
df_str_cols.reset_index(drop=True, inplace=True)
df_cat_enc = pd.get_dummies(df_str_cols, drop_first=True, dtype='int')
df_cat_enc.reset_index(drop=True, inplace=True)
df_cat_enc.head()
```

Now that we have proceeded the columns with one option, we can join the two separate DataFrames into one and continue with further data preparation. In this case, we can first take a complete list of columns to be put in the final DataFrame, followed by the **.concat()** function of Pandas library to append the data by observations, as follows:

```
# join the two separate dataframes
# one with transformed numerical cols
# another with transformed categorical cols

# set all columns
all_columns = []
for each_col in list(df_num_norm.columns):
    all_columns.append(each_col)
for each_col in list(df_cat_enc.columns):
    all_columns.append(each_col)

# prepare final dataframe
x_train_ready = pd.concat([df_num_norm, df_cat_enc], axis=1, ignore_
index=True)
x_train_ready.columns = all_columns

# print sample data of final data
x_train_ready.head()
```

Similarly, we can perform the same preparation activities on the testing data to make sure that they are prepared separately from the training data. It is recommended that we prepare the test data separately from the training data so that we can avoid any form of data leakage as follows:

```
# create dataframe only with numeric columns
# first identify numeric and string columns
str_cols = []
num_cols = []
for each_col in x_test.columns:
    try:
        _ = df_feature_engg[each_col] / 2
        num_cols.append(each_col)
    except Exception as e:
        str_cols.append(each_col)

# now create dataframe only with numeric cols
df_num_cols = x_test[num_cols]

# normalize all columns in the data
df_num_norm = pd.DataFrame(normalize(df_num_cols), columns=df_num_cols.
columns)
df_num_norm.head()

# perform one hot encoding of the string cols.
df_str_cols = x_test[str_cols]
df_str_cols.reset_index(drop=True, inplace=True)
df_cat_enc = pd.get_dummies(df_str_cols, drop_first=True, dtype='int')
df_cat_enc.reset_index(drop=True, inplace=True)
df_cat_enc.head()

# join the two separate dataframes
# one with transformed numerical cols
# another with transformed categorical cols

# set all columns
all_columns = []
for each_col in list(df_num_norm.columns):
    all_columns.append(each_col)
for each_col in list(df_cat_enc.columns):
    all_columns.append(each_col)

# prepare final dataframe
x_test_ready = pd.concat([df_num_norm, df_cat_enc], axis=1, ignore_
index=True)
x_test_ready.columns = all_columns
```

```
# print sample data of final data
x_test_ready.head()
```

Now that we have the data ready for creating our first model. We cannot guarantee that the processing methods we have used (for example, normalization and one hot encoding) are the best suited for our use case, but once we experiment with our first model(s), we can use different feature transformation methods (like standard scaling) to try different versions of the model.

Note: In this particular approach, we have used all the available features, while in the next iteration, we can only selectively use particular features that are correlated to the target (like our correlation plot) to create a different model and compare both of them.

Now that we are ready to fit our first model, let us train the model with our training data, get some predictions on the test data, and evaluate the model performance. Since this is our first model, we should be ready for some surprises.

```
# Create a linear regression model object.
lr_init = LinearRegression()

# fit the model with training data.
lr_init.fit(x_train_ready, y_train)

# get predictions
y_pred = lr_init.predict(x_test_ready)

# calculate the metrics
mae = mean_absolute_error(y_true=y_test,y_pred=y_pred)
rmse = root_mean_squared_error(y_true=y_test,y_pred=y_pred)
r2score = r2_score(y_true=y_test,y_pred=y_pred)

# print the metrics values
print("MAE:",mae)
print("RMSE:",rmse)
print("Adj. R-Squared:",r2score)
```

There are two metrics we specifically made use of; let us quickly define them as follows:

- **MAE**: The average magnitude of errors in a set of predictions, where all individual differences between predictions and actual values have equal weight.

- **RMSE**: The square root of the average squared differences between predictions and actual values, giving greater weight to larger errors.

The preceding metrics values do not represent much if we only look at MAE and RMSE since, by design, the lower these values, the better the model. Since this is our first model, and there are no industry standards to define the so-called golden values of these metrics, we cannot say if our initial model is the best. However, the adjusted R-squared value should ideally be very close to 1, which is not so in our first model, indicating that there is scope to improve the model further. Let us see if (and how) we can improve our initial model.

If we analyze our preceding approach, other than normalizing and one-hot encoding, we have not used any other methods to prepare the data. Also, we have not used any regularization methods yet. More importantly, when we analyzed the data earlier, we saw a handful of features having more correlation to the target than all of the features. Note that regularization is a technique used in machine learning to prevent overfitting, which happens when a model performs well on training data but poorly on new, unseen data. It helps the model generalize better by adding a penalty to the complexity of the model.

Let us try our next model with only the specific set of features, which are more closely related to the target, as follows:

```
# getting data with specific columns
# from the ready dataframe
x_train_select = x_train_ready[['comment', 'like', 'share', 'totalreach',
'engagedusers', 'reach']]
x_test_select = x_test_ready[['comment', 'like', 'share', 'totalreach',
'engagedusers', 'reach']]


# fitting new model & getting predictions
lr_select = LinearRegression()
lr_select.fit(x_train_select, y_train)
y_pred = lr_select.predict(x_test_select)


# calculate the metrics
mae = mean_absolute_error(y_true=y_test,y_pred=y_pred)
rmse = root_mean_squared_error(y_true=y_test,y_pred=y_pred)
r2score = r2_score(y_true=y_test,y_pred=y_pred)

# print the metrics values
print("MAE:",mae)
print("RMSE:",rmse)
print("Adj. R-Squared:",r2score)
```

When we execute this code, we will note that the value of adjusted R-squared has improved, while the values of MAE and RMSE have gone down, which is good. To further improve the model and to make it more realistic, let us apply Lasso regression (also called L1 regularization) to our data and see how it performs, as follows:

```
# Import Lasso Regression algorithm
from sklearn.linear_model import Lasso
```

```
# Load your data
model = Lasso(alpha=0.1)  # alpha is the regularization parameter
model.fit(x_train_select, y_train)

# Make predictions
y_pred = model.predict(x_test_select)

# Get Metrics
mae = mean_absolute_error(y_true=y_test,y_pred=y_pred)
rmse = root_mean_squared_error(y_true=y_test,y_pred=y_pred)
r2score = r2_score(y_true=y_test,y_pred=y_pred)

# Print the metrics
print("MAE:",mae)
print("RMSE:",rmse)
print("Adj. R-Squared:",r2score)
```

When we run this code, we will find that the resultant model has fewer errors (lower values of MAE and RMSE), and the adjusted R-squared value has improved compared to the previous model. Reducing the number of errors in an ML model is of utmost importance for an AI engineer; however, in reality, and mathematically, errors cannot be diminished entirely. Hence, we can say that our revised model is better than the previous model.

Let us see if we can improve the model performance even more using L2 regularization or Ridge regression, using the following code example:

```
# import Ridge regression library
from sklearn.linear_model import Ridge

# Load data
model = Ridge(alpha=0.1)  # alpha is the regularization parameter
model.fit(x_train_select, y_train)

# Make predictions
y_pred = model.predict(x_test_select)

# Get Metrics
mae = mean_absolute_error(y_true=y_test,y_pred=y_pred)
rmse = root_mean_squared_error(y_true=y_test,y_pred=y_pred)
r2score = r2_score(y_true=y_test,y_pred=y_pred)

# Print metrics
print("MAE:",mae)
print("RMSE:",rmse)
print("Adj. R-Squared:",r2score)
```

The model we get is good compared to the Lasso regression model (looking solely at the adjusted R-squared value). In the Lasso model, there are chances of the model becoming biased to the training data, which is common in the real-world (hence, one cannot take any chances). To get the best-performing model (taking the Lasso regression model as the new baseline), we will perform Hyperparameter tuning to find the best value of **alpha** so that we can get a better model. To do so, we will use the grid search cross-validation method. As we will learn later on, hyperparameter tuning is the process of finding the best combination of hyperparameters for a machine learning model to achieve optimal performance. These hyperparameters are settings that are not learned from the training data itself, such as the number of trees in a random forest model.

The grid search cross-validation works as follows:

- Grid search defines a grid of possible values for each hyperparameter we want to tune. In this scenario, it is the value of **alpha**. It then creates and trains multiple models, each with a different combination of hyperparameters from the defined grid.

- Cross-validation is used to evaluate each model's performance. This involves splitting the training data into folds. In each fold, the model is trained on a subset of the data (excluding the fold) and tested on the remaining fold. This process is repeated for all folds, providing a more robust evaluation of the model's generalization ability.

- Grid search calculates a performance metric (e.g., accuracy, R-squared) for each model based on its cross-validation results.

- Finally, it identifies the model with the best performance (according to the chosen metric) and its corresponding hyperparameter combination. This model with the best-found hyperparameters is considered the optimal model for the given problem.

The following is a sample code to generate the best value of **alpha**:

```
# import Grid search Cross-val library
from sklearn.model_selection import GridSearchCV

# define range of alpha values
# between 0.01 until 10
alpha_range = [num / 100 for num in range(1, 1001, 49)]

# Define the parameter grid to search over (alpha values in this case)
param_grid = {'alpha': alpha_range}

# Create a GridSearchCV object with Lasso model and the parameter grid
lasso_grid = GridSearchCV(Lasso(alpha=0.1), param_grid, cv=5)   # cv=5 for
5-fold cross-validation
```

```
# Fit the grid search to the training data
lasso_grid.fit(x_train_select, y_train)
```

```
# Get the best model with the best parameters
best_lasso = lasso_grid.best_estimator_
print("Best Lasso Regression model: {}".format(best_lasso))
```

Now, let us check our updated metrics, as follows:

```
# Use the best model for prediction
y_pred = best_lasso.predict(x_test_select)
```

```
# Get Metrics
mae = mean_absolute_error(y_true=y_test,y_pred=y_pred)
rmse = root_mean_squared_error(y_true=y_test,y_pred=y_pred)
r2score = r2_score(y_true=y_test,y_pred=y_pred)
```

```
# Print metrics
print("MAE:",mae)
print("RMSE:",rmse)
print("Adj. R-Squared:",r2score)
```

This time, we get a tuned model, and since the values of the metrics are somewhat realistic as well, we can consider this as our first acceptable model, which we can export and use.

Note: Even if the adjusted R-squared values have come down (compared to the Lasso model), we will consider the tuned model as a better one because we need a stable model, instead of an overperforming one, to eradicate higher chances of biases and irregularities in the model.

As a part of this use case, let us understand how to export a model as a **pickle** file. In the proceeding use cases, we will discuss how we can load the **pickle** file of the model to make predictions. We will also deploy this **pickle** model into a server in Google Cloud Platform (in the further sections) to run predictions in real-time or batch mode.

We will save or export the model as a **pickle** file as follows:

```
# Importing the pickle library
import pickle
```

```
# Retrieve from GridSearchCV
best_lasso = lasso_grid.best_estimator_
```

```
# Save model to pickle file
filename = 'best_lasso_model_v1.pkl'
with open(filename, 'wb') as file:
    pickle.dump(best_lasso, file)
```

Similarly, we can load an already trained model (like ours) from a given **pickle** file as follows:

```
# Load model from pickle file
with open(filename, 'rb') as file:
    loaded_model = pickle.load(file)

# what's the type of the loaded file?
print(type(loaded_model))
```

Note: From a software engineering perspective, we are not done yet. All of the activities we have performed for our model (including data loading and its massaging) should ideally go into separate utility functions in separate Python files, followed by test cases' scripts for each of them to validate their functionalities.

As we go along the next set of use cases, we will incorporate these items slowly and steadily to make sure that we understand what we are doing, as well as why we are doing so.

Let us now move over to our next sample use case for a classification problem statement, taking an available realistic dataset from the *University of California Irvine (UCI) ML Repository*.

Prediction of heart disease type

For our next use case, let us go through a classification problem of predicting the heart disease type from an available open dataset in the *UCI ML Repository*. The dataset is available here: **https://archive.ics.uci.edu/dataset/45/heart+disease**.

This dataset contains 76 attributes, but all the published experiments refer to using a subset of 14 of them. Goal field refers to the presence of heart disease in the patient. It is the integer value from 0 (no presence) to 4. Experiments with the Cleveland database have concentrated on attempting to distinguish presence (values 1,2,3,4) from absence (value 0). The names and social security numbers of the patients were recently removed from the database and replaced with dummy values.

In this use case, let us follow a different approach right from the beginning. For each activity we perform, we will write a utility function, and instead of manually downloading or extracting the data, we will use the *UCI ML Repository* library in our **requirements. txt** file, which will be shown as follows:

```
ucimlrepo
pandas
numpy
matplotlib
seaborn
scikit-learn
```

```
unittest2
certifi
pytest
```

We should also look at our scaffolding, or the basic directory structure that we are using for this use case, which will be shown as follows:

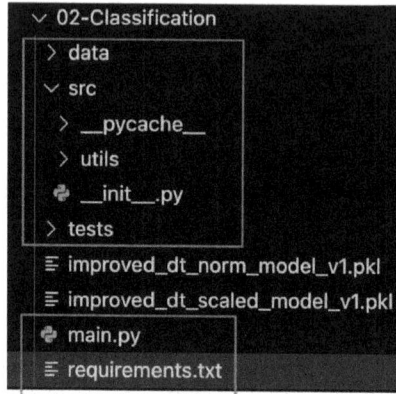

Figure 6.6: Sample skeleton of classification ML task

Let us start with our first utility function, which is to load the data using the **ucimlrepo** library. A sample implementation will look similar to the following code:

```
""" Utility to load data directly from UCI ML Repo """

# Imports
from ucimlrepo import fetch_ucirepo

# Utility definition
def get_data_from_uci(info=True):
    """ Fetch heart disease data from UCI ML Repo """
    # fetch dataset
    heart_disease = fetch_ucirepo(id=45)
    print("Heart Disease Data downloaded from UCI ML Repo.")

    # data (as pandas dataframes)
    features = heart_disease.data.features
    target = heart_disease.data.targets
    print("Datasets for features and target created.")

    # print dataset info if caller wants
    if info:
        # metadata
        print("Metadata for heart disease dataset: ")
```

```
        print(heart_disease.metadata)

        # variable information
        print("Heart Disease dataset's variable information:")
        print(heart_disease.variables)

    # return features and target
    return (features, target)
```

```
# End.
```

In the preceding utility, we are collecting the data directly from the *UCI ML Repository* from its dataset **id = 45** for the heart disease dataset. In the URL provided (at the beginning of this section), we will find sample code from the UCI team themselves, which we have merely reused in our scenario. Rather than only printing the dataset information, our utility function returns the extracted features and target data.

Let us write a test script for the data loader utility as well and test it from the command line. The test script for our **load_data.py** utility is as follows (there are alternative ways of doing the same thing as well):

```
""" Test: load_data.py utility """

# Imports
import unittest
import pandas as pd

from src.utils import load_data

# Test utility
class TestLoadHeartDiseaseData(unittest.TestCase):
    """ Tests for load_data.py utility/function """

    def test_download_and_metadata(self):
        """ Actual test function. Checks for dataset size. """
        features, target = load_data.get_data_from_uci(False)

        # Check for successful download
        self.assertIsNotNone(features)
        self.assertIsNotNone(target)

        # Check data types
        # Both are returned as dataframes
        self.assertIsInstance(features, pd.DataFrame)
        self.assertIsInstance(target, pd.DataFrame)

        # Check basic dimensions
```

```
        self.assertGreater(features.shape[0], 0)   # Ensure at least one row
        self.assertGreater(features.shape[1], 0)   # Ensure at least one
feature
        self.assertEqual(target.shape[0], features.shape[0])   # Ensure
target matches features

# entrypoint for test script
if __name__ == '__main__':
    unittest.main()

# End.
```

Using a test script like this is handy; later, we can automate running all tests at once using Makefile or something similar. Meanwhile, one can use the following command, from the Terminal in the root directory (where all the sub-directories like utils and tests exist), to run the test cases:

```
python -m pytest
```

Note: The command for the pytest library in Python was run using a Terminal window in VS Code. We need to add the pytest library to our requirements.txt file to make this work.

However, for each utility we write (from now onwards), we will write an equivalent test script. Later, we will understand how to automate and run all tests at once.

Note: pytest is a great Python library for running all test scripts (like the aforementioned one) at once. All we need to do is name the test scripts as test_ at the beginning of each file and run the command to run all tests at once from inside the tests folder.

Let us begin by putting all our utilities in different scripts. Starting with the data itself, we need some basic functions to start off, such as to check the data, show its sample, describe its statistics, and so on. To do so, we can create a script in Python in our **utils** directory as follows:

```
# imports
import pandas as pd
import matplotlib.pyplot as plt
import seaborn as sns

# get top 10 rows
def get_top_rows(dataset: pd.DataFrame):

    # print top 10 rows of dataframe
    print(dataset.head(10))

# get 5 point statistics
def describe_data(dataset: pd.DataFrame):
```

```
    # Get description as dataframe
    description_df = dataset.describe(include='all')

    # Print description with expanded width
    print(description_df.to_string(max_colwidth=1000))

    # Get dataset information
    info_df = dataset.info()

    # Print Dataset information
    print(info_df)

# get top 5 value counts
def value_counts(dataset: pd.Series):

    # print top 5 values
    print(pd.DataFrame(dataset.value_counts()).head(5))

# function to return numeric and string columns
def get_col_types(dataset: pd.DataFrame):

    # define empty lists
    num_cols = []
    str_cols = []

    # identify columns
    for each_col in dataset.columns:
        try:
            _ = dataset[each_col] / 2
            num_cols.append(each_col)
        except TypeError as e:
            _ = e
            str_cols.append(each_col)

    # return lists
    return (num_cols, str_cols)

# function to show distribution plots
def get_distribution(dataset: pd.DataFrame):

    # get the num cols and str cols
    num_cols, str_cols = get_col_types(dataset)

    # for each num col, display the displot()
    for each_col in num_cols:
        sns.displot(dataset[each_col])
        plt.plot()

    # for each str col, display the countplot()
    for each_col in str_cols:
```

```
    sns.countplot(dataset[each_col])
    plt.plot()
```

End

Essentially, in all these parts of the same script, we are writing reusable code for all the data, checking activities that we would normally do in a notebook (like our last regression use case). Writing them in the form of reusable functions so that we can use them as many times as we want in a production-like scenario. This also creates a modularized approach and helps maintain (as well as write test cases for each of our utilities) the code much better.

Similarly, we can have another script with a set of utilities to prepare the data before feeding it into an ML algorithm, as shown in the following example:

Note: In the GitHub repository of our book, one gets access to all of these scripts for detailed understanding and analysis.

```
# imports
from src.utils import check_data

import pandas as pd
from sklearn.preprocessing import normalize, StandardScaler
from sklearn.model_selection import train_test_split

# function to remove NULLs from dataset
def remove_nulls(dataset: pd.DataFrame):

    # remove nulls
    dataset.dropna(inplace=True)

    # return dataset
    return dataset

# function to normalize all numeric columns
def normalize_data(dataset: pd.DataFrame) -> pd.DataFrame:

    # get num cols
    num_cols, _ = check_data.get_col_types(dataset)

    # create temp dataframe with
    # the numeric columns only
    df_temp = dataset[num_cols]

    # normalize values of all columns
    # in the temporary dataframe
    df_num_norm = pd.DataFrame(normalize(df_temp), columns=num_cols)
```

```python
    # return normalized dataframe
    return df_num_norm

# function to apply standard scaling to all numeric columns
def standardize_data(dataset: pd.DataFrame) -> pd.DataFrame:

    # get num cols
    num_cols, _ = check_data.get_col_types(dataset)

    # create temp dataframe with
    # the numeric columns only
    df_temp = dataset[num_cols]

    # Create a StandardScaler object
    scaler = StandardScaler()

    # Fit the scaler on the data
    scaler.fit(df_temp)

    # Create a copy to avoid modifying the original DataFrame
    df_standard = df_temp.copy()

    # Transform (standardize) the numerical columns
    df_standard[num_cols] = scaler.transform(df_temp[num_cols])

    # return the final dataframe
    return df_standard

# function to concatenate given dataframes
def concat_datasets(dataset1: pd.DataFrame, dataset2: pd.DataFrame):

    # create empty list of all columns
    # for the final dataset
    all_columns = []

    # set all columns from both the input datasets
    for each_col in list(dataset1.columns):
        all_columns.append(each_col)
    for each_col in list(dataset2.columns):
        all_columns.append(each_col)

    # prepare final dataframe
    df_ready_data = pd.concat([dataset1, dataset2], axis=1, ignore_
index=True)

    # set the column names of the final dataset
    df_ready_data.columns = all_columns
```

```
    # return the final dataset
    return df_ready_data

# Function to split dataset into train/test
def create_train_test(dataset: pd.DataFrame, target_col):

    # create features and target data
    features_data = dataset.drop(target_col, axis=1)
    target_data = dataset[target_col]

    # create train-test split
    x_train, x_test, y_train, y_test = train_test_split(features_data,
target_data, test_size=0.3)

    # return the split
    return (x_train, x_test, y_train, y_test)

# End.
```

Similarly, we can write utilities to train our model, evaluate it, and perform hyperparameter tuning. The initial version of this utility may look as follows:

```
# imports
import warnings
import pandas as pd
from sklearn.tree import DecisionTreeClassifier
from sklearn.metrics import classification_report, confusion_matrix
from sklearn.model_selection import GridSearchCV

# function to fit a Decision tree model
def fit_model(x_train: pd.DataFrame, y_train: pd.Series, model_params: dict
= None):

    # check if model parameters are passed
    # and fit the model accordingly
    if model_params is None:
        # create model object
        dt_model = DecisionTreeClassifier()

        # fit model with training data
        dt_model.fit(x_train, y_train)

    else:
        # unpack model parameters
        max_depth = model_params['max_depth']
```

```
        min_samples_split = model_params['min_samples_split']
        min_samples_leaf = model_params['min_samples_leaf']
        criterion = model_params['criterion']
        max_features = model_params['max_features']

        # create model object with parameters
        dt_model = DecisionTreeClassifier(
            max_depth=max_depth,
            max_features=max_features,
            min_samples_leaf=min_samples_leaf,
            criterion=criterion,
            min_samples_split=min_samples_split
        )

        # fit model with training data
        dt_model.fit(x_train, y_train)

    # return model object
    return dt_model

# function to evaluate model
def evaluate_model(model: DecisionTreeClassifier, x_test:pd.DataFrame, y_
test: pd.Series):

    # get predictions from the model
    y_pred = model.predict(x_test)

    # generate classification report
    class_report = classification_report(y_pred, y_test)

    # generate confusion matrix
    conf_matrix = confusion_matrix(y_pred, y_test)

    # return the metrics
    return (class_report, conf_matrix)

# function to tune hyperparameters
def hp_tuning(model: DecisionTreeClassifier, x_train: pd.DataFrame, y_train:
pd.Series):

    # filter warnings
    warnings.filterwarnings('ignore')

    # define basic set of hyperparameters range
    param_grid = {
        'max_depth': [2, 3, 4, 5, 6, 7, 8],
```

```
        'min_samples_split': [2, 5, 10, 15, 20],
        'min_samples_leaf': [1, 5, 10, 15],
        'criterion': ['gini', 'entropy'],  # Splitting criteria
        'max_features': ['auto', 'sqrt', 'log2']  # Feature selection
    }

    # Create a GridSearchCV object
    grid_dtree = GridSearchCV(estimator=model, param_grid=param_grid,
scoring='accuracy', cv=10)

    # Fit the grid search
    grid_dtree.fit(x_train, y_train)

    # return model, best parameters and best score
    return (grid_dtree.best_params_, grid_dtree.best_estimator_)

# End.
```

Now that we have all the basic utilities in place (for which we can add the test scripts later), let us improve the first version of our **main.py** script. This will be our entry point to the model experimentation.

Firstly, we will import the utilities we have written and the extras like **pandas** and **pickle** library so that we can use the functionalities, as follows:

```
# Imports
import pickle
import pandas as pd
from src.utils import load_data
from src.utils import check_data
from src.utils import process_data
from src.utils import model
```

We can load the data, check the top rows of the features and targets, and check the value counts of the **target** variable as follows:

```
# Main utility
def main():

    # opening log
    print("Started: Heart Disease Prediction.")

    # get features and target
    features, target = load_data.get_data_from_uci(False)
    features = pd.DataFrame(features)
    target = pd.DataFrame(target)
    print("Got features of type: %s", type(features))
```

```
print("Got target of type: %s", type(target))

# Check features data
print("Check features dataset:")
check_data.get_top_rows(features)

# Check value counts of target
print("Check target value counts:")
check_data.value_counts(target.num)

# get target column
target_col = target.columns
print("The target column is: %s", target_col)
```

Furthermore, we can **describe** the dataset, visualize the **features** and **target**, and remove NULLs. To remove NULLs from this dataset, we will join the features and the target in a single DataFrame, remove NULLs, and then start with training and testing splits, as follows:

```
# Describe Features data
print("Describe features' dataset:")
check_data.describe_data(features)

# Get distribution of features
print("Visualising distribution of each feature:")
check_data.get_distribution(features)

# Get distribution of target
print("[Optional] Visualize distribution of target:")
check_data.get_distribution(target)

# Join features + target dataframe
all_data = process_data.concat_datasets(features, target)
print("Features and Target concatenated for NULL removal.")

# remove nulls from combined dataset
data_wo_nulls = process_data.remove_nulls(all_data)
print("Nulls removed from combined dataset of features and target.")
```

Now, we break the data into train and test sets, normalize and scale the features data in both sets separately, and then fit the two models, one with normalized data and one with scaled features data, as follows:

```
# Creating the training and testing sets
x_train, x_test, y_train, y_test = process_data.create_train_test(data_
wo_nulls, target_col)
```

```
print("Broken the data into Training and Testing sets.")

# normalize feature data in the train-test sets
x_train_norm = process_data.normalize_data(x_train)
x_test_norm = process_data.normalize_data(x_test)
print("Features normalized in Training and Test sets.")

# standard scale feature data in train-test sets
x_train_scaled = process_data.standardize_data(x_train)
x_test_scaled = process_data.standardize_data(x_test)
print("Created standard-scaled features in Training and Test sets.")

# fit model with normalized data
dt_norm = model.fit_model(x_train_norm, y_train, None)
print("Model created with Normalized features and as-is target.")

# fit model with scaled data
dt_scaled = model.fit_model(x_train_scaled, y_train, None)
print("Model created with Standard Scaled features and as-is target.")
```

Furthermore, we should evaluate the initial models and get a sense of how good the initial model is.

Note: This specific use case of ours is a multi-class classification.

As a part of the exercise, and also in the real-world, it is obvious that we would get an imbalance of observations (rows in the data) for each class; one or two classes (for example) will have more data, and the rest will have comparatively less data.

This is a classic scenario where we can perform up-sampling methods to improve the model quality, as follows: (We will learn more about this in the proceeding chapters)

```
# evaluate model with norm data
class_report_norm, conf_matrix_norm = model.evaluate_model(dt_norm, x_
test_norm, y_test)
print("Classification Report of Model on Normalized Data:")
print(class_report_norm)
print("Confusion Matrix of Model on Normalized Data:")
print(conf_matrix_norm)

# evaluate model with scaled data
class_report_sc, conf_matrix_sc = model.evaluate_model(dt_scaled, x_
test_scaled, y_test)
print("Classification Report of Model on Standard-scaled Data:")
print(class_report_sc)
```

```
    print("Confusion Matrix of Model on Standard-scaled Data:")
    print(conf_matrix_sc)
```

Lastly, before we export the model, we perform hyperparameter tuning and select a better version of each model(s). The utility we wrote earlier will generate the model itself as part of the tuning exercise, hence, we can return, save, and reuse it for future predictions. Additionally, one should re-generate the metrics to identify how good or how bad the new models are, post hyperparameter tuning as follows:

```
    # tune hyperparameters with norm data
    (
        norm_best_params, norm_best_est
    ) = model.hp_tuning(dt_norm, x_train_norm, y_train)
    print("Performed Hyperparameter tuning of model with normalized
features.")
    print(norm_best_params)

    # tune hyperparameters with scaled data
    (
        scaled_best_params, scaled_best_est
    ) = model.hp_tuning(dt_scaled, x_train_scaled, y_train)
    print("Performed Hyperparameter tuning of model with standard-scaled
features.")
    print(scaled_best_params)

    # evaluate tuned model with norm data
    class_report_norm, conf_matrix_norm = model.evaluate_model(norm_best_
est, x_test_norm, y_test)
    print("Classification Report of Model on Normalized Data:")
    print(class_report_norm)
    print("Confusion Matrix of Model on Normalized Data:")
    print(conf_matrix_norm)

    # evaluate tuned model with scaled data
    class_report_sc, conf_matrix_sc = model.evaluate_model(scaled_best_est,
x_test_scaled, y_test)
    print("Classification Report of Model on Normalized Data:")
    print(class_report_sc)
    print("Confusion Matrix of Model on Normalized Data:")
    print(conf_matrix_sc)
```

Finally, we can save both the models using **pickle** (similar to what we did in the case of regression modeling) on disk as follows, which can then be reused for later predictions:

```
    # export model trained with norm. data
```

```
    filename = 'improved_dt_norm_model_v1.pkl'
    with open(filename, 'wb') as file:
        pickle.dump(norm_best_est, file)

    # export model trained with norm. data
    filename = 'improved_dt_scaled_model_v1.pkl'
    with open(filename, 'wb') as file:
        pickle.dump(scaled_best_est, file)

# Entrypoint
if __name__ == "__main__":
    main()


# End
```

The following are the salient points to remember after completing this experiment:

- From the very beginning, we have made of a rather software engineering approach than a notebook-based approach. This is one great best practice so that we have the right skeleton of our project in place from day one.

- Each activity that we have performed (for example, data analysis, cleaning, model creation, or its evaluation) is put into different utility functions. This helps us create targeted and separate unit tests in Python (using libraries like **pytest** and **unittest**, later on) once the initial versions are in place.

- Next, if one looks at the code closely, it may not be the best in class in terms of performance, but it is quite clean. One should take into account that the clean code guidelines are of prime importance, even in AI and ML Applications.

Note: There is still some scope for improvement. We will put them in the exercises section of this chapter for further practice. In the Exercises section of this chapter, readers will also find useful resources to debug their Python code while working with VS Code.

Now, let us discuss the last use case in this chapter, i.e., unsupervised learning. In this regard, we will take up a notebook-based approach for another common and real-world use case with the available data from the *UCI ML Repository*.

Clustering water treatment plants

We will look into a simple method of unsupervised learning, wherein we take an open-sourced dataset on faults in an urban water treatment plant and its variety of properties. This dataset comes from the daily measures of sensors in an urban wastewater treatment plant. The objective is to classify the operational state of the plant in order to predict faults through the state variables of the plant at each of the stages of the treatment process. There are 527 instances or observations in the dataset, with a total of 38 attributes. There are also some missing values, all of which are unknown. However, all attributes are numeric in nature.

Note: The dataset is downloadable for free from the UCI ML Repository.

Our approach this time will be more of a notebook based approach, but from time to time we will create and make use of reusable functions, so that one gets a flavor of how to create a notebook which can then be converted to a software, in the best way (like we tried in the last use case, on classification).

In this case, let us start with the basics and open a new Jupyter Notebook. To do so, we will use our local system (assuming that we have completed our installations and executed the scripts from the previous sections). In the command line of our workstation, we can traverse to the directory where our previous virtual environment was created using VS Code (or we can choose to create a new one as well) and activate the environment.

In the following figure, we activate the virtual environment and start a **jupyter notebook** instance:

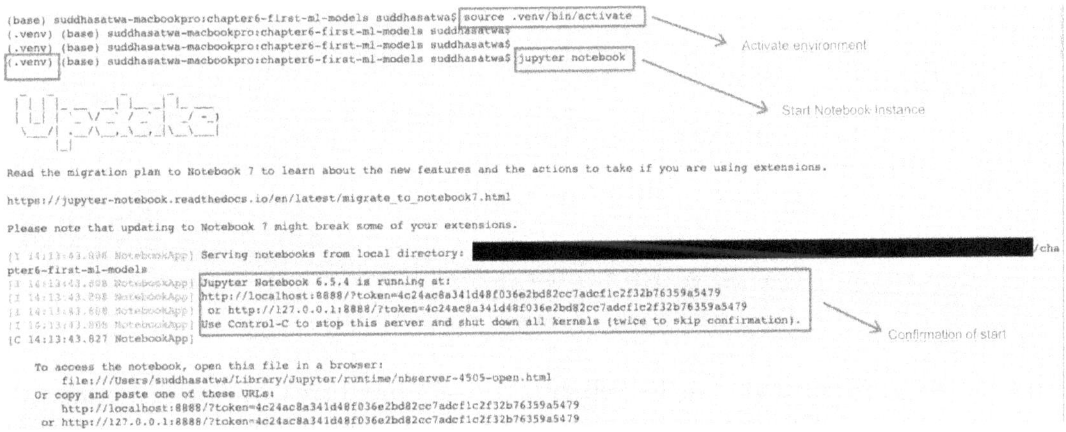

Figure 6.7: Starting up local Jupyter Notebook instance

Now, we will see a new browser window coming up (on the workstation using the default browser, *Edge* or *Chrome*) where we can see the Jupyter Notebook instance with the directory structure.

Note: Alternatively, we could have run this experiment on Google Colab as well, where no local installations would have been required.

We can now create two directories in this folder, where one of them will contain the data and the other, our notebook. It is a good practice to always have folders structured in our experiment folder, on local or elsewhere, so that it is organized and hence easy to find the artifacts later on. At times, this also helps to convert the notebook code cells into scripts and individual Python files while creating a software.

Next, let us see what is downloaded in the data folder. Inside the data folder, one can download the ZIP file from the UCI ML website and unzip or extract the files, which would result in two files, one containing the data and the other containing the metadata.

The first file is the index file, containing some basic version control information on this dataset. Next, we have files named **.data** and **.names**. Typically, this is a common way to annotate open source datasets (and can be used equivocally within organizations and research institutes), where the **.data** file contains the actual delimited dataset and the **.names** file contains the metadata of the dataset. This helps a newcomer in the team to understand the data, although it is highly recommended that AI engineers keep documenting their work elsewhere on a centralized documentation platform, like *Google Docs* or *Confluence*, etc.

We can now come back to our notebooks folder and create a new Jupyter Notebook to run our experiments. We should give meaningful names with some sort of versioning information. We can create new notebooks in any folder in a **Jupyter** instance (like this one) using the **New** ipykernel option, as shown in the following figure:

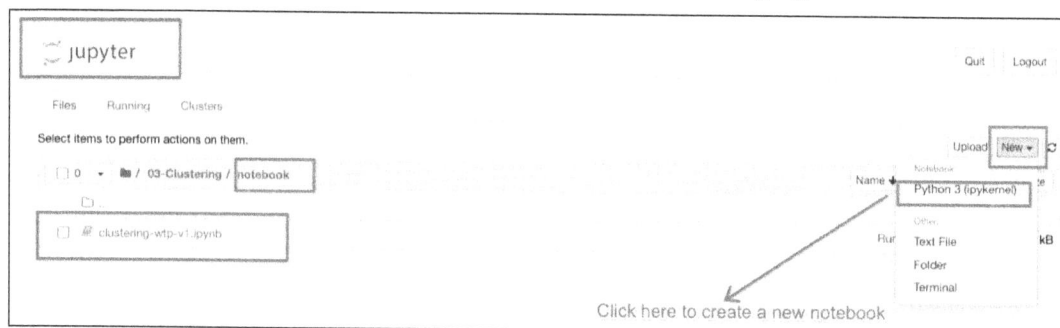

Figure 6.8: Creating notebook for clustering experiment

To start writing the notebook, the first cell should ideally be where we describe the dataset's metadata and the purpose of our experiment. This gives a good introduction to whoever we share this research with.

Note: The same set of keyboard shortcuts are applicable here as well as in a Google Colab environment.

Let us start with our first set of cells in the notebook to load and understand the data. At this stage, we may perform some rudimentary data cleaning as follows:

```
# Import libraries
import warnings
import pandas as pd
import numpy as np
import matplotlib.pyplot as plt
import seaborn as sns
```

```
from sklearn.cluster import KMeans

# setting some general properties
# for all visualizations
plt.rcParams['figure.figsize'] = (5,5)
plt.style.use('ggplot')


# disable warnings.
warnings.filterwarnings('ignore')
```

We can now load the **.data** file from the **data** folder (outside the **notebooks** folder) and start looking at the sample of the data as follows:

```
# load the data as a Dataframe
df_wtp_raw = pd.read_csv('../data/water_treatment_plant/water-treatment.
data')
columns = [
    'date',
    'Q_E','ZN_E','PH_E','DBO_E','DQO_E','SS_E','SSV_E','SED_E','COND_E','PH
_P','DBO_P','SS_P','SSV_P',
    'SED_P','COND_P','PH_D','DBO_D','DQO_D','SS_D','SSV_D','SED_D','COND_D'
,'PH_S','DBO_S','DQO_S',
    'SS_S','SSV_S','SED_S','COND_S','RD_DBO_P','RD_SS_P','RD_SED_P','RD_
DBO_S','RD_DQO_S','RD_DBO_G',
    'RD_DQO_G','RD_SS_G','RD_SED_G'
]
df_wtp_raw.columns = columns
df_wtp_raw.head()
```

From the initial looks, one can identify that almost all columns, other than date, are continuous fields but do contain unknown information denoted by **?**. We can also check the dataset information to see if there are any missing values in the data, as follows:

```
# check dataset information
df_wtp_raw.info()
```

Note: The last screenshot is a snippet of a few columns and not all of them.

We can understand that even if the data is numeric, many of the columns are represented as string, which we should update. Also, we need to find an easy and reusable way to handle the missing information.

Let us create the following reusable function in Python for this purpose:

```
# creating reusable function to impute
# incorrect '?' values with median
```

```
def impute_with_median(df):
    """

    Imputes missing values ('?') in a DataFrame with medians for numeric
columns.

    Args:
        df: A pandas DataFrame.

    Returns:
        A new pandas DataFrame with missing values replaced by medians.
    """

    # Create a copy to avoid modifying the original DataFrame
    df_impute = df.copy()

    # Loop through each column in the copy dataframe
    for col in df_impute.columns:
        filtered_data = df_impute[col][df_impute[col] != '?']
        df_filtered_data = pd.DataFrame(filtered_data)
        median_value = int(df_filtered_data.median().iloc[0])
        print(f"Median value of column '{col}' = '{median_value}'")
        df_impute.loc[df_impute[col] == '?', col] = median_value

    return df_impute
```

In the preceding function, we are taking a Pandas DataFrame as input and making a copy of it, so that we accidentally do not make any alterations to the existing data. To fill the missing values, we use the Median of the rest of the observations. To do so, we filter the data on the rows of each column, where the value is denoted as **?** sign. Then we calculate the median of these observations (using NumPy), print it once (optionally) for clarity, and finally replace the **?** values, with the corresponding median values. Finally, the function returns the cleaned, imputed DataFrame. Let us call this function on our dataset as follows and see how it does:

```
# Calling the utility function to clean data

# creating a copy of the dataframe
df_wtp_copy = df_wtp_raw.copy()

# removing the date col
df_wtp_copy.drop('date', axis=1, inplace=True)

# call utility for cleaning
df_wtp_clean = impute_with_median(df_wtp_copy)

# check dataframe
df_wtp_clean.head()
```

```
# join the date column back into clean dataframe
df_wtp_date = pd.DataFrame(df_wtp_raw['date'])
all_columns = df_wtp_raw.columns
df_wtp_clean_all_cols = pd.concat([df_wtp_date, df_wtp_clean], axis=1,
ignore_index=True)
df_wtp_clean_all_cols.columns = all_columns
df_wtp_clean_all_cols.head()
```

```
# checking dataset information again
df_wtp_clean_all_cols.info()
```

From the outputs, it seems the unknown values are now replaced with the median. One could have used the average or mean value as well for imputation, but in case the data in any column is not already normally distributed (where mean = mode = median), then using the average or mean may add outliers in the data.

Let us now move to the next section of data analysis and perform some more cleaning. Here, one can create a reusable function to take the dataframe as input, and for each column that is not the date column, we can create a histogram to see the distribution of data. Other than histograms, boxplots or violin plots also help identify patterns in each feature or column and detect outliers, as follows:

```
# create reusable function to perform univariate
# analysis of each col other than the 'date' column
def univar_analysis(df: pd.DataFrame):
    """ Takes WTP Dataset as input and prints distplots for each col. """
    for each_col in df_wtp_clean_all_cols.columns:
        # visualize if col. is not date
        if each_col != "date":
            # create dist. plot
            print(f"Dist. Plot for : {each_col}")
            print("=================================")
            plt.hist(df_wtp_clean_all_cols[each_col].astype('str'));
            plt.show();
            print("=================================")
```

```
# Call utility function for dist. plotting
univar_analysis(df_wtp_clean)
```

We have not yet looked into the basic five-point statistics of the features. This can help us understand the distribution of the data and identify any outliers in the data. Let us run the following command and see what we get:

```
# Checking dataset description
df_wtp_clean_all_cols.describe()
```

Note: Since we have not done the proper conversion of columns (from string to real numbers), a majority of the features in the data are wrongly categorized, hence even with an `include='all'` option in the `.describe()` function call, we may not get a good output and understanding of the data.

Now, let us create another function to convert all string columns to numeric columns, where the function can take a DataFrame as an input, and we can convert each column to numeric (with error handling), so that a DataFrame with the right variable types is returned, as shown in the following function:

```
# Reusable function to convert datatypes
# to float64 datatype
def convert_to_float64(df):
    """

    Converts the data types of all columns in a pandas DataFrame to
Float64,
    handling potential errors during conversion.
    """

    # make a copy of the dataframe
    df_copy = df.copy()

    # Iterate over columns and convert
    # dtypes to float64 (with error handling)
    for col in df_copy.columns:
        try:
            df_copy[col] = pd.to_numeric(df_copy[col], errors='coerce')  #
Handle potential errors
        except:
            pass  # Ignore

    # return converted dataframe
    return df_copy
```

Once we call this function, the information on the data looks much better, and the **`describe()`** function output also improves, as follows:

```
# Convert values using the dataset
# without the 'date' column
df_wtp_convert = convert_to_float64(df_wtp_clean)
df_wtp_convert.info()

# Now, describe the dataset
df_wtp_convert.describe()
```

Next, let us begin with K-means clustering (which we discussed in the previous chapters) and see how well we can cluster the dataset.

Note: To create a K-means clustering model, one needs to define the initial value of K, which is also a hyperparameter to the model.

Mathematically, it is nice to get the most appropriate value of K, but operationally (and practically), one should avoid choosing a value that is too small or too big. In case the value of K is too small, the clusters may not accurately represent the variety in the data. If the value of K is too big, the outcomes of the clustering exercise may not help us create any action plans to remediate any issues we learn from these groups. As a start, let us create the object of the K-means clustering class, which we imported earlier from the **scikit-learn** library, and use an initial value of K = 5. We can quickly cross-check if we are about to use the right dataset. Create a copy of it, and while fitting the K-means clustering model on this data, create an additional column in the dataset to store the cluster IDs as follows:

```
# creating a KMeans cluster object
# taking a random value of K=5
kmeans = KMeans(n_clusters=5)

# checking if we selected the right data
df_wtp_convert.head()

# creating a copy of the dataframe
# before creating the cluster labels
df_wtp_clusters = df_wtp_convert.copy()

# Fit the first KMeans clustering model
df_wtp_clusters["cluster"] = kmeans.fit_predict(df_wtp_clusters)
```

Because our dataset is small, it will not take more than a few seconds. Post this, we can mark the cluster IDs as categories and check the dataset once more to find each observation in a new group or cluster. Additionally, we can check which clusters are taking up most of the observations and which ones are low in value as follows:

```
# creating the new column as category
df_wtp_clusters["cluster"] = df_wtp_clusters["cluster"].astype("category")

# Checking the dataset for clusters
df_wtp_clusters.head()

# Checking concentration of records in each cluster
df_wtp_clusters['cluster'].value_counts()
```

Once the clusters are marked on the dataset, one good practice is to take sets of two features at a time (that we would like to use to categorize the data) and visualize the distribution of the clusters, like the following example, where we have taken the input flow to plant and input zinc to plant features, to see how the clusters are coming up:

```
# visualize clusters using 2 features
sns.relplot(
    x="Q_E", y="ZN_E", hue="cluster", data=df_wtp_clusters
);
plt.show();
```

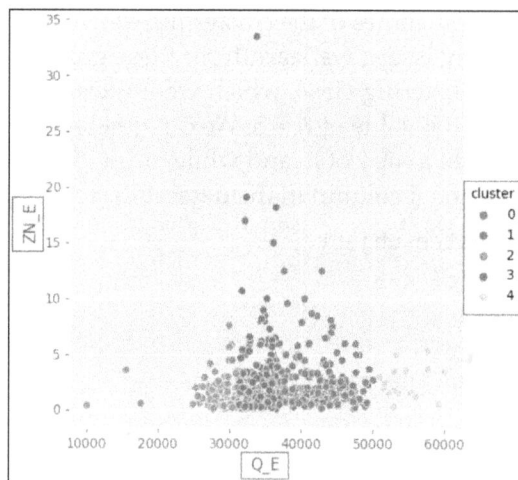

Figure 6.9: Initial K-means clustering model outcome

By looking at the figure, we can start finding good insights from the data. For example, there is one group of failures wherein the flow of zinc in the treatment plant is very low, but the input flow of water is very high. Also, there are clear indications of outliers in the data, especially in cluster 3. Hence, there are multiple ways to understand the data and get insights, and we can communicate actionable results from the experiment.

However, although we do have our first model, we are not sure (by any metric) if our choice of K=5 is mathematically correct (or at least close to being one). Let us try to tune the model by finding a better value of K. To do so, for a range of values of K (starting from 1 until 20, for example), we can create different models on the same data and calculate the WCSS error. WCSS, in simple terms, measures how scattered the data points are within a cluster. The lower the value of WCSS, the tighter the cluster is, which means that the data points are closer together. This gives us elevated confidence that the clusters we have created are more homogenous in nature.

In mathematical terms, we can define it as shown in the following figure, where C is the centroid of the cluster in question, m is the number of data points in total, and p is each data point within the cluster.

$$WCSS(C_j) = \sum_{p_i=1\ \in\ C_j}^{p_m} distance(C_j, p_i)^2$$

Figure 6.10: Formula for WCSS error in clustering

Once we have the WCSS values for all the range values of K, we can choose one value as the right value of K, wherein the errors do not change much drastically if the value of K is increased. When visualized (as shown in the following example), the line chart looks like a hand on a table, and the critical value of K, the elbow:

```
# Elbow method to select K Value
wcss=[]
for k in range(1,21):
    kmeans=KMeans(n_clusters=k,init='k-means++')
    kmeans.fit(df_wtp_convert)
    wcss.append(kmeans.inertia_)

# Checking WCSS values manually
wcss

# plot elbow curve
plt.plot(range(1,21),wcss)
plt.xticks(range(1,21))
plt.xlabel("Number of Clusters (K)")
plt.ylabel("WCSS")
plt.show()
```

From the preceding example code, one may get visual results similar to the following:

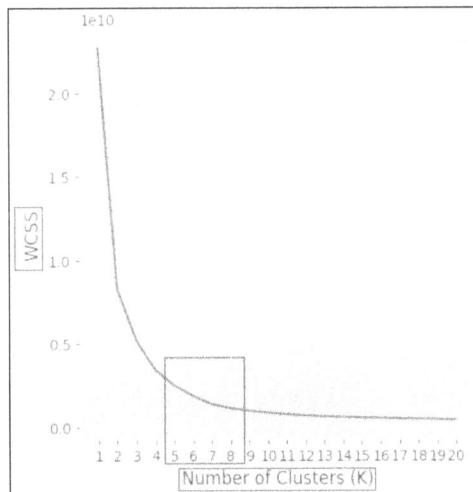

Figure 6.11: Elbow plot to find optimal value of K

From the preceding figure, it is clear, that a value of 6 or 7, or even 8, maybe a good choice for K for our model, given our dataset.

Let us use a value of K=6, fit a new model, and plot the clusters using the same two features again, as follows:

```
# fitting new K-Means model
kmeans = KMeans(n_clusters=6)
```

```
# new copy of the data
df_wtp_clusters_impr = df_wtp_convert.copy()
```

```
# Fit the first KMeans clustering model
df_wtp_clusters_impr["cluster"] = kmeans.fit_predict(df_wtp_clusters_impr)
```

```
# creating the new column as category
df_wtp_clusters_impr["cluster"] = df_wtp_clusters_impr["cluster"].
astype("category")
```

```
# Checking concentration of records in each cluster
df_wtp_clusters_impr['cluster'].value_counts()
```

```
# visualize clusters using 2 features
sns.relplot(
    x="Q_E", y="ZN_E", hue="cluster", data=df_wtp_clusters_impr
);
plt.show();
```

Here is one example of how the final clusters may visually look like:

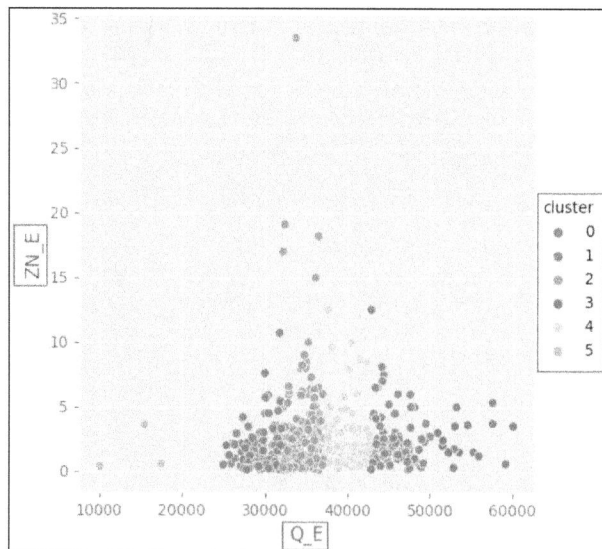

Figure 6.12: *Revised model after selecting K=5*

Now comes the hard part: once the software and modeling are ready, which is merely 5% of the overall exercise, to be honest (and as seen throughout the industry as well), one needs to explain the model's outcome and use it to the best possible extent. Since this is an Unsupervised learning problem, and hence we do not know the ground truth or true labels or labels of the data (different names to the same variable, target), its interpretation is very complex at times as well, especially when we are dealing with datasets like these containing many features (most of which are important in their sense). While we could use WCSS anytime to evaluate the model, and there are other metrics as well, the AI or ML engineers need to spend further time on this analysis alongside a data scientist and colleagues with business acumen and domain knowledge, so that the right set of action plans can be derived out of the insights we get from these models.

Conclusion

In this chapter, we covered the approaches, possible solution(s), and best practices of software engineering for AI or ML to some extent. We have understood how to perform rapid experimentations with Jupyter Notebooks and how to start building an AI application in the format of any other software from its initial days of design and development.

Additionally, we looked into three different real-world use cases of supervised and unsupervised learning (combined) to create effective ML applications and discussed common ways to prepare data, create models, evaluate them, and finally, how to improve them.

In the next chapter, we will discuss computer vision, its applications in machine learning, and how to create AI applications using Python, which solves use cases in the real-world involving visual problem statements.

Exercises

Let us try the following exercises to revise the concepts and to practice more of these ML algorithms:

1. In the regression use case, take each logical section of the notebook, convert it into a Python script, and create the final structure of the project in the same form as we did for the classification use case.

2. Explore the Visual Studio IDE public documentation on how to debug Python programs from here:

    https://code.visualstudio.com/docs/python/debugging

3. In the classification use case, the main.py program does everything in a single place and that too in a sequence. This makes the file quite verbose. Write another version of main.py to make it cleaner. What would one require to achieve this?

    a. Do we need more utilities or functions to make it clean?

    b. Do we need functions within main.py itself to make the code cleaner?

4.   In the clustering exercise, let us try the following:

    a. In the reusable function to replace unknown information (given by ?), make it more generic by adding more functional variables (like the character to be replaced, etc.)

    b. While modeling, we have made use of the K-means clustering model only. Check the scikit-learn documentation and try the DBSCAN model on the same data to see if we get better and lower WCSS values.

Join our book's Discord space

Join the book's Discord Workspace for Latest updates, Offers, Tech happenings around the world, New Release and Sessions with the Authors:

https://discord.bpbonline.com

CHAPTER 7

Computer Vision

Introduction

This chapter explores the various facets of computer vision-related use cases, in which we delve into the important details of **convolutional neural networks** (**CNN**), along with the implementation of some common computer vision use cases in Python, specifically using TensorFlow and Keras libraries. We will start with a review of **artificial neural networks** (**ANN**), which we have briefly defined while learning about the basics of ML. Once we learn its important design principles, including the most important concepts of backpropagation et al., we will explore the mathematical concepts of CNN and understand with practical implementation how many real-world use cases, like object detection and masking, are solved using AI and ML.

Structure

The chapter covers the following topics:

- Artificial neural networks
- Convolutional neural networks
- Real-world object classification
- Transfer learning
- Practical uses and limitations

Objectives

By the end of this chapter, readers will be able to understand how ANNs and CNNs are designed and how their architecture helps solve complex real-world problems using AI and ML systems. One would also understand in depth how to implement such use cases in the real-world using TensorFlow and Keras.

Artificial neural networks

Without learning about ANNs, one would not understand or appreciate CNNs. Let us start with a quick introduction to it and some use cases with its code.

As we have learned briefly earlier, an ANN is a type of ML algorithm that is inspired by how the human brain works and the associated research. They are made up of interconnected nodes that can process information and learn from data. **Neural networks (NNs)** are used in a wide variety of applications, including image recognition, natural language processing, and speech recognition.

ANNs are typically composed of three layers such as an **input** layer, one or many **hidden** layers, and an **output** layer. The input layer receives data from the outside world, the hidden layer(s) processes the data, and the output layer produces a result. The result depends on the problem statement. If we are solving a regression use case, the result is a continuous number, or in the case of a classification problem, it is a set of probabilities of a particular input falling in which class.

Each neuron in the network is connected to the neurons in the previous and following layers by weights. These weights determine how much influence each neuron has on the output of the network. Essentially, when one trains an ANN, we are learning the weights and optimizing them so that with the correct weights, we get the right (as close as possible) output to a given input.

When data is passed through the network, each neuron calculates a weighted sum of its inputs. This sum is then passed through an activation function, which produces an output. The output of each neuron is then passed to the next layer of the network.

There are many different types of neural networks, each with its own strengths and weaknesses. Some of the most common types of neural networks include the following:

- **Feedforward neural networks**:
  - These are the simplest types of neural networks.
  - Data flows from the input layer to the output layer, without any feedback loops.

- **Recurrent neural networks**:
  - These networks are able to remember information from previous inputs.

o This makes them well-suited for tasks such as natural language processing and speech recognition.

- **Convolutional neural networks**:

  o These networks are designed to process data that have a grid-like structure, such as images.

  o They are used in a wide variety of applications, including image recognition and object detection.

Activation functions

Before we progress, let us understand activation functions since they play a vital role in calculating weights in the network. Activation functions essentially determine how neurons respond to the weighted sum of their inputs and introduce non-linearity into the network. This allows ANNs to model complex relationships and make predictions based on patterns in the data, often without any need for feature engineering.

There are numerous activation functions used in neural networks, each with its characteristics and applications. Following are some of the most common ones:

- **Linear: y = x**:

  o Preserves the linear relationship between the input and output.

  o Used in early layers of the NN or for linear regression tasks.

- **Sigmoid: y = 1 / (1 + e^-x)**:

  o A smooth, S-shaped function that squashes the input into a value between 0 and 1.

    Note: We have learned this in the case of logistic regression as well.

  o Used in binary classification problems, such as predicting whether an email is spam or not.

- **Tanh: y = (e^x - e^-x) / (e^x + e^-x)**:

  o Similar to sigmoid, but with a range of -1 to 1.

  o Also used in binary classification and provides a zero-centered output.

- **ReLU: y = max(0, x)**:

  o **ReLU** stands for **rectified linear unit**.

  o A simple and computationally efficient function that sets negative inputs to 0.

  o Widely used in deep neural networks due to its fast training speed and resilience to vanishing gradients.

- **Leaky ReLU: y = max(0.01x, x)**:
  - A variant of ReLU that allows a small amount of gradient flow through the negative region.
  - Helps prevent neurons from dying during training and improves performance on certain tasks.
- **ELU (Exponential Linear Unit): y = x if x >= 0, alpha * (e^x - 1) if x < 0**:
  - A smoother version of ReLU with a negative slope for negative inputs.
  - Has been shown to improve performance on certain image recognition tasks.

The choice of activation function depends on the specific task and network architecture. The following are some general guidelines:

- **Linear**: For linear relationships or regression tasks.
- **Sigmoid and tanh**: For binary classification problems.
- **ReLU and leaky ReLU**: For deep neural networks with multiple layers.
- **ELU**: For image recognition and certain other tasks where smoothness is beneficial.

Some examples of these activation functions getting used can be as follows:

- In a binary classification task where the network predicts whether a customer will purchase a product or not, a sigmoid activation function is often used to output a probability between 0 and 1.
- In a deep neural network for image classification, ReLU activations are commonly used in the hidden layers to introduce non-linearity and improve the network's ability to learn complex features.

Note: The aforementioned activation functions are just a handful of all the activation functions we have in place. There is much more to learn (as we go along with our applications in AI and ML), which one should take up as the basics are clear.

Optimizers

Other than activation functions, optimizers play a crucial role in designing an ANN model. Imagine an optimizer to be the change in approach taken by a good teacher at times; for example, when training students for competitive exams in school or college, this helps to align or customize the learning experience and gives comparatively better results. Optimizers, in a similar sense, are algorithms that guide ANNs on how to adjust the weights and biases in each layer during training. Its only goal is to find the combination of weights and biases that minimizes the loss function. As studied earlier, loss functions are measures to calculate differences between actual and predicted outcomes from a model. The following is how optimizers work:

- **Forward pass**: The network receives input data, processes it through its layers, and generates an output.

- **Loss calculation**: The loss function compares the network's output with the desired output and calculates the error.

- **Backpropagation**: This step calculates how much each parameter (weight or bias) in the network contributed to the error.

- **Optimizer update**: The optimizer uses the backpropagation information to adjust the parameters in a direction that minimizes the loss. Imagine the optimizer nudging the parameters in a way that reduces the error gradually.

The following are some popular optimizers and their use cases:

- **Stochastic Gradient Descent (SGD)**:
  - The simplest optimizer, SGD, updates parameters based on the error of a single data point at a time.
    - Imagine taking a small step in the direction that reduces the error for a single training example.
  - Easy to implement, computationally efficient for large datasets.
  - Can be slow to converge, prone to getting stuck in local minima (suboptimal solutions, especially with complex models).
  - Often used as a baseline or for smaller datasets where computational efficiency is a concern.

- **Root Mean Square Prop (RMSprop)**:
  - Addresses a limitation of SGD where updates can oscillate significantly for parameters with highly varying gradients.
  - RMSprop keeps track of an average squared gradient for each parameter and uses this information to adjust the learning rate for each parameter individually, preventing large oscillations.
  - Often faster and more stable than SGD, particularly for problems with non-stationary gradients (gradients that change significantly during training).
  - Requires tuning a hyperparameter related to the decay rate of the squared gradient average.
  - Effective for tasks with non-stationary gradients, often used in **recurrent neural networks** (**RNNs**) for processing sequential data like text.

- **Adaptive Moment Estimation (Adam)**:
  - Combines ideas from SGD, Momentum, and RMSprop. It maintains an exponentially decaying average of past gradients and squared gradients

for each parameter, adapting the learning rate individually based on these averages.

    o   Often considered a one-size-fits-all optimizer due to its effectiveness across various problems and its ease of use with minimal hyperparameter tuning.

    o   It may not always be the most efficient choice compared to specialized optimizers for specific tasks.

    o   A popular default choice for many neural network architectures due to its robustness and ease of use.

- **Adaptive Gradient Algorithm (Adagrad)**:

    o   Similar to RMSprop, Adagrad adapts the learning rate for each parameter based on the historical sum of squared gradients. However, unlike RMSprop's decaying average, Adagrad accumulates the squared gradients for the entire training process, which can lead to diminishing learning rates later in training.

    o   It can be effective for sparse data problems where some parameters have very infrequent updates.

    o   Learning rates can become very small over time, hindering convergence.

    o   Primarily used for sparse data problems or when dealing with features that have very different scales.

The best optimizer for a specific task depends on factors like the type of network, dataset size, and desired learning rate. Experimentation is often needed to find the optimal choice.

Backpropagation

Another important concept to understand is the process of exactly how an ANN ideally learns the weights in the designed network. This process is called backpropagation and forms the building block of the learning process. Imagine we are training a student for a test, but we cannot directly see their thought process. Backpropagation in neural networks is like having a way to peek into the black box and understand how adjustments are made to improve performance.

Neural networks learn by adjusting internal parameters (weights and biases) during training. These parameters influence how the network transforms input data into output. The goal is to find the optimal combination of parameters that minimizes the error between the network's prediction and the desired output. Backpropagation is a crucial algorithm that enables efficient learning in neural networks with multiple layers. Following is a breakdown of its key steps:

1. **Forward pass**: The network receives input data, processes it through its layers, and generates an output prediction.

2. **Error calculation**: The loss function compares the network's prediction with the desired output and calculates the error (loss value).

3. **Error attribution**: Backpropagation is made use of in this case. It starts at the output layer and works its way backward through the network layer by layer. At each layer, it calculates how much each parameter (weight and bias) in that layer contributed to the overall error.

   Imagine assigning blame for a bad test score in a multi-step calculation. Backpropagation also inherently does a similar analysis to identify how each parameter in the network contributed to the overall error in the output.

4. **Parameter update**: Using the information from backpropagation, the optimizer (a separate algorithm) adjusts the parameters in a direction that minimizes the overall error. Think of the optimizer using the blame assignment from backpropagation to nudge the parameters in a way that reduces the error for future predictions.

As we learned in the preceding section, backpropagation allows the network to learn from its mistakes by iteratively adjusting its internal parameters. With each training iteration, the network becomes better at mapping inputs to desired outputs.

In summary, imagine a maze with multiple exits. Backpropagation helps the network identify which turns in the maze (parameter adjustments) led it to a dead end (high error) and guides it towards the correct exit (minimum loss).

Applications

It is interesting to note that ANNs are used in a wide variety of applications, including the following:

- **Image recognition**: Neural networks can be used to identify objects in images, even if the objects are partially obscured or distorted.

- **Natural language processing**: Neural networks can be used to understand the meaning of text, even if the text is ungrammatical or contains errors.

- **Speech recognition**: Neural networks can be used to recognize spoken words, even if the words are spoken in a noisy environment.

- **Machine translation**: Neural networks can be used to translate text from one language to another.

- **Predictive analytics**: Neural networks can be used to predict future events, such as the weather or the stock market.

With this in mind, let us look at some use cases and write code for them using TensorFlow and Keras. We will (yet again) break these problem statements into different sections of supervised and unsupervised learning.

House price prediction

Let us start with a simple use case, with a built-in dataset, for building a simple regression model in estimating the house prices from labeled data (hence, a supervised learning problem statement), using the TensorFlow and Keras libraries.

Let us start with importing the required libraries:

```
# Load required Python libraries
import pandas as pd
import numpy as np
from TensorFlow.keras.models import Sequential
from TensorFlow.keras.layers import Dense
from sklearn.preprocessing import MinMaxScaler
from sklearn.model_selection import train_test_split
from matplotlib import pyplot as plt
```

Further, let us load the data from GitHub. There are other places, too, from where we could download this, but from GitHub, it becomes quite easy to load **comma-separated value** (CSV) files directly using Pandas. Let us see an example where we take this data from **https://github.com/ywchiu/riii/blob/master/data/house-prices.csv** and load it as a DataFrame. A reference code example is as follows:

```
# Import data as a Pandas Dataframe
data = pd.read_csv("https://raw.githubusercontent.com/ywchiu/riii/master/
data/house-prices.csv")
```

Once you have downloaded the CSV and used it from a data folder in Visual Studio Code IDE, too. Next, let us pre-process the data and create features and targets. For simplicity, we will replace missing values in the data with the average or statistical mean of each numeric column. Although we are not specifically performing any **exploratory data analysis** (EDA) on this data herewith, it is strongly advised that for each experiment we run (irrespective of whether we are using an IDE or a Jupyter Notebook), one should perform a detailed analysis of the data to understand it and find useful nuggets of understanding the data.

Here is an example of data exploration:

```
# Explore data: Analyze data to identify missing values, data types, etc.

# Identify and handle missing values:
# - Numerical columns: replace with Median
# - Categorical columns: replace with Mode

for column in data.select_dtypes(include=['float64', 'int64']):
    median = data[column].median()
    data[column].fillna(median, inplace=True)
```

```
for column in data.select_dtypes(include=['object']):
    mode = data[column].mode()[0]
    data[column].fillna(mode, inplace=True)

# Separate features (X) and target variable (y)
features = data.drop("Price", axis=1)
target = data["Price"]

# Convert categorical variables to one-hot encoded
categorical_cols = [
column for column in features
if features[column].dtype == 'object'
]
features = pd.get_dummies(
features, columns = categorical_cols
)

# Scale numerical features using min-max scaling
scaler = MinMaxScaler()
features = scaler.fit_transform(features)

# Split data into train and test sets
X_train, X_test, y_train, y_test = train_test_split(
features, target, test_size=0.2, random_state=42
)
```

Now, let us build one quick model with three layers in total as a start. We will use one input layer for the data as per its shape, followed by one hidden layer and the final output layer. Let us see an example of how to achieve this:

```
# Define a simple neural network model with Dense layers
model = Sequential()

# Input layer with the same number of neurons as the number of features
model.add(Dense(units=features.shape[1], activation='relu'))

# Hidden layer with 32 hidden neurons
model.add(Dense(units=32, activation='relu'))

# Output layer with a single neuron for predicting sale price (regression
problem)
model.add(Dense(units=1))

# Compile model with optimizer, loss function (MSE) and metrics (MAE)
model.compile(optimizer='adam', loss='mse', metrics=['mae'])
```

```
# fit the model with the training data
history = model.fit(X_train, y_train, epochs=100, batch_size=32, validation_
split=0.2)
```

Note: In the preceding code, we use the ReLU activation function and Adam optimizer, and we are using 100 epochs to train the model initially.

Now that we have the basic model in place, let us evaluate the model by using loss metric as mean squared error (as given in the **model.compile** command in the last section) and mean absolute error to find how well the model is fit. Here is a sample code for model evaluation using mean absolute error:

```
# Evaluate the trained model on the test set
loss, mae = model.evaluate(X_test, y_test, verbose=0)
print(f"Test loss: {loss:.4f}, Mean absolute error: {mae:.2f}")
```

Using the history variable that we have used while training the model, we will now be able to plot the training history along with the losses so that we can estimate a good value of epochs we need to train the model. Usually, if after a certain value of epochs, the losses do not change much, then we can use that specific value as our choice of epochs rather than using a large value of epochs. This helps optimize the training process. Here is a sample code to achieve this:

```
# Visualize training process
plt.plot(history.history['loss'], label='train loss')
plt.plot(history.history['val_loss'], label='val loss')

plt.title("Loss function during training")
plt.xlabel("Epochs")
plt.ylabel("Loss")
plt.legend()

plt.show()
```

Finally, but optionally, we can get the predictions of this model on the test data. Here is an example code snippet:

```
# Get predictions from Test data
predictions = model.predict(X_test)
print(f"Model's predictions on the first 5 test samples: \n
{predictions[:5]}")
```

Further, and as advised in the exercises section, one can explore more variations of optimizers and activation functions to see their effects. For example, we can add more intuitive hyperparameter tuning by adjusting the learning rate.

Note: For a software engineer in the AI or ML space, it is essential to package our work as software.

Hence, when one is using VS Code (after their initial experiments on Jupyter Notebook(s)), we can follow the steps like the following (for example) to package the code:

1. Create a new Python project in visual studio code.

2. Copy all parts of the sample code above into your project directory.

3. Create a virtual environment using the Python extension in VS Code.

4. Install required libraries in the virtual environment.

5. Add a **requirements.txt** file listing all the required libraries and their versions.

6. Add each step of the model-building process as a separate utility under a utils folder.

7. Add a test or folder and add scripts in Python for unit-testing each functionality, like data processing, model creation, model evaluation, etc.

Note: When we run this first model, the output will not be very good. This is to show that simpler networks may not always be the right choice for simple datasets like the one we have used in this example.

Let us move over to our next use case of a classification problem and see how to make it work.

Spam emails

In this use case, we will work on a problem statement on how to classify whether an email is spam or not from a given dataset that is pre-engineered. We will learn more (in *Chapter 8, Natural Language Processing*) how to work with natural language processing tasks and use cases, but at this time, let us imagine that one gets hold of a good volume of emails and extracts the word frequency of some critical words (from the email text or corpus). One can check the *UCI ML Repository* for further information on the dataset. Here, to know about the features and how they were collected for the given study, refer to the link **https://archive.ics.uci.edu/dataset/94/spambase**.

Let us start by importing the libraries we require for this experiment using the following:

```
# Import necessary libraries
import TensorFlow as tf
from TensorFlow import keras
from TensorFlow.keras.layers import Dense, Dropout
from sklearn.model_selection import train_test_split
from sklearn.preprocessing import LabelEncoder, StandardScaler
from sklearn.impute import SimpleImputer
import pandas as pd
import matplotlib.pyplot as plt
```

We can download the data from GitHub, where the same copy of data can be found in the following (or any other similar) repositories. We can read it directly using Pandas and then check some of its basic properties:

```
# Load the spam dataset
data = pd.read_csv("https://raw.githubusercontent.com/ustunb/classification-
pipeline/master/Data/Raw%20Data%20Files/spambase.csv")

# print dataset info
print(data.info())

# Print sample emails
print(data.head())
```

One can perform some further analysis on the data, for example, to check if there are missing values (and impute them as required) and so on. Here is an example:

```
# Check for missing values
print(data.isnull().sum())

# Describe the data
print(data.describe())

# Visualize data distribution
data.hist(figsize=(10, 10))
plt.show()
```

Even if we do not have any missing values in this example dataset, it is always good to use Imputers from the scikit-learn library to replace missing continuous values with the median of that column. Here is an example:

```
# Handle missing values
imputer = SimpleImputer(strategy="median")
data_numeric = data.select_dtypes(include=["number"])
data_numeric = imputer.fit_transform(data_numeric)

# Split data into training and testing sets
X_train, X_test, y_train, y_test = train_test_split(data_numeric,
data["Spam"], test_size=0.2)

# Scale numerical features
scaler = StandardScaler()
X_train = scaler.fit_transform(X_train)
X_test = scaler.transform(X_test)
```

One can now start creating the basic architecture of the ANN model.

Note: In both of these use cases, we have created the overall design of the layers without any guidelines as to what will work for our given use case. Hence, it can be determined as more of an experimentation in terms of how to design the network.

Here is an example code snippet:

```
# Define the model
model = keras.Sequential([
    Dense(64, activation="relu", input_shape=(X_train.shape[1],)),
    Dropout(0.2),
    Dense(32, activation="relu"),
    Dropout(0.2),
    Dense(1, activation="sigmoid")
])

# Compile the model
model.compile(loss="binary_crossentropy", optimizer="adam",
metrics=["accuracy"])
```

Now that we have created the basic model layout, we can train the model and keep its history so that later on, we can plot the training and test losses over epochs to understand the critical value of the Epoch.

Note: The training loss is the mistake we see the model making on the training data, and the test loss is over the test data.

Here is an example code to keep model training history:

```
# Train the model
history = model.fit(X_train, y_train, epochs=20, validation_data=(X_test,
y_test))
```

Let us now evaluate our first model on the test data. The model performs exceptionally well. Hence, one may need to rethink the feature engineering or selection processes that we have applied in this case before considering this model usable:

```
# Evaluate the model
loss, accuracy = model.evaluate(X_test, y_test)
print("Loss:", loss)
print("Accuracy:", accuracy)
```

We can also print the history of the model's training (like the last regression use case) as follows:

```
# Plot epochs vs loss
plt.plot(history.history['loss'])
plt.plot(history.history['val_loss'])
plt.title('Model Loss')
plt.ylabel('Loss')
plt.xlabel('Epoch')
plt.legend(['Train', 'Validation'], loc='upper right')
plt.show()
```

Just like in the last chapter on ML models (where we had solved a few problem statements from scratch), we could also save a trained neural network model on disk so that we can reload it whenever required and use it directly to run the predictions. Here is an example:

```
# Save the model
model.save("spam_classifier.h5")
```

Playground

Who does not like to play? Additionally, what if there is already a website where one can select the problem statement, choose how the data may look in the real-world, add in the features, create a sample ANN architecture, and see how good the output comes through by selecting parameters like activation functions and epochs? The TensorFlow playground provides the same arena. It is accessible over **https://playground.TensorFlow.org**, and, while running an experiment, will look like the following:

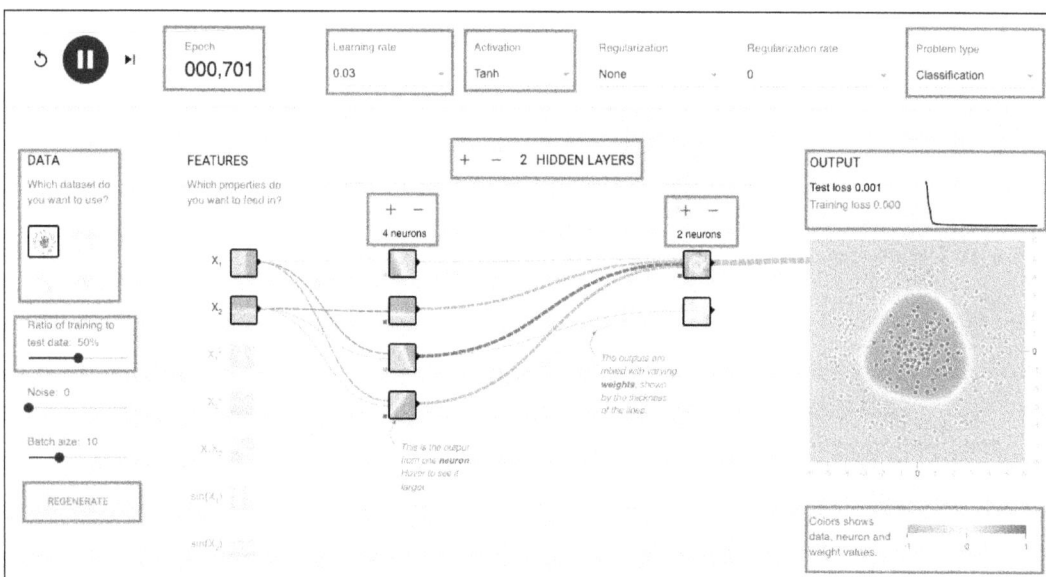

Figure 7.1: TensorFlow playground

Convolutional neural networks

In this section, we will understand a specific type of neural network that helps to solve visual use cases from day-to-day life.

Imagine a network of interconnected neurons inspired by the human brain's visual cortex. This is essentially what CNN is, in simple terms. It is a type of artificial neural network specifically designed to process visual data, like images and videos.

CNNs work by applying filters (small matrices) to the input image, extracting features like edges, shapes, and textures. These filters are like detectives searching for specific patterns in the image. Each filter creates a feature map, highlighting where it found its pattern. Multiple filters are used, generating multiple feature maps, each capturing different aspects of the image.

Pooling layers are used to make the network more efficient. They reduce the dimensionality of feature maps by selecting the maximum or average value from a region. This helps to focus on the most important information and reduces the number of parameters the network needs to learn.

Finally, fully connected layers, similar to traditional neural networks, connect all neurons from the previous layer to every neuron in the current layer. This allows the network to perform classification or regression tasks based on the extracted features.

CNNs are powerful because they can automatically learn and extract meaningful features from images, are robust to object location and orientation, and use parameter sharing for efficiency. They have revolutionized computer vision, enabling machines to see and understand the world around them.

From recognizing objects and faces in images to diagnosing diseases in medical scans, CNNs have a wide range of applications. They are the driving force behind self-driving cars, facial recognition systems, and many other innovative technologies.

Note: In some literature, CNNs are also referred to as ConvNets.

Historically, the research and findings in the area of CNNs started from studies by *Hubel* and *Wiesel*, who found that some neurons in the human brain's visual cortex fire up when presented with light in different directions. Then, there are edge or color or motion, or depth detecting neurons in our brain, too.

Note: Although an in-depth discussion of this particular (and other associated) research is out of scope for this book (since the material is a book by itself), these research areas would essentially form all the building blocks of how CNNs detect or identify, or process images given as inputs to them.

Let us learn each of these particulars. Quickly, let us look at a diagrammatic representation of how the architecture or design of a CNN is realized:

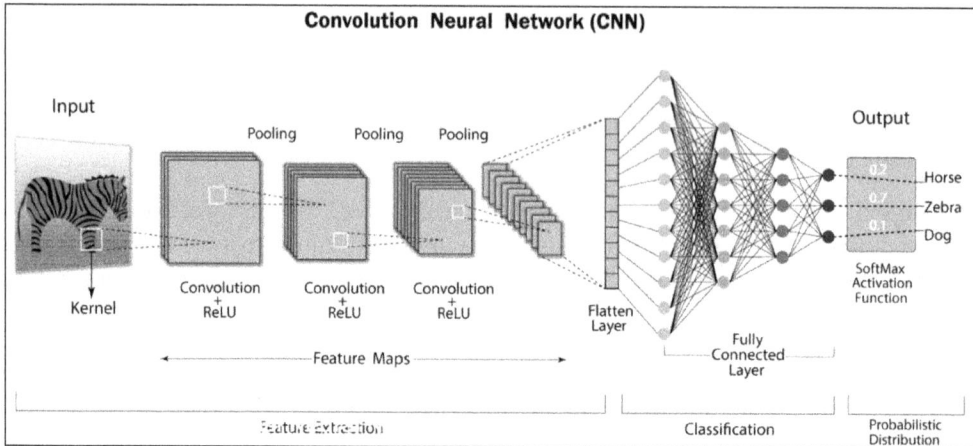

Figure 7.2: Convolutional neural network architecture

Filters

Filters, also called **Kernels** in CNN, are the heart and soul of CNNs. They are typically 3x3 or 5x5 (small) matrices, which scour the input image, searching for patterns of shape and finally extracting meaningful features or properties from any given image. The process of how these kernels slide over an image to find edges and other particulars of the image is called **convolution**. Convolution can be thought of as a generalization of dot products (referring to matrix algebra). Let us understand how they work step by step. Here is an example:

- **Convolution**:
  - The filter slides across the image, performing element-wise multiplication with the underlying pixels.
  - This operation is like comparing the filter's pattern to the local image region.

- **Feature map creation**:
  - The results of the multiplications are summed up, generating a single value.
  - This value represents the filter's response to the specific image region.
  - As the filter slides across the entire image, it generates a map of responses called a feature map.

- **Multiple filters, multiple perspectives**:
  - Different filters are used to detect different features.
  - For example, one filter might detect horizontal edges, while another might detect vertical edges.
  - Each filter creates its feature map, capturing a unique aspect of the image.

- **Depth and channels**:
  - o Filters can have multiple channels, allowing them to process color images.
  - o Each channel corresponds to a color channel (red, green, blue) in the image.
  - o The depth of a filter refers to the number of feature maps it generates.

It is important to understand the properties of these filters or kernels that the aforementioned process uses as follows:

- **Size**: Smaller filters detect fine details, while larger filters capture broader patterns.

- **Stride**:
  - o The step size with which the filter slides across the image.
  - o A stride of 1 means the filter moves one pixel at a time, while a stride of 2 means it skips a pixel.

- **Padding**: Adding pixels around the image border to control the output size of the feature map.

Filters are the key to CNNs' ability to automatically learn and extract meaningful features from images. They act as feature detectors, identifying edges, shapes, textures, and other important visual cues. By analyzing the patterns of activation in different feature maps, the network can understand the content of the image and perform tasks like classification, object detection, and image segmentation. Designing effective filters is crucial for CNN performance. Researchers and practitioners use various techniques to design and optimize filters, including the following:

- **Hand-crafted filters**: Designing filters based on prior knowledge about the task or domain.

- **Learned filters**: Training the filters along with the rest of the network using backpropagation.

- **Transfer learning**: Using pre-trained filters from other CNNs as a starting point.

Note: In the case of a grayscale image input, since there is only one channel in the image, the kernels in this case are 1D and simpler in nature. However, in the case of a color image, where we have three channels (Red, Green, and Blue), the kernel, in this case, is a 3D tensor with three channels. Imagine a Kernel like a cuboid in the latter case.

Pooling

Pooling is an essential component of CNNs, playing a crucial role in reducing the dimensionality of feature maps and improving computational efficiency. It is like a master summarizer, extracting the most important information from a large volume of data while discarding redundant details.

Imagine a CNN analyzing a high-resolution image. The initial convolutional layers extract a wealth of features, resulting in large feature maps. Processing these large maps can be computationally expensive and may lead to overfitting. Pooling comes to the rescue by summarizing the information in these maps, reducing their size and complexity.

Following is how pooling works in a typical CNN:

- **Defining the pooling region**: Pooling operates on a small region of the feature map, typically 2x2 or 3x3 in size. This region can be non-overlapping or overlapping, depending on the pooling method.

- **Extracting the essence**: Within the pooling region, the pooling operation selects a single value that represents the entire region. This value can be calculated using the following methods:

  o **Max pooling**: Selects the maximum value from the region. This is effective for capturing the most prominent features, such as the brightest pixels or the strongest edges.

  o **Average pooling**: Calculates the average value of all pixels in the region. This helps to reduce noise and smooth out the feature map.

  o **L2 pooling**: Computes the square root of the sum of squares of the pixel values in the region. This is less common but can be useful for certain tasks.

- **Creating the summarized map**: The selected value from each pooling region is used to create a new, smaller feature map. This map retains the essential information from the original map but with reduced dimensionality.

Here is a visual view of pooling in CNN, showing how max and average pooling work, for example:

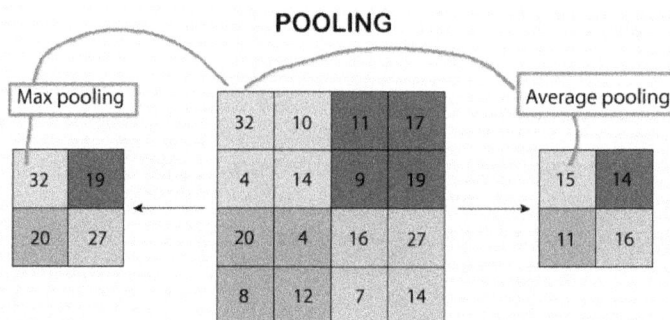

Figure 7.3: Pooling in convolutional neural networks

The benefits of pooling can be summarized as follows:

- **Reduced computational cost**: Smaller feature maps require fewer parameters and computations, making the network more efficient.

- **Improved generalization**: Pooling helps to reduce overfitting by making the network less sensitive to small variations in the input image.

- **Translation invariance**: Max pooling, in particular, makes the network more robust to small translations of objects in the image.

The choice of pooling method depends on the specific task and the characteristics of the data. Max pooling is often preferred for tasks like object detection and image classification, while average pooling can be beneficial for tasks like image segmentation.

Fully connected layers

Fully connected (**FC**) layers are the final stage in a CNN, responsible for making sense of the extracted features and translating them into meaningful outputs. They act as the decision-makers, analyzing the global context and drawing conclusions based on the accumulated knowledge.

Following is (overall) how a fully connected layer will work in a typical CNN design:

- **Flattening the feature maps**: The output of the convolutional and pooling layers consists of multiple feature maps. The FC layer starts by flattening these maps into a single long vector. This vector represents the entire set of extracted features from the input image.

- **Connecting the dots**: Each neuron in the FC layer is connected to every element in the flattened feature vector. This allows the layer to analyze the relationships between different features and consider the global context of the image.

- **Decision time**: The FC layer uses activation functions, such as ReLU or softmax, to transform the weighted sum of inputs into an output. This output can represent a class label for image classification, a bounding box for object detection, or a segmentation mask for image segmentation.

FC layers play a crucial role in integrating the local features extracted by the convolutional layers into a global understanding of the image. They consider the relationships between different features and make decisions based on the overall context. This ability to combine local and global information is essential for complex tasks like object recognition, scene understanding, and image generation.

The number of FC layers in a CNN can vary depending on the complexity of the task and the size of the dataset. A single FC layer is often sufficient for simple tasks, while more complex tasks may require multiple layers to capture the intricate relationships between features. However, adding too many FC layers can lead to overfitting and reduce the network's generalization ability.

FC layers are prone to overfitting, especially when dealing with large datasets. To mitigate this, regularization techniques like dropout and L2 regularization are often employed.

These techniques help to prevent the network from becoming overly reliant on specific features and improve its ability to generalize to unseen data.

In summary, fully connected layers are the final interpreters of visual information in CNNs. They analyze the extracted features, consider the global context, and make decisions based on the accumulated knowledge.

Now, let us move on and write some codes. We will take up a couple of use cases and see how we could solve them using CNNs using the Keras library from TensorFlow.

MNIST handwritten digits

Welcome to the Hello World use case of CNNs using the **Modified National Institute of Standards and Technology (MNIST)** dataset for classifying handwritten digits. The MNIST dataset is a widely used collection of handwritten digits commonly employed for training and evaluating various image processing systems and machine learning algorithms, particularly in the domain of computer vision and deep learning. The full dataset consists of 70,000 grayscale images of handwritten single digits between 0 and 9, with around.

60,000 images form the training set used to train machine learning models, and around 10,000 images comprise the testing set used to evaluate the performance of trained models. Each image is a small square with a dimension of 28 pixels by 28 pixels. Each image has a corresponding label indicating the digit it represents (0-9). The MNIST dataset's simplicity, accessibility, and well-defined structure make it a valuable resource for the following reasons:

- **Benchmarking**: It serves as a standard benchmark for comparing the performance of different image-classification algorithms.

- **Learning tool**: It is a popular starting point for beginners learning image processing and machine learning techniques due to its ease of use and readily available tools and libraries in various programming languages.

- **Development**: It is often used as a foundation for developing and testing more complex image recognition systems for real-world applications.

Let us start by importing the required libraries. Here is an example:

```
# Import necessary libraries
import TensorFlow as tf
from TensorFlow import keras
from TensorFlow.keras.datasets import mnist
from sklearn.model_selection import train_test_split
import matplotlib.pyplot as plt
import numpy as np
```

Next, let us download the MNIST data. This is already available as one of the free datasets in the Keras library. In its default format, the dataset is already available as training and testing sets, hence, one can directly import them as training and testing sets. In real-life scenarios, life will not be this easy; hence, in the next use cases, we will also learn how to prepare datasets, given that the input is a folder of image files. As of now, let us load the data and check how it looks in an already prepared format. Here is an example:

```
# Download and load MNIST dataset
(x_train, y_train), (x_test, y_test) = mnist.load_data()

# Print sample images from the dataset
plt.figure(figsize=(10, 10))
for i in range(25):
    plt.subplot(5, 5, i + 1)
    plt.imshow(x_train[i], cmap="gray")
    plt.title("Class: {}".format(y_train[i]))
plt.show()
```

Before we continue with the process, since this is a set of grayscale images, we will need to reshape the data as per their size and channels. To do so, we use the **.reshape** function from NumPy and convert them using properties, like channels, as the first value and pixel information in the next three values. Here is an example:

```
# Reshape data to 28x28x1 format
x_train = x_train.reshape(-1, 28, 28, 1)
x_test = x_test.reshape(-1, 28, 28, 1)
```

Now, since the image contains pixel values ranging from 0 to 255, one should normalize the pixel values within the range of 0-1 so that the computation in each epoch in these algorithms and designs becomes affordable in terms of computation. Here is an example:

```
# Normalize pixel values to range [0, 1]
x_train = x_train.astype("float32") / 255.0
x_test = x_test.astype("float32") / 255.0
```

Finally, we will encode the labels to categorical values. This will help the fully connected layer at the end of the model design to understand in which class a particular observation gets classified. Here is an example:

```
# One-hot encode labels
y_train = keras.utils.to_categorical(y_train, num_classes=10)
y_test = keras.utils.to_categorical(y_test, num_classes=10)
```

We can also (as a best practice) divide the training data into training and validation data so that we can keep the test data entirely separate from the training process. Here is an example:

```
# Split data into training and validation sets
x_train, x_val, y_train, y_val = train_test_split(x_train, y_train, test_
size=0.2, random_state=42)
```

Now, we can start creating a sample CNN model architecture, similar to what we did in the case of creating an ANN in the last section of this chapter.

Note: The main difference here is that we are no longer creating dense layers from start to finish.

For example, we are creating convolution layers and pooling layers, while at the very end, we conclude the design with a flattened layer and the final fully connected layer using (in this case) a **softmax activation** function. Here is an example:

```
# Define model architecture
model = keras.Sequential([
    keras.layers.Conv2D(32, (3, 3), activation="relu", input_shape=(28, 28,
1)),
    keras.layers.MaxPooling2D((2, 2)),
    keras.layers.Conv2D(64, (3, 3), activation="relu"),
    keras.layers.MaxPooling2D((2, 2)),
    keras.layers.Flatten(),
    keras.layers.Dense(10, activation="softmax")
])

# Compile model
model.compile(loss="categorical_crossentropy", optimizer="adam",
metrics=["accuracy"])

# Print model summary
model.summary()
```

We can now train the model with our training data and use the validation data to validate how the model is doing over each iteration. We can keep the history of model training so that we can plot it later on and find the right value of epoch by plotting the training and validation **loss** v/s the **epochs** using the following:

```
# Train model
history = model.fit(x_train, y_train, epochs=10, validation_data=(x_val,
y_val))

# Plot epochs vs loss to find optimal epochs
plt.plot(history.history["loss"], label="Training Loss")
plt.plot(history.history["val_loss"], label="Validation Loss")
plt.xlabel("Epochs")
plt.ylabel("Loss")
```

```
plt.legend()
plt.show()
```

Finally, one can validate the model (or its first version in this case) using the test data. Here is an example:

```
# Evaluate model on test set
loss, accuracy = model.evaluate(x_test, y_test)
print("Test loss:", loss)
print("Test accuracy:", accuracy)
```

Further in this chapter (in the next section), we will look into some practical real-world use cases of image classification and segmentation involving near to real-world data, and more data processing methods will be introduced.

Real-world object classification

In our first use case, we will try to predict whether a given image is that of a cat or a dog. This sounds childish, but imagine trying to detect the presence of a particular object or any category in a given image with a CNN model trained with enough good-quality data (in this case, labeled images). One would be able to use these networks in a variety of use cases across domains like security features, surveillance, etc. For this use case, we will make use of a labeled set of training and testing data (which we have kept on *Dropbox*) and see how the data is saved or labeled. We will see a unique way of labeling the data by putting them into folders with the name of the class.

Note: For executing this particular use case, we recommend using a graphical processing unit (GPU), which can be available from Google Colab with or without a subscription (readers are recommended to check this in depth before choosing the right option). In this chapter's GitHub repo, readers will find the Jupyter Notebook we have executed over Google Colab (free version).

First, we will start with downloading the data. Here is an example:

```
# this is a free set of Dropbox API where the data is available to all of
us for lifetime.
# contains the labelled training data.
# contains the test data (labelled).
!wget https://www.dropbox.com/s/t4pzwpvrzneb190/training_set.zip
!wget https://www.dropbox.com/s/i37jfni3d29raoc/test_set.zip
```

Once downloaded, let us unzip the data and see its contents. We expect 8005 images belonging to cats and dogs as part of the labeled training data and 2023 images belonging to the same two classes in the test data. Here is an example:

```
!unzip -o training_set.zip
!unzip -o test_set.zip
```

Further, we will check the contents in the test dataset (for example) and take one image of a cat and one of a dog to see how it looks. We can print images as well using the Matplotlib library in Python and, for that matter, some other libraries as well. Here is an example:

```
# Using matplotlib we will take some random images
# and visualise them so that we understand the input data we have
# and the level/type of pre-processing we need to do.
import matplotlib.pyplot as plt
import matplotlib.image as mpimg
img=mpimg.imread('/content/test_set/test_set/cats/cat.4001.jpg')
imgplot = plt.imshow(img)
plt.show()
# perform similar with an example of a Dog image from the Test set.
img=mpimg.imread('/content/test_set/test_set/dogs/dog.4003.jpg')
imgplot = plt.imshow(img)
plt.show()
```

Once the readers run this code, they will find out that the sizes of the randomly chosen images do not match. This means we have to perform pre-processing of the images in such a way that before we train our model, all the images should be of the same dimensions. Otherwise, our CNN architecture cannot be designed.

Now, we can start the actual problem-solving part, which starts with importing the libraries. Here is an example:

```
# importing all the required libraries.
import TensorFlow

# importing Image data generator library to understand the labels in the
images
# as well as to extract the matrix data for each image for training and
testing purposes.
# ImageDataGenerator will also be used to perform Data Augmentation.
from TensorFlow.keras.preprocessing.image import ImageDataGenerator

# usual libraries for ANN
from TensorFlow.keras.models import Sequential

# below, we have also importing the Convolution layer API and the Max
Pooling API.
# RELU or any choice of activation layer is part of the CONV2D API itself.
from TensorFlow.keras.layers import Dense, Conv2D, Flatten, Dropout,
MaxPooling2D, Activation

# below library is for preprocessing of the image.
from TensorFlow.keras.preprocessing import image
```

```
# Perform visualizations.
import matplotlib.pyplot as plt
import matplotlib.image as mpimg
```

Next, we can prepare the variables or parameters that we require to prepare the data. Here is an example:

```
# variables for data processing and modelling
img_width, img_height = 150,150  #width and height of the images
train_data_dir = r"/content/training_set/training_set"
validation_data_dir=r"/content/test_set/test_set"
nb_train_sample =100
nb_validation_samples =100
epochs =20
batch_size= 20
```

Before proceeding further, one needs to know that there are two ways to (overall) represent any color or grayscale image in a 3-dimensional array format. One is called the channel's last format, where we specify the dimensions of the image first, followed by the number of channels, while the other is called channels first, where the number of channels is represented first, followed by the image size.

Note: As we have learned earlier, in the case of a grayscale image, the channel is one, while for a color image, there are three channels.

Accordingly, one can write an example code as follows to find the right way of representation:

```
# let's first define the dimensions of the images.
# in some images, we have channel,width,height --> known as channel_first
representation.
# in some images we have width,height,channel --> otherwise
# that depends on the system from where the image was captured.
import TensorFlow.keras.backend as k
if k.image_data_format()=='channels_first':
    input_shape=(3, img_width, img_height) # fixing the input shape basis
the input images.
else:
    input_shape=(img_width,img_height,3)
print(input_shape)
```

Another important step in data preparation is to increase the variety of the data available to us for training the model and then testing its performance. There are many ways of doing so, while the most common method is called **data augmentation**, where for each given image, we can alter its rotation, or we can rescale it, or change its range, or even change the zoom within the image. These methods of augmenting data can be very helpful in creating 2x, 4x, 8x or even 10x times the available training and testing data. Let us try so on both our training and testing datasets. Here is an example:

```
# Create an object of the ImageDataGenerator
# perform the data augmentation to the training data.
# why? because we need more data during training, even if testing data
volume is comparatively lesser.

# for training data.
train_datagen=ImageDataGenerator (rescale=1. /255, # scaling the pixels in
the range of 0-255
                                  shear_range =0.2,
                                  zoom_range=0.2,
                                  horizontal_flip =True)
# for testing data
test_datagen=ImageDataGenerator (rescale=1. /255) # only scaling, no
augmentation.

# Now this, will generate training generator data
# Target_size = mentioned image_width and image_height
# Batch_size = 20 (already mentioned)
# Class_mode = binary(because here only two classes are there to classify)
train_generator =train_datagen.flow_from_directory(train_data_dir,
                                                    target_size =(img_
width,img_height),

                                                    batch_size=batch_size,
                                                    class_mode='binary',
                                                    classes=['cats','dogs']
                                                    )

# Now, this will generate testing generator data
# Target_size = mentioned image_width and image_height
# Batch_size = 20 (already mentioned)
# Class_mode = binary(because here only two classes are there to classify)
validation_generator =test_datagen.flow_from_directory(validation_data_dir,
                                                        target_size =(img_
width,img_height),

                                                        batch_size=batch_size,
                                                        class_mode='binary')
```

Since we have modified our dataset, we can now check for a handful of sample images by printing them again, just like we had printed a couple of images from the test set earlier. Here is an example:

```
# print some random images from the set of training and validation
datasets.
plt.figure(figsize=(12, 12))
for i in range(0, 15):
    plt.subplot(5, 3, i+1)
    for X_batch, Y_batch in train_generator:
        image = X_batch[0]
        plt.imshow(image)
        break
plt.tight_layout()
plt.show()
```

At this stage, we are ready to create our first CNN model. Let us start with a simple design and see how it performs in the given augmented training and test data. Here is an example:

```
# create a sequential model
# because: we need a sequence of layers to define our CNN components and
further, the ANN components.
# in some literature, or books, we would find the ANN components written as
FCN or fully connected layers.
# output of CNN should be a flatten layer, irrespective of the internal
stages of CNN operations.
model = Sequential()

# Add a convolution layer
# This function CONV2D allows to create convolutional neural network to
extract feature from the images
model.add(Conv2D(64, # number of neurons - i.e., the number of filters or
kernels
                (3,3), # filter size, it can be any size and any type
                input_shape=input_shape)) # 64 neurons with 3*3 filter

# add a RELU layer
model.add(Activation('relu'))

# add a max pooling layer using the MaxPooling2D API
# MaxPooling2D helps to reduce the size of the data
model.add(MaxPooling2D(pool_size=(2,2))) # dimension of the output from
each pool from each filter.

## Here we start with our ANN

# Converts multi dimensional array to 1D channel
# 1D channel = feature vector representation, required for ANN.
# we can call this our Input layer.
```

```
model.add(Flatten())

# first hidden layer
model.add(Dense(64)) # 64 neurons

# Adding the activation layer in our ANN as RELU
model.add(Activation('relu'))

# Output layer
# we can have 1 neuron and use Sigmoid function
# since we have a Binary classification problem
model.add(Dense(1))

# Add the activation function to our Output layer.
model.add(Activation('sigmoid')) # sigmoid activation function

# finally we print the summary of the model.
model.summary()
```

When our readers run the preceding code, one will find the summary of the model design, which can be explained as follows:

- 1792 parameters in the convolution layer are the trainable weights.

- In the RELU layer and max-pooling layer, we are simply performing calculations, hence, nothing is there to learn in back propagation!

- We have weights in the dense layer from the 1D vector representation of our input toward ANN.

  o In our case, we have 22429760 random trainable weights assigned to our input toward the ANN model.

- Inside the ANN model's hidden layer, we have 65 weights to be trained.

Hence, in total, we get 22431617 weights in our model, which will get estimated and re-evaluated over 20 epochs, which we have designed, during the back propagation stage. In the real-world, one will find far more complicated models than this starter design, where many more layers will be carefully designed and experimented with to find state-of-the-art outcomes. Let us now compile the model by defining the optimizer and the loss function. Here is an example:

```
# compilation of our new model (CNN + ANN) is
# exactly the same as we did in case of ANN
# since we have to define global set of hyperparameters for the entire
model.
model.compile(optimizer='rmsprop'
              loss='binary_crossentropy', # binary classification problem
              metrics=['accuracy'])
```

Now, let us call the appropriate function to start the training of our model. Here is an example:

```
# now we can train our model.
training = model.fit(train_generator, # training data which is generated
after augmentation
                    steps_per_epoch=nb_train_sample, # 100
                    epochs=epochs, # 20
                    validation_data=validation_generator,
                    validation_steps=nb_validation_samples # 100
                    )
```

Once the training is completed, one can visualize the **training** and validation **accuracy** as well as **loss** over **epoch**, similar to what we had done in our earlier use cases. Here is an example:

```
# importing library.
import matplotlib.pyplot as plt
# %matplotlib inline

# list all data in training
print(training.history.keys())

# summarize training for accuracy
plt.plot(training.history['accuracy'])
plt.plot(training.history['val_accuracy'])
plt.title('model accuracy')
plt.ylabel('accuracy')
plt.xlabel('epoch')
plt.legend(['train', 'test'], loc='upper left')
plt.show()

# summarize traning for loss
plt.plot(training.history['loss'])
plt.plot(training.history['val_loss'])
plt.title('model loss')
plt.ylabel('loss')
plt.xlabel('epoch')
plt.legend(['train', 'test'], loc='upper left')
plt.show()
```

Once one runs the above initially designed model, we will find a somewhat good outcome. In most cases, we should be able to predict the object (cat or dog) from a given image. However, one should test this at least with a couple of images at first and then improve the model with further design of additional layers in the network. To test how good or bad the initial model performs, one can (for example) use a code like the following:

```
# import the libraries.
from TensorFlow.keras.preprocessing import image
import numpy as np

# load a sample image
img_pred = image.load_img("/content/test_set/test_set/dogs/dog.4006.
jpg",target_size=(150,150))

# represent the sample test image in form of a matrix.
img_pred=image.img_to_array(img_pred)
img_pred=np.expand_dims(img_pred, axis=0)

# capturing the results from our model.
rslt = model.predict(img_pred) # similar .predict() function is used here,
just like we used in ANN or ML.

# print the results.
# the results from the network will be a number : 0 or 1.
# we have to manually convert it back into a readable format.
print(rslt)
if rslt[0][0]==1:
    prediction ="Dog"
else:
    prediction ="Cat"
print('Prediction: ',prediction)

# also along with the predictions display the same image.
img=mpimg.imread('/content/test_set/test_set/dogs/dog.4006.jpg')
imgplot = plt.imshow(img)
plt.show()
```

To further optimize the design, we can introduce some layers specifically to control overfitting. One proven way to do so is to add dropout layers. In simple words, we use dropout layers in any neural network to deactivate some neurons randomly to prevent overfitting of the model. One can add as many layers of dropouts as they see fit, but the final acceptable design remains a matter of experimentation. Other than dropouts, we can also implement a technique called **early stopping**, where during the model's training, it monitors a delta increase in validation accuracy (for example), and if after a certain value of epoch, the value does not change, the training stops. This also saves computation time to get the final model. Here is an example:

```python
# import libraries. (optional)
from keras.models import Sequential

# importing additionally the dropout and the batchnorm layer.
from keras.layers import Conv2D, MaxPooling2D, Dropout, Flatten, Dense,
Activation, BatchNormalization

# more optimization of the model.
# early stopping : stop the iterations when the we have not so
# visible change in accuracy or loss values.
# Learning Rate Reduction: as we approach Global minima,
# let's reduce the learning rate to slow our speed of declining the loss
function val.
from keras.callbacks import EarlyStopping, ReduceLROnPlateau

# one example of early stopping.
earlystop = EarlyStopping(monitor='val_accuracy', # accuracy is the
parameter of interest.
                          patience = 10, # how much time we will wait
                          min_delta = 0.01, # min change expected in the
acc value.
                          mode='max') # overall expectations --> accuracy
of the model should be Max()

# we are creating the network exactly as the previous design.
# we will just add the Dropout layer as a start.
model1 = Sequential()
model1.add(Conv2D(64,(3,3),input_shape=input_shape)) # 64 neurons with 3*3
filter
model1.add(Activation('relu'))
model1.add(MaxPooling2D(pool_size=(2,2)))
model1.add(Flatten()) # link between CNN and ANN
model1.add(Dense(64)) # 64 neurons
model1.add(Activation('relu'))
model1.add(Dropout(0.5))# Prevents overfitting of the model
model1.add(Dense(1)) # output layer
model1.add(Activation('sigmoid')) # sigmoid activation function
model1.summary()

# compile the new CNN model
model1.compile(optimizer='adam', # instead of RMSProp let' use Adam.
               loss='binary_crossentropy',
               metrics=['accuracy'])
```

```
model1.summary()

# fit the CNN model
training = model1.fit(train_generator,
                      steps_per_epoch=nb_train_sample,
                      epochs=10,
                      validation_data=validation_generator,
                      validation_steps=nb_validation_samples,
                      callbacks=[earlystop])
```

To see how well the model worked this time, we could use a similar code as we used previously to plot the **accuracy** and **loss** of the model over **epochs**. Here is an example:

```
import matplotlib.pyplot as plt
# %matplotlib inline

# list all data in training
print(training.history.keys())

# summarize training for accuracy
plt.plot(training.history['accuracy'])
plt.plot(training.history['val_accuracy'])
plt.title('model accuracy')
plt.ylabel('accuracy')
plt.xlabel('epoch')
plt.legend(['train', 'test'], loc='upper left')
plt.show()

# summarize traning for loss
plt.plot(training.history['loss'])
plt.plot(training.history['val_loss'])
plt.title('model loss')
plt.ylabel('loss')
plt.xlabel('epoch')
plt.legend(['train', 'test'], loc='upper left')
plt.show()
```

For brevity, we are not repeating the code for predicting on a couple of sample images of a cat and dog, but we should repeat the step here again to validate how good the new model is, especially with complex images (for example, a cat looking like a dog or vice versa).

Another good method one may implement to better their custom CNN models is batch normalization, which is equally applicable in the case of ANNs as well. Batch normalization in neural networks is like having a pit crew for your data during training. Imagine training data is a bunch of race cars (activations) going through different training stages (layers). The pit crew (batch normalization) standardizes each car's performance (activation) within a small group (mini batch). They tweak things like the engine (weights) to make sure all the cars are on a level playing field (similar distribution) for the next race (training step). This helps the cars learn at a steadier pace (faster convergence) and avoids some common training issues. It is like having a well-oiled training process. Let us see the following sample code of how we can use this technique in our use case:

```python
# Create the next model iteration
# here we will introduce batch normalization along with Dropout
from keras.models import Sequential
from keras.layers import Conv2D, MaxPooling2D, Dropout, Flatten, Dense,
Activation, BatchNormalization
from keras.callbacks import EarlyStopping, ReduceLROnPlateau

# we will continue using Early stopping
earlystop = EarlyStopping(monitor='val_accuracy', patience = 5, min_delta =
0.01, mode='max')

# start of our sequential model
model2 = Sequential()

# stage 1 of CNN --> only in the first stage we need to mention the input
size.
model2.add(Conv2D(32,(3,3),input_shape=input_shape)) # Keras will by
default take RELU which is as per the design/research
#model2.add(Conv2D(32, (3, 3), activation='relu', input_shape=(IMAGE_WIDTH,
IMAGE_HEIGHT, IMAGE_CHANNELS)))
model2.add(BatchNormalization()) # used inside CNN
model2.add(MaxPooling2D(pool_size=(2, 2)))
model2.add(Dropout(0.25))

# Stage 2 of CNN
model2.add(Conv2D(64, (3, 3), activation='relu')) # this is another way to
specify that we would use RELU
model2.add(BatchNormalization())
model2.add(MaxPooling2D(pool_size=(2, 2)))
model2.add(Dropout(0.25))

# Stage 3 of CNN
model2.add(Conv2D(128, (3, 3), activation='relu'))
model2.add(BatchNormalization())
model2.add(MaxPooling2D(pool_size=(2, 2)))
model2.add(Dropout(0.25))
```

```
# Finally we have the ANN.
# we will try this time with Softmax function.
model2.add(Flatten())
model2.add(Dense(512, activation='relu'))
model2.add(BatchNormalization())
model2.add(Dropout(0.5))
model2.add(Dense(1, activation='softmax')) # 2 because we have cat and dog
classes

# compile the new CNN model
model2.compile(optimizer='rmsprop', # falling back from Adam
            loss='binary_crossentropy',
            metrics=['accuracy'])
model2.summary()

# fit the new CNN model
training = model2.fit(train_generator,
                    steps_per_epoch=nb_train_sample,
                    epochs=epochs,
                    validation_data=validation_generator,
                    validation_steps=nb_validation_samples,
                    callbacks=[earlystop])
```

Again, similar code previously used can be reused to plot the **accuracy** v/s **loss** for this model design and check how well all of the components are working together and also if this new design is effective as compared to the previous ones. After all the relevant experimentations are done, one should (as a best practice) offload or save the model. Ideally, this should be done after each design so that we can version them and also test them separately (outside the scope of this experiment) with different datasets. Following is a sample code of how one can save or export a custom CNN model:

```
# load the libraries.
import json
from keras.models import model_from_json
from keras.models import load_model
from keras.preprocessing import image
import numpy as np

# export the model as JSON.
model_json = model2.to_json()
with open("model2.json", "w") as json_file:
    json_file.write(model_json)

# along with the model, we can also save the weights
```

```
# these are the estimated weights or trained weights in our model.
# this is because some applications or libraries may also require the
weights as the input.
model.save_weights('first_try.h5')
print("[INFO] Saved model to disk")
```

Transfer learning

After at least three experiments, we may not have reached a good place with this model. Are there any other efficient ways of tackling such problems? It looks like there is one that is **transfer learning**. The idea is simple. For example, if we have a friend who is an expert in drawing sketches, and we take her help in drawing a new sketch of the objects of my interest, with some customizations? In this case, one does not necessarily invest time in finding a teacher to learn how to sketch themselves. We are simply reusing an existing set of knowledge. This is the same concept we use in the industry in the case of transfer learning, where to avoid the massive amount of computational resources and quality data that production grade CNN models require (in the real-world), we can take help from any of the existing and pre-trained CNN models (which serves our use case).

There are many pre-trained and industry-accepted CNN models, some of which will be looked into now, which are already trained on massive datasets like ImageNet with millions of images. For example, using which an AI engineer can transfer its learned features (like recognizing edges, shapes, and textures) to one's own image recognition or object classification tasks. All we need to do is to optionally fine-tune the final layer(s) of the model specifically with our dataset, allowing our model to specialize in our area of interest or use case. Out of the many benefits of transfer learning, let us look into the following three of the most important ones:

- **Faster training**: Leverage pre-existing knowledge, saving time and resources compared to training from scratch.

- **Improved performance**: Pre-trained models often achieve high accuracy due to the vast datasets they are trained on.

- **Flexibility**: Applicable to various image recognition tasks by fine-tuning the final layers.

Now, let us look into some of the most common and invariably used pre-trained CNN models, along with their pros and cons as follows:

- **Visual Geometry Group 16 (VGG16)**:
    - **Pros**: Renowned for its high accuracy, achieving excellent performance on various image recognition tasks like classification, object detection, and image segmentation. This makes it a popular choice for researchers and developers.

- o **Cons**: The depth (16 layers) translates to higher computational cost. Training and running VGG16 requires significant processing power and memory, making it less suitable for resource-constrained environments or real-time applications.

- **LeNet**:

  - o **Pros**: Lightweight and efficient, making it a great choice for mobile applications or situations with limited resources. Its simplicity allows for faster training compared to deeper models.

  - o **Cons**: Accuracy might not be as high as deeper models, especially for complex tasks with intricate details. For very demanding image recognition problems, LeNet might not be powerful enough.

- **Residual Network (ResNet)**:

  - o **Pros**: Overcomes the vanishing gradient problem that can hinder training in deep networks. This allows ResNet to achieve impressive accuracy even with a high number of layers (often exceeding 100). Offers a good balance between accuracy and computational cost compared to VGG16.

  - o **Cons**: Training can still be computationally expensive due to its depth. Choosing the appropriate depth (number of layers) for your specific task is crucial.

- **Inception (developed by Google)**:

  - o **Pros**: Known for its efficient use of parameters, achieving high accuracy with a relatively smaller number of layers compared to VGG16. This makes it a good compromise between accuracy and efficiency. Inception models often incorporate multiple filter sizes within a single layer, allowing them to capture diverse image features.

  - o **Cons**: Training complexity can be higher compared to simpler models like LeNet. Understanding the architecture might require a deeper grasp of CNN concepts.

- **MobileNet**:

  - o **Pros**: Specifically designed for mobile and embedded devices. Extremely lightweight and efficient, making it ideal for real-time applications with limited resources.

  - o **Cons**: Accuracy might be lower compared to deeper models like VGG16. The trade-off here is prioritizing efficiency over top-notch accuracy for mobile environments.

The optimal model depends on your specific project requirements. The following are some key factors to consider:

- **Task complexity**: For very intricate tasks with high detail, deeper models like VGG16 or ResNet might be preferred.

- **Computational resources**: If processing power and memory are limited, explore lightweight models like LeNet or MobileNet.

- **Dataset size**: Transfer learning is especially beneficial when your dataset is relatively small. Leverage the pre-trained model's knowledge to compensate for limited data.

- **Real-time vs. offline processing**: For real-time applications, prioritize efficiency (MobileNet). For offline tasks where processing power is readily available, accuracy might be a bigger concern (VGG16, ResNet).

Beyond these examples, numerous other pre-trained CNN models exist, each with its unique strengths and suitability for specific scenarios. Frameworks like TensorFlow Hub and PyTorch Hub provide extensive libraries of pre-trained models to explore.

Note: Experimentation is the key. One should try different pre-trained models with transfer learning to see what works best for our image recognition task. By understanding the trade-offs and exploring various options, one can leverage the power of pre-trained CNNs to achieve remarkable results in our projects.

Before concluding this section, let us see the following how we could have used VGG16 as an example in our previous use case of identifying cats or dogs in a given image:

```
from TensorFlow import keras
from TensorFlow.keras.models import Sequential
from TensorFlow.keras import layers
from TensorFlow.keras.layers import Conv2D, MaxPooling2D, Dropout, Flatten,
Dense, Activation,GlobalMaxPooling2D
from TensorFlow.keras import applications
from TensorFlow.keras.preprocessing.image import ImageDataGenerator
from TensorFlow.keras import optimizers
from TensorFlow.keras.applications import VGG16
from TensorFlow.keras.models import Model

image_size = 150
input_shape = (image_size, image_size, 3)

epochs = 20
batch_size = 16

pre_trained_model = VGG16(input_shape=input_shape,
                          include_top=False,
```

```
                        weights="imagenet")

# we don't want to retrain the first 15 layers with our data.
# why? because we are confident that since we have used VGG16 which is
already trained on 1000 class based data
# it already has good knowledge about these objects, which is jmerely our
assumption.
for layer in pre_trained_model.layers[:15]:
    layer.trainable = False

# for our case, we would like to train the last layer
# since VGG16 was trained with 1000 classes but we have binary
classification problem.
for layer in pre_trained_model.layers[15:]:
    layer.trainable = True

last_layer = pre_trained_model.get_layer('block5_pool')
last_output = last_layer.output

# Flatten the output layer to 1 dimension
x = GlobalMaxPooling2D()(last_output) # does the same work as Flatten()
function.

# Add a fully connected layer with 512 hidden units and ReLU activation
x = Dense(512, activation='relu')(x) # functional programming syntax.

# Add a dropout rate of 0.5
x = Dropout(0.5)(x)

# Add a final sigmoid layer for classification
x = layers.Dense(1, activation='sigmoid')(x)

model3 = Model(pre_trained_model.input, # design of VGG16 from GitHub of
Keras.
                x) # adding our own ANN layer.


# compile the new model
model3.compile(loss='binary_crossentropy',
            optimizer=optimizers.SGD(lr=1e-4, momentum=0.9), # homework:
try and see if Adam performs better in this case.
            metrics=['accuracy'])

model3.summary()

# fit the new CNN model with VGG16
training = model3.fit(train_generator,
```

```
                    steps_per_epoch=nb_train_sample,
                    epochs=epochs,
                    validation_data=validation_generator,
                    validation_steps=nb_validation_samples,
                    callbacks=[earlystop])
```

It is recommended that we pay special attention to the code above in understanding how only the final layer(s) of the model is trained on our data of cats and dogs, while the rest of the layers (and hence the pre-trained weights of the VGG16 model) is retained and reused for its already existent vast knowledge.

One can now use the same snippets of code we used earlier to first plot the **accuracy** vs. **loss** over **epoch** and then to check for the accuracy of the model with random complicated images of cats and dogs to see the benefits that transfer learning brings to the table.

Practical uses and limitations

CNNs have revolutionized the field of computer vision, achieving remarkable feats in tasks like image recognition, object detection, and image segmentation. Their ability to learn complex patterns from vast amounts of data has propelled advancements in diverse areas, impacting industries and shaping user experiences. However, CNNs also possess limitations that researchers are actively addressing. This exploration delves into the practical uses, cutting-edge applications, and inherent limitations of CNNs, incorporating recent findings from leading tech companies and research institutions.

Some of the practical implementations (use cases) of CNN are as follows:

- **Image recognition and classification**: CNNs excel at recognizing and classifying objects in images. Google utilizes them in its Google Photos, for example, enabling users to search and organize their photo libraries effortlessly based on content (for example, searching for beach photos). Similarly, Facebook leverages CNNs in its facial recognition technology, allowing users to tag friends in photos with impressive accuracy. A 2021 research paper by Facebook AI (*A Survey on Deep Face Recognition Techniques*. Refer to the link **https://arxiv.org/abs/2004.08185**) explores advancements in facial recognition using CNNs, highlighting their ability to handle pose variations, occlusions, and challenging lighting conditions.

- **Object detection and localization**: CNNs are adept at detecting and pinpointing the location of objects within an image. Microsoft employs this capability in its Microsoft Azure object detection service, enabling developers to build applications that identify and localize objects in real time (for example, identifying cars in traffic footage). Additionally, self-driving car technology heavily relies on CNNs for object detection, allowing autonomous vehicles to recognize pedestrians, traffic signs, and other crucial elements on the road. A 2023 research paper by *Waymo, a self-driving car company owned by Alphabet* (Google's parent company), details how they leverage CNNs for robust object detection in diverse driving scenarios (Waymo research refer to the link **https://waymo.com/research/**).

- **Image segmentation**: CNNs can segment images, separating objects from the background or distinguishing between different parts of an image. This has applications in medical imaging, where CNNs can be trained to segment tumors or specific organs in medical scans. A 2022 study by *Google AI (Exploring the Limits of Weakly-Supervised Segmentation*. Refer to this link **https://arxiv.org/abs/2204.05481**) investigates techniques for improving CNN performance in weakly supervised segmentation tasks, where training data has limited annotations. This research paves the way for more efficient medical image analysis.

- **Video analysis and understanding**: CNNs are increasingly being used for video analysis, enabling applications like action recognition and anomaly detection. For instance, security systems can utilize CNN-powered video analysis to detect suspicious activities. Furthermore, researchers at Facebook AI are exploring the use of CNNs for video summarization, automatically generating concise clips that capture the essence of a longer video (video summarization with attentive 3D CNNs. Refer to this link **https://arxiv.org/abs/1909.12909**).

- **Generative applications**: While primarily used for analysis, CNNs are also venturing into generative tasks, the new kid on the block about whom everyone is equally interested. Techniques like **generative adversarial networks (GANs)**, which utilize CNNs as building blocks, can create realistic images and even manipulate existing ones. Google AI has explored the potential of GANs for artistic style transfer, allowing users to transform images in the style of famous painters (A learned representation for artistic style transfer. Refer to the link **https://arxiv.org/abs/1703.04360**).

Beyond established applications, researchers are continuously exploring novel ways to leverage CNNs as follows:

- **Explainable AI**: A significant focus is on developing explainable AI techniques to understand how CNNs arrive at their decisions. This is crucial for building trust in AI systems, particularly in critical domains like healthcare. A 2023 paper by *Microsoft Research (Towards Interpretable Convolutional Neural Networks*. Refer to this link **https://arxiv.org/abs/2302.11852**) proposes methods for interpreting CNN outputs, providing insights into their reasoning process.

- **Resource efficiency**: As CNNs become more complex, their computational demands soar. training and deploying large models can require significant hardware resources. To address this, researchers are actively exploring the following techniques to make CNNs more efficient:

    o **Model pruning**: This method involves removing redundant connections and filters within the CNN architecture, resulting in a smaller and faster model with minimal accuracy loss. Google AI has published research on pruning frameworks that can accelerate CNNs while maintaining performance (*Pruning Frameworks for Faster and More Accurate CNNs*. Refer to this link **https://arxiv.org/abs/1806.08868**).

o **Quantization**: This technique reduces the precision of weights and activations within the CNN, typically from 32-bit floating-point numbers to lower-precision formats like 8-bit integers. This significantly reduces the model size and computational requirements while enabling deployment on devices with limited resources. Facebook AI has explored quantization techniques for deploying CNNs on mobile and embedded devices (*FBNetV3: Quantized Inverted Bottleneck Net for Mobile and Embedded Vision Applications*. Refer to this link **https://arxiv.org/abs/2103.11629**).

o **Lifelong learning**: Traditional CNNs require retraining on vast amounts of data whenever new information needs to be incorporated. Researchers are exploring techniques for lifelong learning, enabling CNNs to continuously learn and adapt to new data streams without forgetting previously learned knowledge. This is crucial for real-world scenarios where data is constantly evolving. A 2022 paper by Microsoft Research proposes a method for lifelong learning in CNNs using knowledge distillation (*Overcoming Catastrophic Forgetting with Balanced Knowledge Distillation*. Refer to this link **https://arxiv.org/abs/2203.16924**).

o **Transfer learning and few-shot learning**: CNNs pre-trained on massive datasets can be fine-tuned for specific tasks using transfer learning. This significantly reduces the amount of data required for training new models. Additionally, researchers are exploring few-shot learning techniques, enabling CNNs to learn from very limited datasets. This is crucial for scenarios where labelled data is scarce. A 2021 study by Google AI investigates meta-learning approaches for few-shot learning in CNNs (*Benchmarking Few-Shot Visual Learning for Object Recognition*. Refer to this link **https://arxiv.org/abs/2103.10585**).

These are just a few examples of the ongoing research efforts to push the boundaries of CNNs. We can expect even more innovative applications and advancements in this powerful technology in the near future.

Conclusion

In this chapter, we covered the approaches, possible solution(s), and best practices of software engineering for AI or ML to some extent as a start. We have seen how to perform rapid experimentations with Jupyter Notebooks and also how to start building an AI application in the format of any other software from its initial days of design and development. To know how to create effective ML applications, we have looked into three different real-world use cases of supervised and unsupervised learning (combined) and have seen the common ways to prepare data, create models, evaluate them, and finally improve them.

In the next chapter, we are going to start learning about computer vision, its applications in machine learning, and how to create AI applications using Python, which solves use cases in the real-world involving visual problem statements.

Exercises

1. In the regression use case, take each logical section of the notebook, convert it into a Python script, and create the final structure of the project in the same form as we did for the classification use case.

2. In the classification use case, the main.py program does everything in a single place and sequence. This makes the file quite verbose. Write another version of main.py to make it cleaner. What would one require to achieve this? Here are a few areas of improvement:

    a. Do we need more utilities or functions to make it clean?

    b. Do we need functions within main.py itself to make the code cleaner?

3. In the clustering exercise, let us try the following:

    a. In the reusable function to replace unknown information (given by ?), make it more generic by adding more function variables (like the character to be replaced, etc.)

    b. While modeling, we have made use of the K-means clustering model only. Check the scikit-learn documentation and try the DBSCAN model on the same data to see if we get better and lower WCSS values.

4. In the ANN model use-case, try to implement the following examples:

    a. Try adding more layers like dropouts and batch normalization, similar to what we tried in the CNN section, and document cases where they work well and where they do not.

    b. While trying with dropouts, try different values than 0.5 to see variations in model performance.

5. In the CNN example, use the following case of object detection:

    a. Try creating a similar model with your images and one of your friends or family members with their permission.

    b. Document the effects of using a smaller sample size for training a custom model as compared to a pre-trained model like LeNet or VGG16.

CHAPTER 8
Natural Language Processing

Introduction

This chapter explains the basics of **natural language processing** (**NLP**), which is by far one of the most interesting as well as challenging fields of study in AI or ML alongside CNNs. We will learn the basics of how to identify parts of speech and text, followed by various ways of representing textual information in numbers so that we can train ML models. Further, we will see some new neural network architectures in brief, like **recurrent neural networks** (**RNNs**) and **long short-term memory** (**LSTMs**), including the infamous transformer architecture (which powers the recent growth of generative AI applications) with a deep dive in *Chapter 9, Sequence Modelling and Transformers*. We will also discuss the base on the variety of applications (in the form of case studies) of the systems powered by sophisticated NLP tasks and modelling techniques.

Structure

The chapter covers the following topics:

- Importance of natural language processing
- Natural language data analysis
- Introduction to sequential models

- Sentiment analysis
- Case studies

Objectives

By the end of this chapter, the readers will be able to introduce themselves to NLP and its nuances. Further, readers are introduced to the basics of how to analyze and process text, followed by a variety of methods and algorithms to engineer and recognize patterns from textual data. Finally, readers are introduced to useful case studies covering the most built applications around NLP.

Importance of natural language processing

As software engineers, we are accustomed to the precise syntax and structured logic of programming languages. It is equally difficult to realize the technical complexities of human language. This is where NLP, yet another applied and research subfield of AI and ML, steps in.

Note: One should not consider NLP merely as another paradigm in AI/ML, as it is a vast field of study with years of research powering it. Check https://research.google/ for example.

NLP is the art and science of enabling computers to understand, interpret, and generate human language in a way that is both meaningful and useful. It empowers machines to process vast amounts of unstructured textual data, extracting insights, responding to queries, translating between languages, and even generating creative content.

NLP is the driving force behind a wide array of applications you interact with daily. Let us try and understand this with some areas of applications and use cases are as follows:

- **Text understanding**: At its core, NLP helps computers understand written text. It analyzes the structure, meaning, and context of words and sentences.

- **Language modeling**: NLP models are trained to predict the probability of the next word in a sequence. This helps in understanding context and generating coherent sentences.

- **Named entity recognition (NER)**: It identifies and categorizes named entities (like people, organizations, and locations) within a text. For example, in the sentence *Steve Jobs founded Apple in California*, NER would recognize *Steve Jobs* as a person and *Apple* and *California* as organizations and locations, respectively.

- **Sentiment analysis**: This analyzes the sentiment or mood expressed in a piece of text. It could determine if a review is positive, negative, or neutral, for instance.

- **Machine translation**: NLP helps in translating text from one language to another, like Google Translate. It involves understanding the meaning of words and phrases in different languages.

- **Question answering**: NLP can also be used to build systems that answer questions posed in natural language. These systems understand the question, search for relevant information, and provide an accurate answer.

- **Chatbots and virtual assistants**: NLP powers chatbots and virtual assistants like Siri or Alexa. These systems understand spoken commands or written messages and respond accordingly.

- **Summarization**: NLP techniques can be used to summarize large amounts of text into shorter, more concise versions while retaining the essential information.

- **Text generation**: With advancements like OpenAI's ChatGPT or Google's Gemini models, NLP can generate human-like text based on a given prompt. This is used in tasks like writing assistance, content generation, and more.

Note: NLP is a vast and continuously evolving field with applications in various domains, such as healthcare, finance, customer service, and more.

Let us look at some pros and cons of the existing NLP systems based on their state of writing this book.

The following are the pros:

- **Improved communication**: NLP can facilitate more natural and effective communication between humans and machines. This is particularly useful for tasks such as customer service, where chatbots can provide quick and efficient responses to customer inquiries.

- **Enhanced efficiency**: NLP can automate many tasks that were previously done manually, such as data entry and document analysis. This can free up human workers to focus on more complex tasks and improve overall productivity.

- **Greater accessibility**: NLP can make information and services more accessible to people with disabilities. For example, text-to-speech software can help people with visual impairments read online content, while automatic captioning can make videos accessible to people with hearing impairments.

- **Insights from unstructured data**: NLP can unlock valuable insights from unstructured data, such as social media posts, customer reviews, and news articles. This data can be used to improve decision-making, understand customer sentiment, and identify emerging trends.

- **Personalized experiences**: NLP can be used to personalize the user experience across various applications. For example, recommendation systems can suggest products or services that are likely to be of interest to the user, while personalized news feeds can provide users with relevant and timely information.

The following are the cons:

- **Bias and discrimination**: NLP models are trained on large datasets of text and code. If these datasets contain biases, the models can perpetuate and amplify these biases. This can lead to discriminatory outcomes, such as biased hiring decisions or unfair loan approvals.

- **Privacy concerns**: NLP can be used to analyze and interpret personal data, such as emails, social media posts, and browsing history. This raises concerns about privacy and the potential for misuse of personal information.

- **Lack of explainability**: Many NLP models are black boxes, meaning that it is difficult to understand how they arrive at their decisions. This lack of Explainability can make it difficult to trust the results of NLP models and to identify and address potential biases or errors.

- **Limited contextual understanding**: While NLP models can process and understand language to a certain extent, they still lack the full contextual understanding of humans. This can lead to misinterpretations and errors, especially when dealing with complex or nuanced language.

- **High cost of development**: Developing and deploying NLP models can be expensive, requiring significant resources and expertise. This can limit the accessibility of NLP technology to smaller companies and organizations.

NLP is a powerful tool with the potential to revolutionize many aspects of our lives. However, it is important to be aware of the potential drawbacks of NLP and to use it responsibly. By addressing the challenges of bias, privacy, explainability, and cost, we can harness the power of NLP to create a more equitable and efficient future.

Now, let us look at some important aspects of data analysis using NLP. We will start with the basics and then learn hands-on implementation.

Natural language data analysis

Text pre-processing are crucial steps in any NLP task. They are the foundation upon which complex models like language translation, sentiment analysis, and text generation operate. Just as a chef meticulously prepares ingredients before cooking, NLP practitioners must meticulously prepare text data before feeding it to machine learning models. This section will be an introduction to text pre-processing. We will explore various methods and techniques, providing a comprehensive understanding of how text data is transformed into a format suitable for machine learning algorithms.

Imagine a painter starting a masterpiece. Before applying vibrant hues, they meticulously prepare the canvas. Similarly, text pre-processing prepares the raw text data for the painting of ML models. It removes unwanted elements and inconsistencies, ensuring a clean and uniform foundation. Following are the key steps in text pre-processing:

- **Cleaning**: This involves removing noise and irrelevant information from the text. Noise can be anything from punctuation marks and special characters to HTML tags and URLs. Cleaning ensures that the model focuses on the actual content rather than on extraneous elements.

- **Normalization**: This step aims to establish consistency in the text data. It includes tasks like converting text to lowercase, handling different variations of a word (for example, *running*, *ran*, and *runs*), and fixing inconsistencies in spacing and punctuation. Normalization helps the model recognize variations of the same word and treat them similarly.

- **Stop word removal**: Stop words are common words like *the*, *a*, and *is* that carry little meaning. Removing them reduces the data size and improves the efficiency of the model without significantly impacting its performance.

- **Stemming and lemmatization**: These techniques reduce words to their base forms. Stemming removes suffixes and prefixes, while lemmatization returns the dictionary form of a word. Both techniques improve the model's ability to recognize different forms of the same word.

Once the text is cleaned and normalized, it is time to break it down into its fundamental units, that is, tokens. Tokenization essentially splits the text into individual words, sentences, or other meaningful units, depending on the specific task.

The following are some common tokenization methods:

- **Word-level tokenization**: This is the simplest approach, where each word is treated as a separate token. This method is suitable for tasks where word order is crucial, such as sentiment analysis.

- **Sentence-level tokenization**: This method divides the text into sentences, considering punctuation marks as delimiters. This is useful for tasks like text summarization or machine translation.

- **Character-level tokenization**: This method breaks the text into individual characters, regardless of word boundaries. This approach can be beneficial when dealing with unknown words or languages with complex morphology.

- **N-gram tokenization**: This technique involves splitting the text into overlapping sequences of n characters or words. This captures word order and context, making it suitable for tasks like language modeling and text generation.

Text pre-processing and tokenization work together to prepare raw text data for machine learning algorithms. Pre-processing cleans and normalizes the text, removing irrelevant information and inconsistencies. Tokenization then splits the text into meaningful units, depending on the specific task.

Once these essential steps are completed, the processed and tokenized text data can be fed into machine learning models. These models can then perform tasks like sentiment analysis, text summarization, and language translation, extracting valuable insights and generating meaningful outputs from the prepared text data. Let us try to implement some of these concepts using two prominent libraries in Python, such as **Natural Language Toolkit** (**NLTK**) and spaCy.

NLTK is a go-to library for NLP-related tasks in Python. It has many inbuilt datasets, which one can download, along with methods to perform text pre-processing. In the following example, let us take the generally available SMS spam dataset from the *UCI ML Repository*, which essentially contains two fields (separated by tabs). The first one gives the class (ham or spam), and the second one gives the SMS text belonging to that text. This is pre-labelled data available publicly, wherein the occurrence of spam SMS is more than ham. Let us start by importing the libraries that we require for this task, many of which will be required for any experimentations we perform the following use case:

```
# Import all required libraries
import string
import random
import pandas as pd
import numpy as np
import matplotlib.pyplot as plt
import seaborn as sns
import nltk
from nltk.tokenize import word_tokenize
from nltk.probability import FreqDist
from nltk.tokenize import regexp_tokenize
from nltk.stem import PorterStemmer
from nltk.stem import WordNetLemmatizer
from nltk.corpus import stopwords
from nltk import ne_chunk
from sklearn.feature_extraction.text import TfidfVectorizer
from sklearn.feature_extraction.text import CountVectorizer
from sklearn.preprocessing import LabelEncoder
from sklearn.model_selection import train_test_split
from sklearn.naive_bayes import MultinomialNB
from sklearn.metrics import classification_report
from imblearn.over_sampling import SMOTE
```

While one works with the NLTK library, we need to download any required corpus of text, in this case, the collection of stop words. From the NLTK documentation, one can find a list of all corpus available out-of-the-box from the library and then download each of the required datasets for experimentation purposes. Here is a sample code:

```
# Download NLTK stopwords
nltk.download("stopwords")
```

Next, let us load the downloaded SMS spam dataset. A simple Google search on the UCI ML Repository will give one the download link for this dataset, which can be downloaded as a ZIP file and unzipped in the working folder using the following:

```
# load SMS Spam dataset
df = pd.read_csv('SMSSpamCollection', delimiter='\t', names=['class',
'text'])
df.head()
```

We can further check the overall distribution of the classes and also the most frequent SMS text in each class (ham or spam):

```
# check for class value counts
df['class'].value_counts()

# most frequent SMS in each class
df.groupby('class').describe()
```

To perform the basic set of cleaning, let us create a reusable utility function. In this function, we will convert the text to lowercase, remove the stop words, remove the punctuations, perform the stemming of each word, and return the processed text for each SMS text:

```
# Utility function to perform
# basic cleaning of SMS text
def process(text):
    """
    Given the input as the SMS Text, perform initial cleaning.
    """
    # convert to lower case
    text = text.lower()

    # remove punctuations
    text = ''.join([t for t in text if t not in string.punctuation])

    # remove stopwords
    text = [t for t in text.split() if t not in stopwords.words('english')]

    # perform stemming
    port_stem = PorterStemmer()
    text = [port_stem.stem(t) for t in text]

    # return each token
    return text
```

Before we apply the utility function to all the data and chunk them, we can test it on random values of the SMS text, using a code similar to the following. This generates a random number between 0 and the number of rows in the dataset to generate a random index to select an SMS text to be passed into the utility function:

```
# get the no. of rows in the data
df_num_rows = df.shape[0]

# generate a random no. in the range
rand_index = random.randint(0, df_num_rows+1)

# take the random text with
# the random index
text = process(df['text'][rand_index])

# print text
print(f"Original SMS Text: {df['text'][rand_index]}")
print(f"Processed SMS Text: {text}")
```

One sample output from one of our runs (while testing out this code) is as follows. One would find that by this processing, we are getting rid of all the stop words as well as other entities from the text, focusing only on the essential words, which indicate the relevance or essence of the text in a particular SMS text. This method helps to understand what the context is all about in a given text and hence helps us finally to understand if the SMS is spam or ham.

Note: This approach may end up taking away some crucial information, which gives us more context about why a particular statement (in some other equally important use case of NLP) was used. In this book, we will be touching base on methods to chunk the data later on, which helps to maintain the exact sequence of words used in any communication, which helps in those particular use cases wherein the context of what was said matters a lot.

Moving on, and also touching base on the **tokenization** method we have used here, we have broken each SMS text into words, and hence, words are the tokens in this case. What if we would like to consider more than one word or token while breaking the text so that we can retain more information? This is where n-grams will come in handy, where we define a value of **n** and (hence) break any given text in a sequence of **n** words. Simply, in our function above, **n** is 1 (we are reading each word). A sample code is as follows:

```
# Generating Bi-Grams for a random
# SMS Text from the Corpus.

random_sms = df['text'][rand_index]
print(f"Random SMS Text: {random_sms}")

random_sms_words = random_sms.split(" ")
print(f"Broken random SMS into word tokens (n=1): {random_sms_words}")

rand_sms_bigram = list(nltk.bigrams(random_sms_words))
print(f"Bi-Gram SMS Text: {rand_sms_bigram}")
```

A typical output of an approach like the preceding will be similar to the following:

Random SMS Text: Do you know why god created gap between your fingers..? So that, One who is made for you comes & fills those gaps by holding your hand with LOVE..!

Broken random SMS into word tokens (n=1): ['Do', 'you', 'know', 'why', 'god', 'created', 'gap', 'between', 'your', 'fingers..?', 'So', 'that,', 'One', 'who', 'is', 'made', 'for', 'you', 'comes', '&', 'fills', 'those', 'gaps', 'by', 'holding', 'your', 'hand', 'with', 'LOVE..!']

Bi-Gram SMS Text: [('Do', 'you'), ('you', 'know'), ('know', 'why'), ('why', 'god'), ('god', 'created'), ('created', 'gap'), ('gap', 'between'), ('between', 'your'), ('your', 'fingers..?'), ('fingers..?', 'So'), ('So', 'that,'), ('that,', 'One'), ('One', 'who'), ('who', 'is'), ('is', 'made'), ('made', 'for'), ('for', 'you'), ('you', 'comes'), ('comes', '&'), ('&', 'fills'), ('fills', 'those'), ('those', 'gaps'), ('gaps', 'by'), ('by', 'holding'), ('holding', 'your'), ('your', 'hand'), ('hand', 'with'), ('with', 'LOVE..!')]

As one can see, the preceding bigram representation is a combination of two words each since n=2 (hence the prefix **Bi-** with gram). Similarly, for any particular use case, we may want to increase the value of n and create the required tokens. The objective of creating these pairs of words or even single words is to be represented as numbers. There are multiple ways of doing so. Let us start with the most common one, which is called the **bag of words approach**.

Bag of words is a simple and intuitive way of representing text data. The basic idea is to create a vocabulary of unique words from the entire corpus of documents and then represent each document as a numerical vector based on the frequency of words present in that document.

In simple words, we take a list of all unique tokens (words) present across all documents or text across our corpus and count how many times each word or token appears in all of the text in all of the documents.

In this way, one can represent all the text in a corpus as numbers. These can then be used to train ML models for classification and clustering. Additionally, creating a bag of words also helps in information retrieval, where we find the most relevant documents while doing a keyword search on the corpus.

Note: Simply representing each word as the number of times it occurs in the corpus results in loss of context and meaning of the words in use. Not to mention, in case we have a huge vocabulary, then creating this type of representation of data will result in high-dimensionality problems, often making the systems (which are using them) slower.

Let us implement this and see how it works:

```
""" Implement Bag of Words using Count Vectorizer (Approach # 1)"""

# import the required library
from sklearn.feature_extraction.text import CountVectorizer

# create an object of Count Vectorizer
vectorizer = CountVectorizer(stop_words='english', ngram_range=(1,1))

# transform our SMS text data using this object
sms_spam_cv = vectorizer.fit_transform(df['text'])
```

In this example, we make use of an out-of-the-box functionality from the scikit-learn library called **count vectorizer**. Here is how it works overall:

- For each word in the corpus, its occurrence is counted and noted in a vector. This step is commonly known as vectorization.

- The resulting vector is usually very big, considering the amount of vocabulary used in the corpus.

- The result of this operation will be a list of all unique tokens in the corpus, which we can now use as columns in our DataFrame, and the frequency of each word as the values in these columns.

Here is a sample code:

```
# see the final representation of the data.
count_vector_df = pd.DataFrame(
    sms_spam_cv.todense(),
    columns=vectorizer.get_feature_names_out(),
)

# see the dataframe
count_vector_df
```

A typical output will be a huge dataframe in real life, with the number of rows as the number of documents in the corpus and the number of columns as the number of unique tokens or words in the entire corpus. For example, if one runs this code on our data, we get an output similar to the following:

	00	000	000pes	008704050406	0089	0121	01223585236	01223585334	0125698789	02	...	zhong	zindgi	zoe	zogtorius	zoom	zouk	zyada	èn
0	0	0	0	0	0	0	0	0	0	0	...	0	0	0	0	0	0	0	0
1	0	0	0	0	0	0	0	0	0	0	...	0	0	0	0	0	0	0	0
2	0	0	0	0	0	0	0	0	0	0	...	0	0	0	0	0	0	0	0
3	0	0	0	0	0	0	0	0	0	0	...	0	0	0	0	0	0	0	0
4	0	0	0	0	0	0	0	0	0	0	...	0	0	0	0	0	0	0	0
...	...	...	...	...	...	...	...	...	...	...	...	...	...	...	...	...	...	...	...
5567	0	0	0	0	0	0	0	0	0	0	...	0	0	0	0	0	0	0	0
5568	0	0	0	0	0	0	0	0	0	0	...	0	0	0	0	0	0	0	0
5569	0	0	0	0	0	0	0	0	0	0	...	0	0	0	0	0	0	0	0
5570	0	0	0	0	0	0	0	0	0	0	...	0	0	0	0	0	0	0	0
5571	0	0	0	0	0	0	0	0	0	0	...	0	0	0	0	0	0	0	0

5572 rows × 8444 columns

Figure 8.1: *Count vectorizer output on SMS spam dataset*

Specifically, we highlight the shape of the dataframe and one example token or word for reference as follows:

- There are 8444 unique words in this SMS text vocabulary (which is hardly a few MBs in size; imagine the vocabulary for all pages on Facebook on machine learning).

- There are 5572 rows in the dataframe, which is the number of SMS in our dataset.

- One important thing to note here is that any token or word with less than two characters is not considered in the output.

Note: In its Naïve approach, it considers every token in the vocabulary, irrespective of whether they are irrelevant or important. Simply put, the values in the above dataframe are merely the frequency of each word, but not its importance. Just because we use some words more than others in our emails, for example, does not make these specific words more important than others.

To make this better, let us now learn another intuitive way to represent a bag of words, also known as the **term frequency-inverted document frequency (TF-IDF)** vectorizer; but before that, we need to know what TF-IDF is.

TF-IDF can be considered a score of how important a word or token is in a collection of documents. In other words, it helps us identify words that are both frequent in a specific document and rare across the entire corpus. Let us deep dive into what TF-IDF means:

- TF, which is the total number of occurrences of word t in the instances of document d.

  TF, hence, emphasizes any word's prominence in any document in the corpus.

- IDF, which is a logarithm of the total number of documents divided by the number of documents containing the token t.

IDF captures the word's relative scarcity across the entire set of documents.

- TF-IDF, in essence, is the multiplication of TF and IDF calculated for each token in a corpus, hence giving each token's cruciality across all the documents as well as in the documents where they exist.

The coding approach is quite similar to the **CountVectorizer** implementation, with slight differences. Libraries like scikit-learn make these things easy. Here is a sample code:

```python
""" Approach 2: Implement TF-IDF Vectorizer on SMS Spam Data """

# Import library from sklearn.
from sklearn.feature_extraction.text import TfidfVectorizer

# Create a TF-IDF vectorizer
vectorizer = TfidfVectorizer()

# Fit and transform the documents
tfidf_matrix = vectorizer.fit_transform(df['text'])

# Represent the TF-IDF data as a dataframe
sms_tfidf_df = pd.DataFrame(
    tfidf_matrix.todense(),
    columns=vectorizer.get_feature_names_out()
)

# print the dataframe
sms_tfidf_df
```

The output of the preceding TF-IDF DataFrame for the SMS spam dataset is quite comparable to the count vectorizer dataframe, with only the major difference that the values in the TF-IDF dataframe are fractions or decimals representing the actual relevance and importance of each token in the vocabulary. Later, we will learn another interesting and very effective method of converting text to numbers called **word embeddings**. As of now, let us take the TF-IDF vectorized data and see if we could fit a Naïve Bayes classical ML classification model. Let us prepare the data for it:

```python
""" Join the SMS dataset with the TF-IDF dataset """

# getting list of all columns for final dataset
all_columns = df.columns.tolist() + sms_tfidf_df.columns.tolist()

# prepare final dataset with all required columns
joined_df = pd.concat([df, sms_tfidf_df], axis=1, ignore_index=True)
joined_df.columns = all_columns
joined_df.drop('text', axis=1, inplace=True)

# Sample 5 records of the prepared dataset
joined_df.head()
```

Here, we created a DataFrame that contains the **class** of the SMS (which is our label) and all the columns we created as a result of the TF-IDF data preparation strategy. Further, let us prepare our data for model training before splitting it into train and test sets:

```
""" Prepare Final Training data, before split """

# label encoding the target column 'class'
le = LabelEncoder()
class_le = le.fit_transform(df['class'])

# putting the label encoded class into the dataframe
final_train_df = joined_df.copy()
final_train_df.drop('class', axis=1, inplace=True)
final_train_df['class'] = class_le
final_train_df.head()
```

Note: In the preceding code example, we are using label encoding to encode the target or label column into numeric values. Since we have only two unique values in the label (spam or ham), this is a reasonable approach. Keep in mind that 0 represents ham while 1 represents spam in the dataset when we converted the class labels from text to numbers using the label encoding method.

Also, remember that we have seen an example in earlier chapters about one hot encoding, which is not a very bad approach either in this example use case provided we were planning to use an ANN or modeling. We can try that later; meanwhile, let us fit the initial Naïve Bayes model and see how it performs:

```
""" Initial Naive Bayes Model """

# break data into train/test
features = final_train_df.drop('class', axis=1)
target = final_train_df['class']
x_train, x_test, y_train, y_test = train_test_split(features, target, test_size=0.25, random_state=101)

# Fit initial model of Logistic Regression
lr = MultinomialNB().fit(x_train, y_train)

# Predict from Test data
y_pred = lr.predict(x_test)

# generate classification report
print(classification_report(y_pred, y_test))
```

When one runs the preceding code example, we expect to get a classification report, which shows good performance of the model with only one caveat, since one of the classes (ham) has more examples than the other (spam). Hence, there is a class imbalance in the data, which affects its ability to learn enough patterns for each class. Here is an (example) output of the classification report:

```
              precision    recall  f1-score   support

           0       1.00      0.95      0.98      1287
           1       0.64      1.00      0.78       106

    accuracy                           0.96      1393
   macro avg       0.82      0.98      0.88      1393
weighted avg       0.97      0.96      0.96      1393
```

Let us discuss one of the most common ways to deal with imbalanced datasets, which is the **Synthetic Minority Oversampling Technique (SMOTE)**. Specifically, a random example from the minority class is first chosen. Then, k of the nearest neighbors for that example are found (typically k=5). A randomly selected neighbor is chosen, and a synthetic example is created at a randomly selected point between the two examples in the feature space. Let us see if this improves the performance of the model. So, before we use it, we should install the library either from outside the notebook, or in the following example, from within our notebook as a code cell:

```
!pip install imbalanced-learn
```

Once installed, let us import the library, create a client object, pass the training data into it, and retrain our Naïve Bayes model:

```
""" Perform SMOTE on Training data """

# import the library
from imblearn.over_sampling import SMOTE

# perform SMOTE on training data
# by creating an object
sms_smote = SMOTE()
x_train_smote, y_train_smote = sms_smote.fit_resample(x_train, y_train)
```

Let us now predict our test set and see the improvement in the classification report:

```
""" Fit another Naive Bayes model on SMOTE data """

# Fit initial model of Logistic Regression
lr_new = MultinomialNB().fit(x_train_smote, y_train_smote)

# Predict from Test data
y_pred_smote = lr_new.predict(x_test)

# generate classification report
print(classification_report(y_pred_smote, y_test))
```

When one looks at the classification report now, it is much better than the previous model:

	precision	recall	f1-score	support
0	0.98	0.99	0.99	1223
1	0.91	0.89	0.90	170
accuracy			0.98	1393
macro avg	0.95	0.94	0.94	1393
weighted avg	0.98	0.98	0.98	1393

However, one should be careful while using SMOTE in scenarios such as if there are a good amount of overlaps in the feature space (that is, the properties of the features constituting one class as compared to the other) for both or all the classes labels, then the oversampling done by SMOTE may result into bias in the data (since the superficial data points for one class may overlap on the other class). In such cases, other statistical methods can be used to oversample the data, or in case we have a very large amount of examples, we can (optionally, but not recommended) perform down-sampling of the class label with a higher amount of examples.

Now, let us head over to learn an interesting type of neural network architecture, which is very well suited (by their design) to solve NLP (as well as time series) problems.

Introduction to sequential models

In this section of the chapter, we will briefly introduce sequential models and the important ones in this arena. Sequential models are a cornerstone of deep learning and represent a linear stack of layers in neural networks, facilitating the construction of complex architectures for diverse tasks like image recognition and NLP. The next chapter (*Chapter 9, Sequential Modeling and Transformers*) of our book is completely dedicated to these models, where we will go in depth with hands-on coding examples.

Recurrent neural networks

In many real-world NLP problems, it is very important to cater to the sequence of words. Imagine a part of one's review about their first iPhone: *iPhone has a very fast processor*. In this case, the word *fast* actually relates to the *iPhone* word used in this sentence, while the word *very* relates again to the word *fast*. Processing any of such text using our bag of words methods like count vectorizer or TF-IDF vectorizer completely discards the sequence information, and hence, for any applicable use cases where sequences will be important, we will never be able to get a very good model. The same ideology applies to time series data as well. Imagine creating a model for demand forecasting for an e-retailer where the model should be trained in such a way that it is able to recognize the effects of religious events in the target country or city on the demand for a particular set of products.

Note: These events affecting the demand may happen a handful of times during the year, while we may have the historical demand data on a daily aggregation level for the past X years. One can think of many more real-world examples that require models to recognize entities present in a sequence, like machine translation (for example, Google Translate), image captioning (with input as an input and output as a sentence or more describing the image), &/or speech recognition.

In this context, one makes use of RNN, which, unlike feedforward networks, which process information in a linear, one-way direction, RNNs have internal memory that allows them to retain information over time.

The key to RNNs' memory lies in their recurrent connections. Each unit in an RNN receives not only the current input but also the output from the previous unit, creating a loop that allows information to persist. This loop enables the network to learn patterns and relationships within sequences, making it adept at handling temporal data.

The following is a simplified breakdown of an RNN's architecture:

- **Input layer**: Receives the current input data.

- **Hidden layer**: Contains the recurrent units with internal memory. Each unit processes the current input and the output from the previous unit, generating a new output.

- **Output layer**: Produces the final output based on the information processed by the hidden layer.

To understand the detailed architecture of RNNs, let us break down their key components:

The basic building block of an RNN is an artificial neuron, similar to the neurons in an ANN. Each neuron receives input from other neurons, performs a weighted sum of these inputs, and applies an activation function to produce an output. However, unlike ANNs, RNN neurons have an additional input, like their own internal state from the previous time step. This internal state, also known as the **hidden state**, allows the neuron to remember information from past inputs and use it to influence its current output.

The key feature of RNNs is the **recurrent connection**, which allows the network to maintain its internal state over time. This connection feeds the output of the neuron back into itself as input at the next time step. This feedback loop allows the network to learn temporal dependencies in the data, making it possible to process sequences of information.

To understand how RNNs process sequential data, imagine unfolding the network across time. Each time step represents a new layer in the network, with the hidden state from the previous layer being passed as input to the current layer. This unfolding allows the network to process the sequence one element at a time while maintaining a memory of the previous elements.

Taking a direct reference from the *Stanford CS230* notes on RNN architecture by *Shervine Amidi* (refer to link **https://rb.gy/xg3yw0**), here is a quick and simple architecture of an RNN:

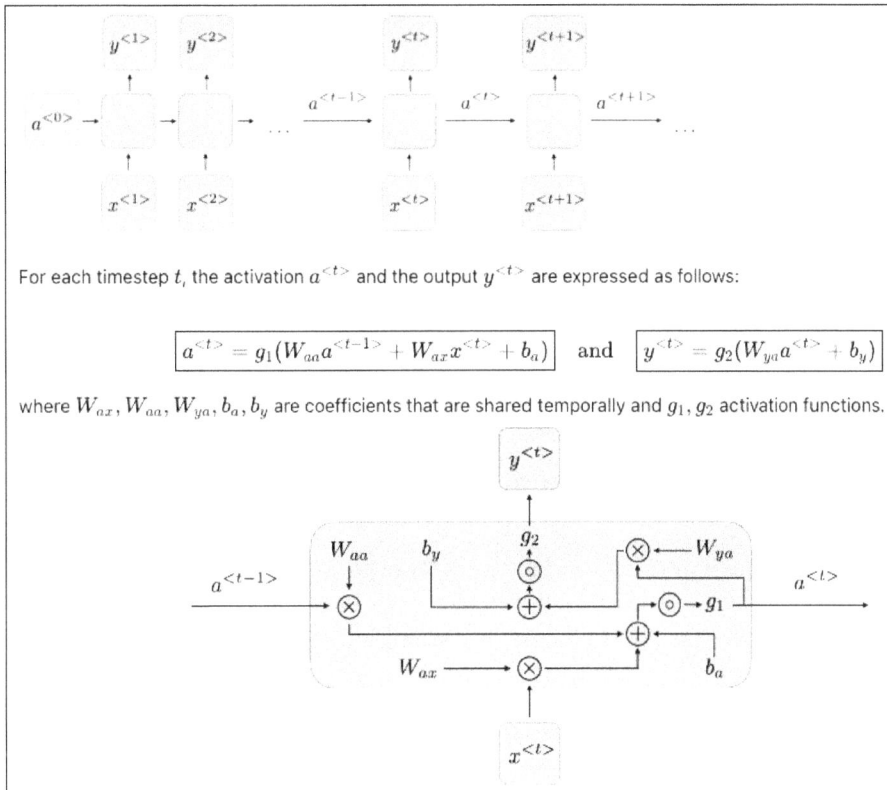

For each timestep t, the activation $a^{<t>}$ and the output $y^{<t>}$ are expressed as follows:

$$a^{<t>} = g_1\left(W_{aa}a^{<t-1>} + W_{ax}x^{<t>} + b_a\right) \quad \text{and} \quad y^{<t>} = g_2\left(W_{ya}a^{<t>} + b_y\right)$$

where $W_{ax}, W_{aa}, W_{ya}, b_a, b_y$ are coefficients that are shared temporally and g_1, g_2 activation functions.

Figure 8.2: *Typical RNN architecture*

To ensure we have understood this properly, the following is a step-by-step breakdown of how RNNs work in each stage, given any use case that requires sequential data:

1. **Initialization**: The RNN starts with an initial hidden state, which is a vector of numbers that represents the network's internal memory. This hidden state is typically initialized with zeros or random values.

2. **Input processing**:

    a. At each time step, the RNN receives an input, which could be a word, a sound, or a data point.

    b. This input is combined with the previous hidden state and passed through a series of layers, typically including a hidden layer and an output layer.

3. **Hidden state update**: The hidden state is updated based on the current input and the previous hidden state. This update is performed using a special function

called a **recurrent function**, which allows the network to retain information from previous inputs.

4. **Output generation**: The output layer generates an output based on the current hidden state. This output could be a prediction, a classification, or a new element in the sequence.

5. **Iteration**:

   a. The process of input processing, hidden state update, and output generation is repeated for each element in the sequence.

   b. This allows the RNN to learn long-term dependencies and relationships within the data.

6. **Backpropagation**:

   a. After processing the entire sequence, the RNN calculates the error between its predictions and the actual values.

   b. This error is then propagated back through the network, adjusting the weights and biases of the neurons to improve the network's performance.

Imagine an assembly line where each station represents a layer in the RNN. The input enters the first station, gets processed, and then passes to the next station along with the information from the previous station. This process continues until the final station, where the output is generated.

The main advantage of using an RNN architecture is that we can now process input of any length. Additionally, since we are using a single layer to perform multiple iterations, the model size will never increase with the increasing size of the input. The computation takes into account the historical information, and during training, the weights are shared across time. However, it is often seen that depending on the data in question, the computation of RNNs can be slow.

One should also keep in mind that there are four types of RNNs by design, as follows:

- **One to one**: This is where we have one output for each given input. This is a typical example of a traditional neural network.

- **One to many**: This is where we have one input resulting in multiple outputs. A typical example of this is music generation.

- **Many to one**: This is where we have many inputs resulting in a single output, an example of which includes sentiment classification.

- **Many to many**: This is where many inputs result in many outputs. A typical use case is named entity recognition or machine translation.

Keeping this background information about RNNs in mind, let us look at one interesting type of RNNs or sequential models, which addresses a very specific problem.

Vanishing gradients

One common issue seen in RNNs is that, by design, they do not have any neurons that can retain any information. Why is keeping a memory important? There are times when a given input (such as a sentence in English) is quite long, and to understand what word comes next or to understand what kind of sentence this is (happy or unhappy, for example, assuming we were solving a sentiment analysis use case) it is important to remember, or read, or assimilate the entire sentence at once or some words from the very beginning of the sentence. This is where RNNs show a typical problem of **vanishing gradients**. Let us try to understand this briefly.

RNNs use backpropagation, a technique to adjust the network's weights based on the error in its predictions. This involves calculating gradients for each weight, which are then used to update the weights. However, in RNNs, gradients are multiplied repeatedly as they flow backward through the network's recurrent connections.

The following are a couple of the most common problems with the design of RNNs:

- **Activation functions**: RNNs typically use activation functions like sigmoid or tanh, which squash values between 0 and 1. These functions have a derivative that is less than 1, meaning that each multiplication in the backpropagation process reduces the gradient's magnitude.

- **Long sequences**: When dealing with long sequences, the repeated multiplication of gradients can lead to extremely small values, effectively vanishing the gradient signal. This makes it difficult for the network to learn long-term dependencies in the data.

The consequences of the vanishing gradients problem are as follows:

- **Slow learning**: The network struggles to learn from past information, leading to slow convergence and poor performance.

- **Inability to capture long-term dependencies**: The network fails to recognize patterns that span across long sequences, limiting its ability to understand complex relationships in the data.

Think of the vanishing gradient problem similar to a whisper getting fainter and fainter as it travels through a long hallway. To know more about this matter, our readers are suggested to go through the research paper detailing its characteristics and impact on RNNs here: **https://arxiv.org/abs/1609.04501**. There are many tried and tested solutions for the vanishing gradient problem, some of which are as follows:

- **LSTM**:
  - LSTMs introduce a **memory cell** that can store information over long periods, mitigating the vanishing gradient problem.

- They use gating mechanisms to control the flow of information, allowing gradients to flow more effectively through time.

- **Gated recurrent unit (GRU)**:

  - GRUs are a simplified version of LSTMs, offering similar benefits with fewer parameters.

  - They use a single gate to control the flow of information, making them computationally more efficient.

- **ReLU**: Using ReLU as the activation function can help alleviate the vanishing gradient problem, as its derivative is either 0 or 1, preventing the gradient from shrinking too rapidly.

- **Gradient clipping**: This technique limits the magnitude of gradients to prevent them from exploding or vanishing. It helps stabilize the training process and improve performance.

For its wide variety of applications, we will introduce the LSTM architecture specifically and see how it can help us solve use cases where there can be big sequences of data as input.

Long short-term memory

Imagine trying to understand a conversation. We do not just focus on the last word spoken. We will consider the entire context of the conversation, remembering previous sentences and their relationships. This is the essence of LSTM networks in the context of AI and ML.

LSTMs are a special type of RNN designed to excel at processing sequential data like text, audio, or time series. Unlike traditional RNNs, LSTMs have a unique internal structure that allows them to remember information over long periods.

At the heart of an LSTM lies the memory cell, a special unit that stores information over time. This cell is controlled by the following three gates:

- **Forget gate**: Decides which information from the past should be discarded. Think of it as a filter that removes irrelevant details.

- **Input gate**: Determines which new information from the current input should be added to the memory cell. It acts like a selective gate, allowing only the most important information to pass through.

- **Output gate**: Controls which information from the memory cell is passed on to the next step in the network. It acts as a communicator, sharing the relevant information with the rest of the network.

Imagine a conveyor belt carrying information. Each step on the belt represents a time step in the sequence. The LSTM cell sits beside the belt, constantly processing the information. Follow these steps:

1. The forget gate examines the previous memory cell's contents and decides which information is no longer relevant. It forgets this information, effectively removing it from the memory cell.

2. The input gate analyzes the current input and the previous memory cell's contents. It decides which new information is important and adds it to the memory cell.

3. The output gate combines the updated memory cell's contents with the current input and produces an output. This output can be used for further processing or as the final prediction.

What about the actual learning algorithm in an LSTM architecture? LSTMs use a technique called **backpropagation through time (BPTT)** to learn from their mistakes. This involves calculating the error at each time step and adjusting the weights of the network to minimize this error. This process allows the LSTM to learn complex patterns and relationships within the sequential data. Let us understand how this works in detail:

- Instead of treating the LSTM as a single unit, we imagine it as a series of interconnected units, one for each time step. Each unit receives the input for that time step and passes its output to the next unit.

- This unfolding allows us to calculate the error at each time step and propagate it back through the entire sequence. This way, the network can learn how its parameters affect the output at every point in the sequence, not just the current one.

The overall process is as follows:

- **Forward pass**: The input sequence is fed through the unfolded LSTM, one time step at a time. At each step, the LSTM updates its internal state and produces an output.

- **Error calculation**: The output of the LSTM is compared to the target output for each time step, and the error is calculated.

- **Backward pass**: The error is propagated back through the unfolded LSTM, starting from the last time step and moving backward. This involves calculating the gradients of the error with respect to the network's parameters at each time step.

- **Parameter update**: The gradients are used to update the network's parameters using an optimization algorithm like gradient descent.

Some of the straight-away advantages of using BPTT are as follows:

- **Learning long-term dependencies**: BPTT allows LSTMs to learn complex relationships between elements that are far apart in the sequence.

- **Improved accuracy**: By considering the error at all time steps, BPTT helps LSTMs achieve higher accuracy on tasks involving sequential data.

However, there are a few challenges of BPTT as well, like the ones mentioned in the following:

- **Vanishing gradients**: As the sequence gets longer, the gradients can become very small, making it difficult for the network to learn long-term dependencies. This is known as the vanishing gradient problem.

- **Computational cost**: BPTT requires processing the entire sequence, which can be computationally expensive for long sequences.

To address these challenges while using BPTT in LSTMs, one must have a couple of solutions. They are as follows:

- **Gradient clipping**: This technique limits the magnitude of gradients to prevent them from becoming too small or too large.

- **Truncated BPTT**: Instead of backpropagating through the entire sequence, we can truncate the sequence and only backpropagate through a fixed number of time steps. This reduces the computational cost but can also limit the network's ability to learn long-term dependencies.

Keeping our background knowledge in mind, one should be aware that LSTMs have revolutionized various fields:

- **Machine translation**: Google Translate uses LSTMs to translate text between languages, capturing the nuances of grammar and meaning.

- **Speech recognition**: Amazon Alexa and Google Assistant rely on LSTMs to understand your voice commands and respond accordingly.

- **Financial forecasting**: LSTMs are used to predict stock prices, identify market trends, and manage investment portfolios.

LSTMs are powerful tools for tackling complex sequential data. Their ability to remember information over long periods and learn from past experiences makes them ideal for a wide range of applications. By understanding the inner workings of LSTMs, you can unlock their potential and build intelligent systems that can process and understand sequential data like never before.

Sentiment analysis

Imagine one is scrolling through social media, and we see a post about a new product. We want to know if people are excited about it or not. This is where **sentiment analysis** comes in.

Sentiment analysis is a powerful tool in the field of NLP that helps us understand the emotional tone behind the text. It is like having a super-powered translator that can decipher the feelings expressed in words, whether it is positive, negative, or neutral.

At its core, sentiment analysis relies on ML algorithms trained on massive datasets of text labeled with their corresponding sentiment. These algorithms learn to identify patterns in words, phrases, and even emojis that indicate a particular emotion. The following is a simplified breakdown:

- **Data collection**: We gather a large dataset of text, like reviews, tweets, or social media posts.

- **Data pre-processing**: This involves cleaning the data by removing irrelevant information like punctuation, stop words (common words like *the* or *a*) and converting everything to lowercase.

- **Feature extraction**: We extract meaningful features from the text, such as the presence of specific words, the frequency of certain words, or the overall length of the text.

- **Model training**: We train a machine learning model on the pre-processed data using algorithms like Naïve Bayes, SVM, or deep learning models like RNNs.

- **Sentiment prediction**: Once the model is trained, we can feed it new text, and it will predict the sentiment expressed in that text.

There are a few common types of approaches of sentiment analysis that are used across industries; the most important ones are as follows:

- **Document-level**: Analyzing the overall sentiment of an entire document, like a product review or a news article.

- **Sentence-level**: Analyzing the sentiment of individual sentences within a document.

- **Aspect-based**: Identifying the sentiment toward specific aspects of a product or service, like price or customer service.

Although there can be many practical applications of sentiment analysis, the following are a few industries and use cases where it is used predominantly:

- **Social media monitoring**: Understanding public opinion about brands, products, or events.

- **Customer feedback analysis**: Identifying customer satisfaction levels and areas for improvement.

- **Market research**: Gaining insights into consumer preferences and trends.

- **Political analysis**: Tracking public sentiment towards political candidates or policies.

- **Healthcare**: Analyzing patient feedback and identifying potential health risks.

It is essential to present the outcomes of our ML experiments in an easy visual format(s) for the end users to make the most sense of it. Sentiment analysis outcomes can also be visualized using various techniques, such as:

- **Word clouds**: Visualizing the most frequent words in a dataset, with the size of each word representing its frequency.

- **Sentiment bar charts**: Showing the distribution of positive, negative, and neutral sentiment across different categories or periods.

- **Sentiment heatmaps**: Visualizing the sentiment of different parts of a document, like individual sentences or paragraphs.

With all the good things that we learnt aforesaid, one should also be worried about some important challenges that an AI engineer will encounter while implementing a sentiment analysis solution. A few of these are as follows:

- **Sarcasm and irony**: Detecting sarcasm and irony can be challenging for sentiment analysis models as they often rely on context and linguistic nuances.

- **Subjectivity**: Some text may express opinions or beliefs without explicitly stating a positive or negative sentiment.

- **Data bias**: The training data used for sentiment analysis models can influence their performance and potentially lead to biased results.

Keeping this background knowledge in mind, let us now try and implement one sentiment analysis problem statement using an **Internet Movie Database** (**IMDb**) movie review dataset. We will download it from the *Stanford* website, extract the required data file, and run our notebook with it. Let us start with the basics first, which is importing the required libraries:

```
# Import necessary libraries
import TensorFlow as tf
from TensorFlow import keras
from TensorFlow.keras.preprocessing.text import Tokenizer
from TensorFlow.keras.preprocessing.sequence import pad_sequences
from sklearn.model_selection import train_test_split
from sklearn.metrics import accuracy_score
import pandas as pd
import numpy as np
```

Let us now download the data from its source, unpack it, and define some paths and variables, which we will use throughout this experiment to load and work with the data:

```
# Download dataset
!wget https://ai.stanford.edu/~amaas/data/sentiment/aclImdb_v1.tar.gz
```

```
# unpack the dataset
!tar -xf aclImdb_v1.tar.gz

# Define paths to data
train_path = "aclImdb/train/"
test_path = "aclImdb/test/"

# Define parameters
max_words = 10000
max_len = 200
batch_size = 32
epochs = 10
```

Before proceeding further, we could write a reusable Python function to load the data properly since this dataset is in its current format. We have a huge amount of text corpus and their labels, both of which are stored separately in different folders alongside the labels, which are put inside sub-folders of whether the sentiment was positive or negative, given by folder names like **pos** and **neg**:

```
# Function to read data from files
def read_data(path):
    """
    Reads data from the specified path and returns lists of reviews and
labels.

    Args:
        path: Path to the data directory.

    Returns:
        reviews: List of movie reviews.
        labels: List of sentiment labels (0 for negative, 1 for positive).
    """

    # import libraries
    import os

    # create variables for returning
    # reviews and their labels
    reviews = []
    labels = []

    # Reading the data
    for sentiment in ["pos", "neg"]:
```

```
        sentiment_path = path + sentiment + "/"
        for filename in os.listdir(sentiment_path):
            with open(os.path.join(sentiment_path, filename), "r",
encoding="utf-8") as f:
                reviews.append(f.read())
                labels.append(1 if sentiment == "pos" else 0)

    # return the reviews and their labels
    return reviews, labels
```

Using our function, let us now read the training and testing data:

```
# Read training and testing data
train_reviews, train_labels = read_data(train_path)
test_reviews, test_labels = read_data(test_path)
```

For the sake of simplicity, we can make use of the out-of-the-box tokenizer functionality from the Keras library and tokenize the sentences. Once that is done, we can convert them into sequences of tokens and pad them:

```
# Preprocess text data
tokenizer = Tokenizer(num_words=max_words)
tokenizer.fit_on_texts(train_reviews)
train_sequences = tokenizer.texts_to_sequences(train_reviews)
test_sequences = tokenizer.texts_to_sequences(test_reviews)
train_padded = pad_sequences(train_sequences, maxlen=max_len)
test_padded = pad_sequences(test_sequences, maxlen=max_len)
```

Let us break the available data into train-test validation sets. Once done, we will use an LSTM model this time, for example, to see its performance on a textual data use case like this one and compile the model.

Note: While designing the initial model (again), we are keeping the original design simple enough for later experimentation.

```
# Split data into training and validation sets
train_data, val_data, train_labels, val_labels = train_test_split(train_
padded, train_labels, test_size=0.2)

# Create the model
model = keras.Sequential([
    keras.layers.Embedding(max_words, 128, input_length=max_len),
    keras.layers.LSTM(64),
    keras.layers.Dense(1, activation="sigmoid")
])
```

```
# Compile the model
model.compile(loss="binary_crossentropy", optimizer="adam",
metrics=["accuracy"])
```

Let us now train the model and keep a history of the training so that we can visualize this information later on and optimize any inputs or designs if required:

```
# Train the model
train_labels = np.array(train_labels)
val_labels = np.array(val_labels)
history = model.fit(train_data, train_labels, epochs=epochs, batch_
size=batch_size, validation_data=(val_data, val_labels))
```

Finally, we could verify the performance of the model with our test data, which we have not used during the training phase at all, and plot the history of training for **loss** versus **epochs**:

```
# Evaluate the model
test_labels = np.array(test_labels)
test_loss, test_acc = model.evaluate(test_padded, test_labels)
print("Test accuracy:", test_acc)

# Plot epochs vs loss
import matplotlib.pyplot as plt
plt.plot(history.history['loss'])
plt.plot(history.history['val_loss'])
plt.title('Model loss')
plt.ylabel('Loss')
plt.xlabel('Epoch')
plt.legend(['Train', 'Validation'], loc='upper left')
plt.show()
```

As we see here, this was a simple example of how to implement an LSTM model for resolving use cases like the sentiment of a movie review on IMDb. As we go further, we will look at even more such implementations in the next chapter.

Case studies

Let us now look at a couple of applications of NLP in day-to-day life that are very critical. One of these belongs to the conversational AI area of work in AI or ML, which is as critical today as creating models for regression and classification. The other is merely to translate natural language from one language to another, but its applications and implications are tremendous, with use cases spreading across industries.

Chatbots

Chatbots have emerged as powerful tools for businesses to enhance customer service, streamline operations, and personalize user experiences. Let us examine two compelling case studies that demonstrate the transformative potential of chatbots:

- **Duolingo: Language learning companion**

  Duolingo, the popular language learning platform, leverages a chatbot named Duo to provide a more engaging and interactive learning experience. Duo acts as a virtual language partner, offering personalized feedback, answering questions, and motivating users to continue their language journey.

  While one uses this platform, the following are some of the characteristics it provides. This list acts as a good reference for what a similar chatbot solution's high-level design should look like:

  - **Adaptive learning**: Duo personalizes the learning experience by adapting to the user's progress and learning style.

  - **Conversational practice**: Users can engage in natural language conversations with Duo, practicing their speaking and listening skills.

  - **Error correction and feedback**: Duo provides immediate feedback on user responses, helping them identify and correct mistakes.

  - **Motivation and encouragement**: Duo offers encouragement and celebrates user achievements, keeping them motivated to learn.

  Duolingo's chatbot has significantly improved user engagement and retention. The personalized learning experience and conversational practice opportunities have made language learning more accessible and enjoyable for millions of users worldwide.

- **Koninklijke Luchtvaart Maatschappij (KLM) Royal Dutch Airlines**:

  KLM Royal Dutch Airlines utilizes a chatbot named BlueBot to provide 24/7 customer support and travel assistance. BlueBot assists passengers with various tasks, including booking flights, checking in, managing reservations, and answering travel-related questions.

  Some of the design aspects of a chatbot like this will include the following, if not more:

  - **Multilingual support**: BlueBot supports multiple languages, catering to a global audience.

  - **Real-time information**: BlueBot provides up-to-date flight information, including delays, cancellations, and gate changes.

- o **Personalized assistance**: BlueBot can access user profiles to offer personalized recommendations and assistance.

- o **24/7 availability**: BlueBot is available 24/7, ensuring passengers receive assistance whenever needed.

KLM's chatbot has significantly improved customer satisfaction and reduced the workload on human customer service agents. BlueBot's ability to handle routine inquiries and provide real-time information has streamlined the travel experience for passengers.

Machine translation

Machine translation (MT) has revolutionized the way we communicate and access information across language barriers. Let us explore two case studies that showcase the power of MT in different contexts:

- **Google Translate**: Google Translate, the world's most popular MT platform, provides real-time translation for over 100 languages. It empowers users to communicate with people from different cultures, access information in various languages, and overcome language barriers in their daily lives.

   Let us understand at least some of the most important high-level designs included in Google Translate as of today:

   - o **Real-time translation**: Google Translate instantly translates text, speech, and images, enabling seamless communication.

   - o **Multiple language support**: It supports over 100 languages, covering a vast majority of the world's population.

   - o **Contextual understanding**: Google Translate utilizes advanced algorithms to understand the context of the text, providing more accurate and natural translations.

   - o **Integration with other Google products**: Google Translate seamlessly integrates with other Google products like Gmail, Chrome, and Search, making it readily accessible.

   Google Translate has democratized access to information and communication, breaking down language barriers and fostering global understanding. It has empowered individuals and businesses to connect with people worldwide, expanding their reach and opportunities.

- **DeepL for businesses and professionals**: DeepL is a specialized MT platform that focuses on providing high-quality translations for businesses and professionals. It utilizes advanced neural network technology to deliver accurate and nuanced translations, particularly for technical and industry-specific content.

Some of the background design aspects of this platform are as follows:

- o **Neural network technology**: DeepL employs advanced neural networks trained on massive datasets, resulting in more accurate and natural-sounding translations.

- o **Industry-specific dictionaries**: DeepL offers specialized dictionaries for various industries, ensuring accurate terminology and domain-specific language.

- o **Collaboration features**: DeepL provides collaboration tools for teams to work on translations together, streamlining the translation process.

- o **Security and privacy**: DeepL prioritizes data security and privacy, making it suitable for handling sensitive information.

DeepL has become quite a valuable tool for businesses and professionals who require high-quality translations for their work. Its accuracy, industry-specific focus, and collaboration features have made it a preferred choice for organizations that demand precision and efficiency in their communication.

The intention of providing these examples to our readers in this chapter is to encourage thinking in terms of high-level design aspects, as a start, of such similar and many other use cases and applications, which can be created to benefit from natural language inputs. One should not limit oneself to thinking only in terms of written language but should also consider audio and video formats as input types, along with the inherent complexities in each of the natural languages that humans speak. How about a Sanskrit-to-Hindi translation system?

Conclusion

In this chapter, we covered the introduction to NLP and some of the common ways to tokenize language data. Further, we looked into some of the methods used very frequently in the industry to represent words to numbers, alongside how to use them while creating models to tackle use cases like sentiment analysis or sentiment classification. Further, we introduced a special type of ANN called sequential models, wherein designs like RNN and LSTM help to retain the context of long text inputs as well. Finally, we looked into some common use cases of NLP in the real-world, which are of prime importance as of today, keeping in mind the sort of applications required by businesses around the world.

In the next chapter, we are going to study and design sequential models, understand the mathematics behind them in depth, and implement some use cases using Python. We will also introduce transformers and attention mechanisms with a quick introduction to generative AI, and finally, we will read about various real-world case studies.

Exercises

Let us now try the following exercises to revise the concepts and to practice more of these ML algorithms:

1. In the classical ML implementation of the SMS spam classifier:

    a. Take the same data, with the same pre-processing steps, and fit an ANN. Is the ANN model better than our Naïve Bayes model(s)? Explore available research to find possible reasons for these differences.

    b. Can you try to fit another ANN without pre-processing steps? Does it work?

    c. Lastly, what other methods of over-sampling of data can we apply, other than SMOTE, in scenarios like these?

2. In the section on RNNs and LSTMs:

    a. Take the same data of IMDB movie ratings and perform detailed data exploration. To do so, explore libraries in Python like Pandas profiling, AutoViz and SweetViz, for example. Note the pros and cons of using each of these libraries w.r.t computation resources and time.

    b. In the LSTM sample code, change the initial design by adding more neurons or layers and see their impact.

Join our book's Discord space

Join the book's Discord Workspace for Latest updates, Offers, Tech happenings around the world, New Release and Sessions with the Authors:

https://discord.bpbonline.com

CHAPTER 9

Sequence Modelling and Transformers

Introduction

This chapter introduces the world of natural language processing by studying more about the importance of sequence models and use cases like forecasting and language translation where there is an increasing use of sequence models. We will be re-introduced to forecasting, one of the most common methods used across industries for planning and demand management, followed by modelling language as a sequence of events. We introduce readers to GANs, which are broadly used in language and image use cases. Finally, readers are introduced to what is today the core functionality of generative AI systems, also known as **transformers**, covering the attention mechanism. All of these aforementioned topics are implemented hands-on using TensorFlow and Keras for practical realization.

Structure

The chapter covers the following topics:

- Introduction to sequential models
- Time series forecasting
- Forecasting
- Language modelling

- Generative adversarial networks
- Transformers and attention mechanism
- Real-world case studies

Objectives

By the end of this chapter, the readers will be able to apply RNNs and LSTMs for traditional forecasting and natural language generation use cases. We will learn about which sequential networks are best for which areas of work. We will also come to know about language modelling fundamentals, along with introductory knowledge on GANs, to get them started on applicable generative use cases. Further, we will learn about transformers and how they are paving the way for the generative AI hype. Finally, as part of every learning, we will be implementing hands-on solutions for specific real-world use cases using these algorithms and architectures.

Introduction to sequential models

Sequential models are the workhorses of deep learning, particularly in tasks involving sequence-based data. These models, much like a well-choreographed dance, process information step-by-step, taking into account the order of elements to arrive at informed predictions and decisions. We introduced RNNs and LSTMs in *Chapter 8, Natural Language Processing,* and even saw and hands-on example. Further, in this chapter, we will explore the intricacies of these models, including:

- **Power of time series**: Unraveling the role of ordering in sequential data and how models leverage this structure for accurate predictions.

- **Building blocks of sequence**: Discovering the core elements like RNNs and LSTM networks driving these models.

- **Applications in real life**: Witnessing the versatility of sequential models in diverse spheres like language translation, speech recognition, video analysis, and weather forecasting.

- **Training and tuning**: Mastering the process of guiding these models toward optimal performance with suitable training methodologies and parameter adjustments.

Time series forecasting

Sequential data holds a distinct characteristic: **the order matters**. Imagine a stock market sequence like analyzing fluctuations without considering past trends that can lead to misleading conclusions. This is where time series analysis steps in, recognizing the crucial role of order in making sense of sequential data.

Consider stock prices at consecutive points, weather readings over time, or daily customer transactions. Time series data captures the dynamic nature of information, where each data point has a unique timestamp and potentially influences the future.

We, however, do have a small problem in that is analyzing this data without recognizing the temporal dependence, which can result in inaccurate predictions or missed insights. Sequential models address this challenge by leveraging the inherent order within the data to uncover hidden patterns and predict future trends with greater accuracy.

In this chapter, we will learn about time series forecasting. At this time, let us remember quickly, as learned in *Chapter 8*, how RNNs and LSTMs can help solve a forecasting problem.

Note: The core concept of RNNs is that they remember past sequences. It processes information sequentially, feeding the output of one step as input to the next, retaining a memory of previous information. One can think of it as an internal echo within the network, allowing for a dynamic understanding of the sequence.

However, traditional RNNs have limitations in remembering long sequences due to vanishing gradients. This is where LSTM networks come in. LSTMs are a type of RNN with additional features like gates, enabling them to learn and retain long-term dependencies more effectively than their simpler counterparts.

Further, by their design, LSTMs are equipped with gates that act as regulators of information flow within the networks. These gates learn to determine what information should be kept in the memory, what should be forgotten, and what should be used for future prediction.

These architectural details allow LSTMs and other RNN-based models to excel in processing and understanding complex sequential data. This is also how they immensely help in solving time series forecasting problems, which, for the record, is one of the most critical business use cases across industries like financial institutions, e-commerce, and retail, amongst many others.

Training and tuning sequential models

To achieve optimal performance from our sequential model, training and tuning play a critical role:

- **Dataset preparation**: We start with a carefully curated dataset that accurately represents the sequences you intend to analyze. We need to ensure that our data is well-structured and pre-processed, free from inconsistencies or noise that can impede training. We will see examples of these as we start solving more use cases.

- **Loss function and optimization algorithm**: During our experiments, we select a loss function, like mean squared error or cross-entropy, to quantify the model's errors during training. We will learn more about how to choose the right ones as we go along and implement use cases.

- **Hyperparameter optimization**: During our experiments, we will be required to fine-tune hyperparameters like learning rate, batch size, and hidden layer structure to achieve efficient convergence and minimize errors during training.

- **Model monitoring**: Monitoring our model's performance with metrics suitable for sequential tasks, such as perplexity for language modeling or mean absolute error for time series forecasting, is crucial. By carefully analyzing and iteratively optimizing, one can refine your model to achieve its full potential.

Let us look into each of these areas in detail before starting to implement a hands-on example for a particular real-world use case.

Dataset preparation

For preparing data for any given use case (like forecasting), the following are some guidelines one can follow:

Note: These are general guidelines for any AI or ML application design, and one must be flexible in their approach to redesign them as required.

- **Understanding your data**: Before diving into the preparation process, it is crucial to understand the nature of your data. We must ask ourselves (and sometimes our customers for whom we might be building the solution) the following questions:

  o What type of data are you dealing with? Is it text, audio, video, or sensor readings?

  o What is the format of the data? Is it raw, pre-processed, or labeled?

  o What is the size of the data? Is it a small dataset or a large one?

  o What is the quality of the data? Is it clean or noisy?

  Understanding these aspects will guide our choices in the subsequent preparation steps.

- **Data cleaning and pre-processing**: Data cleaning and pre-processing are essential for ensuring the quality of our training data. This involves:

  o **Handling missing values**: Filling in missing data points with appropriate strategies like mean imputation, interpolation, or deletion.

  o **Removing outliers**: Identifying and removing data points that deviate significantly from the norm, as they can negatively impact model performance.

  o **Normalizing data**: Scaling your data to a specific range, often between 0 and 1, to improve training efficiency and prevent issues caused by features with vastly different scales.

  o **Tokenization**: For text data, converting words into numerical representations using techniques like word embedding or character-level encoding.

- o **Padding sequences**: Adjusting the length of sequences to a fixed size, as RNNs require consistent input lengths. This can be done by padding shorter sequences with zeros or by truncating longer ones.

- **Feature engineering**: Feature engineering involves creating new features from existing ones to improve model performance. This can be particularly helpful for RNNs, as they can benefit from additional information that captures the context and relationships within the data. Some common features of engineering techniques include:

  - o **Extracting features from raw data**: For example, extracting features like pitch and volume from audio data.

  - o **Combining features from different sources**: For example, combining text and image features for sentiment analysis.

  - o **Creating n-grams**: Generating sequences of *n* consecutive words or characters to capture local context.

  - o **Using word embedding techniques**: Representing words as dense vectors that capture their semantic relationships.

- **Data splitting**:

  - o Once our data is clean and pre-processed, it is crucial to split it into training, validation, and test sets. This allows us to evaluate the performance of your model on unseen data and avoid overfitting. A common split ratio is 70% for training, 15% for validation, and 15% for testing.

  - o We have been doing this all along and will continue following the best practices in all the upcoming use cases as well.

- **Data augmentation**:

  - o Data augmentation involves artificially increasing the size and diversity of our training data. We made use of this when we were coding use cases for CNN.

  - o This can be particularly helpful when dealing with limited datasets, as it helps prevent overfitting and improves model generalizability.

  - o Some common data augmentation techniques for RNNs include:

    - **Randomly dropping words**: Simulating missing data scenarios.

    - **Swapping words**: Changing the order of words within a sentence.

    - **Inserting synonyms**: Replacing words with synonyms to increase vocabulary diversity.

    - **Back-translation**: Translating text into another language and then back to the original language to introduce variations.

Loss functions and optimizers

Let us now understand the types of loss functions and optimizers that are essential in case of using RNNs and LSTMs in a given use case. This is very important to experiment with since the choices in these two areas will affect the model outcome a lot.

To revise, a loss function measures the discrepancy between the model's predictions and the actual target values. It guides the optimization process by quantifying the **badness** of the model's current state. Choosing the right loss function is crucial for effective training. The most common loss functions for RNNs or LSTMs are as follows:

- **Mean squared error (MSE)**: Calculates the average squared difference between predicted and actual values. Suitable for regression tasks where the output is a continuous value.

- **Cross-entropy loss**: Measures the difference between the predicted probability distribution and the true distribution. Commonly used for classification tasks where the output is a categorical variable.

- **Hinge loss**: Similar to cross-entropy loss but less sensitive to outliers. Used in **support vector machines** (**SVMs**) and other classification tasks.

- **Negative log-likelihood (NLL)**: Measures the negative probability of the true labels given the model's predictions. Often used in conjunction with softmax activation for multi-class classification.

The choice of loss function depends on the specific task and the nature of the data. For example, MSE is preferred for regression tasks, while cross-entropy is more suitable for classification.

Again, as we have understood in earlier chapters, optimization algorithms iteratively adjust the model's parameters to minimize the loss function. They guide the model toward better performance by finding the optimal set of weights and biases. The most popular optimization algorithms for RNNs or LSTMs are as follows:

- **Stochastic Gradient Descent (SGD)**: A simple yet effective algorithm that updates parameters based on the gradient of the loss function for each parameter.

- **Adam**: An adaptive learning rate optimization algorithm that adjusts the learning rate for each parameter individually, leading to faster convergence.

- **Root Mean Square Propagation (RMSprop)**: Another adaptive learning rate algorithm that addresses the vanishing gradient problem often encountered in RNNs.

- **Adaptive Gradient Algorithm (Adagrad)**: An optimization algorithm that adapts the learning rate based on the historical gradients of each parameter.

The choice of optimization algorithm depends on factors like the size and complexity of the model, the nature of the data, and the desired convergence speed.

Before we move further, one needs to remember a couple of very important aspects of training RNNs and LSTMs, one of which we have already been doing in our earlier use cases:

- **Gradient clipping**:
  - o RNNs and LSTMs can suffer from exploding gradients, where the gradients become increasingly large during training, leading to instability and divergence.
  - o Gradient clipping mitigates this issue by setting a threshold on the maximum gradient value.
  - o When the gradient exceeds the threshold, it is scaled down to the specified limit.

- **Visualizing loss and optimization**:
  - o Visualizing the loss function and optimization process can provide valuable insights into the training progress.
  - o Plotting the loss curve over time helps identify convergence and potential issues like overfitting or underfitting.
  - o Additionally, visualizing the gradients can reveal exploding or vanishing gradient problems.

Hyperparameter optimization

Before learning optimization techniques, let us quickly revise what hyperparameters are. In the context of RNNs and LSTMs, or for that matter, for any ML models we come up with, hyperparameters are settings that control the learning process and the model's architecture. They are distinct from the model's weights and biases, which are learned during training.

The following are some key hyperparameters for RNNs and LSTMs, which are equally applicable to any other artificial neural network architectures:

- **Learning rate**: This determines the step size the optimizer takes during training. A high learning rate can lead to faster convergence but may also cause instability and overshooting the optimal solution. A low learning rate can lead to slow convergence and getting stuck in local minima.

- **Number of hidden units**: This defines the complexity of the model. More hidden units allow the model to learn more complex relationships but also increase the risk of overfitting.

- **Number of layers**: This determines the depth of the model. Deeper models can capture longer-term dependencies in the data but also require more training data and computational resources.

- **Activation function**: This introduces non-linearity into the model, allowing it to learn complex patterns. Common choices include ReLU, tanh, and sigmoid.

- **Batch size**: This defines the number of samples used in each training iteration. Larger batch sizes can lead to faster training but may require more memory and can be less stable.

- **Optimizer**: This algorithm updates the model's weights and biases based on the calculated gradients. Popular choices include Adam, RMSprop, and SGD.

- **Regularization techniques**: These methods help prevent overfitting by penalizing model complexity. Common techniques include L1 and L2 regularization, dropout, and early stopping.

Now that we understand the key hyperparameters, let us explore different optimization techniques, some of which are used in some of our traditional ML use cases in earlier chapters:

- **Grid search**: This is a brute-force approach where you define a grid of values for each hyperparameter and train the model with every possible combination. While simple to implement, it can be computationally expensive, especially for models with many hyperparameters.

- **Random search**: This method randomly samples values for each hyperparameter within a defined range. It can be more efficient than a grid search, especially when the optimal values are not evenly distributed.

- **Bayesian optimization**: This technique uses a probabilistic model to guide the search for optimal hyperparameters. It iteratively updates the model based on the performance of previously evaluated configurations, focusing on promising areas of the hyperparameter space.

- **Gradient-based optimization**: This approach uses the gradient of the loss function with respect to the hyperparameters to guide the search. Techniques like hyperband and **population-based training** (PBT) fall under this category.

- **Automated machine learning (AutoML)**: These tools automate the hyperparameter optimization process, often using a combination of the techniques mentioned above. They can be helpful for beginners or for quickly finding good hyperparameters but may not always achieve the best possible performance.

It is crucial to visualize and analyze the results of your hyperparameter optimization process. This can be done by plotting the performance of different configurations on metrics like accuracy, loss, or F1 score. Additionally, techniques like learning curves and confusion matrices can provide valuable insights into the model's behavior.

Finally, the following are some best practices and tips for hyperparameter optimization:

- **Start with a baseline**: Begin with a simple model and optimize its hyperparameters before moving to more complex architectures.

- **Use a validation set**: Always use a separate validation set to evaluate the performance of different hyperparameter configurations.

- **Log your experiments**: Keep track of the hyperparameters you tried and their corresponding performance to avoid repeating experiments and learn from past results.

- **Consider early stopping**: Stop training if the validation performance does not improve for a certain number of epochs to avoid overfitting.

- **Use libraries and tools**: Several libraries and tools like Keras Tuner, Optuna, and Hyperopt can automate and simplify the hyperparameter optimization process.

Forecasting

Before we go any further, we will learn one of the most important and compelling business problems across domains, which is how to forecast the values of a temporal variable. These are use cases, like demand forecasting, for example, where we are trying to estimate values of a continuous variable, which changes over time. To solve these problems, we make use of time series forecasting models, where sequential ANNs play a vital role.

Time series forecasting models are powerful tools used to predict future values based on historical data. These models analyze trends, seasonality, and other patterns in time-based data to make informed predictions about what might happen next. From predicting stock prices to forecasting weather patterns, time series forecasting models have a wide range of applications across various industries.

Imagine we have data on the daily sales of a particular product over the past year. This data represents a time series, where each data point corresponds to a specific date and the corresponding sales value. A time series forecasting model would analyze this data to identify patterns and relationships between sales and various factors like seasonality, promotions, or economic trends. Based on these insights, the model would then predict future sales for the coming weeks or months.

There are numerous time series forecasting models, each with its strengths and weaknesses. This is critical to understand since forecasting problems are equally approachable using traditional ML as well as deep learning methods. Some popular models include the following:

- **Autoregressive (AR) models**: These models predict future values based on past values of the same time series. For example, an AR model might use the sales data from the past week to predict sales for the upcoming week.

- **Moving average (MA) models**: These models consider the average of past values to predict future values. For instance, a moving average model might use the average sales of the past month to predict sales for the next month.

- **Autoregressive integrated moving average (ARIMA) models**: These models combine the features of AR and MA models, incorporating both past values and the average of past errors to make predictions. ARIMA models are widely used for their versatility and accuracy.

- **Exponential smoothing models**: These models assign exponentially decreasing weights to past observations, giving more importance to recent data. This approach is particularly useful when dealing with data that exhibits trends or seasonality.

- **Neural network models**: These models, inspired by the human brain, can learn complex relationships within the data and make highly accurate predictions. They often require large amounts of data and computational resources for training.

The choice of the most suitable time series forecasting model depends on several factors, including the characteristics of the data, the desired level of accuracy, and the available computational resources. Some key considerations include the following:

- **Stationarity**: The data should be stationary, meaning its statistical properties, like mean and variance, remain constant over time. If the data is non-stationary, it might require transformations before applying certain models.

- **Trend and seasonality**: The presence of trends and seasonality in the data can influence the choice of model. Some models are specifically designed to handle these patterns.

- **Model complexity**: More complex models like neural networks can achieve higher accuracy but require more data and computational power. Simpler models might be sufficient for less demanding tasks.

Once a model is trained, it is crucial to evaluate its performance on unseen data to assess its accuracy and generalizability. Common metrics used for evaluation include the following:

- **Mean squared error (MSE)**: Measures the average squared difference between predicted and actual values.

- **Root mean squared error (RMSE)**: Like MSE but in the same units as the data, making it easier to interpret.

- **Mean absolute error (MAE)**: Measures the average absolute difference between predicted and actual values.

By analyzing these metrics, we can determine how well the model performs and identify areas for improvement.

Time series forecasting models have numerous applications across various domains:

- **Finance**: Predicting stock prices, market trends, and customer behavior.

- **Retail**: Forecasting sales, inventory management, and demand planning.

- **Weather forecasting**: Predicting temperature, precipitation, and other weather patterns.

- **Healthcare**: Predicting disease outbreaks, patient readmissions, and resource utilization.

- **Energy**: Forecasting energy consumption, demand, and prices.

Let us take a sample use case and try to implement the solution in Python using sequential models to solve a forecasting problem. We will take a sample dataset of daily minimum air temperature and try to create a model that can estimate temperatures in any given period in the future. To do so, let us start by importing the required libraries:

```
# Import required libraries
import pandas as pd
import numpy as np
from TensorFlow import keras
from TensorFlow.keras.layers import LSTM, Dense
from sklearn.preprocessing import MinMaxScaler
from matplotlib import pyplot as plt
```

As seen here, we are importing only the basic libraries so that we can explore the core functionalities rather than packaging the solution as software (which we will let be an exercise for our readers). Further, our target dataset is available on GitHub in this case, hence, we can use its URL to directly read it as a Pandas DataFrame:

```
# Download the data
url = "https://raw.githubusercontent.com/jbrownlee/Datasets/master/daily-min-temperatures.csv"
data = pd.read_csv(url)
data.head()
```

Let us look at the data itself, now that it has been downloaded, by running a code snippet like given in the following. We will see that the data almost follows a particular pattern. Interestingly, the patterns also repeat themselves. These are the seasonal and cyclicity patterns, which are sometimes evident from the nature of the available data when we try to visualize it using temporal charts like these. Basic EDA like this also helps to decide which modeling technique will be most suitable for the given scenario:

```
# Plot the time series data
plt.plot(data['Temp'])
plt.show()

# Check for missing values
print(data.isnull().sum())
```

Here is an example output one might find after running the last part of the code:

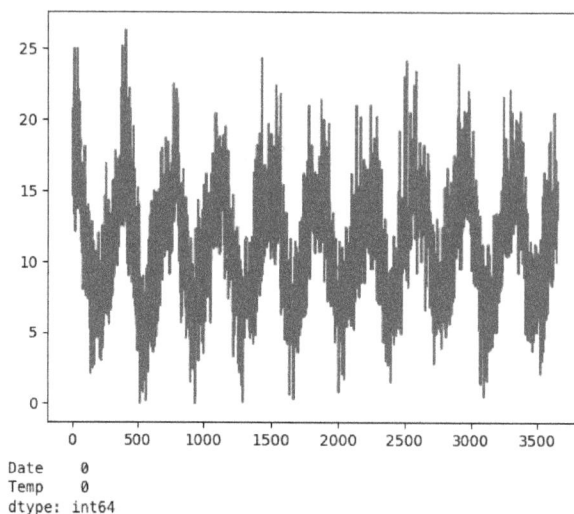

```
Date     0
Temp     0
dtype: int64
```

Figure 9.1: *Temperature data properties*

Before we proceed with the modeling, one needs to scale the data so that it fits within an acceptable range of calculations. This will speed up the computation process as well as allow us to process outliers in the data. Here is a sample code:

```
# Scale the data using MinMaxScaler
scaler = MinMaxScaler(feature_range=(0, 1))
data['Temp'] = scaler.fit_transform(data['Temp'].values.reshape(-1, 1))

# Create the training and testing datasets
train_size = int(len(data) * 0.8)
train_data = data[:train_size]
test_data = data[train_size:]
```

As we see in the preceding code, for this example use case, we are dividing the data only into train and test sets. In any given use case similar to this, one may divide the data into train, test, and validate sets so that we can keep the test set completely aside for predictions and getting the model metrics on unknown data. Further, we create a look-back variable, which allows us to capture past data points. Then, we can iterate through the training data, starting from the index as the look-back value. Inside the loop, we extract a sequence of past temperature values from the training data using slicing. This creates the input sequence for the LSTM model we want to fit soon, representing the past look-back temperatures. Finally, we convert the training data into arrays since LSTMs typically work better with efficient numerical data structures, and finally, we reshape the training data to a 3D structure of sorts, which is required by most LSTM implementations. Here is an example implementation:

```
# Create the input and output sequences
look_back = 10
X_train, Y_train = [], []
for i in range(look_back, len(train_data)):
    X_train.append(train_data['Temp'][i-look_back:i])
    Y_train.append(train_data['Temp'][i])
X_train, Y_train = np.array(X_train), np.array(Y_train)

# Reshape the input data for LSTM
X_train = np.reshape(X_train, (X_train.shape[0], X_train.shape[1], 1))
```

Finally, we can now create the model and keep a tab on the history so that we can plot it later on to understand how well we did during the process.

Note: To keep the example simple enough, we are not using early stopping or similar controls.

Here is a sample code to create the model architecture:

```
# Define the LSTM model
model = keras.Sequential([
    LSTM(50, return_sequences=True, input_shape=(look_back, 1)),
    LSTM(50),
    Dense(1)
])

# Compile the model
model.compile(loss='mean_squared_error', optimizer='adam')

# Train the model
history = model.fit(X_train, Y_train, epochs=100, batch_size=32, validation_
split=0.2)
```

Once the training is over, we can plot the training history to see the model loss with training and validation data over time. Ideally, their differences, as we know by now, should be ignorable. Here is one example of how we can plot the model performance over time:

```
# Plot the loss over epochs
plt.plot(history.history['loss'])
plt.plot(history.history['val_loss'])
plt.title('Model Loss')
plt.ylabel('Loss')
plt.xlabel('Epoch')
plt.legend(['Train', 'Validation'], loc='upper right')
plt.show()
```

An example output may look like the following:

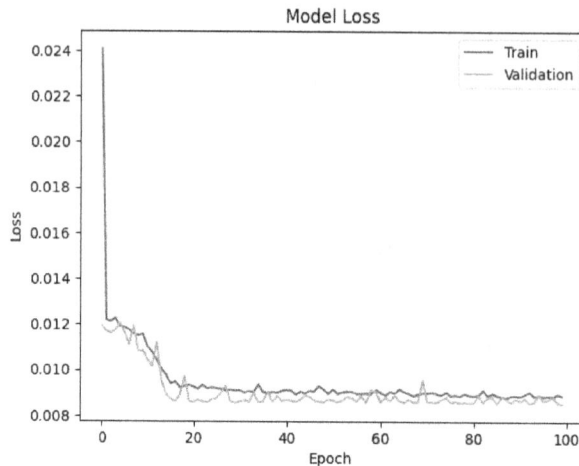

Figure 9.2: *LSTM training history*

Finally, we can take the test data, make predictions on it, and save it in a variable so that we can compare the predicted test values with actuals using a visual:

```
# Make predictions on the test data
test_data = test_data['Temp'].values
X_test = []
for i in range(look_back, len(test_data)):
    X_test.append(test_data[i-look_back:i])
X_test = np.array(X_test)
X_test = np.reshape(X_test, (X_test.shape[0], X_test.shape[1], 1))
predictions = model.predict(X_test)
```

Now, to get the correct and relatable estimations, since we had used a MinMax scaler, we need to reverse the transformation we did to the data so that we can compare apples to apples. Once it is inverted, a common best practice is to plot the actuals versus the predictions superimposed on each other so that we can gauge how similar or different they look. Here is a sample implementation:

```
# Invert the scaling to get the original values
predictions = scaler.inverse_transform(predictions)
test_data = scaler.inverse_transform(test_data.reshape(-1, 1))

# Plot the predictions against the actual values
plt.plot(test_data, label='Actual')
plt.plot(predictions, label='Predicted')
plt.title('LSTM Predictions')
plt.ylabel('Temperature')
```

```
plt.xlabel('Time')
plt.legend()
plt.show()
```

The output plot may look like the following:

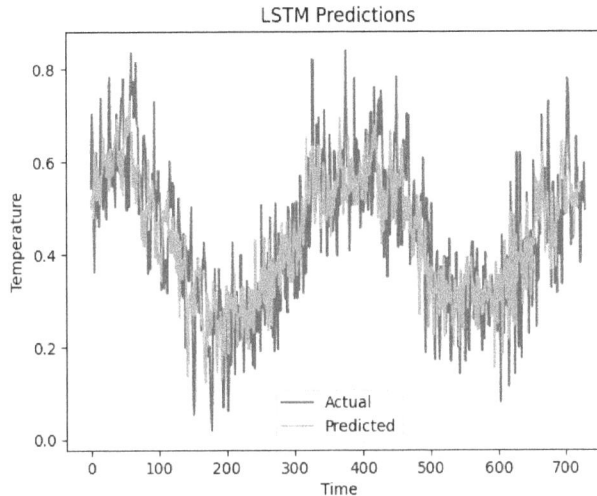

Figure 9.3: *Predictions from LSTM*

As we see, out of the box, with a mediocre initial design of the network, an LSTM model works out the temporal properties of the data (like trend, seasonality, and cyclicity, wherever applicable) very neatly, and the predictions are quite close to the actual observations. This makes sequential models very powerful, even for use cases like forecasting, where the resulting values are dependent on time.

Language modelling

In this section of the chapter, we will introduce another very compelling and extremely useful application of sequential models.

Imagine a machine that can understand and generate human language. That is precisely what **language modelling** aims to achieve. It is a branch of AI focused on building statistical methods that can predict the next word in a sequence, given the preceding words. These models analyze vast amounts of text data to learn the patterns and relationships between words, enabling them to generate coherent and contextually relevant text.

At their core, language models are based on probability theory. They assign probabilities to different possible continuations of a given sequence of words. The model with the highest probability for the next word is considered the most likely continuation. This process is repeated iteratively, generating text word by word.

There are two main approaches to language modelling:

- **Statistical language models**: These models rely on statistical methods like n-grams to predict the next word. N-grams consider the preceding n words to predict the next one, with higher n values capturing longer-range dependencies.

- **Neural language models**: These models utilize artificial neural networks, particularly RNNs and transformers, to learn complex relationships between words. They can capture long-range dependencies and generate more fluent and coherent text compared to statistical models.

Language models are of different types, each with its strengths and weaknesses:

- **Autoregressive models**: These models generate text sequentially, predicting the next word based on the preceding words. Examples include n-gram models, RNNs, and transformers.

- **Autoencoding models**: These models learn a compressed representation of the input text and then use it to generate new text. Examples include **variational autoencoders** (**VAEs**) and GANs.

- **Contextual language models**: These models consider the entire context of a sentence or document when predicting the next word, leading to more accurate and nuanced predictions. Examples include **Bidirectional Encoder Representations from Transformers** (**BERT**) and **generative pre-trained transformer 3** (**GPT-3**).

Overall, language models have revolutionized various fields, including the following:

- **NLP**: Language models power tasks like machine translation, text summarization, sentiment analysis, and question answering.

- **Text generation**: They can generate creative content like poems, stories, and articles, as well as personalized responses in chatbots and virtual assistants.

- **Code generation**: Language models can assist programmers by generating code snippets or completing code based on natural language instructions.

- **Data analysis**: They can analyze large amounts of text data to identify patterns, trends, and insights.

Looking at its unprecedented popularity and varied range of applications in the current day, not to mention the ever-increasing amount of research taking place day to day, let us learn the internal workings of contextual language models.

Contextual language modeling (**CLM**) is a powerful technique in NLP that has revolutionized the way we interact with machines. Unlike traditional language models that treat each word in isolation, CLMs consider the context of surrounding words to understand the meaning of a sentence. This allows them to generate more natural and coherent text, perform complex tasks like question answering and summarization, and even translate languages.

At the heart of CLMs lies the concept of **word embeddings**. Each word is represented as a vector of numbers, where each dimension captures different aspects of the word's meaning. These vectors are learned from large amounts of text data, allowing the model to understand the relationships between words and their context.

The most common type of CLM is the **transformer**, a neural network architecture that has achieved state-of-the-art results in various NLP tasks. Transformers use an **encoder-decoder** structure, where the encoder reads the input text and generates a hidden representation of its meaning, and the decoder uses this representation to generate the output text.

During training, the CLM is fed a large corpus of text and learns to predict the next word in a sequence based on the preceding words. This process allows the model to capture the statistical relationships between words and their context.

There are various types of CLMs, each with its strengths and weaknesses:

- **Autoregressive models**: These models generate text one word at a time, predicting the next word based on the previously generated words. Examples include GPT-3 and BERT.

- **Autoencoding models**: These models learn a compressed representation of the input text and then try to reconstruct the original text from this representation. Examples include **Bidirectional and Auto-Regressive Transformers** (**BART**) and **Text-to-Text Transfer Transformer** (**T5**).

- **Masked language models**: These models are trained to predict masked words in a sentence, forcing them to learn the context of surrounding words. Examples include BERT and RoBERTa.

CLMs have a wide range of applications in NLP, including:

- **Text generation**: Generating creative text formats like poems, code, scripts, musical pieces, emails, letters, etc.

- **Machine translation**: Translating text from one language to another.

- **Question answering**: Answering questions based on a given context.

- **Text summarization**: Summarizing large amounts of text into concise summaries.

- **Sentiment analysis**: Determining the emotional tone of a piece of text.

- **Dialogue systems**: Creating chatbots that can engage in natural conversations with humans.

On the positive side, CLMs provide some interesting advantages, leading to their successful applications in a variety of NLP and other use cases, like the following:

- **High accuracy**: CLMs can achieve high accuracy on various NLP tasks.

- **Versatility**: CLMs can be used for a wide range of applications.

- **Contextual understanding**: CLMs can understand the context of surrounding words, leading to more natural and coherent outputs.

On the other side of the coin, however, CLMs do have their fair share of limitations, such as the following:

- **Bias**: CLMs can inherit biases from the data they are trained on.

- **Computational cost**: Training and running CLMs can be computationally expensive.

- **Lack of explainability**: It can be difficult to understand how CLMs make decisions.

Further, we will now explore some very applied (and interesting) areas of sequential models in the following sections of this chapter.

Generative adversarial networks

GANs, introduced in 2014 by *Ian Goodfellow et al.* (refer to the link **https://arxiv.org/pdf/1406.2661**), are a powerful class of deep learning models capable of generating new data that closely resembles the training data. They have gained immense popularity in recent years due to their ability to produce realistic images, videos, music, and even text.

Overall, a GAN consists of two main components:

- **Generator**: This network takes a random noise vector as input and generates new data that resembles the training data.

- **Discriminator**: This network takes both real data and generated data as input and tries to distinguish between the two.

The generator and discriminator are trained in an adversarial manner, where the generator tries to fool the discriminator, and the discriminator tries to improve its ability to distinguish real from generated data. This competition drives both networks to improve, leading to the generator producing increasingly realistic data.

Some of the important key concepts related to GANs are as follows:

- **Generative model**: A model that learns the underlying distribution of the data and can generate new data samples from that distribution.

- **Adversarial training**: A training process where two models compete against each other, leading to the improvement of both models.

- **Loss function**: A function that measures the difference between the generated data and the real data.

- **Backpropagation**: A technique used to update the weights of the generator and discriminator networks based on the loss function.

The architecture of a GAN can vary depending on the specific application. However, a typical GAN architecture consists of the following components:

- **Input layer**: This layer takes a random noise vector as input for the generator.

- **Hidden layers**: These layers process the input data and generate the output data.

- **Output layer**: This layer produces the final generated data.

- **Discriminator input layer**: This layer takes both real data and generated data as input.

- **Discriminator hidden layers**: These layers process the input data and try to distinguish between real and generated data.

- **Discriminator output layer**: This layer outputs a probability indicating whether the input data is real or generated.

Further, the training process of a GAN involves the following steps:

1. Sample a random noise vector.

2. Feed the noise vector to the generator to generate new data.

3. Feed both the real data and the generated data to the discriminator.

4. Calculate the loss function for both the generator and the discriminator.

5. Update the weights of the generator and discriminator using backpropagation.

6. Repeat steps 1-5 until the generator produces realistic data.

As per the outcomes of the initial research by *Ian Goodfellow et al.*, the generator outcomes post-training on various datasets like CIFAR-10, for example, can be seen in *Figure 9.4*. This gives a fair idea of how GANs can be used to generate Images as an output modality, for example.

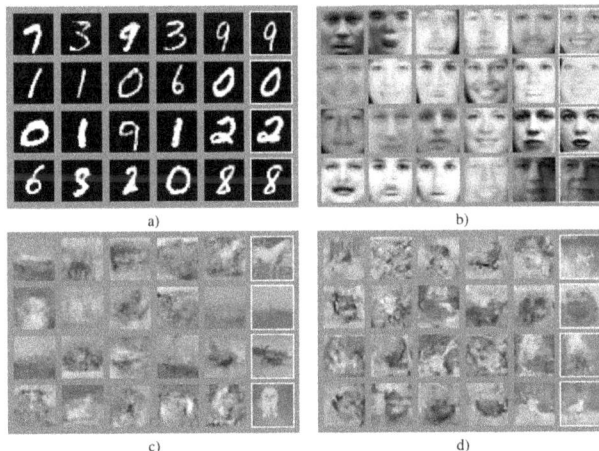

Figure 9.4: Sample generator outcomes from initial training

At the end of the day, GANs have a wide range of applications, including:

- **Image generation**: Generating realistic images of faces, objects, and scenes.

- **Video generation**: Generating realistic videos of people, objects, and events.

- **Music generation**: Generating new music pieces in different styles.

- **Text generation**: Generating realistic text, such as news articles, poems, and code.

- **Data augmentation**: Increasing the size and diversity of a dataset by generating new data samples.

Despite their impressive capabilities, GANs also face several challenges:

- **Training instability**: GANs can be difficult to train due to the adversarial nature of the training process.

- **Mode collapse**: The generator may collapse into generating only a limited variety of data.

- **Ethical concerns**: GANs can be used to generate fake images and videos, which can be used for malicious purposes.

Overall, GANs are a powerful tool for generating new data that closely resembles the training data. They have a wide range of applications and have the potential to revolutionize many industries. However, they also face several challenges that need to be addressed. As research in GANs continues, we can expect to see even more impressive results in the future.

Transformers and attention mechanism

Transformers are a type of neural network architecture that has revolutionized the field of NLP in recent years. They have achieved state-of-the-art results on a wide range of NLP tasks, including machine translation, text summarization, question answering, and sentiment analysis. Let us look at a detailed introduction to transformers, covering their architecture, training process, and applications.

Transformers are a type of neural network architecture that rely on the self-attention mechanism to process and understand sequences of data, such as text or speech. Unlike traditional RNNs, which process data sequentially, transformers can process all elements of a sequence simultaneously, allowing them to capture long-range dependencies and relationships between elements. The research on transformers came to light from the seminal research paper called *Attention is all you need* by *Vaswani et al.*, which is available for reference at **https://arxiv.org/pdf/1706.03762**.

The transformer architecture consists of two main components:

- **Encoder**: The encoder takes the input sequence and processes it to generate a representation of the sequence.

- **Decoder**: The decoder takes the encoded representation from the encoder and generates the output sequence.

Both the encoder and decoder consist of multiple layers stacked on top of each other. Each layer consists of two sub-layers:

- **Multi-head attention**: This sub-layer allows the model to attend to different parts of the input sequence simultaneously.

- **Feed-forward network**: This sub-layer applies a non-linear transformation to the output of the multi-head attention layer.

From the research paper, here is a quick overview of what a transformer architecture looks like. At first, this is quite overwhelming for one starting off with this style of ANNs, but once we understand its layers and how they function, it becomes easy to realize their applications and benefits. Here is the overall transformer architecture:

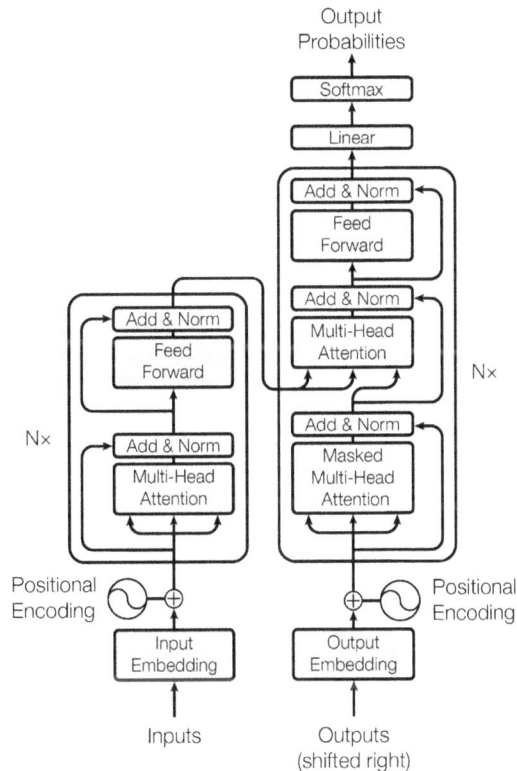

Figure 9.5: *Architecture of transformers*

At the heart of transformers, we have the self-attention mechanism. The self-attention mechanism is the core of the transformer architecture. It allows the model to attend to different parts of the input sequence and learn how they relate to each other. The self-attention mechanism works as follows:

- **Query, key, and value**: The input sequence is first split into three parts:

  o Query

  o Key

  o Value

- **Attention scores**: The model calculates attention scores between each element in the query and each element in the key. The attention scores measure how relevant each element in the key is to each element in the query.

- **Weighted sum**: The model then takes a weighted sum of the values, where the weights are the attention scores. This weighted sum represents the context vector for each element in the query.

In general, and as per research, the attention mechanism or module can either be represented or designed as scaled dot-product attention or multi-head attention, as one can learn from the figure representation in the following:

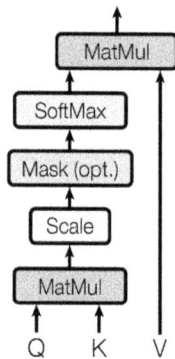

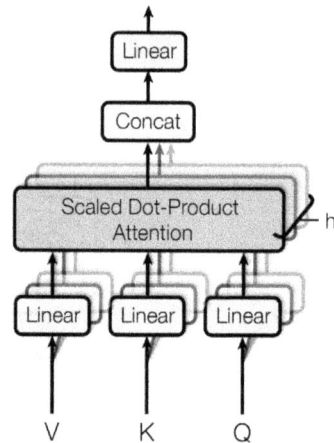

Figure 9.6: *Types of attention mechanisms*

Transformers are typically trained using a supervised learning approach. This means that the model is trained on a dataset of labelled examples, where each example consists of an input sequence and a corresponding output sequence. The model is trained to minimize the difference between the predicted output sequence and the actual output sequence. Training a transformer requires carefully preparing our data. Following is a breakdown of the key steps:

- **Tokenization**: Break down your text data into individual tokens, which can be words, sub-words, or characters.

- **Vocabulary creation**: Build a vocabulary of all unique tokens encountered in your data.

- **Encoding**: Convert each token into a numerical representation using the vocabulary.

- **Padding**: Ensure all sequences have the same length by padding shorter sequences with special tokens.

- **Batching**: Group your data into batches for efficient training.

Now, let us discuss the training process:

- **Initializing the model**: Start with a pre-trained transformer model or initialize a new model from scratch.

- **Defining the loss function**: Choose a suitable loss function to measure the difference between the model's predictions and the ground truth. Common choices include cross-entropy loss for classification tasks and mean squared error for regression tasks.

- **Optimizer selection**: Select an optimizer, like Adam or SGD, to update the model's parameters based on the calculated loss.

- **Training loop**: Iterate through your training data in batches, feeding each batch to the model and calculating the loss. Update the model's parameters using the optimizer to minimize the loss.

- **Monitoring and evaluation**: Track the model's performance on a validation set during training to assess its generalization ability. Early stopping can be implemented to prevent overfitting.

- **Fine-tuning**: Once the model is trained, you can fine-tune it for your specific task using a smaller learning rate.

The following are some valuable tips to enhance our transformer training experience:

- **Regularization**: Employ techniques like dropout and weight decay to prevent overfitting.

- **Learning rate scheduling**: Adjust the learning rate during training to optimize convergence.

- **Gradient clipping**: Prevent exploding gradients by clipping their magnitude.

- **Data augmentation**: Increase the size and diversity of your training data using techniques like back-translation or synonym replacement.

- **Transfer learning**: Leverage pre-trained models and fine-tune them for your specific task.

Mostly, and since it is quite costly to train transformers from scratch (both in terms of the data and compute we require), generally in the industry, one tends to use a pre-trained version of a transformer model or even the models, which are based on the transformer architecture. To give some context:

- The original transformer, as per the research paper shared earlier, was trained on the standard *Workshop on Statistical Machine Translation (WMT)* 2014 English-German dataset consisting of about 4.5 million sentence pairs. Here is the process followed:

  o Sentences were encoded using byte-pair encoding, which has a shared source target vocabulary of about 37000 tokens.

  o For English-French translation testing, we used the significantly larger WMT 2014 English-French dataset consisting of 36M sentences and split tokens into a 32000-word-piece vocabulary.

  o Sentence pairs were batched together by approximate sequence length. Each training batch contained a set of sentence pairs containing approximately 25000 source tokens and 25000 target tokens.

- Again, the research team trained the initial models on one machine with 8 NVIDIA P100 GPUs.

  o For the base models using the hyperparameters described throughout the research paper, each training step took about 0.4 seconds.

  o They trained the base models for a total of 100,000 steps or 12 hours.

  o For the big models, the step time was 1.0 second. The big models were trained for 300,000 steps (3.5 days).

Again, for a detailed study and further understanding of transformers and how they work (along with how the attention mechanism is used sparingly in its design), we would recommend reading *Jay Alammar's* inevitable resource on understanding transformers in an illustrated manner (refer to this link **https://jalammar.github.io/illustrated-transformer/**).

Transformers have been successfully applied to a wide range of NLP tasks, including:

- **Machine translation**: Translating text from one language to another.

- **Text summarization**: Generating a concise summary of a longer text.

- **Question answering**: Answering questions based on a given context.

- **Sentiment analysis**: Determining the sentiment of a piece of text.

- **Text generation**: Generating new text that is like a given text.

Generative artificial intelligence

With all the knowledge of GAN and transformers that we have briefly gained in this chapter in the previous sections, let us now discuss the most impactful change around us, which these seminal research and architectures are bringing to the table. The area we are referring to is the ever-growing and fascinating world of generative AI.

Generative AI empowers machines to create entirely new content, be it text, images, music, or even code. Unlike traditional AI models that primarily focus on analyzing and understanding existing data, generative AI leaps forward by generating novel outputs that have not been seen before. This opens a world of possibilities, allowing us to explore uncharted creative territories and push the boundaries of human imagination.

At its core, generative AI relies on deep learning and (especially) transformers. These deep learning models are trained on massive datasets of the type of content they are expected to generate. For instance, a text-generating AI might be trained on a dataset of millions of books and articles, while an image-generating AI might be trained on a dataset of billions of photographs.

During training, the model learns to identify the underlying patterns and structures within the data. It analyzes how words are combined to form sentences, how pixels are arranged to form images, or how notes are sequenced to form music. This knowledge is then used to generate new content that statistically resembles the training data but is not an exact copy of anything it has seen before.

The world of generative AI is diverse, encompassing a wide range of models with varying capabilities and applications. Let us discuss some of the most prominent types:

- **GANs**: As learned in the last sections of this chapter, these models pit two neural networks against each other in a competitive game. One network, the generator, attempts to create new data that resembles the training data. The other network, the discriminator, tries to distinguish between real data and the generator's creations. This adversarial process pushes both networks to improve, ultimately leading the generator to produce increasingly realistic and convincing outputs.

- **VAEs**: VAEs take a different approach, focusing on compressing and encoding the essential information within the training data into a lower-dimensional latent space. This latent space acts as a compressed representation of the data, capturing its key features and variations. The model then learns to sample from this latent space, generating new data points that share the same underlying characteristics as the training data.

- **Autoregressive models**: These models generate data sequentially, one element at a time. They predict the next element based on the previously generated elements, building up the output piece by piece. This approach is particularly effective for generating text, music, and code, where the order of elements plays a crucial role.

- **Diffusion models**: These models work by gradually adding noise to an existing data point until it becomes unrecognizable. They then learn to reverse this process, progressively removing the noise and reconstructing the original data point. This **denoising** process can be used to generate new data points that share similar characteristics with the original data.

The applications of generative AI are vast and continuously expanding, touching upon various aspects of our lives. The following are a few examples:

- **Creative industries**: Generative AI is revolutionizing creative fields like writing, music composition, and visual arts. AI-powered tools can assist artists in overcoming creative blocks, generating new ideas, and exploring uncharted artistic territories.

- **Drug discovery**: Generative AI can accelerate the discovery of new drugs by designing novel molecules with desired properties. This can significantly reduce the time and cost associated with traditional drug development processes.

- **Personalized education**: Generative AI can personalize the learning experience for each student by creating adaptive learning materials and providing tailored feedback. This can improve student engagement and learning outcomes.

- **Data augmentation**: Generative AI can be used to generate synthetic data that resembles real-world data. This can be particularly useful in situations where real data is scarce or difficult to obtain.

- **Generative design**: Generative AI can be used to design and optimize products and systems, considering various constraints and objectives. This can lead to more efficient and sustainable designs.

Generative AI is still in the early stages of development, but its potential is immense. As the technology continues to advance, we can expect to see even more innovative and transformative applications emerge. From creating personalized learning experiences to designing life-saving drugs, generative AI has the potential to reshape our world in profound ways.

However, it is important to acknowledge the potential risks and challenges associated with generative AI. Issues like bias, misinformation, and deep fakes need to be addressed responsibly to ensure that this powerful technology is used for good.

As we move forward and continue using these systems, it is crucial to strike a balance between embracing the potential of generative AI and mitigating its risks. By doing so, we can harness this transformative technology to create a better future for all. In the context of this book especially, we will not learn in-depth about using any of the generative AI systems, like Google Gemini or OpenAI ChatGPT. However, here is a comprehensive list of the most popular generative AI systems available for users and enterprises:

- **Text generation**:
  - **For users**:
    - **ChatGPT**: Developed by OpenAI, ChatGPT is a powerful language model capable of generating human-quality text in response to a wide range of prompts. It excels in tasks like writing stories, poems, and even code.

- **Jasper**: This AI writing assistant helps users create high-quality content for various purposes, including blog posts, social media captions, and marketing copy. Its user-friendly interface and diverse templates make it accessible to both beginners and experienced writers.

- **Rytr**: Rytr is a budget-friendly option that offers a variety of text-generation tools, including article writing, blog post outlines, and product descriptions. Its free plan allows users to experiment with the platform before committing to a paid subscription.

- **For enterprises**:

  - **GPT-3**: OpenAI's GPT-3 is a highly advanced language model with a vast knowledge base and the ability to generate human-like text in multiple languages. Enterprises can leverage its capabilities for tasks like content creation, customer service chatbots, and product descriptions.

  - **Cohere**: This platform provides access to various AI models, including text generation, translation, and summarization. Its enterprise-grade features ensure security, scalability, and customization for businesses of all sizes.

  - **Wordsmith**: Wordsmith specializes in generating personalized marketing content at scale. Its AI-powered platform allows businesses to create targeted email campaigns, social media posts, and landing pages that resonate with their audience.

- **Image generation**:

  - **For users**:

    - **DALL-E 2**: Developed by OpenAI, DALL-E 2 is a cutting-edge AI system that can generate realistic images from text descriptions. Its ability to create high-quality, original artwork has made it a popular tool for artists, designers, and anyone seeking creative inspiration.

    - **Midjourney**: This AI image generator allows users to create stunning images based on text prompts. Its Discord community provides a platform for sharing creations, collaborating with other users, and exploring the potential of AI-generated art.

    - **NightCafe**: NightCafe offers a user-friendly interface for generating images using various AI models. Its diverse features, including style transfer and artistic filters, cater to both beginners and experienced users.

- ○ **For enterprises**:
  - ▪ **Jasper Art**: This AI image-generation tool is integrated with the Jasper writing assistant (Jasper AI), allowing users to create visuals that complement their written content. Its ability to generate images based on specific brand guidelines makes it valuable for marketing and advertising campaigns.

  - ▪ **Synthesia**: Synthesia specializes in creating AI-generated videos featuring realistic human avatars. Businesses can use this technology to personalize marketing messages, create engaging training materials, and enhance customer interactions.

  - ▪ **Pictory**: This AI video editing platform allows users to automatically generate video content from text scripts. Its features include adding voiceovers, music, and visuals, making it a powerful tool for creating engaging video content at scale.

- **Music generation**:
  - ○ **For users**:
    - ▪ **Jukebox**: Developed by OpenAI, Jukebox is an AI system that can generate music in various styles, including classical, jazz, and pop. Its ability to create original compositions and mimic the styles of famous artists makes it a fascinating tool for music enthusiasts and aspiring musicians.

    - ▪ **Amper Music**: This AI-powered music platform allows users to create custom soundtracks for videos, podcasts, and other projects. Its vast library of AI-generated music and sound effects provides a diverse range of options to suit any creative need.

    - ▪ **MuseNet**: MuseNet is a large-scale neural network trained on a massive dataset of musical compositions. It can generate music in various styles and instruments, offering a unique way to explore and experiment with musical creation.

  - ○ **For enterprises**:
    - ▪ **Amper Music**: Amper Music's enterprise-grade features allow businesses to create and manage large-scale music libraries for various applications, including marketing campaigns, in-store experiences, and video content.

    - ▪ **Jukebox**: OpenAI offers access to Jukebox through its API, enabling businesses to integrate AI-generated music into their products and services. This opens up possibilities for personalized music experiences and innovative applications in the entertainment industry.

- **Landr**: Landr is an AI-powered mastering platform that helps musicians and producers achieve professional-quality sound for their music. Its AI algorithms analyze and enhance audio tracks, ensuring a polished and consistent sound across all platforms.

- **Video generation**:
  - For users:
    - **Synthesia**: Synthesia's AI video generation capabilities allow users to create personalized videos featuring realistic human avatars. This technology can be used for educational purposes, creating engaging presentations, or even generating personalized video messages.

    - **Pictory**: Pictory's AI video editing platform allows users to automatically generate video content from text scripts. Its features include adding voiceovers, music, and visuals, making it a powerful tool for creating engaging video content at scale.

    - **DeepBrain AI**: DeepBrain AI offers a range of AI-powered video generation tools, including video editing, animation, and special effects. Its user-friendly interface and diverse features make it accessible for both beginners and experienced video creators.

  - For enterprises:
    - **Synthesia**: Synthesia's enterprise-grade features allow businesses to create and manage large-scale video libraries for various applications, including marketing campaigns, training materials, and customer interactions.

    - **Pictory**: Pictory's enterprise plans offer advanced features, such as team collaboration, custom branding, and bulk video generation, making it suitable for large organizations with high video production needs.

    - **DeepBrain AI**: DeepBrain AI's enterprise solutions provide businesses with access to its powerful AI video generation tools, enabling them to create high-quality video content for various marketing, training, and communication purposes.

Let us now continue to the last section of this chapter to explore some of the most common case studies of sequential models, transformers, GANs, and generative AI offerings.

Real-world case studies

Let us now discuss and try to realize the existing solutions all around us so that from time to time, we can take inspiration and references in the use cases that we are going to approach.

Sequential models

Case study 1: Language translation

- **Model**: RNNs, specifically LSTM networks
- **Organization**: Google Translate
- **Link: https://ai.googleblog.com/2016/09/a-neural-network-for-machine.html**
- **Description**: Google Translate utilizes LSTMs to translate languages by learning the relationships between words in a sentence. This enables accurate and fluent translations across multiple languages.

Case study 2: Speech recognition

- **Model: Hidden Markov Models (HMMs)** and **deep neural networks (DNNs)**
- **Organization**: Apple Siri
- **Link: https://www.apple.com/siri/**
- **Description**: Siri employs HMMs and DNNs to recognize spoken language and convert it into text. This allows users to interact with their devices using voice commands.

Transformers

Case study 1: Text summarization

- **Model**: Transformer-based models like BART
- **Organization**: Facebook AI
- **Link: https://arxiv.org/abs/1910.13461**
- **Description**: Facebook AI uses BART for text summarization, generating concise summaries of lengthy documents while preserving key information.

Case study 2: Machine translation

- **Model**: Transformer-based models like T5
- **Organization**: Google AI
- **Link: https://research.google/blog/exploring-transfer-learning-with-t5-the-text-to-text-transfer-transformer/**
- **Description**: Google AI leverages T5 for machine translation, achieving high accuracy and fluency in translating between multiple languages.

GANs

Case study 1: Image generation

- **Model**: **Generative adversarial network 2 (StyleGAN2)**

- **Organization**: NVIDIA

- **Link**: **https://arxiv.org/abs/1912.04958**

- **Description**: NVIDIA's StyleGAN2 generates high-fidelity images of faces, landscapes, and other objects, pushing the boundaries of photorealism.

Case study 2: Text-to-image generation

- **Model**: DALL-E 2 (GPT-3)

- **Organization**: OpenAI

- **Link**: **https://openai.com/dall-e-2/**

- **Description**: OpenAI's DALL-E 2 generates images from textual descriptions, enabling users to create visual representations of their ideas and concepts.

Generative artificial intelligence offerings

Case study 1: Content creation

- **Model**: Jasper

- **Organization**: Jasper.ai

- **Link**: **https://www.jasper.ai/**

- **Description**: Jasper is a generative AI platform that assists in creating various types of content, including blog posts, social media captions, and marketing copy.

Case study 2: Code generation

- **Model**: GitHub Copilot

- **Organization**: GitHub

- **Link**: **https://copilot.github.com/**

- **Description**: GitHub Copilot is an AI pair programmer that suggests code completions and assists developers in writing more efficient and accurate code.

Conclusion

In this chapter, we covered the applications of sequential models, understood yet again how they function, the use cases they can solve, and practical use cases using Python. Further, we learned about transformers, GANs, and their designs, which can help us approach particular use cases in translation and generation across modalities like text, images, audio, and video. Then, we have investigated a brief introduction to generative AI and how it is shaping the world as we speak into more innovative approaches to solve problems across domains and organizations.

In the next chapter, we are going to explore the operational side of AI and ML, starting with understanding what MLOps is, and how we can, in the practical world, deploy these applications that we create, the designs we require, the automation we should follow and the best practices, both in an on-premises setup context as well as on cloud platforms.

Exercises

1. Try to implement an RNN similar to the LSTM model we have created and compare the performance of both models.

2. In an LSTM, try to separate data into train, test, and validate datasets and also try to implement early stopping with a large value of epochs.

3. Explore the various hyperparameters we can tune in an LSTM.

4. Read through the given research papers and blogs in depth.

5. Look through GitHub and see if you can find geniuses implementing these networks from scratch. (**Hint**: Look for an amazing engineer and researcher named *Andrez Karpathy*)

6. Explore the more enterprise-ready generative AI solutions, especially the ones offered by AWS, Google Cloud, Azure, and Oracle Cloud Infrastructure.

   a. Can you list the primary enterprise differences between these offerings and the open-source or free offerings?

   b. Can you also list the specific security features that differentiate these enterprise offerings from others?

7. Create an account in Hugging Face and try out their spaces.

   a. Try at least three variations of image generation, text generation, text summarization, and language translation models.

   b. Give a special look at Gemma (2B and 7B) models on Hugging Face and see what users are applying these models to achieve. (For example, translation of international text to Indic languages.)

CHAPTER 10

MLOps and Deployment

Introduction

Imagine a well-oiled machine, data scientists meticulously build and train models, engineers seamlessly integrate them into production environments, and operations teams monitor and maintain their performance. This is the essence of MLOps: fostering collaboration and automation to accelerate the delivery of valuable ML solutions. One can consider this as DevOps for AI/ML applications and platforms.

This chapter explores the interesting field of MLOps and its principles. We learn about what MLOps is, how it is essential, why every AI and ML engineer should use it in their day-to-day operations, what value it brings to the software development lifecycle for AI and ML applications, and finally, a few tools and frameworks that all readers of this book should be aware of.

Structure

The chapter covers the following topics:

- Introduction to MLOps
- AI and ML deployment
- Model monitoring

- CI/CD for ML
- TensorFlow Extended
- Kubeflow
- Containers, Docker, and Kubernetes

Objectives

By the end of this chapter, readers of our book should be familiar with the importance and areas of application of MLOps, which is more of an approach than a specific technology, and how to apply it while building AI and ML applications. We will cover the various stages of the MLOps maturity model, followed by learning about containerization with Docker and orchestration of production workloads using Kubernetes. Inclusively, we will look at code examples for references.

Introduction to MLOps

When we build software systems, we not only think of functionalities but also about operationalizing. While operationalizing software, we think about how to deploy it, how to track code changes, and perhaps automatically push these changes to an environment where they can be tested without much intervention, using automated test cases. Furthermore, we think about how to monitor and track the performance and usage of the system when the software is used by all users. All of the tools, frameworks, and automation that are used in this respect are from the world of DevOps when it comes to building software systems. We can also do something similar for our AI and ML applications.

MLOps is a set of practices that aim to streamline and automate the process of deploying and managing machine learning models in production. It bridges the gap between the development and operations teams, creating a continuous workflow for building, deploying, and monitoring ML models effectively. There are several reasons why MLOps has become crucial in the modern world. Some are mentioned as follows:

- **Increased complexity**: ML models are becoming increasingly complex, with intricate architectures and large datasets. Managing such models manually is cumbersome and error-prone.

- **Faster iteration**: Businesses need to deploy and update models faster to stay competitive. Traditional software development methods are too slow for this rapid iteration.

- **Improved reliability**: ML models in production require constant monitoring to ensure optimal performance and catch potential issues early.

- **Collaboration**: MLOps promotes collaboration between data scientists, engineers, and operations teams, fostering knowledge sharing and better decision-making.

Most of the important concepts that we build upon are summarized in this whitepaper from *Google*, which we recommend all of our readers to be familiar with:

https://services.google.com/fh/files/misc/practitioners_guide_to_mlops_whitepaper. pdf

Several key components come together to form the MLOps framework; some are mentioned as follows:

- **Version control and configuration management**: Tracking changes in code, data, and model configurations is essential for reproducibility and traceability. Tools like Git and MLflow play a crucial role here.

- **Continuous integration/continuous delivery (CI/CD)**: Automating the testing, building, and deployment of models ensures faster and more efficient delivery pipelines. Existing CI/CD tools like Jenkins can be adapted for ML workflows.

- **Model monitoring**: Continuously evaluating model performance in production helps identify any degradation or unexpected behavior. Tools like Prometheus and Grafana provide real-time insights into model metrics.

- **Experimentation and feature management**: Enabling controlled experimentation with different model versions and features allows for rapid iteration and data-driven decision-making. Platforms like Kubeflow and Feast facilitate this process.

- **Infrastructure orchestration**: Managing the underlying infrastructure for ML workloads, including cloud resources and containerization, requires tools like Kubernetes and Docker for efficient scaling and resource allocation.

- **Security and governance**: Implementing security measures for data and models is crucial to mitigate risks and ensure model explainability and fairness. Techniques like differential privacy and federated learning contribute to this aspect.

Adopting MLOps brings a multitude of benefits to organizations; some are mentioned as follows:

- **Increased efficiency**: Automating workflows and managing models effectively leads to faster deployment and reduced development overhead.

- **Improved model quality**: Continuous monitoring and experimentation ensure high-performing models while identifying potential biases or issues early on.

- **Enhanced collaboration**: Breaking down silos between teams fosters better communication and shared responsibility for successful model operation.

- **Reduced operational costs**: Streamlined processes and automation minimize manual effort and optimize cost in the long run.

- **Faster time-to-market**: Rapid iteration and efficient deployment pipelines enable quicker adaptation to market demands and quicker delivery of solutions.

When implementing MLOps in our organization, we can start by following these steps:

1. Assess current ML development and deployment processes. Identify areas for improvement and potential challenges in adopting MLOps practices.

2. Choose appropriate tools and technologies. Research and compare different options for version control, CI/CD, monitoring, and model management based on our specific needs and infrastructure.

3. Start with small, manageable experiments. Introduce MLOps concepts gradually with a few models in a controlled environment, before scaling up across the organization.

4. Train the on-ground team on MLOps best practices. Educate data scientists, engineers, and operation teams on the importance and benefits of MLOps and how it can transform their workflow.

5. Iterate and continuously improve MLOps processes. As we gain experience and insights, we adjust the MLOps implementation to optimize efficiency and adapt to emerging technologies and challenges.

As we explore MLOps in this chapter, here is what a typical MLOps lifecycle might look like:

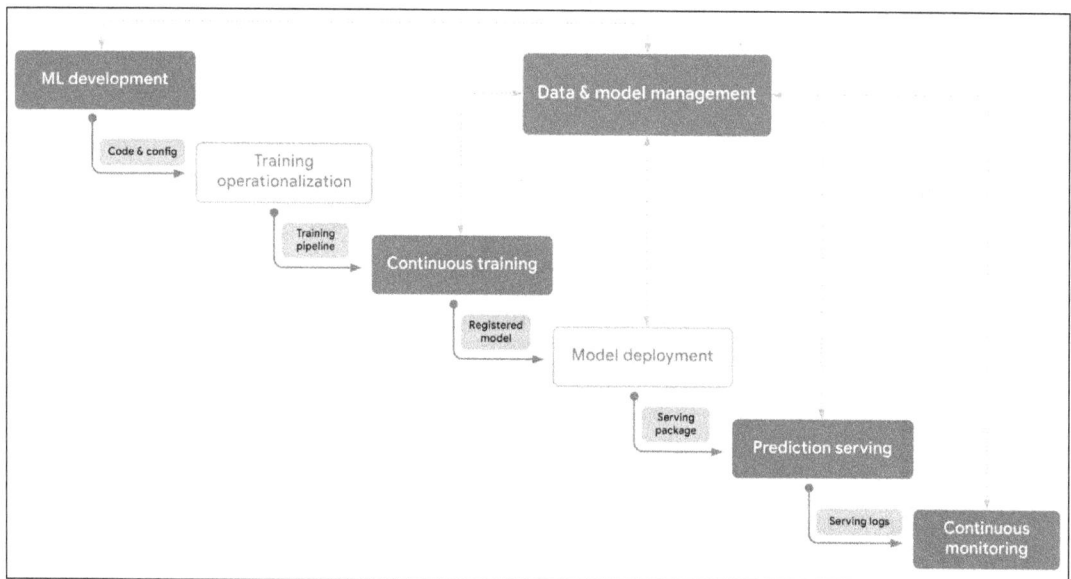

Figure 10.1: MLOps lifecycle overview

This is not a waterfall workflow that has to sequentially pass through all the processes. The processes can be skipped, or the flow can repeat a given phase or a subsequence of the processes. The flowchart in the previous figure has been explained as follows:

- The core activity during the ML development phase is experimentation. As data scientists and ML researchers prototype model architectures and training routines, they create labeled datasets, and they use features and other reusable ML artifacts that are governed through the data and model management process. The primary output of this process is a formalized training procedure, which includes data pre-processing, model architecture, and model training settings.

- If the ML system requires continuous training (repeated retraining of the model), the training procedure is operationalized as a training pipeline. This requires a CI/CD routine to build, test, and deploy the pipeline to the target execution environment.

- The continuous training pipeline is executed repeatedly based on retraining triggers, and it produces a model as output. The model is retrained as new data becomes available or when model performance decay is detected. Other training artifacts and metadata that are produced by a training pipeline are also tracked. If the pipeline produces a successful model candidate, that candidate is then tracked by the model management process as a registered model.

- The registered model is annotated, reviewed, and approved for release and is then deployed to a production environment. This process might be relatively opaque if you are using a no-code solution, or it can involve building a custom CI/CD pipeline for progressive delivery.

- The deployed model serves predictions using the deployment pattern that you have specified: online, batch, or streaming predictions. In addition to serving predictions, the serving runtime can generate model explanations and capture serving logs to be used by the continuous monitoring process.

- The continuous monitoring process monitors the model for predictive effectiveness and service. The primary concern of effective performance monitoring is detecting model decay, for example, data and concept drift. The model deployment can also be monitored for efficiency metrics like latency, throughput, hardware resource utilization, and execution errors.

Before we look at the aspects of MLOps and how they are implemented, let us try to see the various stages of the MLOps maturity model. This will give a fair idea of where a particular team stands and how to evolve to the next level as we continue to improve ourselves.

Level 0: Manual process

Many teams will have excellent data scientists and researchers who build state-of-the-art models for the given use case, but their process of building and deploying the ML models is almost entirely manual in many cases. This is what we will refer to as the **basic level of maturity** or **Level 0**. This is where almost all the steps in the process are performed manually with the use of some tools, although there will be pieces of operations that will contain script-driven approaches. Here is a visual look at this level of MLOps maturity:

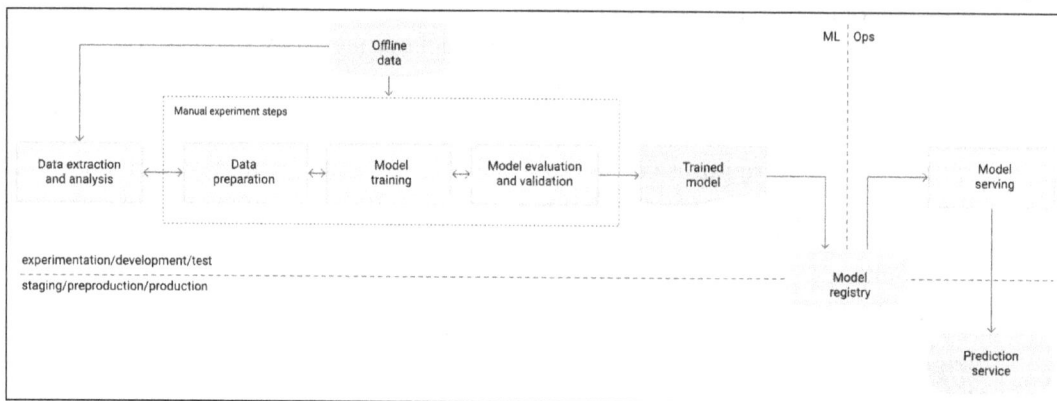

Figure 10.2: MLOps Level 0

The explanation of the figure is mentioned as follows:

- Almost all the steps are manual, requiring manual execution in each step and manual transition from one step to the other.

- This is where most of our Jupyter Notebook-based lifecycles will live until we find a better way of implementation.

  o There is also a complete disconnection between ML and operations.

- There are no CI or automated tests and no CDs, which might not even be applicable.

- Other than some unknown or hidden handoffs between the data scientists who are building the systems and the AI engineers who are putting the solutions to a target system in the form of a prediction service, like a REST API Microservice, there are no systems in this stage that monitor the lifecycle and performance of the ML model as well as the other important parts of the system.

  o Hence, there is no feedback coming back to the model development stage, which we can use to help improve the systems.

This is usually the first stage in the ML lifecycle or maturity for many organizations that are starting off to apply AI and ML to their business use cases. One should note that this stage of Level 0 may be well sufficient when models are to be rarely trained or changed. However, many times, when an ML model is deployed in the real-world with actual data (that skews and drifts all the time or over a period of time), these ML models (that worked so well in our notebooks) start to fail. An interesting read on this aspect can be found on the Forbes website here: **https://www.forbes.com/sites/forbestechcouncil/2019/04/03/ why-machine-learning-models-crash-and-burn-in-production/**. Let us see if we are able to address some of these challenges and limitations in the next levels.

Level 1: Pipeline automation

The primary objective at this level is to perform continuous automated model training, preferably using a well-designed ML pipeline. This will let us achieve a CD of models for the given prediction service. The ML pipeline can be (and usually is) an automated replica of the training experiments run by the data scientists, with an additional step of data extraction.

At this level, we aim to achieve a system where there should be some trigger to initiate the ML training (ideally driven by a monitor of the model's performance or drifts in production data). There are other components expected in this design, like a store for features to be used in and across similar ML models, a registry to version control each iteration of model training, some metadata store to store information about the pipeline executions or model versions, and so on. An ideal overview of the stage is shown in the following figure:

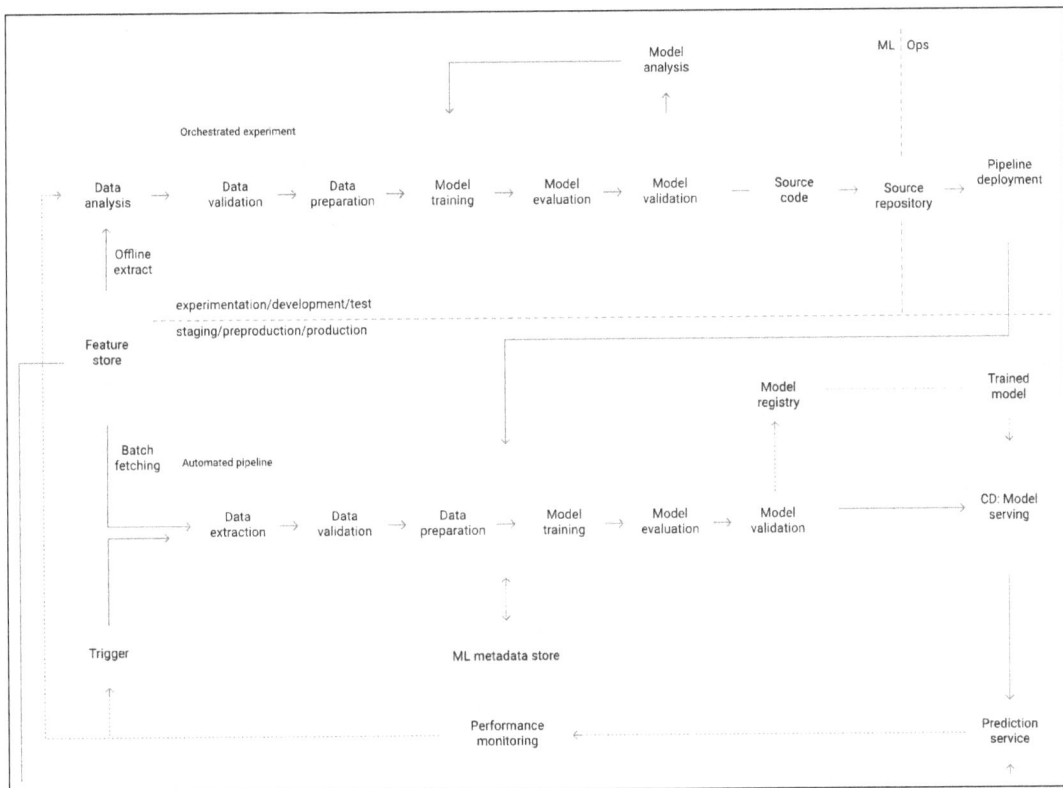

Figure 10.3: MLOps Level 1

Some of the salient features of this design are as follows:

- Each stage of ML experimentation is orchestrated, while the training between each step of experimentation is automated to a good extent. This leads to rapid iteration of model development towards target-serving environments.

- Each iteration of the ML model is automatically and continuously trained in production using fresh data based on live pipeline triggers. This design aspect is called **continuous training**. We will learn more about these triggers in due course.

- The same pipelines that are automated and used in non-production environments are used in production environments as well, unifying DevOps methodologies in ML.

- Each of the components in these pipelines should be reusable and shareable across ML pipelines. Hence, while EDA can still be performed using Jupyter Notebooks, all the source codes of the components that make up the pipeline should be modularized and ideally containerized. We will learn about Docker and how to containerize enterprise ML applications by the end of this chapter.

- Either based on a schedule or ideally triggered by detected changes in model performance in production, there are CD pipelines at this level that deploy ML models trained on new data from production into serving endpoints. As we know, these delivery pipelines are also automated.

The key difference one should acknowledge is, while in Level 0, one would deploy a trained model as a prediction endpoint to production, in Level 1, we aim to deploy the whole training pipeline, which should then automatically run to serve the trained ML model in and as the prediction endpoint service. By the term endpoint, we are referring simply to services or VM, etc., which are hosting the models and are ideally accessible over REST API calls by applications that like to leverage the ML models in question. Imagine the Google Translate UI making an API call in the backend-served translation model with the user's input language to return the translated version into the chosen target language. During this time, one should consider the various components we require to add in the Level 1 stage of MLOps maturity, which can enable continuous training and deployment of any given ML model. Let us discuss the most important components as follows:

- **Data and model validation**:
  - **Data validation**: It ensures data quality before model training. It checks for schema skews (unexpected features, missing features, or incorrect values) and data value skews (significant changes in data patterns).
  - **Model validation**: It evaluates the trained model's performance against a test dataset, comparing it to previous models. It also ensures consistent performance across different data segments and checks for deployment compatibility.

- **Feature store**:
  - A centralized repository for features used in training and serving.
  - It provides APIs for high-throughput batch and low-latency real-time serving.

- o It enables feature discovery, reuse, and consistency, preventing training-serving skew.

- o It is an optional component unless someone is sharing features across models.

- **Metadata management**:

  - o Records information about each pipeline execution, including versions, timestamps, parameters, artifacts, and evaluation metrics.

  - o Facilitates lineage tracking, reproducibility, debugging, and model rollbacks.

- **ML pipeline triggers**: They define when the pipeline should be executed:

  - o **On demand**: This requires manual execution.

  - o **On schedule**: This requires regular retraining based on data availability.

  - o **On new data**: This requires retraining triggered by new data arrival.

  - o **On performance degradation**: This requires retraining when the model performance drops.

  - o **On data drift**: This requires retraining when significant changes in data distributions occur.

Overall, these additional components in Level 1 help to emphasize the importance of automation and validation in ML pipelines to ensure reliable and efficient model deployment and CI. For infrequent pipeline deployments and a small number of pipelines, manual or semi-automated testing and deployment are sufficient. However, for rapid iteration of ML ideas (especially new ones, rather than only updating existing ones) and managing numerous pipelines for both old and new pipelines, a CI/CD setup is essential for automated build, test, and deployment. This is where we need to use Level 2 of the MLOps maturity model.

Level 2: CI/CD

We will focus more on the fast update of the pipelines in production at this level. In order to do so, we require a CI/CD system to be in place, similar to what we do in the case of software engineering solutions using DevOps frameworks and tools. This automation will assist our ML engineers in performing rapid experimentation and further automatically build, test, and deploy new pipeline components. Here is an overview of the CI/CD setup we are aiming for at this level:

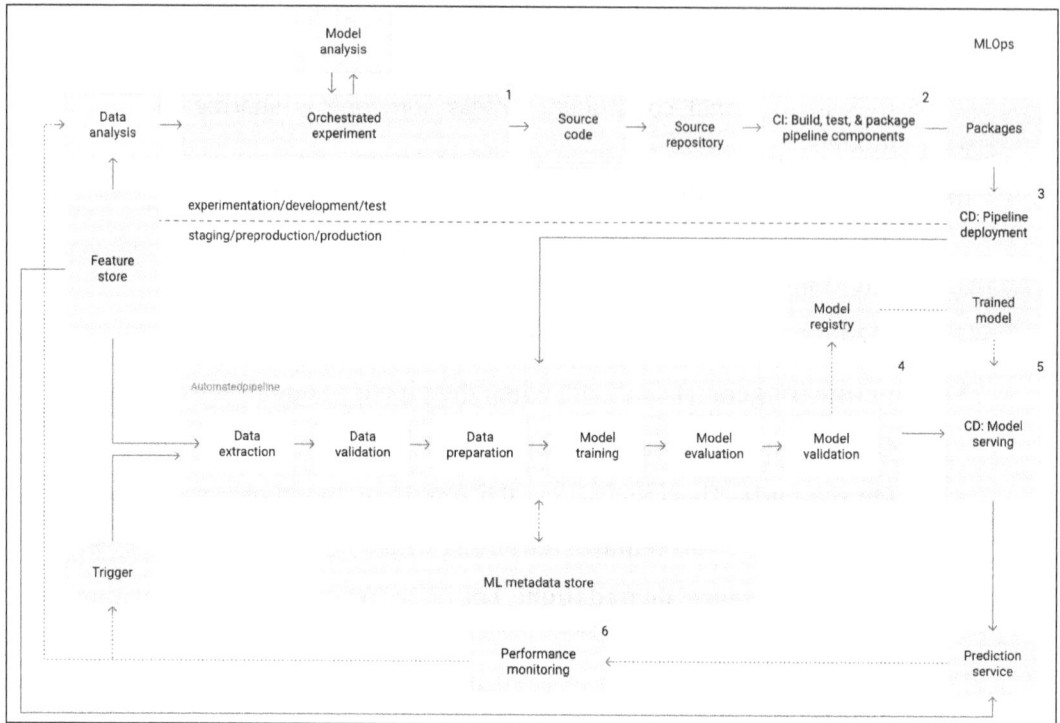

Figure 10.4: *MLOps Level 2*

As evident from the preceding architecture, in this stage, the ML pipeline consists of the following six stages:

- **Development and experimentation**: Here, the iterative development and testing of new ML algorithms and models takes place, resulting in source code for pipeline steps.

- **Pipeline CI**: This stage includes building and testing the source code and producing pipeline components (packages, executables, and artifacts) for deployment.

- **Pipeline CD**: This stage involves deploying the CI artifacts to the target environment, resulting in a deployed pipeline with the new model implementation.

- **Automated triggering**: Here, the automatic pipeline execution is based on schedules or triggers, producing a trained model stored in a model registry.

- **Model continuous delivery**: Serving the trained model as a prediction service for generating predictions occurs in this stage.

- **Monitoring**:The last stage is collecting performance statistics on the model using live data, triggering either pipeline execution or a new experiment cycle.

While the pipeline automates most of the process, the data and model analysis remain manual tasks performed by data scientists before and after each experiment cycle.

As we are considering CI at this level, the following are the several key tasks included in the process:

- **Unit testing**: This includes testing individual components like feature engineering logic and model methods.

- **Model training convergence**: This ensures the model's loss decreases with iterations and does not overfit on limited data.

- **Data integrity**: This checks for errors like missing values caused by division by zero or handling of extreme values.

- **Artifact validation**: This verifies that each pipeline component produces the expected outputs.

- **Integration testing**: This ensures seamless interaction between different pipeline components.

At this level, our system should continuously deliver new pipeline implementations to target environments, which should make prediction-ready endpoint services of newly trained models (as found during experimentations). The key steps include the following:

1. **Pre-deployment verification**:

    a. **Compatibility check**: It ensures the target infrastructure meets the model's requirements (packages, resources).

    b. **Prediction service testing**: It validates the service API with expected inputs and outputs, especially when updating model versions.

    c. **Performance testing**: It evaluates service performance under load, measuring metrics like **queries per second** (**QPS**) and latency.

    d. **Data validation**: It ensures data quality for retraining or batch prediction.

    e. **Performance target verification**: It confirms the model meets desired predictive performance levels.

2. **Deployment stages**:

    a. **Automated deployment (test environment)**: It is triggered by code pushes to the development branch.

    b. **Semi-automated deployment (pre-production)**: It is triggered by merges to the main branch after review or any other configured feature branch other than the main branch in some cases.

    c. **Manual deployment (production)**: It happens after successful runs in the pre-production environment.

This structured approach emphasizes thorough testing and gradual deployment, minimizing risks and ensuring a smooth transition to production.

Level 2 of MLOps maturity emphasizes that deploying ML in production goes beyond simply deploying a model as an API for predictions. It necessitates the deployment of a complete ML pipeline that automates the retraining and deployment of new models. This pipeline should be integrated with a CI/CD system to ensure automated testing and deployment of new pipeline implementations.

The benefits of this approach are significant:

- **Adaptability**: The automated pipeline allows for quick adaptation to changes in data and business environments, ensuring the model remains relevant and effective.

- **Efficiency**: Automation streamlines the entire ML development and production process, reducing manual effort and potential errors.

- **Scalability**: The CI/CD system enables seamless scaling of the ML pipeline to handle increasing data volumes and model complexity.

This level of maturity also encourages a gradual implementation of these practices, allowing organizations to improve the automation of their ML systems incrementally. This approach allows for a smoother transition and minimizes disruption to existing processes.

AI and ML deployments

AI/ML deployments encompass the essential processes of taking a trained AI/ML model and putting it into production. This entails packaging the model, deploying it to the appropriate infrastructure, and integrating it with existing systems or applications. This section will explore three critical aspects of AI/ML deployments:

- On-premises installations
- Data and model security
- Effective operations design

On-premises installations involve setting up and running our AI/ML models within our infrastructure rather than using cloud-based services. This provides greater control over data and models, which can be beneficial for industries with stringent security or privacy requirements. Some of the common pros and cons are as follows:

- **Advantages**:
  - **Data security**: On-premises installations offer enhanced data security, especially for sensitive information, by keeping all data within our network.
  - **Customization**: You have complete control over the infrastructure and can customize it to suit our specific needs and requirements.
  - **Reduced latency**: On-premises installations can minimize latency, especially when real-time responsiveness is crucial.

- ○ **Offline capabilities**: Our AI/ML models can operate even in situations with limited or no internet connectivity.

- **Disadvantages**:

  - ○ **Costly setup**: On-premises installations require significant upfront investments for hardware and software resources.

  - ○ **Maintenance complexity**: Managing our infrastructure adds to the complexity and requires dedicated IT personnel.

  - ○ **Scalability challenges**: Scaling our infrastructure to accommodate future needs can be more difficult with on-premises installations.

One must be aware of a few considerations for on-premises installations, as follows:

- **Data security requirements**: We must assess the sensitivity of our data and the regulatory requirements for its protection.

- **Infrastructure capabilities**: In parallel, we should evaluate our current IT infrastructure and its ability to support AI/ML deployments.

- **Budget constraints**: Finally, one should consider the costs associated with hardware, software, and personnel needed to manage an on-premises deployment.

Data and model security are equally important in AI/ML deployments. Protecting sensitive data and model integrity ensures the ethical, reliable, and responsible operation of our systems. Some of the best practices when it comes to data and model security are as follows:

- **Data encryption**: Encrypt data at rest and in transit to safeguard against unauthorized access.

- **Access control**: Implement strong access control measures to ensure only authorized users can access sensitive data.

- **Auditing and logging**: Regularly monitor activity logs to detect potential security vulnerabilities and breaches.

- **Data minimization**: Collect and store only the minimal amount of data required for our AI/ML models.

- **Model versioning**: Track and control different model versions to maintain reproducibility and facilitate rollbacks if needed.

- **Vulnerability assessment**: Regularly test our models for potential vulnerabilities that could lead to adversarial attacks.

- **Explainable AI**: Use techniques to understand how models make decisions, allowing for more transparent and accountable operations.

Effective operational design ensures our AI/ML models run smoothly, efficiently, and reliably in production environments. This involves monitoring model performance, managing resources, and automating tasks for smoother workflows.

Some of the key considerations for better operational design are as follows:

- **Monitoring**: Implement systems to continuously monitor model performance metrics and data quality to detect and address potential issues.

- **Resource management**: Optimize resource utilization for cost efficiency and scalability, adjusting infrastructure based on actual usage patterns.

- **Automation**: Automate routine tasks, such as model retraining, data preparation, and deployment processes, for increased efficiency and reduced manual intervention.

- **Logging and error handling**: Implement comprehensive logging and error handling processes for effective troubleshooting and problem resolution.

Some of the upfront benefits of having a tangible operational design are as follows:

- **Proactive issue identification**: Early detection of anomalies and issues allows for timely intervention, reducing potential downtime and errors.

- **Cost optimization**: Efficient resource management and automation minimize operational expenses.

- **Improved reliability and scalability**: A well-managed system is more robust and adaptable to changes in demand or data volume.

Some common tools and technologies that are involved in this entire process are as follows:

- **Monitoring systems**: Prometheus, Grafana, Datadog.
- **Resource management Tools**: Kubernetes, Docker Swarm.
- **Automation frameworks**: Airflow, Prefect, Luigi.

AI/ML deployments require careful consideration of various factors, including on-premises vs. cloud deployments, data and model security measures, and effective operational design. Carefully evaluating each element ensures the successful integration and smooth operation of our AI/ML models in production, achieving the desired business value and impact.

Model monitoring

In this section of the chapter, we will investigate monitoring ML models and how to do so effectively. Monitoring may sound more operational than creating state-of-the-art models, but they are as essential as any other aspect of ML engineering. This is where we watch the health of our models and track the changes in their lifecycles in order to keep them updated. Let us first look at the types of monitoring one should be looking at for any given AI/ML installation.

We will start by taking care of data monitoring, which involves tracking the data our model is trained on and used for predictions. It checks for the following points:

- **Data drift**: It occurs when the distribution of our data changes over time, potentially leading to inaccurate predictions. Imagine our model is trained on images of sunny days but suddenly encounters mostly rainy-day images. Its performance might suffer.

- **Data quality**: It monitors for missing values, outliers, or inconsistencies in our data that could negatively impact model training and predictions.

- **Data bias**: It checks for biases in our data that could lead to unfair or discriminatory outcomes. For example, a model trained on loan applications might exhibit bias against certain demographics if the data reflects historical biases.

Next up is model monitoring, which focuses on the model itself, tracking its performance and behavior, as follows:

- **Model performance**: Monitors metrics like accuracy, precision, recall, and F1 score to ensure the model continues to perform well on new data.

- **Model explainability**: Tracks how the model makes decisions, providing insights into its reasoning and potential biases. This helps to understand why the model makes certain predictions and identifies areas for improvement.

- **Model health**: Monitors for issues like overfitting, where the model performs well on training data but poorly on new data, and degradation, where the model's performance deteriorates over time.

Lastly, there is infrastructure monitoring, which is where one monitors the infrastructure supporting our model, ensuring it runs smoothly and efficiently:

- **Resource utilization**: Tracks resource usage like CPU, memory, and network bandwidth to identify potential bottlenecks and optimize performance.

- **System health**: Monitors for system failures, errors, and security vulnerabilities to ensure the infrastructure remains stable and secure.

All of these types of monitoring need to be put in place to some extent as a start and then improved over a period of time for any type of AI/ML platform, irrespective of the use case we are trying to resolve. Let us look at some examples and see how (for the different types of models that we have learned so far) one can put monitoring systems in place and the specific KPIs that one would like to monitor, as follows:

- **Classification models**:
  - **Fraud detection**: Monitor the accuracy of a fraud detection model to ensure it correctly identifies fraudulent transactions.

- **Spam filtering**: Monitor the precision and recall of a spam filtering model to ensure it effectively filters spam emails while minimizing false positives.

- **Medical diagnosis**: Monitor the F1 score of a medical diagnosis model to ensure it accurately diagnoses diseases with high precision and recall.

- **Regression models**:

  - **Sales forecasting**: Monitor the MSE of a sales forecasting model to ensure it accurately predicts future sales figures.

  - **Stock price prediction**: Monitor the RMSE of a stock price prediction model to ensure it accurately predicts future stock prices.

  - **Customer churn prediction**: Monitor the AUC of a customer churn prediction model to ensure it accurately identifies customers at risk of churn.

- **Clustering models**:

  - **Customer segmentation**: Monitor the silhouette score of a customer segmentation model to ensure it effectively groups customers into distinct segments.

  - **Anomaly detection**: Monitor the *Calinski-Harabasz* index of an anomaly detection model to ensure it effectively identifies unusual data points.

  - **Image classification**: Monitor the *Davies-Bouldin* index of an image classification model to ensure it effectively groups images into distinct categories.

- **NLP models**:

  - **Machine translation**: Monitor the BLEU score of a machine translation model to ensure it accurately translates text between languages.

  - **Text summarization**: Monitor the ROUGE score of a text summarization model to ensure it accurately summarizes text while preserving key information.

  - **Sentiment analysis**: Monitor the accuracy of a sentiment analysis model to ensure it accurately identifies the sentiment of text data.

- **Computer vision models**:

  - **Object detection**: Monitor the accuracy of an object detection model to ensure it accurately identifies and locates objects in images.

  - **Image classification**: Monitor the precision and recall of an image classification model to ensure it accurately classifies images into different categories.

o **Facial recognition**: Monitor the F1 score of a facial recognition model to ensure it accurately identifies individuals in images with high precision and recall.

This list is endless, but in the real-world, the KPIs we choose for monitoring an AI/ML platform not only encompass the technical working and health of the models but also the business metrics that need to be taken into consideration. Although one cannot jot down a comprehensive list of all that we would want to monitor, as a best practice, such KPIs should be identified and monitored from day one of the implementation of any AI/ML system.

Several cloud frameworks provide comprehensive tools and services for model monitoring. Here are some popular options:

- **Amazon SageMaker**:

    o **Model monitor**: Continuously monitors deployed models for data quality, model quality, and model explainability. It provides real-time insights and alerts for potential issues.

    o **Clarify**: Helps understand and interpret model predictions, providing insights into model behavior and potential biases.

- **Google Cloud Platform, Vertex AI**:

    o **Vertex AI monitoring**: It monitors model performance and data quality in real time, providing insights into model drift, data skew, and feature importance.

    o **Explainable AI**: It provides tools and techniques for understanding and interpreting model predictions, including feature importance and counterfactual explanations.

- **Microsoft Azure Machine Learning**:

    o **Model explainability**: It provides tools and techniques for understanding and interpreting model predictions, including feature importance and LIME explanations.

    o **Model management**: It enables versioning, deployment, and monitoring of models, ensuring consistency and traceability.

Choosing the right cloud framework for model monitoring depends on several factors, including the following:

- **Type of models**: Different frameworks offer varying levels of support for different types of models.

- **Monitoring needs**: Consider the specific metrics and insights you need to track for our models.

- **Integration with existing infrastructure**: Choose a framework that integrates seamlessly with our existing cloud environment.

- **Cost and scalability**: Evaluate the pricing models and scalability options offered by different frameworks.

In addition to the preceding cloud frameworks, several open-source tools and libraries can be used for model monitoring. These include the following:

- **Prometheus**: This is a monitoring system that collects and stores metrics from various sources.

- **Grafana**: This is a data visualization tool that can be used to create dashboards for monitoring model performance.

- **MLflow**: This is an open-source platform for managing the machine learning lifecycle, including model monitoring.

Let us look at how to implement CI/CD for ML platforms, keeping in mind the different levels of MLOps that we have already learned.

CI/CD for ML

As we have learned about the various levels of maturity in MLOps practices, a typical CI/CD pipeline for ML models includes the following stages:

- **Code commit**: The developer commits the code for the ML model to a version control system, such as Git.

- **Build**: The system builds the ML model from the code. This may involve downloading dependencies, compiling code, and training the model.

- **Test**: The system tests the ML model to ensure that it meets the required quality standards. This may involve running unit tests, integration tests, and performance tests.

- **Deploy**: The system deploys the ML model to production. This may involve deploying the model to a cloud platform, such as AWS or Azure, or deploying it to an on-premises server.

- **Monitor**: The system monitors the ML model in production to ensure that it is performing as expected. This may involve collecting metrics on the model's performance and alerting the developers if there are any problems.

Some of the common tools we generally use while implementing CI/CD for AI/ML models are as follows:

- **Jenkins**: This is an open-source tool that can be used to automate the build, test, and deployment of ML models.

- **GitHub Actions**: This tool is integrated with GitHub. It can be used to automate the build, test, and deployment of ML models.

- **MLflow**: This is an open-source platform for managing the ML lifecycle. It can be used to track experiments, manage models, and deploy models to production.

- **Kubeflow**: This is an open-source platform for deploying and managing ML models using containers for each of its components on Kubernetes.

- **TensorFlow Extended (TFX)**: A TFX pipeline is a sequence of components that implement an ML pipeline that is specifically designed for scalable, high-performance machine learning tasks. Components are built using TFX libraries, which can also be used individually.

We will explore TFX and Kubeflow in the coming sections of this chapter. Specific cloud platforms like Azure, Google Cloud, and AWS may also have their cloud service offerings, which can be used to design the CI/CD required for AI/ML installations on those specific cloud platforms.

TensorFlow Extended

TFX is an open-source end-to-end platform for building, managing, and deploying ML pipelines. It provides a comprehensive set of tools and libraries that streamline the ML development process, making it easier and faster to build and deploy reliable, production-ready ML models.

In this section, we will learn the basics of TFX, covering its key features, architecture, components, and benefits. We will also explore how TFX can be used to build and deploy ML pipelines in various scenarios. Later, we will see sample code implementations of how to employ TFX in ML engineering

Let us look at some key features of TFX to understand why one needs to be aware of them and, further, how to make the best use of them, as follows:

- **End-to-end ML pipeline orchestration**: TFX provides a framework for defining, managing, and executing ML pipelines, encompassing all stages from data ingestion to model deployment.

- **Modular and extensible architecture**: TFX is built on a modular architecture, allowing users to easily customize and extend the platform to meet their specific needs.

- **Versioning and reproducibility**: TFX ensures that all components and artifacts within an ML pipeline are versioned, enabling the reproducibility and traceability of results.

- **Scalability and performance**: TFX is designed to handle large-scale ML workloads, leveraging distributed computing frameworks like Apache Beam and Kubernetes for efficient execution.

- **Integration with the TensorFlow ecosystem**: TFX seamlessly integrates with other TensorFlow libraries and tools, providing a unified platform for ML development.

TFX follows a modular architecture, consisting of the following key components:

- **Components**: These are reusable building blocks that represent individual steps within an ML pipeline, such as data ingestion, pre-processing, training, evaluation, and deployment.

- **Orchestrator**: This component manages the execution of the ML pipeline, coordinating the execution of different components and ensuring dependencies are met.

- **Driver**: This component provides a command line interface for interacting with the TFX platform, allowing users to define, run, and monitor ML pipelines.

- **Metadata store**: This component stores information about the ML pipeline, including its components, artifacts, and execution history.

TFX offers a rich set of components covering various stages of the ML pipeline, as follows:

- **Data validation**:

  - **StatisticsGen**: It analyzes your data to generate statistics like mean, standard deviation, and cardinality.

  - **SchemaGen**: It infers the schema of your data, including data types and missing values.

  - **ExampleValidator**: It checks if your data adheres to the defined schema and flags any inconsistencies.

- **Transformation**:

  - **Transform**: It applies transformations like normalization, discretization, and feature engineering to your data.

  - **Imputer**: It handles missing values in your data using techniques like mean or median imputation.

- **Training**:

  - **Trainer**: This trains your model using the transformed data and chosen hyperparameters.

  - **Tuner**: This optimizes hyperparameters for your model to achieve the best performance.

  - **Evaluator**: This evaluates the trained model's performance on unseen data using various metrics.

- **Serving**:
  - o **Model validator**: It validates the trained model before deployment to ensure it meets quality standards.
  - o **Pusher**: It pushes the validated model to a serving environment for real-world predictions.

- **Infra and metadata**:
  - o **Orchestrator**: This manages the execution of your pipeline, including scheduling and resource allocation.
  - o **Resolver**: This handles dependencies between components and retrieves necessary data artifacts.
  - o **Metadata**: This stores information about your pipeline, including lineage, parameters, and metrics.

The following components seamlessly work together to build a complete ML pipeline in any ideal production environment:

  - o **Data ingestion**: Data is ingested from various sources like CSV files, databases, or cloud storage.
  - o **Data validation**: Data is validated to ensure completeness, consistency, and adherence to the defined schema.
  - o **Transformation**: Data is transformed using pre-processing techniques to prepare it for training.
  - o **Training**: The transformed data is used to train the ML model, with hyperparameters optimized for best performance.
  - o **Evaluation**: The trained model is evaluated on unseen data to assess its accuracy and generalizability.
  - o **Serving**: The validated model is deployed to a serving environment, ready to make predictions on live data.

There are some upfront benefits of using TFX as follows:

- **Increased productivity**: TFX automates many repetitive tasks in ML development, allowing data scientists and engineers to focus on more strategic aspects.

- **Improved model quality**: TFX provides tools and best practices for ensuring data quality, model fairness, and explainability.

- **Reduced time to market**: TFX streamlines the ML deployment process, enabling faster delivery of models to production.

- **Enhanced collaboration**: TFX facilitates collaboration among different teams involved in ML development by providing a centralized platform for managing and sharing artifacts.

- **Cost optimization**: TFX helps optimize resource utilization by efficiently managing compute resources and reducing infrastructure costs.

Before we proceed further, it is important to note that, as of writing this chapter, the TFX library is only supported to run on Linux and Macintosh OS (Apple) but not on Windows. Also, the latest version of TFX, which is equally compatible with other required Python libraries, is best suited for the Python 3.9.16 version. So, to set up TFX, one can follow these steps first (on their Linux environments, like CentOS or Ubuntu or RHEL, for example) to configure Python 3.9.16. Note that this is one of the many ways of running specific Python version(s) on Linux environments.

Firstly, we can install the **pyenv** library using a command like the following from the terminal:

```
curl -fsSL https://pyenv.run | bash
```

Once the installation finishes, it gives a text like the following, which needs to be added in the **~/.bash_profile** file so that we can use PyEnv to create specific Python environments:

```
# Load pyenv automatically by appending
# the following to
# ~/.bash_profile if it exists, otherwise ~/.profile (for login shells)
# and ~/.bashrc (for interactive shells) :

export PYENV_ROOT="$HOME/.pyenv"
[[ -d $PYENV_ROOT/bin ]] && export PATH="$PYENV_ROOT/bin:$PATH"
eval "$(pyenv init - bash)"

# Restart your shell for the changes to take effect.

# Load pyenv-virtualenv automatically by adding
# the following to ~/.bashrc:

eval "$(pyenv virtualenv-init -)"
```

Note that we can use the vi editor to add these lines to the **~/.bashrc** file. Once this file is updated, we can **source** it so that we can load the required settings:

```
source ~/.bashrc
```

Next, to select the specific version of Python, we can run the following command on the Terminal to get a list of all available versions. This is optional and can be skipped to save time, although it is a good-to-know command:

```
pyenv install -l
```

Now, let us install the specific Python version using a command like the following:

```
pyenv install 3.9.16
```

Once the installation is complete, let us create a new virtual environment so that we can install the TFX library. To do so, we can use the following commands in sequence:

```
python3 -m venv ~/tfx3
source ~/tfx3/bin/activate
which pip
which python
python --version
pip install tfx
pip install jupyter ipython
```

In the preceding commands, we created a new virtual environment called **tfx3** for Python and activated it. Note that we can give any name to this virtual environment! Next, we activated the environment, checked if we were using the right **pip** and **python** command line utilities from the new environment, checked the Python version, and finally installed the TFX library.

Once the library is installed, we can use the following setting on the command line to suppress a known bug that is still open and unresolved. This known issue is related to TensorFlow and Keras, whose discussion is not relevant at this moment.

```
export TF_USE_LEGACY_KERAS=1
```

Finally, we can open a Jupyter Notebook environment (locally) on our Linux OS using the following command within the newly created **tfx3** virtual environment:

```
cd Downloads
jupyter notebook
```

Now that the environment is set up for us, let us look at a quick official example of how to make use of TFX pipelines. As a part of this implementation, we will take a small pre-labeled dataset called the **Penguins** dataset and run a custom ML training on the dataset to see TFX in action. The pipeline will consist of three essential TFX components: **ExampleGen** (to work with the training data), **Trainer** (to run the actual training pipeline), and **Pusher** (to finally push a validated model toward a deployment target or endpoint, which in this example will be local disk).

To start, we can place the provided Jupyter Notebook file from this book's GitHub repository from the relevant folder of *Chapter 10* into the **Downloads** folder of our Linux OS. Furthermore, we will check the versions of TensorFlow and TFX. This is optional, but it helps in case one gets any errors in execution to check for logs and support in the developer communities. Here is a sample code:

```
# Import TensorFlow libraries
import TensorFlow as tf
print('TensorFlow version: {}'.format(tf.__version__))
from tfx import v1 as tfx
print('TFX version: {}'.format(tfx.__version__))
```

Before we start loading the data, we will define the required parameters to create the pipeline definition. These are required variables to define a TFX pipeline. By default, all output from the pipeline will be generated under the current directory, as follows:

```
# create pipeline definition
import os

PIPELINE_NAME = "penguin-simple"

# Output directory to store artifacts generated from the pipeline.
PIPELINE_ROOT = os.path.join('pipelines', PIPELINE_NAME)
# Path to a SQLite DB file to use as an MLMD storage.
METADATA_PATH = os.path.join('metadata', PIPELINE_NAME, 'metadata.db')
# Output directory where created models from the pipeline will be exported.
SERVING_MODEL_DIR = os.path.join('serving_model', PIPELINE_NAME)

from absl import logging
logging.set_verbosity(logging.INFO)  # Set default logging level.
```

Now that we have the very basic setup in place, we will download our penguins dataset from GitHub in this case, which is already labeled. Refer to the following code for a better understanding:

```
# download the data
import urllib.request
import tempfile

DATA_ROOT = tempfile.mkdtemp(prefix='tfx-data')  # Create a temporary
directory.
_data_url = 'https://raw.githubusercontent.com/TensorFlow/tfx/master/tfx/
examples/penguin/data/labelled/penguins_processed.csv'
_data_filepath = os.path.join(DATA_ROOT, "data.csv")
urllib.request.urlretrieve(_data_url, _data_filepath)
```

Here, we are downloading the sample data. In this particular example, we will skip the EDA part of the dataset since it is dummy data used for this specific example use case. While working on Colab, one can optionally check the data that gets downloaded using the Linux **head** command, as shown in the following example:

```
# Check downloaded data file
!head {_data_filepath}
```

In this example, we will create a trainer Python script and use the **%%writefile** magic function directive so that we can save the file in the local directory and call it as part of our TFX pipeline:

```
# create variable for training module
_trainer_module_file = 'penguin_trainer.py'

%%writefile {_trainer_module_file}

from typing import List
from absl import logging
import TensorFlow as tf
from TensorFlow import keras
from TensorFlow_transform.tf_metadata import schema_utils

from tfx import v1 as tfx
from tfx_bsl.public import tfxio
from TensorFlow_metadata.proto.v0 import schema_pb2

_FEATURE_KEYS = [
    'culmen_length_mm', 'culmen_depth_mm', 'flipper_length_mm', 'body_
mass_g'
]
_LABEL_KEY = 'species'

_TRAIN_BATCH_SIZE = 20
_EVAL_BATCH_SIZE = 10

# Since we're not generating or creating a schema, we will instead create
# a feature spec.  Since there are a fairly small number of features this
is
# manageable for this dataset.
_FEATURE_SPEC = {
    **{
        feature: tf.io.FixedLenFeature(shape=[1], dtype=tf.float32)
            for feature in _FEATURE_KEYS
        },
    _LABEL_KEY: tf.io.FixedLenFeature(shape=[1], dtype=tf.int64)
}

def _input_fn(file_pattern: List[str],
                data_accessor: tfx.components.DataAccessor,
                schema: schema_pb2.Schema,
                batch_size: int = 200) -> tf.data.Dataset:
    """Generates features and label for training.
```

```
   Args:
     file_pattern: List of paths or patterns of input tfrecord files.
     data_accessor: DataAccessor for converting input to RecordBatch.
     schema: schema of the input data.
     batch_size: representing the number of consecutive elements of returned
       dataset to combine in a single batch

   Returns:
     A dataset that contains (features, indices) tuple where features is a
       dictionary of Tensors, and indices is a single Tensor of label
indices.
   """

   return data_accessor.tf_dataset_factory(
       file_pattern,
       tfxio.TensorFlowDatasetOptions(
           batch_size=batch_size, label_key=_LABEL_KEY),
       schema=schema).repeat()

def _build_keras_model() -> tf.keras.Model:
   """Creates a DNN Keras model for classifying penguin data.

   Returns:
     A Keras Model.
   """

   # The model below is built with Functional API, please refer to
   # https://www.TensorFlow.org/guide/keras/overview for all API options.
   inputs = [keras.layers.Input(shape=(1,), name=f) for f in _FEATURE_KEYS]
   d = keras.layers.concatenate(inputs)
   for _ in range(2):
     d = keras.layers.Dense(8, activation='relu')(d)
   outputs = keras.layers.Dense(3)(d)

   model = keras.Model(inputs=inputs, outputs=outputs)
   model.compile(
       optimizer=keras.optimizers.Adam(1e-2),
       loss=tf.keras.losses.SparseCategoricalCrossentropy(from_logits=True),
       metrics=[keras.metrics.SparseCategoricalAccuracy()])

   model.summary(print_fn=logging.info)
   return model

# TFX Trainer will call this function.
```

```
def run_fn(fn_args: tfx.components.FnArgs):
  """Train the model based on given args.

  Args:
    fn_args: Holds args used to train the model as name/value pairs.
  """

  # This schema is usually either an output of SchemaGen or a manually-
curated
  # version provided by pipeline author. A schema can also derived from TFT
  # graph if a Transform component is used. In the case when either is
missing,
  # `schema_from_feature_spec` could be used to generate schema from very
simple
  # feature_spec, but the schema returned would be very primitive.
  schema = schema_utils.schema_from_feature_spec(_FEATURE_SPEC)

  train_dataset = _input_fn(
      fn_args.train_files,
      fn_args.data_accessor,
      schema,
      batch_size=_TRAIN_BATCH_SIZE)
  eval_dataset = _input_fn(
      fn_args.eval_files,
      fn_args.data_accessor,
      schema,
      batch_size=_EVAL_BATCH_SIZE)

  model = _build_keras_model()
  model.fit(
      train_dataset,
      steps_per_epoch=fn_args.train_steps,
      validation_data=eval_dataset,
      validation_steps=fn_args.eval_steps)

  # The result of the training should be saved in `fn_args.serving_model_
dir`
  # directory.
  model.save(fn_args.serving_model_dir)
```

In this script, we first define the columns or features in the dataset, train the model using Keras (suggesting that TFX will work with our existing ML libraries as well), and finally save the model in TensorFlow format. Before we execute this trainer, the **ExampleGen** and

Pusher modules of TFX and other required components. We will create a reusable function to execute the TFX pipeline with all the required parameters. Refer to the following code for clarity:

```
# utility to create the TFX pipeline
def _create_pipeline(pipeline_name: str, pipeline_root: str, data_root:
str,
                        module_file: str, serving_model_dir: str,
                        metadata_path: str) -> tfx.dsl.Pipeline:
  """Creates a three component penguin pipeline with TFX."""
  # Brings data into the pipeline.
  example_gen = tfx.components.CsvExampleGen(input_base=data_root)

  # Uses user-provided Python function that trains a model.
  trainer = tfx.components.Trainer(
      module_file=module_file,
      examples=example_gen.outputs['examples'],
      train_args=tfx.proto.TrainArgs(num_steps=100),
      eval_args=tfx.proto.EvalArgs(num_steps=5))

  # Pushes the model to a filesystem destination.
  pusher = tfx.components.Pusher(
      model=trainer.outputs['model'],
      push_destination=tfx.proto.PushDestination(
          filesystem=tfx.proto.PushDestination.Filesystem(
              base_directory=serving_model_dir)))

  # Following three components will be included in the pipeline.
  components = [
      example_gen,
      trainer,
      pusher,
  ]

  return tfx.dsl.Pipeline(
      pipeline_name=pipeline_name,
      pipeline_root=pipeline_root,
      metadata_connection_config=tfx.orchestration.metadata
      .sqlite_metadata_connection_config(metadata_path),
      components=components)
```

Finally, we can run the pipeline and check the serving model directory once the job finishes. In the following example, the TFX Pusher component is used to put the trained model (as a TensorFlow file format) in the local directory defined by the **serving_model_dir** variable:

```
# Run the TFX pipeline
tfx.orchestration.LocalDagRunner().run(
  _create_pipeline(
      pipeline_name=PIPELINE_NAME,
      pipeline_root=PIPELINE_ROOT,
      data_root=DATA_ROOT,
      module_file=_trainer_module_file,
      serving_model_dir=SERVING_MODEL_DIR,
      metadata_path=METADATA_PATH))

# List files in created model directory.
!find {SERVING_MODEL_DIR}
```

This example shows how one can design and run a TFX component for a given ML use case. One can find this and similar examples from the TensorFlow GitHub public repository here: **https://github.com/TensorFlow/tfx/blob/master/docs/tutorials/tfx/**. In the next section, we will learn about another interesting and very popular library that makes use of containers under the hood to run ML pipelines.

Kubeflow

Both TensorFlow and TFX are designed for production systems, which can lead to the perception of a steep learning curve. However, they provide a comprehensive set of APIs and functions necessary for various tasks related to machine learning engineering right out of the box. This is where Kubeflow comes in.

Kubeflow is an open-source platform for deploying and managing ML pipelines in production environments. Built on top of Kubernetes (which we will learn briefly in the next section of this chapter), Kubeflow aims to simplify and streamline the ML workflow, enabling data scientists and engineers to focus on building better models rather than worrying about the infrastructure and deployment complexities.

Kubeflow offers a range of services for the entire ML lifecycle, including the following:

- **Data preparation and pre-processing**: It includes tools for ingesting, cleaning, and transforming data.

- **Model training**: It includes scalable and distributed training using various frameworks like TensorFlow, PyTorch, and XGBoost.

- **Model deployment and serving**: It efficiently serves models for real-time predictions.

- **Model monitoring and explainability**: It observes model performance and understands its behavior.

- **Pipeline management and orchestration**: It automates and manages the entire ML workflow.

Kubeflow provides several key advantages for deploying ML models in production; some are as follows:

- **Scalability**: It leverages the power of Kubernetes to scale ML workloads across multiple nodes and clusters.

- **Portability**: It runs on various platforms, including public clouds, private data centers, and hybrid environments.

- **Extensibility**: It offers a modular architecture with numerous components easily configurable and integrated with existing workflows.

- **Open-source**: It is freely available and benefits from community contributions, fostering innovation and rapid development.

- **Security**: It utilizes Kubernetes' security features to protect ML models and data.

At its core, Kubeflow functions by leveraging Kubernetes as the underlying container orchestration platform. The ML workflow is broken down into individual steps or components, each packaged as a container. Kubernetes then schedules and manages these containers across the cluster, ensuring efficient resource utilization and scalability.

The Kubeflow architecture comprises several key components, as follows:

- **Kubeflow pipelines**: This declares and automates ML workflows using declarative configurations.

- **Jupyter hub**: This enables interactive notebooks for data exploration and model experimentation.

- **KFServing**: This serves ML models in production for real-time predictions.

- **Central dashboard**: This provides a unified view of all ML components and resources.

To understand how it works on the ground, we will again use a Google Colab-based notebook to run a typical ML use case. While we will use **Kubeflow Pipelines** (**KFP**) to execute the orchestration, we will use sklearn to build the model components and package them together. If any of our readers would like to try this example on their workstations, we recommend installing Docker and Docker Desktop and installing Minikube. The respective installations are simplistic and very well documented on their respective websites. Additionally, we recommend following the local installation guidelines of Kubeflow from the Kubeflow public documentation page. **Minikube**, in this context, is a mini-version of how a Kubernetes cluster would look in a production-like setup. In the later section of this chapter, we will learn more about Docker and Kubernetes in some depth.

Let us start by installing the required libraries as follows:

```
# install Kubeflow
!pip install kfp --upgrade -q
# install UCI ML Repo
!pip install ucimlrepo -q
```

In this use case, we will make use of a spam dataset from the *UCI ML Repository*. Let us start by importing the required libraries of Kubeflow to create the pipeline and its components:

```
# Import necessary libraries
import kfp
from kfp import dsl
from kfp.dsl import component
```

In this case, Kubeflow was imported. We imported its **dsl** library so that we could create individual components of the pipeline and the component decorator itself. Each activity we perform as part of our ML lifecycle is packaged as a component in Kubeflow. They get separate containers to execute, and hence, they do not affect each other's operation. For each of these components, we need to define the base image as if we are creating a Docker container and specify the libraries we require to run the functionality inside the container. Let us start by creating the component for loading and pre-processing data:

```
# Define a function to load and preprocess data
@component(base_image='python:3.9', packages_to_install=['pandas',
'numpy'])
def load_and_preprocess_data() -> str:
    import numpy as np
    import pandas as pd
    url = 'https://archive.ics.uci.edu/ml/machine-learning-databases/
spambase/spambase.data'
    data = pd.read_csv(url, header=None)

    columns = ["word_freq_make", "word_freq_address", "word_freq_all",
"word_freq_3d", "word_freq_our",
                "word_freq_over", "word_freq_remove", "word_freq_internet",
"word_freq_order", "word_freq_mail",
                "word_freq_receive", "word_freq_will", "word_freq_people",
"word_freq_report", "word_freq_addresses",
                "word_freq_free", "word_freq_business", "word_freq_email",
"word_freq_you", "word_freq_credit",
                "word_freq_your", "word_freq_font", "word_freq_000", "word_
freq_money", "word_freq_hp",
```

```
            "word_freq_hpl", "word_freq_george", "word_freq_650", "word_
freq_lab", "word_freq_labs",
            "word_freq_telnet", "word_freq_857", "word_freq_data",
"word_freq_415", "word_freq_85",
            "word_freq_technology", "word_freq_1999", "word_freq_parts",
"word_freq_pm", "word_freq_direct",
            "word_freq_cs", "word_freq_meeting", "word_freq_original",
"word_freq_project", "word_freq_re",
            "word_freq_edu", "word_freq_table", "word_freq_conference",
"char_freq_;", "char_freq_(",
            "char_freq_[", "char_freq_!", "char_freq_$", "char_freq_#",
"capital_run_length_average",
            "capital_run_length_longest", "capital_run_length_total",
"spam"]
    data.columns = columns

    # Save preprocessed data to CSV
    data.to_csv('preprocessed_data.csv', index=False)
    return 'preprocessed_data.csv'
```

Irrespective of the simple logic of the function here, we use a Python decorator to specify that this function will be used as a Kubeflow component and the libraries it requires to run the function. Similarly, we continue to define all the required components, and then later/finally, we can stitch them together in the form of a **directed acyclic graph** (**DAG**). Let us create the next component for performing the EDA and saving its results:

```
# Define a function for exploratory data analysis
@component(base_image='python:3.9', packages_to_install=['pandas',
'numpy'])
def eda(preprocessed_data_path: str):
    import pandas as pd
    import numpy as np
    data = pd.read_csv(preprocessed_data_path)

    # Print data information and description
    print(data.info())
    print(data.describe())

    # Save the info and describe to a text file
    with open('eda_output.txt', 'w') as f:
        f.write(str(data.info()) + '\n' + str(data.describe()))
```

Next, let us define the feature engineering component that we want to have as part of our ML pipeline in the following example:

```
# Define a function for feature engineering
@component(base_image='python:3.9', packages_to_install=['pandas', 'numpy',
'scikit-learn'])
def feature_engineering(preprocessed_data_path: str) -> str:
    import pandas as pd
    import numpy as np
    from sklearn.impute import SimpleImputer
    from sklearn.model_selection import train_test_split
    from sklearn.preprocessing import StandardScaler
    data = pd.read_csv(preprocessed_data_path)

    # Handle missing values
    imputer_num = SimpleImputer(strategy='median')
    imputer_cat = SimpleImputer(strategy='most_frequent')

    numeric_features = data.select_dtypes(include=[np.number]).columns
    categorical_features = data.select_dtypes(exclude=[np.number]).columns

    data[numeric_features] = imputer_num.fit_transform(data[numeric_
features])
    data[categorical_features] = imputer_cat.fit_transform(data[categorical_
features])

    # Splitting the data
    X = data.drop('spam', axis=1)
    y = data['spam']

    X_train, X_test, y_train, y_test = train_test_split(X, y, test_
size=0.2, random_state=42)

    # Standardizing the data
    scaler = StandardScaler()
    X_train = scaler.fit_transform(X_train)
    X_test = scaler.transform(X_test)

    # Save engineered features
    np.savez('engineered_features.npz', X_train=X_train, X_test=X_test, y_
train=y_train, y_test=y_test)
    return 'engineered_features.npz'
```

Let us now define the model training component similarly:

```
# Define a function for model training
@component(base_image='python:3.9', packages_to_install=['numpy',
'TensorFlow', 'keras'])
```

```
def model_training(engineered_features_path: str) -> str:
    import numpy as np
    import TensorFlow as tf
    from TensorFlow import keras
    from TensorFlow.keras.models import Sequential
    from TensorFlow.keras.layers import Dense
    data = np.load(engineered_features_path)
    X_train = data['X_train']
    X_test = data['X_test']
    y_train = data['y_train']
    y_test = data['y_test']

    model = Sequential()
    model.add(Dense(64, input_dim=X_train.shape[1], activation='relu'))
    model.add(Dense(32, activation='relu'))
    model.add(Dense(1, activation='sigmoid'))

    model.compile(loss='binary_crossentropy', optimizer='adam',
metrics=['accuracy'])

    history = model.fit(X_train, y_train, epochs=50, batch_size=10,
validation_split=0.2)

    # Save the trained model
    model.save('spam_classification_model.h5')

    # Save the training history
    np.savez('training_history.npz', history=history.history)
    return 'spam_classification_model.h5'
```

Now, let us add the model evaluation part of our ML pipeline:

```
# Define a function for evaluating the model
@component(base_image='python:3.9', packages_to_install=['numpy',
'TensorFlow', 'keras'])
def model_evaluation(trained_model_path: str, engineered_features_path:
str):
    import numpy as np
    import TensorFlow as tf
    from TensorFlow import keras
    from TensorFlow.keras.models import Sequential
    from TensorFlow.keras.layers import Dense
    import matplotlib.pyplot as plt
```

```
    data = np.load(engineered_features_path)
    X_test = data['X_test']
    y_test = data['y_test']

    model = keras.models.load_model(trained_model_path)
    loss, accuracy = model.evaluate(X_test, y_test)
    print(f'Test Loss: {loss}')
    print(f'Test Accuracy: {accuracy}')

    history_data = np.load('/mnt/data/training_history.npz', allow_
pickle=True)
    history = history_data['history'].item()

    plt.plot(history['loss'], label='train_loss')
    plt.plot(history['val_loss'], label='val_loss')
    plt.xlabel('Epochs')
    plt.ylabel('Loss')
    plt.legend()
    plt.savefig('/mnt/data/loss_plot.png')
```

Note: When we are working on a cloud platform, like AWS, Azure, or GCP, we store outcomes of each stage into a bucket or Blob Storage so that the components can still be idempotent and communicate with each other with respect to data stored securely on the cloud.

Now, once we have created our components, we can package them as a pipeline using the DSL functionality of Kubeflow as follows:

```
# Define the pipeline
@dsl.pipeline(
    name='Spam Classification Pipeline',
    description='A pipeline to train and classify emails as spam or not
spam'
)
def spam_classification_pipeline():
    preprocessed_data_task = load_and_preprocess_data()
    eda(preprocessed_data_path=preprocessed_data_task.output)
    engineered_features_task = feature_engineering(preprocessed_data_
path=preprocessed_data_task.output)
    trained_model_task = model_training(engineered_features_
path=engineered_features_task.output)
    model_evaluation(trained_model_path=trained_model_task.output,
engineered_features_path=engineered_features_task.output)
```

```
# Compile the pipeline
kfp.compiler.Compiler().compile(spam_classification_pipeline, 'spam_
classification_pipeline.yaml')
```

In the background, Kubeflow considers each component as a container, and while executing them in the sequence we define in the pipeline (as seen previously), it gets executed in a Kubernetes cluster. We will study the containers Docker and Kubernetes in the next and final section of this chapter. Additionally, we need to compile our pipeline as a YAML file so that we can install this YAML in our Kubeflow service running on a Kubernetes cluster. This starts the pipeline, and one can visualize its outcome in the form of a DAG. One way to do this programmatically, provided we are running this experiment on a local workstation, is as follows:

```
# Creating the KFP client, since the pipeline is compiled
client = kfp.Client()

# Specify experiment name
experiment_name = "spam_classification_experiment"
experiment = client.create_experiment(name=experiment_name)

# Submit the pipeline run
run_name = "spam_classification_run"
run_result = client.run_pipeline(
    experiment_id=experiment.id,
    job_name=run_name,
    pipeline_package_path='spam_classification_pipeline.yaml'
)
```

Let us now understand what containers are, how to use Docker, and how Kubernetes helps to orchestrate fleets of such deployments and applications with or without the cloud.

Containers, Docker, and Kubernetes

Let us explore what containers are and how they will help to implement AI and ML solutions at scale. We will learn in depth about containers, introduce the workings of Docker, and finally learn about how Kubernetes helps in productionizing AI/ML applications in an ideal production environment.

Containers

Containers are a lightweight and portable way to package and run applications. They provide a consistent environment for applications to run, regardless of the underlying infrastructure. This makes them ideal for deploying applications in the cloud, on-premises, or in hybrid environments.

A container is a standardized unit of software that packages up code and all its dependencies, such as libraries, frameworks, and configuration files. This allows the application to run consistently on any system that supports containers. The concept of containers is not new, but it gained significant traction with the advent of **Docker** in 2013. Docker revolutionized containerization by providing a comprehensive platform for creating, distributing, and managing containers. Since then, other containerization technologies, such as Kubernetes, have further enhanced the capabilities of container orchestration, making it easier to manage large-scale container deployments.

Containers are isolated from each other and the host operating system. Due to this, they cannot access each other's files or processes or modify the host operating system. This isolation makes containers more secure and reliable than traditional VMs. Unlike traditional VMs, containers share the host system's operating system kernel and isolate the application processes from the underlying infrastructure. This approach provides several advantages, including reduced overhead, faster start-up times, and improved resource utilization.

Containers are based on the concept of operating system virtualization. This means that they use the host operating system's kernel to run, but they have their own isolated user space. This isolation is achieved through a technology called **namespaces**.

Namespaces provide a way to isolate different parts of the operating system, such as the file system, network, and processes. This means that each container has its view of the operating system, and it cannot see or access the resources of other containers or the host operating system.

In addition to namespaces, containers also use other technologies to provide isolation and security. These technologies include the following:

- **Control groups (cgroups)**: They limit the resources that a container can use, such as CPU, memory, and disk space. This helps to ensure that containers do not consume too many resources and impact the performance of other containers or the host operating system.

- **Security capabilities**: They allow containers to be run with specific privileges. This helps to reduce the risk of containers being compromised by malicious actors.

There are many overall benefits to using containers, including the following:

- **Portability**: Containers can be run on any system that supports containers, regardless of the underlying infrastructure. This makes them ideal for deploying applications in the cloud, on-premises, or in hybrid environments.

- **Isolation**: Containers are isolated from each other and the host operating system. This makes them more secure and reliable than traditional virtual machines.

- **Scalability**: Containers are lightweight and can be easily scaled up or down. This makes them ideal for applications that need to be able to handle varying workloads.

- **Efficiency**: Containers share the host operating system's kernel, which makes them more efficient than virtual machines.

- **Fast start-up times**: Containers start up much faster compared to virtual machines.

Overall, there are two main types of containers as follows:

- **Docker containers**: They are the most popular type of container. They are based on the Docker platform, which provides a set of tools and technologies for building, running, and managing containers.

- **LXC containers**: They are a type of container that is based on the Linux kernel. They are less popular than Docker containers, but they offer more flexibility and control.

Containers are used for a variety of purposes, including the following:

- **Deploying applications**: Containers are a popular way to deploy applications in the cloud, on-premises, or in hybrid environments.

- **Microservices**: Containers are ideal for building and deploying microservices, which are small, independent services that can be easily scaled and updated.

- **CI/CD**: Containers can be used to automate the build, test, and deployment of applications.

- **Development and testing**: Containers can be used to create isolated development and testing environments.

AI and ML engineering involves a complex interplay of various components, including data pre-processing, model training, evaluation, and deployment. Each stage of the AI/ML lifecycle requires specific software libraries, frameworks, and configurations, which can vary significantly depending on the use case and the underlying hardware. Containers offer a robust solution to streamline this complexity by providing a consistent and reproducible environment across different stages of the AI/ML workflow as follows:

- **Consistency and reproducibility**:

  - One of the primary challenges in AI/ML projects is ensuring that experiments are reproducible. Variations in software versions, dependencies, and hardware configurations can lead to discrepancies in results, making it difficult to validate and compare different models.

  - Containers address this issue by encapsulating the entire runtime environment, including the operating system, libraries, and dependencies, ensuring that the application behaves consistently across different environments.

- **Scalability and resource management**:

  - AI/ML workloads often require significant computational resources, particularly during the model training phase. Training deep learning models, for instance, can involve processing large datasets and performing complex mathematical computations that demand high-performance hardware, such as GPUs and TPUs. Containers facilitate efficient resource management and scalability by enabling the dynamic allocation of resources based on workload requirements.

o Kubernetes, an open-source container orchestration platform, plays a crucial role in managing containerized AI/ML applications at scale. Kubernetes provides mechanisms for automated deployment, scaling, and management of containerized applications, allowing organizations to utilize their computational resources efficiently. For instance, Kubernetes can automatically scale the number of containers based on the workload, ensuring that the system can handle varying levels of demand without manual intervention.

o Moreover, Kubernetes supports GPU scheduling, enabling seamless integration of GPU resources into the containerized environment. This capability is particularly beneficial for AI/ML workloads, where GPU acceleration can significantly reduce training times and improve model performance. By leveraging Kubernetes, organizations can create scalable and efficient AI/ML pipelines that can handle large-scale data processing and model training tasks.

- **Isolation and security**:

  o In multi-tenant environments, such as cloud-based AI/ML platforms, isolation and security are critical considerations. Containers provide process-level isolation, ensuring that each application runs in its isolated environment without interfering with other applications on the same host. This isolation enhances security by reducing the attack surface and preventing potential conflicts between applications.

  o Furthermore, containers enable fine-grained access control and resource limitations, allowing organizations to enforce security policies and manage resource usage effectively. For instance, Kubernetes supports **role-based access control** (**RBAC**), enabling administrators to define granular access permissions for different users and applications. This capability is essential for maintaining the security and integrity of AI/ML workflows, particularly in environments with multiple users and shared resources.

- **Portability and deployment flexibility**:

  o AI/ML projects often transition through various stages, from development and testing to production deployment. Each stage may involve different environments, such as local development machines, on-premises servers, or cloud-based infrastructure. Containers offer a high degree of portability, enabling seamless transitions between different environments without the need for extensive reconfiguration.

- ○ Containerization also simplifies the process of CI/CD for AI/ML applications. By integrating containers into the CI/CD pipeline, organizations can automate the testing, validation, and deployment of models, ensuring that new models and updates are seamlessly integrated into the production environment. This approach accelerates the development cycle and enables rapid iteration and experimentation, which are critical for AI/ML innovation.

- **Collaboration and sharing**:

  - ○ AI/ML projects often involve collaboration among data scientists, engineers, and domain experts, who may work on different aspects of the project, such as data pre-processing, feature engineering, model development, and evaluation. Containers facilitate collaboration by providing a standardized and reproducible environment that can be easily shared among team members.

  - ○ Moreover, containers enable the sharing of pre-trained models and AI/ML pipelines through container registries. Organizations can publish container images that include pre-trained models and inference pipelines, allowing other teams or external collaborators to integrate these models easily into their applications. This capability promotes the reuse of models and accelerates the development of AI/ML solutions by leveraging existing work.

Containers have been widely adopted in various AI/ML use cases, demonstrating their versatility and effectiveness in different scenarios. Some notable use cases include the following:

- **Model training and hyperparameter tuning**: Training ML models often involves experimenting with different hyperparameters and configurations to optimize model performance. Containers enable the creation of isolated and reproducible environments for each experiment, ensuring that the results are consistent and comparable.

- **Model inference and serving**: Deploying ML models for inference requires a robust and scalable infrastructure that can handle incoming requests with low latency and high availability. Containers provide a flexible solution for deploying and scaling inference services, ensuring that the models can be served reliably in production.

- **Data pre-processing and ETL pipelines**: Data pre-processing is a crucial step in the AI/ML lifecycle, involving tasks such as data cleaning, transformation, and feature extraction. Containers facilitate the creation of standardized and reproducible data pre-processing pipelines that can be easily integrated into the overall workflow.

- **Experiment tracking and reproducibility**: Tracking experiments and ensuring reproducibility are critical aspects of AI/ML research and development. Containers enable the encapsulation of the entire experiment environment, including the code, dependencies, and configurations, ensuring that the experiments can be reproduced and validated.

- **Edge AI and IoT**: Edge AI involves deploying AI models on edge devices, such as IoT sensors, mobile devices, and embedded systems, to enable real-time inference and decision-making. Containers provide a lightweight and portable solution for deploying AI models on edge devices, ensuring that the models can run efficiently with limited resources.

Let us now understand Docker and take a quick tutorial on how to use it.

Docker

Docker offers a self-contained container that encapsulates our application along with all its dependencies, libraries, frameworks, runtime environments, and configurations. It is a platform that allows you to package your application and its dependencies into **containers**. These containers are lightweight and isolated, ensuring consistent and reliable execution across different environments.

Some of the key concepts when it comes to understanding and using Docker are as follows:

- **Docker engine**: This is the core component of Docker, responsible for building, running, and managing containers.

- **Docker image**: This is a read-only template containing the instructions for creating a container. It includes the application code, libraries, and configurations.

- **Docker container**: This is a running instance of a Docker image. It is an isolated environment with its own file system, processes, and network.

- **Dockerfile**: This is a text file containing instructions for building a Docker image. It specifies the steps to install dependencies, copy files, and configure the environment.

- **Docker hub**: This is a public registry where you can find and share Docker images.

Let us understand step by step how Docker is made to work, as follows:

1. **Building an image**: You write a Dockerfile with instructions for building your application environment.

2. **Running a container**: Using the docker run command, you create a container from the image. The container starts running the application with all its dependencies.

3. **Managing containers**: Docker provides commands to manage containers, including starting, stopping, restarting, and removing them.

Some of the out-of-the-box benefits of using Docker are as follows:

- **Portability**: Docker containers run consistently across different environments, from development machines to production servers.

- **Isolation**: Each container runs in its isolated environment, preventing conflicts between applications and their dependencies.

- **Scalability**: Docker makes it easy to scale applications by running multiple containers on a single host or across multiple hosts.

- **Reproducibility**: Docker ensures that your application runs the same way in every environment, regardless of the underlying infrastructure.

- **Efficiency**: Docker containers are lightweight and share the host operating system's kernel, making them efficient in terms of resource utilization.

To get started with Docker, let us follow these steps, most of which are already well-documented in the official Docker documentation:

1. **Install Docker**: Download and install Docker on your system from the official website (**https://www.docker.com/**).

2. **Explore Docker Hub**: Browse the Docker Hub (**https://hub.docker.com/**) to find pre-built images for various applications and tools.

3. **Write a Dockerfile**: Create a Dockerfile for your application, specifying the steps to build the environment.

4. **Build an image**: Use the `docker build` command to build an image from your Dockerfile.

5. **Run a container**: Use the `docker run` command to start a container from your image.

Refer to *Chapter 5, Machine Learning Algorithms,* once more to refresh your initial knowledge of how to write a Dockerfile. Here, we will take a quick look at an example. Let us create a directory and a very basic Flask application in Python. This is typically what an AI or ML engineer does to showcase their demos or applications that utilize ML models in the background. In this example, we will create a Hello World Flask app to demonstrate how to use Docker:

```
mkdir flask-app
cd flask-app
```

Let us imagine we have a **Flask** app that looks like the following code:

```
from flask import Flask

app = Flask(__name__)

@app.route('/')
```

```
def hello_world():
    return 'Hello, World!'

if __name__ == '__main__':
    app.run(host='0.0.0.0', port=5000)
```

As seen in the previous code, we want a Web UI to run on our workstation or **localhost** where it simply prints **Hello World** text on the browser. To package this, let us create a requirements file as well:

echo "Flask==2.0.2" > requirements.txt

Furthermore, in the same directory, let us create a **Dockerfile** file. This file can have any custom name as well, but typically, software engineers name them as **Dockerfile** for each reference. Refer to the following code for a better understanding:

```
# Use an official Python runtime as a parent image
FROM python:3.9-slim

# Set the working directory in the container
WORKDIR /app

# Copy the current directory contents into the container at /app
COPY . /app

# Install any needed packages specified in requirements.txt
RUN pip install --no-cache-dir -r requirements.txt

# Make port 5000 available to the world outside this container
EXPOSE 5000

# Define environment variable
ENV FLASK_APP=app.py

# Run app.py when the container launches
CMD ["python", "app.py"]
```

We are asking **Docker** to create an **Image** where our Flask app will run on Port **5000** using the **app.py** script that we created previously. At this stage, our working directory will have the following structure:

```
flask-app/
├── app.py
├── Dockerfile
└── requirements.txt
```

Next, let us build the image on our workstation using the **docker** command from the same directory where we have our **Dockerfile** file:

docker build -t flask-app .

Now, we are ready to run the image as a container. To do so, we can use the following command:

```
docker run -d -p 5000:5000 flask-app
```

We can open **http://localhost:5000** on our local browser to check the application we just created if all goes well.

Now that we are aware of how to create basic containers from Docker images, let us learn more about Kubernetes and see how AI and ML applications are deployed on production-like systems using Kubernetes.

Kubernetes

Containers have emerged as the preferred packaging format. They offer portability, scalability, and resource efficiency, making them ideal for modern application development. However, managing containers at scale can be a daunting task. This is where Kubernetes comes to the rescue.

Kubernetes provides a robust platform for container orchestration, offering numerous benefits. Some are as follows:

- **Automated deployment and scaling**: Kubernetes automates the deployment and scaling of containerized applications, eliminating manual intervention and ensuring efficient resource utilization.

- **High availability**: Kubernetes ensures the high availability of applications by automatically restarting failed containers and scheduling them on healthy nodes.

- **Service discovery and load balancing**: Kubernetes facilitates service discovery and load balancing, enabling seamless communication and traffic distribution among containerized applications.

- **Storage orchestration**: Kubernetes integrates with various storage solutions, providing persistent storage for containerized applications.

- **Declarative configuration**: Kubernetes uses declarative configuration files, allowing developers to define the desired state of their applications, and it also takes care of achieving and maintaining that state.

- **Self-healing capabilities**: Kubernetes automatically detects and replaces unhealthy containers, ensuring continuous application uptime.

- **Extensibility**: Kubernetes offers a rich ecosystem of extensions and plugins, allowing customization and integration with various tools and technologies.

Kubernetes is built on a master-node architecture, consisting of two primary components as follows:

- **Master node**: This acts as the central control plane, managing the cluster and making decisions about container scheduling and resource allocation. It comprises several components, including the API server, scheduler, controller manager, and etcd (a distributed key-value store).

- **Worker nodes**: These are the workhorses of the cluster, responsible for running containerized applications. Each worker node hosts a container runtime environment (e.g., Docker, containerd) and a kubelet, which communicates with the master node to receive instructions and manage containers.

To utilize Kubernetes effectively, understanding its core concepts is crucial. Here is a quick overview of the core parts of Kubernetes:

- **Pods**: It is the smallest unit of deployment in Kubernetes. It represents a group of one or more containers that share resources and network space.

- **Services**: They provide a stable endpoint for accessing pods, regardless of their underlying IP addresses or container instances.

- **Deployments**: They manage the lifecycle of pods, ensuring that the desired number of pods are running and updated in a controlled manner.

- **Namespaces**: They provide logical partitions within a cluster, allowing multiple users or applications to share resources without interfering with each other.

- **Labels and selectors**: They are key-value pairs used to organize and identify resources within the cluster.

- **Volumes**: They provide persistent storage for containerized applications, allowing them to retain data even after the container restarts.

There are several ways to get started with Kubernetes. Here are 2 of the most common ones:

- **Local Kubernetes cluster**: You can set up a local Kubernetes cluster using tools like Minikube or Docker Desktop.

- **Managed Kubernetes services**: Cloud providers like Google Cloud, Amazon Web Services, and Microsoft Azure offer managed Kubernetes services, taking care of the infrastructure and cluster management.

Let us take our previous example of the sample Flask App and extend it to run on Kubernetes. Similar steps are usually followed even for medium to large-scale applications. Before we do so, let us tag and push the Image we created earlier to the Docker Hub (in this example). Instead, or when one is working with a cloud environment, we usually choose to push our Images in a secured repository, like Artifact Registry in Google Cloud, for example. Before doing the steps, we must install at least the Minikube setup on the local workstation by referring to its public documentation.

Now, to push our image to Docker Hub, one can follow these commands:

```
docker login
docker tag flask-app your-dockerhub-username/flask-app:latest
docker push your-dockerhub-username/flask-app:latest
```

In order to deploy any service like our Flask app on Kubernetes, we need a couple of YAML files. Firstly, we should create the **deployment.yaml** file where we mention specifics of how the service (or our application) will be deployed, with properties like replicas, labels, our image, the application port number, etc. Here is an example configuration file:

```
apiVersion: apps/v1
kind: Deployment
metadata:
  name: flask-app-deployment
spec:
  replicas: 2
  selector:
    matchLabels:
      app: flask-app
  template:
    metadata:
      labels:
        app: flask-app
    spec:
      containers:
      - name: flask-app
        image: your-dockerhub-username/flask-app:latest
        ports:
        - containerPort: 5000
```

Now, we will create a **service.yaml** file, wherein we provide metadata information along with any load-balancing requirements for our Web UI:

```
apiVersion: v1
kind: Service
metadata:
  name: flask-app-service
spec:
  selector:
    app: flask-app
  ports:
  - protocol: TCP
    port: 80
```

```
      targetPort: 5000
  type: LoadBalancer
```

Now that we have created the YAML files, our local directory should look like the following code:

```
flask-app/
├── app.py
├── Dockerfile
├── requirements.txt
├── deployment.yaml
└── service.yaml
```

From here, let us apply our YAML files:

```
kubectl apply -f deployment.yaml
```

```
kubectl apply -f service.yaml
```

Let us check if our pods were created, as they serve as the primary components running our web application. Here is an actual command:

```
kubectl get pods -A
```

In the output of the previous command, we should see the flask-app running on the locally installed Kubernetes setup. We can check the status of the services that we deployed using the following command:

```
kubectl get services
```

That was a quick example of how to deploy containers on Kubernetes. There is far more to be explored, but that would be mostly driven by the needs of the AI or ML application that one designs to resolve a particular use case.

Conclusion

In this chapter, we covered what MLOps is, where it fits into building enterprise-scale AI and ML applications, and some of the tools that one can use to engineer systems of this nature. In the next chapter, we are going to explore how to serve models and scale them in production and how to tackle real-world challenges like customer adoption and deployment strategies with a variety of options to serve models as per the application where they fit.

Exercises

1. Study the Google whitepaper on MLOps and how it is to be rightly implemented, especially on a Cloud Platform.

2. Pick any one of the previous use cases on ML from the last chapters in our book and try to implement the same use case using TensorFlow Extended pipelines. Note the challenges in this migration.

3. Install Docker, Minikube, and Kubeflow on your local workstation, and try the example use case given in the Kubeflow section of this chapter. Note the system requirement limitations wherein the YAML deployment or pipeline run fails.

4. Take any sample web application from GitHub that is already open-sourced by its developer and try to create a container on your workstation using the Docker utility. Select an application that does not already have a Dockerfile available.

5. Take the same application from the last steps and follow the steps shown in the example of how to deploy them on a Kubernetes cluster. Now, on the same cluster, try deploying more than one application, and note the challenges we face while doing so.

Join our book's Discord space

Join the book's Discord Workspace for Latest updates, Offers, Tech happenings around the world, New Release and Sessions with the Authors:

https://discord.bpbonline.com

## CHAPTER 11

Model Serving and Scalability

Introduction

Imagine we have trained a fantastic machine learning model that can predict customer churn with remarkable accuracy. However, this model remains dormant within our training environment, unable to interact with real users. This is where **model serving** comes into play. It acts as the bridge between our trained model and the real-world, allowing it to receive user input, generate predictions, and ultimately deliver value.

The process of model serving involves packaging our trained model into a format suitable for deployment. This typically involves converting the model into a format compatible with specific serving frameworks or platforms. Additionally, we might need to integrate the model with APIs or web applications to enable user interaction.

As our application gains traction and the user base expands, our model needs to be able to handle the increasing load without sacrificing performance. This is where **scalability** becomes paramount. A scalable model serving system can dynamically adjust its resources to accommodate growing demand, ensuring that predictions are delivered promptly and efficiently.

Scalability can be achieved through various techniques, such as horizontal scaling (adding more servers) or vertical scaling (increasing resources on existing servers). Additionally, techniques like model compression and quantization can help reduce the model's size and computational requirements, further enhancing scalability.

Model serving and scalability are intertwined concepts. Effective model serving ensures that our model is readily available for user interaction, while scalability guarantees that it can handle increasing demand without performance degradation. Together, they form the backbone of a robust and reliable machine learning application. This is exactly what we aim to learn in this chapter of our book.

Structure

The chapter covers the following topics:

- Introduction to model serving
- Model serving options
- Deployment strategies
- Real-world challenges

Objectives

By the end of this chapter, readers of our book should be familiar with how to effectively design scalable serving infrastructure and design for any given ML model in the real-world, both using in-house IT infrastructure and/or any popular cloud platform, like Google Cloud.

Introduction to model serving

Model serving is the process of deploying a trained ML model to production, where it can be used to make predictions on new data. This involves a series of steps, including preparing the model, choosing the right serving platform, and integrating the model into our application.

There are several design patterns for model serving, each with its advantages and disadvantages. Here are some of the most common patterns:

- **REST API**: This is the most common pattern, where the model is exposed as a REST API endpoint. Clients can send requests to the API with new data, and the model will return predictions. This pattern is simple to implement and can be used with a variety of programming languages and frameworks.

- **Batch inference**: This pattern is used when we need to make predictions on a large number of data points at once. The model is loaded into memory, and then a batch of data is sent to the model for prediction. This pattern can be more efficient than REST API for large datasets, but it requires more memory and processing power.

- **Real-time inference**: This pattern is used when we need to make predictions on new data as it arrives. The model is loaded into memory, and then each new data point is sent to the model for prediction. This pattern is the most responsive, but it also requires the most resources.

- **Streaming inference**: This pattern is used when we need to make predictions on a continuous stream of data. The model is loaded into memory, and then the data stream is sent to the model for prediction. This pattern is useful for applications that require real-time predictions on large amounts of data.

There are a number of ways to customize the model serving to meet our specific needs. Here are some of the most common customizations:

- **Model versioning**: This allows us to deploy multiple versions of our model and switch between them as needed. This is useful for A/B testing new models or rolling back to a previous version if necessary.

- **Model monitoring**: This allows us to monitor the performance of our model in production and identify any issues that may arise. This is important for ensuring that our model is performing as expected and that it is not being used in a way that could lead to bias or discrimination.

- **Model explainability**: This allows us to understand how our model is making predictions. This is important for debugging our model and for ensuring that it is making fair and unbiased decisions.

Model serving is a critical part of deploying machine learning models to production. By understanding the different design patterns and customizations available, one can choose the best approach for our specific needs. Let us look now at what options we have to serve ML models.

Model serving options

Model serving is the process of deploying a trained ML model to production so that it can be used to make predictions on new data. This is a critical step in the ML pipeline, as it allows models to be used in real-world applications. There are a variety of model-serving options available, each with its advantages and disadvantages. The choice of which option to use will depend on the specific needs of the application.

There are three main types of models serving options as follows:

- **On-premises serving**: It is the most traditional model serving option. This involves deploying the model to a server that is located on the premises of the organization using the model. This option offers the highest level of control and security, but it can also be the most expensive and time-consuming to set up and maintain.

- **Cloud-based serving**: It is a more modern model serving option. This involves deploying the model to a cloud platform, such as **Amazon Web Services** (**AWS**), Microsoft Azure, or **Google Cloud Platform** (**GCP**). This option is more scalable and cost-effective than on-premises serving, but it can also be less secure.

- **Edge serving**: It is the most recent model serving option. This involves deploying the model to a device at the edge of the network, such as a smartphone or an IoT device. This option offers the lowest latency and highest responsiveness, but it can also be the most challenging to set up and maintain.

There are several factors to consider when choosing a model serving option, including the following:

- **Latency**: The amount of time it takes for the model to make a prediction.

- **Throughput**: The number of predictions the model can make per second.

- **Scalability**: The ability of the model to handle increasing amounts of data.

- **Cost**: The cost of deploying and maintaining the model.

- **Security**: The level of security required for the model.

Model serving is a critical step in the ML pipeline. There are a variety of model-serving options available, each with its advantages and disadvantages. The choice of which option to use will depend on the specific needs of the application.

There are a variety of techniques that can be used for model serving, including the following:

- **REST APIs**: REST APIs are a common way to serve models. They allow clients to send requests to the model and receive predictions in response.

- **gRPC**: **Google Remote Procedure Calls (gRPC)** is a high-performance RPC framework that can be used to serve models. It offers lower latency and higher throughput than REST APIs.

- **Model zoos**: Model zoos are repositories of pre-trained models that can be used for serving. They can be a good option for organizations that do not have the resources to train their models.

Let us now explore the effective strategies of deploying models in a variety of setup conditions.

Deployment strategies

In this part of the chapter, we will explore TensorFlow Serving and Vertex AI on GCP, which is by far the two most common yet powerful ways to productionize deployments of ML models for small to large scale setups, keeping in mind the various facets of model scalability that we have learned until now in this chapter. Let us start with TensorFlow Serving and see how to make it work.

TensorFlow Serving

TensorFlow Serving is a powerful tool for deploying and serving ML models in production environments. It provides a flexible and scalable framework for managing and serving models, allowing one to easily deploy and update models, manage different versions, and handle high-volume requests. This section of our chapter will provide a detailed explanation of model serving using TensorFlow Serving, covering its key concepts, architecture, and how to use it in practice.

As a start, let us learn some key concepts about TensorFlow Serving to understand the components that underpin its design as follows:

- **Model**: A trained ML model that can be used to make predictions on new data.
- **Model version**: A specific version of a model, typically identified by a unique identifier.
- **Model server**: A server that hosts and serves models.
- **Client**: An application or service that sends requests to the model server for predictions.
- **Request**: A message containing the input data for a prediction.
- **Response**: A message containing the prediction results.

Overall, TensorFlow Serving has a modular architecture consisting of the following components:

- **ModelServer**: The main component responsible for managing and serving models.
- **Servable**: A unit of serving that encapsulates a model and its associated resources.
- **Loader**: A component responsible for loading models into the ModelServer.
- **Source**: A component responsible for providing models to the Loader.
- **Manager**: A component responsible for managing the lifecycle of models and Servables.
- **Scheduler**: A component responsible for scheduling model loading and unloading.

One of the critical components of TensorFlow service is how it orchestrates an ML model in terms of both preparing it (training, exporting, loading, etc.) as well as serving it to end systems or users. The workflow for serving a model using TensorFlow Serving is as follows:

1. **Model training**: Train an ML model using TensorFlow or another framework.
2. **Model export**: Export the trained model to a format compatible with TensorFlow Serving.
3. **Model loading**: Load the exported model into the ModelServer using a Loader.

4. **Model serving**: Send prediction requests to the ModelServer.

5. **Prediction generation**: The ModelServer uses the loaded model to generate predictions for the requests.

6. **Response generation**: The ModelServer sends the prediction results back to the client.

To use TensorFlow Serving, we need to:

1. **Install TensorFlow Serving**: Follow the instructions on the official TensorFlow Serving website to install the necessary software.

2. **Export our model**: Export our trained model to a SavedModel format.

3. **Start a ModelServer**: Start a ModelServer instance and configure it to load our model.

4. **Send prediction requests**: Send prediction requests to the ModelServer using the TensorFlow Serving API or gRPC.

Some of the key benefits of using TensorFlow Serving can be summarized as follows:

- **Scalability**: TensorFlow Serving can handle high-volume requests by scaling horizontally across multiple servers.

- **Flexibility**: TensorFlow Serving supports various model formats and can be easily integrated with different applications and services.

- **Versioning**: TensorFlow Serving allows us to manage different versions of our models and easily switch between them.

- **Monitoring**: TensorFlow Serving provides tools for monitoring model performance and resource utilization.

In the *References* section of this chapter, we have provided some useful links to learn about TensorFlow Serving even in more depth and some hands-on exercises for starters to know about how to make it work. Note that similar to TensorFlow itself, the learning curve can be a bit stiffer than other available alternatives, one of which is going to be explored next.

Vertex AI in Google Cloud

Vertex AI is a unified ML platform on Google Cloud that simplifies the entire ML lifecycle, from data preparation and model training to deployment and monitoring. It offers a wide range of tools and services to help us build, deploy, and manage our ML models at scale on Google Cloud. In this section, although we will not be performing a deep dive analysis of how Vertex AI is to be made to work, we will understand it enough so that one can start their AI/ML implementations in the cloud.

Some of the key features of Vertex AI are as follows:

- **Unified platform**: Vertex AI brings together all the tools and services we need for ML under one roof, eliminating the need to manage multiple disparate tools and services.

- **Simplified workflow**: Vertex AI provides a streamlined workflow for building and deploying ML models, making it easier for data scientists and ML engineers to collaborate and iterate quickly.

- **Automated tasks**: Vertex AI automates many of the tedious and time-consuming tasks involved in ML, such as data preparation, model training, and hyperparameter tuning.

- **Scalability and flexibility**: Vertex AI is built on Google Cloud's infrastructure, which means it can scale to meet our needs and offers a variety of deployment options, including on-premises, cloud, and hybrid environments.

- **Security and compliance**: Vertex AI is built with security and compliance in mind, and it offers a variety of features to help us protect our data and models.

Vertex AI consists of several key components, some of which are as follows:

- **Vertex AI workbench**: A Jupyter Notebook-based environment for data exploration, model training, and experimentation.

- **Vertex AI pipelines**: A managed service for building and orchestrating ML pipelines.

- **Vertex AI training**: A managed service for training ML models on various hardware accelerators, including GPUs and TPUs.

- **Vertex AI prediction**: A managed service for deploying and serving ML models.

- **Vertex AI explainable AI**: A set of tools for understanding and explaining the predictions made by ML models.

Now, let us understand some of the key benefits of using Vertex AI as follows:

- **Increased productivity**: Vertex AI can help us build and deploy ML models faster and more efficiently.

- **Improved model quality**: Vertex AI provides tools and services that can help us build better-performing ML models.

- **Reduced costs**: Vertex AI can help us reduce the cost of building and deploying ML models.

- **Enhanced collaboration**: Vertex AI provides a platform for data scientists and ML engineers to collaborate more effectively.

- **Simplified compliance**: Vertex AI can help us meet our compliance requirements for data security and privacy.

To get started with Vertex AI, one can create a free trial account on Google Cloud. Once we have an account, we can access the Vertex AI console and start exploring the various tools and services. For beginners at Google Cloud, we strongly recommend starting off with the Vertex AI tutorials, the link to which is available in the *References* section of this chapter. In addition to the aforementioned, readers are to acknowledge the fact that Vertex AI, with many of its components, including the generative AI offerings, are open for automations and deployments using infrastructure as code libraries and platforms like Terraform.

Deployment strategies

Depending on multiple factors, like users and applications who would be interacting with our ML solutions, the scale at which it needs to operate, or the **total cost of ownership** (**TCO**) of any ML solutions, the strategy to deploy an ML system to production will change, and rightly needs to change as well.

ML in production using containers

Let us start with how to make effective deployments of ML models using containers. We have studied containers in *Chapter 10, MLOps and Deployment,* so we will not necessarily repeat the basics of containers and how they work! Several strategies can be employed for deploying machine learning models using containers in production. Here are some common approaches:

- **Single-container deployment**: This approach packages the model, its dependencies, and the prediction code into a single container. It is suitable for simple models and straightforward deployments.

- **Multi-container deployment**: This approach separates the model, dependencies, and prediction code into different containers. This allows for modularity and easier scaling of individual components.

- **Microservices architecture**: This approach decomposes the machine learning pipeline into independent microservices, each deployed as a separate container. This enables greater flexibility and scalability for complex workflows.

To ensure the successful and efficient deployment of ML models using containers, consider the following best practices:

- **Use a container registry**: Store our container images in a secure and accessible container registry like Docker Hub or Google Container Registry.

- **Automate build and deployment process**: Use tools like CI/CD pipelines to automate the container build, testing, and deployment process, ensuring consistency and efficiency.

- **Monitor and log container activity**: Monitor the performance and resource utilization of our containers to identify potential issues and optimize resource allocation.

- **Implement security measures**: Secure our containers by implementing access controls, vulnerability scanning, and encryption.

- **Consider cloud-based container platforms**: Leverage cloud-based container platforms like Amazon ECS, Google Kubernetes Engine, or Azure Kubernetes Service for easier management and scalability.

Note that what we present here are a few of many ways in which we can productionize ML models using containers, but we cover the most important of them. Let us now look at some of the common design patterns in which one may find ML models deployed in production while served in custom or cloud-based container services as follows:

- **HTTP service**:
  - The ML model is deployed as a RESTful API or gRPC service within a container.
  - Clients can send requests to the service, and the model processes them to generate predictions.
  - **Pros**:
    - **Real-time predictions**: Ideal for applications that require immediate responses, such as recommendation systems or fraud detection.
    - **Scalability**: Containers can be easily scaled horizontally to handle increased traffic.
    - **Flexibility**: Supports various programming languages and frameworks.
  - **Cons**:
    - **Higher latency**: For batch processing, the latency might be noticeable.
    - **Resource consumption**: Requires continuous resource allocation, even during idle periods.

- **Message queue**:
  - The ML model is deployed as a consumer on a message queue.
  - Producers send requests to the queue, and the model processes them asynchronously.

- Pros:

  - **Decoupling**: Separates producers and consumers, allowing for asynchronous processing.

  - **Scalability**: Can handle large volumes of data without overwhelming the model.

  - **Batch processing**: Suitable for tasks that can be processed in batches, such as image classification or natural language processing.

- Cons:

  - **Latency**: Might introduce latency due to the asynchronous nature of the process.

  - **Complexity**: Requires additional infrastructure for managing the message queue.

- **Batch process**:

  - The ML model is deployed as a batch job within a container.

  - A scheduled task triggers the execution of the job, which processes a large dataset to generate predictions.

  - Pros:

    - **Cost-effective**: Ideal for tasks that do not require real-time predictions, as it can leverage off-peak resources.

    - **Efficiency**: Can process large datasets efficiently.

    - **Data consistency**: Ensures data consistency by processing batches of data.

  - Cons:

    - **Latency**: Not suitable for real-time applications.

    - **Manual intervention**: Requires manual scheduling and monitoring of batch jobs.

The best deployment method depends on the specific requirements of our ML model. One must consider factors such as the following before choosing a method:

- **Latency**: How quickly do we need predictions?

- **Throughput**: How much data do we need to process?

- **Scalability**: How much will our workload grow?

- **Cost**: What is our budget for infrastructure and operations?

ML in production using GCP

In similar lines, now let us look at how one may choose to deploy ML models on GCP, which is one of the best choices for AI/ML and data applications. GCP offers a comprehensive suite of tools and services to facilitate this process, enabling us to seamlessly integrate our models into real-world applications.

Let us start with some of the key considerations for ML model deployment on GCP:

- **Scalability**: Ensure our models can handle increasing workloads and adapt to changing demands. GCP's scalable infrastructure allows us to scale our resources up or down as needed.

- **Security**: Implement robust security measures to protect our models and data. GCP offers various security features, including encryption, access control, and compliance tools.

- **Automation**: Automate our ML workflows to streamline the deployment process and reduce manual effort. GCP provides tools like Cloud Build and Cloud Functions for automating tasks.

- **Monitoring and alerting**: Monitor our models' performance and receive alerts for any anomalies. GCP offers tools like Cloud Monitoring and Cloud Logging for comprehensive monitoring capabilities.

Keeping this in mind, let us go through some of the common yet important best practices for ML model deployment on GCP as follows:

- **Choose the right infrastructure**: Select the appropriate GCP services based on our model's requirements and workload. Consider options like cloud TPUs for high-performance training, cloud GPUs for inference acceleration, and Cloud Run for serverless deployments.

- **Effective versioning and tracking**: Implement version control for our models and code to track changes and facilitate rollbacks. GCP offers tools like Cloud Source Repositories and Cloud Build for version management.

- **Robust testing and validation**: Thoroughly test our models before deployment to ensure they meet our performance and accuracy requirements. GCP provides tools like Vertex AI for model testing and validation.

- **CI/CD**: Automate our deployment process using CI/CD pipelines to ensure consistent and reliable deployments. GCP offers tools like Cloud Build and Cloud Deploy for CI/CD automation.

- **Model monitoring and management**: Monitor our models' performance in production and take corrective actions when necessary. GCP offers tools like Vertex AI Model Monitoring and Vertex Explainable AI for model monitoring and interpretability.

Choosing an appropriate service on any cloud platform to deploy our AI/ML solutions is often a daunting task, not only because of the plethora of available options but also because we would like to tie in our business objectives and cost of ownership considerations to the solution we build, ultimately. Here are a few GCP services that we would end up using while creating and deploying an ML solution on GCP more often:

- **Vertex AI**: A unified platform for building, training, deploying, and managing ML models.

- **Cloud TPUs**: Specialized hardware accelerators for high-performance ML training.

- **Cloud GPUs**: High-performance GPUs for accelerating ML inference.

- **Cloud Run**: A serverless platform for deploying containerized ML models.

- **Cloud Functions**: A serverless platform for deploying event-driven ML models.

- **Cloud Storage**: A scalable and secure storage service for storing ML models and data.

- **Cloud Monitoring**: A comprehensive monitoring service for tracking ML model performance and health.

- **Cloud Logging**: A centralized logging service for collecting and analyzing ML model logs.

- **Cloud Scheduler**: A service for scheduling automated tasks, such as model retraining.

Again, let us look at some of the common design patterns used by AI/ML applications deployed on GCP in general, as follows:

- **Model as a service (MaaS)**:

  o **Concept**: Deploy our model as a web service or API that can be accessed by other applications.

  o **GCP services**:

    ▪ **AI Platform Prediction**: A managed service for serving models with low latency and high throughput.

    ▪ **Cloud functions**: Serverless compute platform for event-driven functions.

    ▪ **App engine**: Platform for building and deploying web applications.

  o **Best practices**:

    ▪ **Containerize model**: Package model and dependencies into a Docker container for portability and scalability.

- **Use a managed service**: Leverage AI Platform Prediction for its scalability, reliability, and managed infrastructure.

- **Optimize for performance**: Consider factors like batching, caching, and hardware acceleration.

- **Batch prediction**:

  - **Concept**: Process large datasets offline and store the predictions for later use.

  - **GCP services**:

    - **Cloud Dataflow**: A fully managed service for data processing and analysis.

    - **Cloud Dataproc**: A managed Hadoop and Spark service for big data processing.

  - **Best practices**:

    - **Optimize data pipelines**: Ensure efficient data ingestion, transformation, and storage.

    - **Leverage batch processing frameworks**: Utilize Cloud Dataflow or Cloud Dataproc for scalable and fault-tolerant batch jobs.

    - **Schedule jobs**: Automate batch prediction tasks using Cloud Scheduler.

- **Edge deployment**:

  - **Concept**: Deploy models directly on edge devices like IoT sensors or mobile phones for real-time processing.

  - **GCP services**:

    - **Cloud IoT core**: A managed service for connecting, controlling, and monitoring IoT devices.

    - **Cloud machine learning engine**: Train and deploy custom models for edge devices.

  - **Best practices**:

    - **Optimize model size**: Reduce model complexity and size to fit on edge devices.

    - **Consider latency and bandwidth constraints**: Design models that can operate with limited resources.

    - **Ensure security**: Protect sensitive data and prevent unauthorized access.

- **MLOps pipeline**:

  - o **Concept**: Automate the entire machine learning lifecycle, from data ingestion to model deployment.

  - o **GCP services**:

    - ▪ **Cloud build**: A fully managed CI/CD service.

    - ▪ **Cloud composer**: A managed Apache Airflow service for workflow orchestration.

    - ▪ **Vertex AI**: A unified platform for building, deploying, and managing machine learning models.

  - o **Best practices**:

    - ▪ **Version control**: Track model versions, training data, and code changes.

    - ▪ **Experiment tracking**: Log experiment parameters, metrics, and artifacts.

    - ▪ **Continuous integration and delivery**: Automate testing, deployment, and monitoring.

Model service strategies

Irrespective of the method or cloud platform one chooses to deploy, service, and scale ML solutions, it is critical to keep in mind how one can securely expose the ML model as a service, preferably using APIs. This is where model services play a crucial role. Model services are APIs that expose machine learning models as services. These services can be used to make predictions or classifications on new data. To ensure the effectiveness and scalability of model services, several design patterns and strategies can be employed.

Let us start with some of the common strategies, like the following:

- **A/B testing**:

  - o **Purpose**: To compare the performance of different models or versions of a model. How it works (or is made to work) is as follows:

    - ▪ **Divide traffic**: Split incoming traffic between the current model and a new candidate model.

    - ▪ **Measure performance**: Track key metrics like accuracy, precision, recall, and latency for both models.

    - ▪ **Analyze results**: Compare the performance of the two models. If the new model significantly outperforms the old one, it can be deployed to all traffic.

- o **Benefits**:

    - **Risk mitigation**: Helps identify potential issues with new models before they are deployed to all users.

    - **Continuous improvement**: Encourages a culture of experimentation and innovation.

- **Endpoint sharing**:

    - o **Purpose**: To share a single endpoint for multiple models, allowing for dynamic routing of requests based on certain criteria. How it works overall can be understood as follows:

        - **Define routing rules**:

            - Establish rules that determine which model to use for a given request.

            - These rules can be based on factors like user attributes, input data characteristics, or time of day.

            - Note that on matured cloud platforms, like AWS, Azure, or GCP, these rules are available to be implemented out of the box without much additional engineering effort.

        - **Implement routing logic**:

            - Develop a mechanism to route incoming requests to the appropriate model based on the defined rules.

        - **Monitor performance**:

            - Track the performance of each model and adjust the routing rules as needed.

    - o **Benefits**:

        - **Flexibility**: Allows for dynamic model selection based on changing conditions.

        - **Efficiency**: Reduces the number of endpoints required.

Some of the other commonly used design patterns are as follows:

- **Canary releases**: A gradual rollout strategy where a new model is initially deployed to a small subset of users.

- **Blue-green deployments**: A technique where two identical production environments are maintained. One environment is used for the current model, while the other is used for the new model.

- **Shadowing**: A method where both the old and new models are deployed, but only the old model is used to serve requests. The new model can be used for evaluation or experimentation.

- **Model composition**: Combining multiple models to create a more powerful or flexible model.

- **Model chaining**: Using the output of one model as the input to another model.

At the end of the day, the strategy we make use of is all dependent on the overall architecture that we are planning to deliver or create for our services or end users or customers. Typically, in a large-scale organization, the creation of such strategies will involve Enterprise Architects as well so that the overall design can be in line with the needs.

Real-world challenges

Some of the most common real-world challenges we face while effectively serving ML models are related to scalability design in the first place. Let us explore this area before looking into other possible reasons for concern.

Scalability design

As ML models become increasingly complex and data volumes grow, the ability to serve these models efficiently and at scale becomes critical. Scalable model serving ensures that models can handle high volumes of requests with low latency and high availability, even during peak periods.

Several challenges arise when designing scalable model-serving architectures, as follows:

- **High concurrency**: Models need to handle a large number of concurrent requests without impacting response times.

- **Low latency**: Predictions need to be delivered with minimal delay, especially for real-time applications.

- **High availability**: The serving system should be resilient to failures and maintain continuous operation.

- **Resource efficiency**: The system should utilize resources efficiently to minimize costs.

- **Model updates**: The system should be able to seamlessly integrate new model versions without disrupting service.

To address these challenges, several design principles guide the development of scalable model serving architectures as follows:

- **Horizontal scaling**: Distribute the workload across multiple servers to handle increased traffic.

- **Load balancing**: Distribute requests evenly across servers to prevent bottlenecks.

- **Caching**: Store frequently accessed data in memory for faster retrieval.

- **Model compression**: Reduce model size to minimize memory footprint and improve inference speed.

- **Asynchronous processing**: Process requests asynchronously to improve throughput.

- **Monitoring and logging**: Continuously monitor system performance and log events for troubleshooting.

Several architectures can be used to achieve scalability in model serving as follows:

- **Serverless architectures**: Utilize cloud-based serverless functions to dynamically scale resources based on demand. This approach eliminates the need to manage server infrastructure and reduces costs.

- **Containerized architectures**: Package models and their dependencies in containers for portability and ease of deployment. This approach allows for efficient scaling and resource management.

- **Microservice architectures**: Break down the serving system into smaller, independent services that can be scaled independently. This approach improves modularity and fault tolerance.

- **Hybrid architectures**: Combine elements of different architectures to achieve the desired level of scalability and performance.

Several best practices can be implemented to ensure a scalable model serving as follows:

- **Choose the right infrastructure**: Select cloud platforms or on-premise hardware that can handle the expected load.

- **Optimize model size and inference speed**: Use model compression techniques and efficient inference libraries to reduce latency.

- **Implement caching and pre-fetching**: Cache frequently accessed data and pre-fetch data likely to be needed in the future.

- **Monitor and analyze performance**: Continuously monitor system performance and analyze logs to identify bottlenecks and optimize resource utilization.

- **Automate deployments and updates**: Automate model deployment and updates to minimize downtime and ensure smooth transitions.

Designing scalable model serving architectures requires careful consideration of various factors, including concurrency, latency, availability, resource efficiency, and model updates. By implementing the design principles, architectures, and best practices discussed in this chapter, organizations can ensure their ML models can serve predictions efficiently and at scale, even as data volumes and user demands grow.

Performance considerations

Another important area of challenge in the real-world is to measure and improve the performance of an ML system over time. The performance of an ML model is not just about achieving high accuracy on a test set. It also involves a nuanced balance of various metrics and considerations that reflect the model's ability to generalize from training data to real-world scenarios. This balance ensures that models perform well not only on paper but also in actual deployment, where they impact real decisions and real lives.

Some of the most critical aspects of performance considerations for ML model serving are:

- **Data quality and feature engineering**: The importance of high-quality data and effective feature engineering in enhancing model performance.

- **Model optimization and selection**: Techniques for optimizing model architecture and selecting the right algorithm for the task at hand.

- **Serving infrastructure and optimization**: Strategies for optimizing the serving infrastructure, including hardware and software considerations.

- **Monitoring and evaluation**: The importance of continuous monitoring and evaluation to ensure model performance and address potential issues.

The adage **garbage in, garbage out** is particularly apt in the context of ML. The quality and quantity of data used to train ML models are fundamental to their success. Good data fuels the model's ability to learn effectively and make accurate predictions, while poor data can lead to misleading results and failed projects.

Some of the most important aspects to check when it comes to data quality are as follows:

- **Accuracy**: Data with errors or inaccuracies can mislead the training process, causing the model to learn incorrect patterns and apply them inappropriately.

- **Completeness**: Missing values can significantly impact the performance of many ML algorithms, as they rely on a full dataset to discern patterns accurately.

- **Representativeness**: Data must reflect the real-world diversity and range of scenarios that the model will face. Data that is not representative can cause the model to perform well in a test environment but fail in real-world applications.

Similarly, for data quantity, let us look at some of the crucial areas as follows:

- **Volume**: More data provides more examples from which the model can learn, improving its ability to generalize and reducing the likelihood of overfitting.

- **Variability**: Large datasets that include a wide range of input variations give the model a broader perspective and a better ability to handle unseen data.

Effective **feature selection and engineering** are pivotal in enhancing a machine learning model's accuracy and efficiency. By carefully choosing which features to include and finding innovative ways to transform and combine existing information, data scientists can significantly boost model performance. This process not only helps in making the model more robust but also more adaptable to complex real-world scenarios.

Similarly, **algorithm selection** is pivotal in the machine learning pipeline. The choice of algorithm can significantly impact the model's performance, training time, and ability to generalize to new data. Selecting the right algorithm involves understanding the strengths and weaknesses of each and matching them to the specific needs of the dataset and problem at hand.

Some of the important factors to consider while choosing algorithms and performing feature engineering are as follows:

- **Problem type**: Different algorithms excel at different types of problems. For example, linear regression is suitable for regression tasks, while decision trees are better for classification problems.

- **Data size and complexity**: Some algorithms are more computationally expensive than others and may not be suitable for large datasets or complex problems.

- **Accuracy requirements**: The desired level of accuracy will influence the choice of algorithm. Some algorithms are inherently more accurate than others, but they may also require more training data or computational resources.

- **Interpretability**: Some algorithms are more interpretable than others, meaning it is easier to understand how they make predictions. This can be important for applications where understanding the model's reasoning is crucial.

Next comes the hurdle of optimizing models. This is where we tune them according to our data and use cases and try to make them better. Some of the aspects of this activity are as follows:

- **Hyperparameter tuning**: Adjusting the hyperparameters of a model can significantly impact its performance. This involves finding the optimal values for parameters such as learning rate, regularization strength, and number of hidden layers.

- **Early stopping**: This technique prevents overfitting by stopping the training process when the model's performance on the validation set starts to degrade.

- **Regularization**: Regularization techniques help to prevent overfitting by penalizing models that are too complex.

Finally, the **serving infrastructure** plays a critical role in ensuring that ML models can be deployed and used effectively in production. This infrastructure includes the hardware, software, and networking components that are required to run the model and serve predictions to users.

Some of the serving infrastructure aspects to be aware of are as follows:

- **CPU vs. GPU**: CPUs are general-purpose processors that handle sequential tasks well but struggle with parallel computations. GPUs, on the other hand, are specialized for parallel processing, making them ideal for ML workloads that involve matrix operations. For many ML models, especially deep neural networks, GPU inference can be orders of magnitude faster than CPU inference.

- **Memory**: ML models can require significant amounts of memory, especially during training. It is important to ensure that the serving infrastructure has sufficient memory to handle the model's requirements.

- **Storage**: The serving infrastructure also needs to have adequate storage capacity to store the model, training data, and other relevant files.

In line with the hardware, one needs to be aware of some of the software engineering considerations as well, like the following:

- **Model serving frameworks**: There are a variety of model serving frameworks available, such as TensorFlow Serving, PyTorch Serve, and MLflow. These frameworks provide tools and APIs for deploying and managing ML models in production.

- **Containerization**: Containerization technologies such as Docker and Kubernetes can help to simplify the deployment and management of ML models. They provide a consistent and isolated environment for running models, making it easier to scale and manage them in production.

- **Monitoring and logging**: It is important to monitor the performance of ML models in production and to log any errors or issues that occur. This information can be used to troubleshoot problems and improve the model's performance over time.

Practically, it is not enough to track the health and throughput of our deployed ML service alone. In order to maintain the accuracy and effectiveness of our model, we need to continuously evaluate its performance and identify regressions so that we can retrain, fine-tune, and redeploy at an optimal cadence.

Some of the key technical metrics that we will often refer to as a refresher are as follows:

- **Accuracy**: This is the most common metric for evaluating the performance of a classification model. It measures the percentage of predictions that are correct.

- **Precision**: This metric measures the proportion of positive predictions that were correct.

- **Recall**: This metric measures the proportion of actual positive cases that were correctly identified.

- **F1 score**: This metric is the harmonic mean of precision and recall, providing a balance between the two.

- **AUC-ROC**: This metric is used to evaluate the performance of binary classification models. It measures the area under the **receiver operating characteristic (ROC)** curve.

Using the metrics discussed above, we can apply selective and interesting monitoring techniques like the following:

- **Data drift monitoring**: This technique monitors the distribution of the input data over time to detect any changes that could impact the model's performance.

- **Prediction drift monitoring**: This technique monitors the distribution of the model's predictions over time to detect any changes that could indicate a degradation in performance.

- **Model explainability**: This technique helps to understand how the model makes predictions, which can be useful for debugging and improving the model's performance.

Performance considerations are crucial for ensuring that ML models are effective and reliable in production. By carefully considering the factors discussed in this chapter, one can optimize our model's performance and ensure that it meets the needs of our business.

Best practices

Before we conclude our learning on model serving, let us go through the various best practices that we have learned in this chapter in a summary as follows:

- **Plan for scalability**: Design the serving layer with scalability in mind, utilizing technologies like containerization and cloud platforms to handle increasing workloads.

- **Optimize for latency**: Minimize the time it takes for the model to generate predictions by optimizing the serving infrastructure and using techniques like caching and pre-processing.

- **Ensure reliability**: Implement robust error handling and recovery mechanisms to minimize downtime and ensure consistent predictions.

- **Prioritize security**: Implement security measures like encryption, authentication, and authorization to protect the model and its predictions.

- **Monitor and analyze**: Continuously monitor the model's performance, including metrics like accuracy, latency, and resource utilization. Analyze the data to identify potential issues and opportunities for improvement.

- **Automate the deployment process**: Automate the deployment process to streamline the transition from development to production. This reduces manual effort and minimizes errors.

- **Version control**: Implement version control for the model and its serving infrastructure to track changes and facilitate rollbacks if necessary.

- **Use a model serving framework**: Leverage existing model serving frameworks like TensorFlow Serving, PyTorch Serve, or MLflow to simplify the deployment process and benefit from built-in features.

- **Consider cloud-based solutions**: Cloud platforms like AWS SageMaker and Azure Machine Learning offer managed model-serving solutions that can simplify deployment and management.

- **Invest in infrastructure**: Invest in a robust and scalable infrastructure that can support the demands of the model serving process. This includes hardware, networking, and storage resources.

In the real-world, these best practices should be tailored to our platform, organization, and business needs, keeping a tap on the TCO of any solution. In line with this, we should be aware of the common pitfalls that we can avoid from the early days of implementation as follows:

- **Underestimating scalability needs**: Failing to plan for scalability can lead to performance issues and bottlenecks as the model receives more requests.

- **Ignoring latency concerns**: High latency can lead to poor user experience and hinder the adoption of the model.

- **Neglecting security measures**: Inadequate security measures can expose the model and its predictions to unauthorized access and manipulation.

- **Lack of monitoring and analysis**: Failing to monitor the model's performance can lead to undetected issues and missed opportunities for improvement.

- **Manual deployment process**: A manual deployment process is prone to errors and inconsistencies, making it difficult to maintain a reliable and efficient serving environment.

- **Lack of version control**: Without version control, it becomes challenging to track changes and revert to previous versions if necessary.

- **Ignoring infrastructure needs**: Insufficient infrastructure can lead to performance bottlenecks and limit the model's ability to scale.

Conclusion

In this chapter, we covered what model serving is, how it is done in the real-world, and how it should be properly designed and architected both in an on-premise setup as well as in prominent cloud platforms like Google Cloud.

In the next chapter, we will discuss how to squeeze our ML models so that they can run on handhelds and mobile devices.

Exercises

Let us now try the following exercises to revise the concepts and practice model serving:

1. Read in depth the official PyTorch documentation on model service and the various options or features it provides to ML engineers. The link is provided in the *References* section of this chapter.

2. Go through the Vertex AI tutorials in the link provided in the *References* section to understand more about how to effectively design and develop AI and ML systems on GCP.

    a. This gives a fair idea of how other cloud platforms can be effectively used as well.

3. Can you find a dedicated book or GitHub repository (even an online course!) that focuses only on MLOps? This should be a must in your reading list.

References

Here are the various references used in this chapter. We highly encourage our readers to go through all of them for more references and examples:

1. PyTorch model serving: **https://pytorch.org/serve/**

2. TensorFlow Serving GitHub repository: **https://github.com/TensorFlow/serving**

3. TensorFlow Serving tutorial: **https://www.TensorFlow.org/tfx/serving/serving_basic**

4. Vertex AI tutorials: **https://cloud.google.com/vertex-ai/docs/tutorials**

Join our book's Discord space

Join the book's Discord Workspace for Latest updates, Offers, Tech happenings around the world, New Release and Sessions with the Authors:

https://discord.bpbonline.com

## CHAPTER 12

Model Deployment for Mobile

Introduction

Now that we have learned to a good extent how to create usable ML solutions, can we scale our solutions to run on millions of mobile devices? These can be a variety of handhelds that one uses day to day. There is no doubt that the ubiquitous presence of mobile devices in our lives has opened up exciting possibilities for integrating ML into everyday tasks. This chapter discusses deploying ML models on mobile devices, empowering you to develop intelligent applications that leverage the power of AI directly on your smartphone, tablet, or smartwatch.

While we learn in detail about how to effectively package models for mobile devices, we will explore the design patterns commonly used for deploying ML models on mobile devices. These patterns address the unique challenges and constraints of mobile environments, ensuring efficient and effective model execution.

We also need to focus on the technical aspects of how to design and implement ML-powered mobile applications. This is where one needs to know of tools and frameworks that facilitate the design and development process.

Structure

The chapter covers the following topics:

- Machine learning on mobile
- Design and implementation

Objectives

By the end of this chapter, readers of our book should be familiar with how to effectively design ML and AI-powered applications for handheld devices and how to package them so that they fit into the device and operate without loss of performance or accuracy. In turn, we learn the various frameworks that enable us to deliver such solutions, how to integrate them with the operating systems of these handheld devices, and some common case studies.

Machine learning on mobile

Running ML applications on mobile devices requires comprehensive design. Let us first start looking into the patterns that underpin these ML applications on handhelds. This will help us ensure that we design for optimal performance and user experience while creating such systems. Some of the most common patterns include the following:

- **Local inference**: This pattern involves running the ML model directly on the device, leveraging the device's processing power for real-time predictions. This approach is ideal for applications where low latency and offline functionality are critical.

- **Cloud inference**: In this pattern, the ML model resides on a remote server, and the mobile device sends data to the server for predictions. This approach is suitable for computationally intensive models or situations where the device lacks sufficient processing power.

- **Hybrid inference**: This pattern combines local and cloud inference, leveraging the strengths of both approaches. For instance, the model's core functionality might run locally while complex tasks are offloaded to the cloud.

The applications of ML on mobile devices are vast and diverse, spanning various domains. Here are some prominent examples:

- **Image recognition**: Mobile apps can use image recognition to identify objects, landmarks, or faces in real time, enabling features like augmented reality or personalized recommendations.

- **Natural language processing (NLP)**: NLP-powered mobile apps can understand and respond to natural language, facilitating voice assistants, text translation, and sentiment analysis.

- **Predictive maintenance**: ML models can analyze sensor data from mobile devices to predict potential equipment failures, enabling proactive maintenance and preventing downtime.

- **Personalized recommendations**: Mobile apps can leverage ML to personalize recommendations for products, services, or content based on user preferences and behavior.

Understanding the capabilities and limitations of mobile devices is crucial for designing and deploying ML models effectively. Factors like processing power, memory, battery life, and network connectivity need to be considered. Additionally, studying user interaction patterns and preferences helps tailor the ML experience to user needs.

The design and implementation of ML-powered mobile applications involve several key steps:

1. **Model selection**: Choosing the right ML model for the specific use case is crucial. Factors like accuracy, computational complexity, and model size need to be considered.

2. **Model optimization**: Optimizing the model for mobile deployment is essential for ensuring efficient performance and low resource consumption. Techniques like quantization and pruning can be employed to reduce model size and improve inference speed.

3. **Mobile framework integration**: Integrating the ML model with the chosen mobile development framework (e.g., **TensorFlow Lite** (**TFLite**) for Android, Core ML for iOS) is necessary for running the model on the device.

4. **User interface design**: Designing an intuitive and user-friendly interface that seamlessly integrates with the ML functionality is crucial for a positive user experience.

One of the most commonly used frameworks when it comes to developing ML applications for mobile platforms is TFLite. TFLite is a popular open-source framework specifically designed for deploying ML models on mobile and embedded devices. It offers several advantages, including the following:

- **Optimized for mobile**: TFLite models are optimized for low latency and low power consumption, making them ideal for mobile applications.

- **Cross-platform support**: TFLite supports various mobile platforms, including Android, iOS, and embedded devices.

- **Easy integration**: TFLite provides APIs and tools for easy integration with mobile development frameworks.

Integrating ML models with Android and iOS applications involves specific steps and considerations for each platform, as follows:

- **Android**:
    - TFLite provides the necessary libraries and tools for integrating ML models into Android apps.
    - The **Android Neural Networks API (NNAPI)** can be used to accelerate ML inference on compatible devices.
- **iOS**:
    - Core ML is Apple's framework for deploying ML models on iOS devices.
    - TFLite models can be converted to Core ML format for integration with iOS apps.

Before we jump on to learning more about design patterns and implementations, to illustrate the practical application of ML on mobile devices, let us explore the following case studies:

- **Mobile app recommendation**: This case study demonstrates how ML can be used to recommend relevant apps to users based on their preferences and usage patterns. The ML model analyzes user data, such as app installations, usage history, and device characteristics, to generate personalized recommendations.

- **Web-based image recognition**: This case study showcases how ML can be used to recognize objects in images captured by mobile devices. The ML model is trained on a dataset of labeled images and deployed on the device, enabling real-time object recognition capabilities.

Now, we will learn about the design and implementation of such systems using TFLite and see how we can integrate our ML applications in handheld devices.

Design and implementation

In the following sections, we will explore TFLite with code examples and see design guidelines on how to package ML applications for Android and iOS. Further, we will also explore some real-world applications around us that use ML systems in mobile and handheld devices for multiple use cases.

TensorFlow Lite

TFLite is a powerful tool for deploying machine learning models on a wide range of devices, including mobile phones, embedded devices, and **Internet of Things (IoT)** devices. It enables on-device ML inference with low latency and small binary size, making it ideal for real-time applications. TFLite is an open-source machine learning framework that allows developers to deploy machine learning models on a wide range of devices. It is a lightweight version of TensorFlow designed to be fast and efficient on devices with limited computational resources.

Some of the most important features of TFLite are as follows:

- **Model conversion**: TFLite can convert existing TensorFlow models into a format that can be executed on devices with limited computational resources. This process, called **model conversion**, allows developers to take advantage of the vast ecosystem of pre-trained TensorFlow models and deploy them on their own devices.

- **Low latency**: TFLite reduces inference time, making it ideal for real-time applications. This is crucial for applications that require immediate responses, such as object detection and image recognition.

- **Small binary size**: TFLite models are small and efficient, making them suitable for deployment on devices with limited storage space. This is important for mobile devices and embedded systems, where storage space is often limited.

- **Cross-platform support**: TFLite supports a wide range of platforms, including Android, iOS, Linux, and embedded systems. This makes it a versatile tool for developers who want to deploy their models on a variety of devices.

- **Optimization tools**: TFLite provides several tools and libraries for optimizing and improving the performance of ML models. These tools include quantization, which reduces the precision of model parameters to reduce the size and improve the performance of the model, and pruning, which removes redundant or unnecessary connections in the model to make it more efficient.

The TFLite workflow consists of two main steps as follows:

1. **Model conversion**: The first step is to convert the TensorFlow model into a TFLite model. This is done using the TFLite Converter, which optimizes the model for deployment on devices with limited computational resources.

2. **Inference**: Once the model has been converted, it can be used for inference on the target device. This is done using the TFLite Interpreter, which executes the model and returns the results.

TFLite can be used to build and deploy a wide range of ML applications, including the following:

- **Image classification**: TFLite can be used to classify images in real time, such as identifying objects in photos or videos.

- **Object detection**: TFLite can be used to detect objects in images and videos, such as identifying people, cars, and other objects.

- **NLP**: TFLite can be used for NLP tasks, such as text translation and sentiment analysis.

- **Speech recognition**: TFLite can be used for speech recognition tasks, such as transcribing audio to text.

- **Recommendation systems**: TFLite can be used to build recommendation systems that suggest products or content to users.

Some of the advantages of using TFLite for mobile applications are as follows:

- **Low latency**: TFLite models run quickly on devices with limited computational resources, making them ideal for real-time applications.

- **Small binary size**: TFLite models are small and efficient, making them suitable for deployment on devices with limited storage space.

- **Cross-platform support**: TFLite supports a wide range of platforms, making it a versatile tool for developers who want to deploy their models on a variety of devices.

- **Open-source**: TFLite is an open-source framework, which means that it is free to use and distribute. This makes it a popular choice for developers who are looking for a cost-effective solution for deploying machine learning models.

Before we look at an approach to how to package Android or iOS applications with such ML models, let us build a quick ML model using TensorFlow and export it as a TFLite file. To start, we import the required libraries as follows:

```
"""Importing libraries"""
import TensorFlow as tf
from TensorFlow import keras
from TensorFlow.keras.layers import Conv2D, MaxPooling2D, Flatten, Dense
from TensorFlow.keras.preprocessing.image import ImageDataGenerator
from sklearn.model_selection import train_test_split
import matplotlib.pyplot as plt
import numpy as np
```

Once imported, let us capture and prepare the required data for training the model. In this example, we will reuse the MNIST dataset:

```
"""Capturing and Preparing the data"""
# Load MNIST data
(x_train, y_train), (x_test, y_test) = tf.keras.datasets.mnist.load_data()

# Normalize pixel values
x_train = x_train.astype('float32') / 255.0
x_test = x_test.astype('float32') / 255.0

# Reshape data for CNN input
x_train = x_train.reshape(-1, 28, 28, 1)
x_test = x_test.reshape(-1, 28, 28, 1)
```

```
# One-hot encode labels
y_train = tf.keras.utils.to_categorical(y_train, num_classes=10)
y_test = tf.keras.utils.to_categorical(y_test, num_classes=10)

# Split data into training and validation sets
x_train, x_val, y_train, y_val = train_test_split(x_train, y_train, test_
size=0.2, random_state=42)
```

Further, let us now train the model with a basic architecture and see how it performs:

```
"""Training the Model"""
# Define the model
model = keras.Sequential([
    Conv2D(32, (3, 3), activation='relu', input_shape=(28, 28, 1)),
    MaxPooling2D((2, 2)),
    Conv2D(64, (3, 3), activation='relu'),
    MaxPooling2D((2, 2)),
    Flatten(),
    Dense(10, activation='softmax')
])

# Compile the model
model.compile(loss='categorical_crossentropy', optimizer='adam',
metrics=['accuracy'])

# Print model summary
model.summary()

"""Initiate Model Training"""
# Data augmentation
train_datagen = ImageDataGenerator(rotation_range=40, width_shift_
range=0.2, height_shift_range=0.2, shear_range=0.2, zoom_range=0.2,
horizontal_flip=True, fill_mode='nearest')

# Train the model
history = model.fit(train_datagen.flow(x_train, y_train, batch_size=32),
epochs=10, validation_data=(x_val, y_val))
```

We can evaluate the model by comparing the training and validation **accuracy** and **loss** over the **epoch** for which the model was trained:

```
"""Model Evaluation"""
# Evaluate the model
loss, accuracy = model.evaluate(x_test, y_test, verbose=0)
```

```
print('Test loss:', loss)
print('Test accuracy:', accuracy)

# Plot training and validation accuracy
plt.plot(history.history['accuracy'])
plt.plot(history.history['val_accuracy'])
plt.title('Model accuracy')
plt.ylabel('Accuracy')
plt.xlabel('Epoch')
plt.legend(['Train', 'Validation'], loc='upper left')
plt.show()

# Plot training and validation loss
plt.plot(history.history['loss'])
plt.plot(history.history['val_loss'])
plt.title('Model loss')
plt.ylabel('Loss')
plt.xlabel('Epoch')
plt.legend(['Train', 'Validation'], loc='upper left')
plt.show()
```

Before we export the model, we can also run a sample test with an unseen input:

```
"""Sample Predictions"""
# Predict on a sample image
img = x_test[0]
prediction = model.predict(np.expand_dims(img, axis=0))
print('Predicted class:', np.argmax(prediction))

# Show the sample image
plt.imshow(img, cmap='gray')
plt.show()
```

Finally, we export the model. Instead of exporting the model as a pickle file, which we have done multiple times earlier in our book, we use TFLite format during export:

```
"""Export Model - Smaller version for Mobiles"""
converter = tf.lite.TFLiteConverter.from_keras_model(model)
converter.target_spec.supported_ops = [tf.lite.OpsSet.TFLITE_BUILTINS]
tflite_model = converter.convert()

with open('model.tflite', 'wb') as f:
    f.write(tflite_model)
```

Note that this is one example of exporting the model to disk. There are other methods that TFLite provides.

Models on Android and iOS

Let us now look into how we can approach putting a trained ML model on Android devices. This is an example approach and does not focus on any particular use case. Overall, these steps are followed:

1. **Train and export your TensorFlow model**: Ensure you have a trained TensorFlow neural network for image classification. Export this trained model as a TensorFlow Lite (**.tflite**) model. This lightweight format is optimized for mobile deployment.

2. **Import the .tflite model into Android Studio**: In Android Studio, right-click on the app in the project view, navigate to New | Other | TensorFlow Lite Model, and select your downloaded **.tflite** file.

3. **Design your app layout**: Create a user interface in your Android app for image classification. Include an ImageView to display selected images, a TextView to show classification results and buttons for users to capture images from the camera or choose from the gallery.

4. **Handle image capture and selection**: Implement the functionality for users to take pictures using the device camera or select existing images from their gallery. Ensure your app requests necessary permissions for camera and storage access.

5. **Preprocess the input image**: Before feeding the image to your model, resize it to match the input dimensions expected by your TFLite model. In the provided example, the model expects images of size 32x32 pixels. Also, convert the image from a Bitmap to a ByteBuffer format, which is the required input format for the TFLite model.

6. **Run inference with the TensorFlow Lite model**: Use the TFLite Interpreter to load your **.tflite** model and run inference on the pre-processed image. This step involves creating a ByteBuffer to store the pixel data of the input image. The ByteBuffer is then fed to the TFLite Interpreter, which performs the image classification.

7. **Retrieve and display classification results**: Extract the output probabilities or confidence scores from the model's output. Identify the class with the highest confidence score, which represents the model's prediction. Finally, display this predicted class label to the user in the app's user interface.

Packaging the entire application will require specialized skills in Android development. The same is applicable in case we are trying to create applications on iOS. One such example for the Android application is available here on GitHub: **https://github.com/IJ-Apps/Image-Classification-App-with-Custom-TensorFlow-Model/tree/main**.

Please note, while considering referring to any such experimentation, one should note the attribution guidelines before any sort of commercial use. Similarly, if one would need to make use of GCP and Google AI services for packaging ML applications for Android or iOS, here are some guidelines and instructions that we can follow: **https://ai.google.dev/ edge/litert/libraries/task_library/image_classifier**.

In the ideal scenario, we will often find separate teams in our organization(s) taking care of Android and iOS development. An AI/ML engineer is hence expected to create the best-in-class model and export it in a lightweight format so that the integration, performance, and latency of the application are no longer a concern.

Real-world applications

Now, let us look at a variety of practical use cases and applications all around us that make use of ML within mobile and handheld devices. This gives one a clear picture of the various domains where ML is applied, as follows:

- **Creativity tools**:
  - ML is empowering users to express their creativity in new and exciting ways. Popular apps like *Snapchat* and *Prisma* utilize on-device ML to power real-time AR effects and artistic style transfer, respectively. These features allow users to transform their photos and videos with stunning visual effects, adding a layer of fun and personalization to their content.
  - **Other examples include**:
    - **Momento GIFs**: This app uses image segmentation to blend AR effects around people in scenes, creating unique and engaging GIFs.
    - **Octi**: This app uses image segmentation and pose estimation to track people in videos, enabling users to add fun effects and animations.
    - **Panda**: This app combines AR masks with speech recognition, allowing users to trigger effects by speaking specific words.
  - These creativity tools demonstrate the potential of ML to enhance user engagement and provide new avenues for self-expression.
- **Core UI/UX enhancements**:
  - ML is also transforming the core **user interface and user experience (UI/ UX)** of mobile apps. Apps like *Superimpose X* utilize image segmentation to power an auto-masking tool, simplifying the process of editing photos. *Subreddit Suggester* leverages *Create ML* to automatically suggest relevant subreddits based on a post title, saving users time and effort.

- o **Other examples include**:

    - **HomeCourt**: This app uses pose detection and other ML models to automatically track basketball analytics, providing valuable insights for players and coaches.

    - **PlantVillage**: This app utilizes ML to identify and diagnose plant diseases, assisting farmers and gardeners in maintaining healthy crops.

    - **Polarr**: This app uses on-device ML to enhance photo composition, editing, and organization in real time, streamlining the photo editing process.

  - o These examples showcase how ML can improve the efficiency and effectiveness of various mobile app functionalities, enhancing the overall user experience.

- **Efficiency and productivity**:

  - o ML is also driving efficiency and productivity in various mobile applications. Apps like *Evernote* and *Todoist* utilize ML to analyze user behavior and suggest relevant actions, such as creating reminders or prioritizing tasks. This intelligent assistance helps users stay organized and manage their time effectively.

  - o **Other examples include**:

    - **Grammarly**: This app uses ML to check grammar and spelling in real-time, improving the accuracy and clarity of written communication.

    - **Google Assistant**: This virtual assistant uses ML to understand user queries and provide relevant information or complete tasks, such as making appointments or setting reminders.

    - **Microsoft Translator**: This app uses ML to translate text and speech in real-time, facilitating communication across language barriers.

  - o These examples showcase how ML can automate tasks and provide intelligent assistance, enhancing user productivity and efficiency.

- **Health and wellness**:

  - o ML is making significant contributions to health and wellness apps like *MyFitnessPal* and *Headspace* utilize ML to provide personalized fitness and meditation recommendations, respectively. These apps empower users to take control of their health and well-being.

  - o **Other examples include**:

    - **Sleep Cycle**: This app uses ML to analyze sleep patterns and wake users up at the optimal time, improving sleep quality.

- **MoodPath**: This app uses ML to track mood and provide personalized insights and recommendations for managing mental health.

- **WebMD**: This app uses ML to provide accurate and up-to-date health information, empowering users to make informed decisions about their health.

o These examples demonstrate how ML can promote healthy habits and provide valuable support for individuals seeking to improve their well-being.

- **Security and privacy**:

  o ML also plays a crucial role in enhancing security and privacy on mobile devices. Apps like *Lookout* and *Avast Mobile Security* utilize ML to detect and prevent malware and phishing attacks, protecting users from online threats.

  o **Other examples include**:

    - **Google Photos**: This app uses ML to identify and categorize photos, making it easier to find specific images and manage storage space.

    - **Apple Face ID**: This facial recognition system uses ML to securely unlock iPhones and iPads, providing an additional layer of security.

    - **Samsung Knox**: This security platform utilizes ML to detect and prevent unauthorized access to sensitive data on Samsung devices.

  o These examples showcase how ML can safeguard user data and protect devices from malicious activities.

Conclusion

In this chapter, we introduced how to deploy ML models and make them work on mobile (or related remote) devices. In turn, we introduce TFLite, along with design and development samples and/or guidelines, to develop and package ML model-driven applications for mobile devices. Finally, we covered the integration of such applications (driven by ML) on Android and iOS platforms, alongside a couple of interesting case studies on two of the most common current world applications.

In the next chapter, we will provide a quick recap of the summary of all the chapters we have gone through in this book so far and some real-world experiences of how to make use of this knowledge in the best possible way.

Exercises

Let us now try the following exercises to revise the concepts and practice how to prepare models for mobile devices:

1. Read into documentations, README files, and other software artifacts in GitHub about open-source implementations of mobile applications for ML.

2. Are there any specific CNN networks that are designed specifically for mobile or handheld devices' ML applications? Find them from the *arXiv* portal and study their architectures to understand why their design is suitable for mobile apps.

References

Here are the various references used in this chapter. We highly encourage our readers to go through all of them for more references and examples:

1. TensorFlow Lite: **https://ai.google.dev/edge/litert**

2. Google Research: **https://scholar.google.co.in/ scholar?q=machine+learning+on+mobile+applications&hl=en&as_sdt=0&as_ vis=1&oi=scholart**

Join our book's Discord space

Join the book's Discord Workspace for Latest updates, Offers, Tech happenings around the world, New Release and Sessions with the Authors:

https://discord.bpbonline.com

CHAPTER 13
Summary, Future, and Resources

Introduction

During this book, we have learned in depth about ML, applications of AI/ML in various industries, use cases of AI/ML, tools and frameworks used in building AI/ML systems, and how to package AI/ML solutions for production use cases on cloud or in-house servers as well as on mobile platforms.

In this chapter, we will perform a brief review of all that we have learned so far in this book in stages. We will revisit each important concept as a refresher and try to understand the bigger picture of fitting in the solutions powered by AI/ML solutions.

Structure

The chapter covers the following topics:

- Overview and insights
- Future of AI and ML
- Resources

Objectives

By the end of this chapter, readers of our book should get a recap of all the concepts learned in this book. Readers are re-introduced to the current state of AI and ML implementations as a revision/summary as well as a realization, along with a variety of interesting implications and uses, like generative AI, in the current world. Finally, readers are encouraged with the right amount of additional resources for professional growth in the ever-growing field of AI and ML, including an additional focus on AI ethics and data privacy in the age of ChatGPT and similar.

Overview and insights

Let us start the first section of this chapter with a quick summary of all of the previous learnings in our book until now. Later, we will understand briefly how to architect AI/ML solutions powered by these algorithms well and by employing solid software engineering principles, followed by research and resources in this field.

Machine learning

As we have studied, ML is a type of AI that allows computers to learn from data without being explicitly programmed. This means that ML algorithms can identify patterns and relationships in data and then use these patterns to make predictions about new data. ML is used in a wide variety of applications, including fraud detection, image recognition, and NLP.

There are many different types of ML algorithms, each with its own strengths and weaknesses. Some of the most common types of ML algorithms include the following:

- **Supervised learning**: In supervised learning, the algorithm is trained on a dataset that includes both input data and the desired output. The algorithm then learns to map the input data to the output data. This type of learning is often used for tasks such as classification and regression.

- **Unsupervised learning**: In unsupervised learning, the algorithm is not given any labeled data. Instead, it must learn to identify patterns and relationships in the data on its own. This type of learning is often used for tasks such as clustering and dimensionality reduction.

- **Reinforcement learning**: In reinforcement learning, the algorithm learns by interacting with its environment. The algorithm is given a reward or penalty for its actions, and it learns to take actions that maximize its rewards. This type of learning is often used for tasks such as game playing and robot control.

ML has many benefits, including the following:

- **Improved accuracy**: ML algorithms can often achieve higher accuracy than traditional methods, especially when dealing with complex data.

- **Automation**: ML can automate many tasks that would otherwise be done manually, saving time and money.

- **Personalization**: ML can be used to personalize experiences for individual users, such as recommending products or providing customer support.

- **Innovation**: ML is driving innovation in many industries, from healthcare to finance to transportation.

ML is used in a wide variety of applications, including the following:

- **Fraud detection**: ML can be used to detect fraudulent transactions in real time, helping to prevent financial losses.

- **Image recognition**: ML can be used to recognize objects and faces in images, which can be used for tasks such as security and marketing.

- **NLP**: ML can be used to understand and generate human language, which can be used for tasks such as machine translation and chatbots.

- **Predictive maintenance**: ML can be used to predict when equipment is likely to fail, which can help prevent costly downtime.

- **Personalized recommendations**: ML can be used to recommend products or services to individual users based on their past behavior.

ML is a powerful tool, but it also has some challenges. These challenges include the following:

- **Data quality**: ML algorithms are only as good as the data they are trained on. If the data is of poor quality, the algorithm will not be able to learn effectively.

- **Model complexity**: ML models can become very complex, which can make them difficult to understand and interpret.

- **Bias**: ML algorithms can be biased, reflecting the biases of the data they are trained on. This can lead to unfair or discriminatory outcomes.

- **Security**: ML models can be vulnerable to security attacks, such as poisoning attacks.

Deep learning

Deep learning draws inspiration from the structure and function of the human brain. It utilizes artificial neural networks, composed of interconnected layers of nodes, to process information hierarchically. Each layer learns to extract increasingly abstract features from the data, allowing the network to develop a sophisticated understanding of the underlying patterns. Unlike traditional machine learning algorithms that rely on hand-crafted features, deep learning models automatically discover these features through the learning process. This enables them to handle complex, high-dimensional data, such as images, videos, and natural language, with remarkable accuracy.

The applications of deep learning are vast and continuously expanding. Here are a few prominent examples:

- **Computer vision**: Deep learning algorithms power image recognition systems, object detection, and facial analysis, enabling applications like self-driving cars, medical diagnosis, and security systems.

- **NLP**: Deep learning models are revolutionizing the way we interact with computers. These models power chatbots, machine translation, sentiment analysis, and text summarization, making human-computer interaction more natural and intuitive.

- **Speech recognition**: Deep learning has significantly improved the accuracy of speech recognition systems, leading to advancements in voice assistants, dictation software, and real-time language translation.

- **Fraud detection**: Deep learning algorithms are used to detect fraudulent activities in financial transactions, online payments, and insurance claims, enhancing security and reducing financial losses.

- **Personalized recommendations**: Deep learning models are used by e-commerce platforms and streaming services to personalize recommendations for products, movies, and music, leading to a more engaging and satisfying user experience.

The field of deep learning is rapidly evolving, with breakthroughs and applications emerging constantly. Some exciting areas of future development include the following:

- **Generative AI**: Deep learning models are being used to generate realistic images, videos, and even music, opening up possibilities for creative applications and personalized content generation.

- **Explainable AI**: As deep learning models become increasingly complex, there is a growing need to understand their decision-making process. Explainable AI aims to provide insights into how these models arrive at their conclusions, enhancing trust and transparency.

- **Neuromorphic computing**: Inspired by the human brain, neuromorphic computing aims to develop hardware architectures that mimic the brain's structure and function, potentially leading to more efficient and powerful deep learning systems.

Computer vision

Computer vision is a fascinating field within AI that enables computers to see and understand the visual world. It involves developing algorithms and techniques to extract meaningful information from images, videos, and other visual inputs, allowing computers to perform tasks that were previously only possible for humans. Computer vision systems typically rely on a combination of machine learning and deep learning techniques. These techniques allow computers to learn from vast amounts of visual data and identify patterns that can be used to recognize objects, classify images, and understand the content of visual scenes.

Computer vision has a wide range of applications across various industries, including the following:

- **Manufacturing**: Automating quality control, defect detection, and robotic manipulation.

- **Healthcare**: Assisting in medical diagnosis, image analysis, and surgical procedures.

- **Retail**: Enabling self-checkout systems, product recognition, and personalized recommendations.

- **Security**: Implementing facial recognition, object detection, and surveillance systems.

- **Transportation**: Developing self-driving cars, traffic monitoring, and autonomous navigation.

Despite its significant advancements, computer vision still faces several challenges as follows:

- **Data quality**: The accuracy of computer vision systems depends heavily on the quality of the data they are trained on. Poorly labelled or noisy data can lead to inaccurate results.

- **Computational resources**: Training and running complex computer vision models require significant computational resources, which can be expensive and time-consuming.

- **Ethical concerns**: The use of computer vision raises ethical concerns related to privacy, bias, and discrimination. It is important to ensure that these systems are used responsibly and ethically.

Sequential models

Sequence models are a type of ML model that is specifically designed to handle sequential data. This type of data is characterized by its order, meaning that the elements of the data have a specific relationship to each other. Examples of sequential data include text, audio, video, and time series data. Sequence models can be used to translate languages, generate text, predict stock prices, and even create music.

There are many different types of sequence models, but they all share a common characteristic: they use an RNN to process the data. RNNs are a type of neural network that has a loop in its architecture, which allows it to remember information from previous time stamps. This makes them ideal for processing sequential data, as they can take into account the context of the data when making predictions.

Sequence models have a wide range of applications, including the following:

- **NLP**: Machine translation, text generation, sentiment analysis, and chatbots.

- **Time series analysis**: Stock price prediction, weather forecasting, and anomaly detection.

- **Speech recognition**: Speech-to-text and voice assistants.

- **Image captioning**: Generating descriptions of images.

- **Video analysis**: Action recognition and object tracking.

Sequence models can be challenging to train as they require a large amount of data and can be computationally expensive. Additionally, they can be susceptible to vanishing gradients, which can make it difficult to learn long-term dependencies in the data.

Sequence models are a rapidly evolving field, and new techniques are being developed all the time. In the future, we can expect to see even more powerful and versatile sequence models that can be used to solve a wide range of problems.

Machine learning operations

Machine learning operations (**MLOps**) is a set of practices designed to streamline the process of building, deploying, and managing ML models in production. It aims to bridge the gap between development and operations for machine learning, ensuring that models are developed, tested, and deployed consistently and reliably. By automating and standardizing the machine learning lifecycle, MLOps can help organizations:

- **Reduce costs**: MLOps can help organizations reduce costs by automating and optimizing the machine learning lifecycle, reducing the need for manual intervention.

- **Improve model quality**: MLOps can help organizations improve model quality by providing a framework for tracking experiments, managing data versions, and deploying models in a controlled manner.

- **Increase agility**: MLOps can help organizations increase agility by automating the deployment and monitoring of machine learning models, allowing them to respond to changes in the market more quickly.

- **Reduce risk**: MLOps can help organizations reduce risk by providing a framework for managing model governance, compliance, and security.

MLOps is based on several key principles, including the following:

- **Automation**: MLOps aims to automate as much of the machine learning lifecycle as possible, from data preparation to model deployment and monitoring.

- **Collaboration**: MLOps requires collaboration between data scientists, engineers, and operations teams.

- **Versioning**: MLOps requires careful versioning of data, models, and code to ensure reproducibility and traceability.

- **Monitoring**: MLOps requires continuous monitoring of models in production to detect any issues or degradation in performance.

- **Security**: MLOps requires security measures to protect data, models, and code from unauthorized access.

There are several tools and technologies available to support MLOps, including the following:

- **Model management platforms**: These platforms provide a central repository for storing, versioning, and deploying machine learning models.

- **CI/CD tools**: These tools can be used to automate the building, testing, and deployment of machine learning models.

- **Monitoring tools**: These tools can be used to monitor the performance of machine learning models in production and detect any issues.

- **Cloud platforms**: Cloud platforms can provide the infrastructure and resources needed to run MLOps pipelines.

Model deployment and scaling

Model deployment is the process of making a trained machine learning model available for use in a production environment. This involves integrating the model into an existing system or application so that it can start making predictions based on new data. Deployment ensures that the model can interact with other components, such as databases and user interfaces, to deliver real-time insights and automated decisions. Model deployment strategies allow organizations to leverage the power of their models to solve real-world problems and create new business opportunities.

Deploying ML models can be challenging. Some of the common challenges include the following:

- **Data availability and quality:** High-quality data is essential for model performance. Ensuring that we have access to comprehensive and clean datasets is crucial.

- **System design**: Designing the right infrastructure for a given application is important. This includes considerations such as scalability, security, and performance.

- **Monitoring and maintenance**: Maintaining the model post-deployment is important for its long-term success. This includes monitoring for model drift, retraining, and redeployment.

There are several different strategies for deploying machine learning models. Some of the most common include the following:

- **Batch deployment**: This involves deploying the model to a server where it can process data in batches. This is a good option for applications where latency is not a concern.

- **Real-time deployment**: This involves deploying the model to a server where it can process data in real time. This is a good option for applications where latency is a concern.

- **Cloud deployment**: This involves deploying the model to a cloud platform, such as Google Cloud or Amazon Web Services. This can be a good option for applications that require scalability and flexibility.

Model scalability refers to the ability of a model to handle increasing amounts of data and traffic. As our application grows, we will need to ensure that our model can scale to meet the demand. There are several ways to achieve model scalability, including the following:

- **Horizontal scaling**: This involves adding more servers to our infrastructure.

- **Vertical scaling**: This involves adding more resources to our existing servers.

- **Model optimization**: This involves optimizing our model to reduce its resource requirements.

Model deployment on mobile

Model deployment can be done on a variety of platforms, including mobile devices. Mobile devices are becoming increasingly powerful and ubiquitous, making them an ideal platform for deploying ML models.

TFLite is a lightweight framework for deploying machine learning models on mobile devices. It is a subset of the TensorFlow library, which is a popular framework for ML development. TFLite is designed to be small and efficient, making it ideal for use on mobile devices.

There are a few things to consider when designing and developing a mobile application that uses a machine learning model. First, we need to choose the right framework for deploying our model. TFLite is a good option for many mobile applications. Second, we need to design our application to be efficient and use as little battery power as possible. Finally, we need to make sure that our application is secure and protects the privacy of our users.

Integrating an ML model into a mobile application can be a complex task. There are a few things to consider, such as how to handle data preprocessing, how to make predictions, and how to handle errors. There are a number of resources available to help us with this process, including the TFLite documentation and the TFLite GitHub repository.

There are a number of interesting case studies of machine learning models being deployed on mobile devices. For example, Google Translate uses an ML model to translate text between languages. This model is deployed on mobile devices, allowing users to translate text on the go. Another example is Google Assistant, which uses an ML model to understand natural language. This model is deployed on mobile devices, allowing users to interact with the Assistant using their voice.

Future of AI and ML

The past decade has witnessed an explosion in the development and adoption of AI/ML technologies. This growth is driven by several factors, including the following:

- **Increased computing power**: The availability of powerful and affordable computing resources, such as GPUs and cloud computing platforms, has made it possible to train and deploy complex AI/ML models.

- **Advances in algorithms**: Researchers have developed new and improved algorithms for various AI/ML tasks, such as image recognition, natural language processing, and predictive modeling.

- **Availability of data**: The increasing availability of large datasets has enabled the training of more accurate and robust AI/ML models.

Generative AI, a subset of AI that focuses on creating new content, is rapidly gaining traction. Generative AI models can generate text, images, videos, and even music. This technology has the potential to revolutionize various industries, including the following:

- **Content creation**: Generative AI can be used to create realistic and engaging content for marketing, advertising, and entertainment purposes.

- **Drug discovery**: Generative AI can be used to design new drugs and therapies.

- **Product design**: Generative AI can be used to design new products and prototypes.

As AI/ML systems become more pervasive, it is crucial to address ethical and data privacy concerns. These concerns include the following:

- **Bias and fairness**: AI/ML models can perpetuate biases present in the data they are trained on.

- **Privacy violations**: AI/ML systems can collect and use personal data without proper consent or knowledge.

- **Transparency and explainability**: It can be difficult to understand how AI/ML models make decisions, which can lead to a lack of trust and accountability.

Effective governance frameworks are needed to ensure the responsible development and deployment of AI/ML systems. These frameworks should address issues such as:

- **Data governance:** Establishing clear guidelines for data collection, storage, and use.

- **Model governance**: Ensuring that AI/ML models are developed and deployed safely and ethically.

- **Algorithmic transparency**: Making AI/ML models more transparent and explainable.

Developing and deploying AI/ML systems in production environments requires careful planning and execution. Here are some best practices to follow:

- **Model development and training**:

  o **Define clear objectives**: Clearly define the goals and objectives of the AI/ML model.

  o **Use high-quality data**: Train the model on high-quality, labeled data that is representative of the real-world use case.

  o **Validate and test the model**: Thoroughly validate and test the model to ensure its accuracy and robustness.

  o **Monitor the model's performance**: Continuously monitor the model's performance in production and make adjustments as needed.

- **Model deployment and monitoring**:

  o **Choose the right deployment environment**: Select the appropriate deployment environment based on the model's requirements and the organization's infrastructure.

  o **Automate the deployment process**: Automate the deployment process to ensure consistency and repeatability.

  o **Monitor the model's health**: Continuously monitor the model's health and performance in production.

  o **Implement rollback mechanisms**: Implement rollback mechanisms to revert to previous versions of the model if necessary.

- **Data management and security**:

  o **Implement data security measures**: Implement appropriate data security measures to protect sensitive data.

  o **Use data encryption**: Encrypt data at rest and in transit.

  o **Control access to data**: Limit access to data to authorized personnel.

  o **Regularly audit data security practices**: Regularly audit data security practices to ensure compliance with regulations.

- **Explainability and interpretability**:

  o **Make models more interpretable**: Develop models that are more interpretable and explainable.

  o **Provide explanations for model decisions**: Provide explanations for model decisions to stakeholders.

  o **Use visualization tools**: Use visualization tools to help understand model behavior.

  o **Continuous improvement and iteration**: Continuously iterate on the model based on feedback and new data.

  o **Improve the data quality**: Improve the quality of the data used to train the model.

  o **Refine the model architecture**: Refine the model architecture to improve its performance.

Several reference architectures can be used for deploying AI/ML systems in production. These architectures include the following:

- **Cloud-based architectures:** Cloud-based architectures offer scalability, flexibility, and ease of deployment. In this architecture, the AI/ML model is deployed on a cloud platform, such as **Amazon Web Services** (**AWS**), Microsoft Azure, or **Google Cloud Platform** (**GCP**).

- **On-premises architectures:** On-premises architectures offer more control and security. In this architecture, the AI/ML model is deployed on servers located on-premises.

- **Hybrid architectures**: Hybrid architectures combine the benefits of cloud-based and on-premises architectures. In this architecture, some components of the AI/ML system are deployed on the cloud, while others are deployed on-premises.

- **Microservices-based architectures:** Microservices-based architectures break down the AI/ML system into smaller, independent services. This approach makes the system more modular, scalable, and maintainable.

Resources

Here are some resources to make our learning more complete as we go along. It is imperative to keep a tap on the ongoing developments in the field of AI/ML. Here are a few resources to always keep handy, as a start, out of many:

- **Google Research**: **https://research.google/.** This is one shop destination of a continual process of open sourcing research ideas and discussions from Google, which it has been consistently doing for the last 26 years, as of writing this book.

As of today, there are more than 7,000+ research studies published by Google over a variety of software engineering and related fields, including AI/ML.

- **arXiv: https://www.arxiv.org** . Maintained by *Cornell University*, arXiv is a free distribution service and an open-access archive for nearly 2.4 million scholarly articles in the fields of physics, mathematics, computer science, quantitative biology, quantitative finance, statistics, electrical engineering and systems science, and economics.

Conclusion

In this chapter, we revised the concepts of ML and neural networks, revisited the core concepts of solid software engineering principles, and had a relook at how to design effective deployment methodologies. We also understood where AI/ML is progressing and how generative AI is having a world-scale impact across industries. Lastly, we made us remember about the AI ethics and how to imbibe them well in our day-to-day operations with AI/ML solutions and their design.

References

For this chapter specifically, the references section is of much more importance. Herewith, we can get a list of important reusable assets and code references for the implementation of a variety of AI/ML solutions:

1. Deep learning book: **https://www.deeplearningbook.org/**

2. Stanford University's deep learning tutorial: **https://www.wetube.com/ watch?v=pTbXg8a2e98**

3. MIT's deep learning course: **https://deeplearning.mit.edu/**

4. Google's deep learning research blog: **https://ai.googleblog.com/**

5. OpenAI's deep learning resources: **https://openai.com/resources/deep-learning/**

6. MLOps with Vertex AI: **https://github.com/GoogleCloudPlatform/mlops-with-vertex-ai**

7. AI/ML on Vertex AI in Google Cloud: **https://github.com/ GoogleCloudPlatform/vertex-ai-samples**

8. AWS AI solution kit: **https://github.com/awslabs/aws-ai-solution-kit**

9. Azure AI samples: **https://github.com/Azure-Samples/azureai-samples**

Index

www.ingramcontent.com/pod-product-compliance
Lightning Source LLC
Chambersburg PA
CBHW061743210326
41599CB00034B/6773